An Object-Oriented Approach to Programming Logic and Design

Second Edition

Joyce Farrell

THOMSON

COURSE TECHNOLOGY

THOMSON

COURSE TECHNOLOGY

An Object-Oriented Approach to Programming Logic and Design, *Second Edition*

Joyce Farrell

Vice President, Technology and Trades:
Dave Garza

Director of Learning Solutions:
Sandy Clark

Acquisitions Editor:
Amy Jollymore

Managing Editor:
Tricia Coia

Development Editor:
Dan Seiter

Product Marketing Manager:
Bryant Chrzan

Editorial Assistant:
Patrick Frank

Content Project Manager:
Heather Furrow

Cover Designer:
Steve Deschene

Compositor:
International Typesetting and Composition

Manufacturing Coordinator:
Julio Esperas

BRIEF CONTENTS

TABLE OF CONTENTS

PREFACE

An Object-Oriented Approach to Programming Logic and Design, Second Edition provides the beginning programmer with a guide to developing object-oriented program logic. This textbook assumes no programming language experience. The writing is nontechnical and emphasizes good programming practices. The examples are business examples; they do not assume mathematical background beyond high school business math. Additionally, the examples illustrate one or two major points; they do not contain so many features that students become lost following irrelevant and extraneous details.

The examples in *An Object-Oriented Approach to Programming Logic and Design* have been created to provide students with a sound background in logic, no matter what programming languages they eventually use to write programs. This book can be used in a stand-alone logic course that students take as a prerequisite to a programming course, or as a companion book to any object-oriented programming language text using any language such as Java, Visual Basic, C++, or C#.

ORGANIZATION AND COVERAGE

An Object-Oriented Approach to Programming Logic and Design, Second Edition introduces students to programming concepts, enforcing good style, and logical thinking. General programming concepts are introduced in Chapter 1. In Chapter 2, students are introduced to the advantages of structured programming, such as creating methods that include sequence, selection, and loop structures. Chapters 3, 4, and 5 provide a solid background in programming universals—decision-making, looping, and handling arrays. Chapter 6 introduces methods; the student becomes familiar with parameter passing, overloading methods, and the concept of ambiguity. With the background acquired in the first six chapters, the student is well-prepared to start thinking in an object-oriented manner.

In Chapter 7, the student is presented with a thorough foundation in object-oriented programming techniques, including class design, private and public access of class members, instance and static class members, and constructors and destructors. The later chapters provide the student with a background in a wide variety of programming techniques used in modern object-oriented applications. Chapter 8 describes programming with graphical user interface (GUI) objects and handling the events they generate. Chapter 9 provides background in the object-oriented concepts of polymorphism and inheritance, Chapter 10 describes managing program errors using the object-oriented technique called exception handling, and Chapter 11 teaches the basics of system design, introducing the Unified Modeling Language. Finally, Chapter 12 provides advanced array applications, including a variety of sorting techniques, handling arrays of objects, and using multidimensional arrays.

In addition to the 12 chapters, four appendices allow students to gain extra experience with structuring large unstructured programs, using the binary numbering system, working with large decision tables, and understanding some of the issues involved in software testing.

An Object-Oriented Approach to Programming Logic and Design, Second Edition combines text explanations with flowcharts and pseudocode examples to provide students with alternative means of expressing structured logic. Numerous detailed, full-program exercises at the end of each chapter illustrate the concepts explained within the chapter, and reinforce understanding and retention of the material presented.

The book is a language-independent introduction to programming logic beginning with object-oriented principles. It distinguishes itself from other programming logic texts in the following ways:

» Object-oriented programming terminology is explained in easy-to-understand language, using everyday real-life examples as well as programming examples. Students learn traditional programming concepts such as variables, data types, decisions, loops, and arrays, and learn object-oriented concepts such as classes, objects, inheritance, and polymorphism before they are burdened with the syntax of a specific programming language.

» Object-oriented terminology is explained as it refers to GUI objects used in visual languages as well as to business objects.

» No programming experience is assumed.

» Examples are language-independent; this text can be used in a logic course, or as a companion text in courses in any object-oriented programming language such as Java, Visual Basic, C++, or C#.

» Examples are everyday business examples; no mathematics beyond high school algebra is required. This is not a computer science text; it is an introduction to logic for CIS students who want to get up to speed and quickly develop useful programs.

» Examples are simple; the point under discussion is not lost in overly detailed examples.

» The student will understand data types and gain a solid foundation in the declaration, definition, and use of variables, arithmetic operations, and other basic programming concepts. Within methods, structure is stressed; students will become proficient in recognizing and using sequences, selections, and loops, and will use arrays.

» Many more types of exercises are provided than in most other texts. In addition to programming problems, this book provides objective review questions, essay-type discussion questions, and a running case project.

» This book is written for the student who will go on to study an object-oriented language such as C++, Java, C#, or Visual Basic. The book uses conventions that are appropriate for object-oriented languages, including using modern identifier naming conventions, teaching arrays as zero-based, and using parentheses with method names; these features are not used in competing texts. Also, this book ignores topics covered by other texts that do not apply as readily to object-oriented applications, such as stacks, queues, and control break processing.

The second edition improves on the first in the following ways:

NEW!

The second edition features a "gentler" introduction to object-oriented programming concepts. For many students, the first edition covered too much theory too quickly before providing a thorough grounding in programming basics. The topics in the second edition have been reordered to provide a superior first exposure to programming for most students. Students are provided with a thorough grounding in the important concept of structure that applies to every method in every program, whether the program is written in a procedural or object-oriented language.

Although the introduction to object-oriented programming is gentler, it is still present from the start. For example, classes are used immediately, although in early examples they might have only a `main()` method.

NEW!

The second edition provides many more diagrams than the first. Especially in the early chapters, flowcharts are used along with pseudocode. Almost every example of decision-making and looping uses both tools. Seeing a flowchart diagram and reading pseudocode that accomplishes the same tasks helps different types of learners and reinforces concepts for all learners.

NEW!

The second edition provides images of running programs where appropriate. Screen shots are included that show both command-line, text-based interfaces and GUI interfaces. Seeing these interfaces will give the student a firmer grasp of what input and output look like.

NEW!

The second edition provides more complete programs. The first edition often showed only a method to illustrate a concept such as decision making, looping, or array handling. The new edition shows several full programs when illustrating concepts like these, helping the student to see how programming structures fit into the big picture.

NEW!

In addition to the wealth of exercises and review questions that follow each chapter, discussion questions have been added. These can be used as written exercises to encourage writing across the curriculum, to promote discussion among students in online classes, or as oral exercises that promote classroom participation.

NEW!

The second edition is more visually pleasing than the first, aided by the use of color to enliven diagrams and help distinguish key features.

NEW!

It is sometimes illustrative to show an example of how NOT to do something—for example, having a dead code path in a program. However, students do not always read carefully and sometimes pattern their logic on the book's "bad" examples. When the instructor is critical, the frustrated student says, "But that's how they did it in the book!" Therefore, although the text will continue to describe and identify bad examples, we also include a new "Don't do it" icon that provides a visual jolt to the student, emphasizing that particular figures are NOT to be emulated.

NEW!

The second edition contains a new appendix that covers some of the issues of software testing, which is a growing employment market.

NEW!

FEATURES OF THE TEXT

An Object-Oriented Approach to Programming Logic and Design is a superior textbook because it includes the following features:

» **Objectives**—Each chapter begins with a list of objectives so the student knows the topics that will be presented in the chapter. In addition to providing a quick reference to topics covered, this feature provides a useful study aid.

» **Flowcharts and pseudocode**—This book has plenty of figures and illustrations, including flowcharts that provide the reader with a visual learning experience, rather than one that involves simply studying text.

» **Complete class example**—The book provides a complete class example in most chapters to demonstrate the application of the topics learned.

» **Notes**—These tips provide additional information such as other locations in the book that expand on a topic or common errors to avoid.

» **Chapter summaries**—A summary recaps the programming concepts and techniques covered in the chapter. This feature provides a concise means for students to review and check their understanding of the main points in each chapter.

» **Key terms**—A collection of all the key terms ends each chapter. Definitions are also included in sentence format and in the order in which the key terms appear in the chapter.

» **Review questions**—Twenty review questions at the end of each chapter reinforce the main ideas introduced in the chapter. Successfully answering these questions will demonstrate mastery of the concepts and information presented.

» **Exercises**—Each chapter includes meaningful programming exercises that provide students with additional practice of the skills and concepts they learned in the lesson. These exercises increase in difficulty and are designed to allow students to explore logical programming concepts. Each exercise can be completed using flowcharts or pseudocode; in addition, instructors can choose to assign the exercises as programming problems to be coded and executed in an object-oriented programming language.

» **Case project**—Each chapter concludes with a running case project involving a hypothetical business. By applying the current chapter's concepts to the continuing business example, the student discovers that the concepts learned in each chapter contribute to the development of a complete business system.

» **Up for Discussion questions**—Each chapter provides some thought-provoking questions that can be used to spark classroom or online discussion.

» **Glossary**—All the key terms are explained in a glossary at the back of the book.

TEACHING TOOLS AND SUPPLEMENTS

The following supplemental materials are available when this book is used in a classroom setting. All of the teaching tools available with this book are provided to the instructor on a single CD-ROM. The book includes the following features:

» **Electronic Instructor's Manual**—The Instructor's Manual that accompanies this textbook provides additional instructional material to assist in class preparation, including items such as sample syllabi, chapter outlines, technical notes, lecture notes, quick quizzes, teaching tips, discussion topics, and key terms.

» **ExamView®**—This textbook is accompanied by ExamView, a powerful testing software package that allows instructors to create and administer printed, computer (LAN-based), and Internet exams. ExamView includes hundreds of questions that correspond to the topics covered in this text, enabling students to generate detailed study guides that include page references for further review. The computer-based and Internet testing components allow students to take exams at their computers, and save the instructor time by grading each exam automatically.

» **PowerPoint presentations**—This book comes with Microsoft PowerPoint slides for each chapter. These are included as a teaching aid for classroom presentation, to make available to students on your network for chapter review, or to be printed for classroom distribution. Instructors can add their own slides for additional topics they introduce to the class.

» **Solutions**—Suggested solutions to review questions and exercises are provided on the Teaching Tools CD-ROM and on the Course Technology Web site at *www.course.com*. The solutions are password protected.

» **Distance learning**—Cengage is proud to present online test banks in WebCT and Blackboard to provide the most complete and dynamic learning experience possible. Instructors are encouraged to make the most of the course, both online and offline. For more information on how to access the online test bank, contact your local Cengage sales representative.

ACCOMPANYING SOFTWARE

» **Microsoft® Office Visio® Professional 2007, 60-day version**—Visio 2007 is a diagramming program that helps users create flowcharts and diagrams easily while working through the text, enabling them to visualize concepts and learn more effectively. A 60-day version of Visio 2007 comes with each new, unused copy of the text.

» **Visual Logic™, version 2.0**—Visual Logic™ is a simple but powerful tool for teaching programming logic and design without traditional high-level programming language syntax. Visual Logic uses flowcharts to explain essential programming concepts, including variables, input, assignment, output, conditions, loops, procedures, graphics, arrays, and files. It also has the ability to interpret and execute flowcharts, providing students with immediate and accurate feedback about their solutions. By executing student solutions, Visual Logic combines the power of a high-level language with the ease and simplicity of flowcharts. You may purchase Visual Logic along with your text. Please contact your Cengage sales representative for more information.

ACKNOWLEDGMENTS

I would like to thank all of the people who helped to make this book a reality, especially Dan Seiter, Development Editor, whose sense of humor made this project fun, and whose attention to detail made this book a superior teaching tool. Thanks also to Tricia Coia, Managing Editor; Amy Jollymore, Acquisitions Editor; Heather Furrow, Content Project Manager; and Green Pen QA, Technical Editors. It is a pleasure to work with so many people who are dedicated to producing quality textbooks.

I am grateful to the many reviewers who provided helpful and insightful comments during the development of this book, including Nelson Capaz, Pasco Hernando Community College; JoAnn Shoemaker-Cooper, Hinds Community College; Peter van der Goes, Rose State College; and Melinda White, Seminole Community College.

Thanks, too, to my husband, Geoff, who handles everything else when I have a chapter to complete. This book is dedicated to him and to our daughters, Andrea and Audrey.

Joyce Farrell

AN OVERVIEW OF COMPUTERS AND LOGIC

In this chapter, you will:

Learn about computer components and operations

Learn about the evolution of programming techniques

Learn about the steps involved in the programming process

Learn about flowcharts and pseudocode statements

Create an application class with a `main()` method

Use and name variables

Assign values to variables

Describe data types

Learn about various forms of input

UNDERSTANDING COMPUTER COMPONENTS AND OPERATIONS

The two major components of any computer system are its hardware and its software. **Hardware** is the equipment, or the devices, associated with a computer. For a computer to be useful, however, it needs more than equipment; a computer needs to be given instructions. The instructions that tell the computer what to do are called **software**, or programs, and are written by programmers. This book focuses on the process of writing these instructions.

> **»NOTE** Software can be classified as application software or system software. **Application software** comprises all the programs you apply to a task—word-processing programs, spreadsheets, payroll and inventory programs, and even games. **System software** comprises the programs that you use to manage your computer, including operating systems such as Windows or UNIX and other utility programs not used directly by end users. This book focuses on the logic used to write application software programs, although many of the concepts apply to both types of software.

Together, computer hardware and software accomplish four major operations:

1. Input
2. Processing
3. Output
4. Storage

> **»NOTE** Printed computer output is called **hard copy**. Screen output is **soft copy**.

Hardware devices that perform input include keyboards and mice. **Input devices** provide the ways that **data**, or facts, enter the computer system. **Processing** data items may involve organizing them, checking them for accuracy, or performing mathematical operations on them. The piece of hardware that performs these sorts of tasks is the **central processing unit**, or **CPU**. After data items have been processed, the resulting **information** is sent to a printer, monitor, or some other **output device** so that people can view, interpret, and use the results. Often, you also want to store the output information on **storage devices**—hardware such as magnetic disks, compact discs, or USB drives. Computer software consists of all the instructions that control how and when data is input, how it is processed, and the form in which it is output or stored.

> **»NOTE** Data includes all the text, numerical information, or other information that is processed by a computer. However, many computer professionals reserve the term *information* for data that has been processed. For example, your name, Social Security number, and hourly pay rate are data items, but your paycheck holds information.

Computer hardware by itself is useless without a programmer's instructions, or software, just as your stereo equipment doesn't do much until you provide music on a CD or tape. You can buy prewritten software that is stored on a disk, you can download software from the Web, or you can write your own software instructions. You can enter instructions into a computer system through any of the hardware devices you use for data; most often, you type your instructions using a keyboard and store them on a device such as a disk or CD.

You write computer instructions in a computer **programming language** such as Visual Basic, C#, C++, Java, Pascal, COBOL, RPG, or Fortran. Just as some people speak English and others speak Japanese, programmers also write programs in different languages. Some programmers work exclusively in one language, while others know several and use the one that seems most appropriate for the task at hand.

No matter which programming language a computer programmer uses, the language has rules that govern its word usage and punctuation. These rules are called the language's **syntax**. If you ask, "How the get to store do I?" in English, most people can figure out what you probably mean, even though you have not used proper English syntax. However, computers are not nearly as smart as most people; with a computer, you might as well have asked, "Xpu mxv ot dodnm cadf B?" Unless the syntax is perfect, the computer cannot interpret the programming language instruction at all.

Every computer operates on circuitry that consists of millions of on-off switches. Each programming language uses a piece of software to translate the specific language into the computer's on-off circuitry language, or **machine language**. The language translation software is called a **compiler** or **interpreter**, and it tells you if you have used a programming language incorrectly. Therefore, syntax errors are relatively easy to locate and correct—the compiler or interpreter you use highlights every syntax error. If you write a computer program using a language such as C++, but spell one of its words incorrectly or reverse the proper order of two words, the compiler lets you know it found a mistake by displaying an error message as soon as you try to run the program.

>> **NOTE** Although there are differences in how compilers and interpreters work, their basic function is the same—to translate your programming statements into code the computer can use. When you use a compiler, an entire program is translated before it can execute; when you use an interpreter, each instruction is translated just prior to execution. Usually, you do not choose which type of translation to use—it depends on the programming language.

For a program to work properly, you must give the instructions to the computer in a specific sequence, you must not leave any instructions out, and you must not add extraneous instructions. By doing this, you are developing the **logic** of the computer program. Suppose you instruct someone to make a cake as follows:

```
Stir
Add two eggs
Add a gallon of gasoline
Bake at 350 degrees for 45 minutes
Add three cups of flour
```

Even though you have used the English language syntax correctly, the instructions are out of sequence, some instructions are missing, and some instructions belong to procedures other than baking a cake. If you follow these instructions, you are not going to end up with an edible cake, and you may end up with a disaster. Logical errors are much more difficult to locate than syntax errors; it is easier for you to determine whether "eggs" is spelled incorrectly in a recipe than it is for you to tell if there are too many eggs or they are added too soon.

>> **NOTE** Programmers often call logical errors **semantic errors**. For example, if you misspell a programming-language word, you commit a syntax error, but if you use a correct word that does not make any sense in the current context, you commit a semantic error.

Just as baking directions can be given correctly in French, German, or Spanish, the same logic of a program can be expressed in any number of programming languages. This book is almost exclusively concerned with the logic development process. Because this book is not concerned with any specific language, the programming examples could have been written in Japanese, C++, or Java. The logic is the same in any language. For convenience, the book uses English!

Once instructions have been input into the computer and translated into machine language, a program can be **run**, or **executed**. You can write program instructions that take a number (an input step), double it (processing), and provide you with the answer (output) in a programming language such as Java or C++, but if you were to write it using English-like statements, it would look like this:

```
Get inputNumber.
Compute calculatedAnswer as inputNumber times 2.
Print calculatedAnswer.
```

NOTE
You will learn why spaces are eliminated between words like input and Number in the next few pages.

The instruction to Get inputNumber is an example of an input operation. When the computer interprets this instruction, it knows to look to an input device to obtain a number. Computers often have several input devices: such as a keyboard, a mouse, a CD drive, and two or more disk drives. When you learn a specific programming language, you learn how to tell the computer which of those input devices to access for input. Logically, however, it doesn't really matter which hardware device is used, as long as the computer knows to look for a number. The logic of the input operation—that the computer must obtain a number for input, and that the computer must obtain it before multiplying it by 2—remains the same regardless of any specific input hardware device. The same is true in your daily life—if you follow the instruction "Get eggs from store," it does not really matter if you are following a handwritten instruction from a paper list or a voice-mail instruction left on your cell phone—the process of getting the eggs, and the result of doing so, are the same.

NOTE
Many computer professionals categorize disk drives and CD drives as storage devices rather than input devices. Such devices can be used for input, storage, and output.

Processing is the step that occurs when inputNumber is doubled; the statement Compute calculatedAnswer as inputNumber times 2 represents processing. Mathematical operations are not the only kind of processing, but they are very typical. After you write a program, it can be used on computers of different brands, sizes, and speeds. Whether you use an IBM, Macintosh, Linux, or UNIX operating system, and whether you use a personal computer on your desk or a mainframe that costs hundreds of thousands of dollars and resides in a special building in a university, multiplying by 2 is the same process. The hardware is not important; the processing will be the same.

NOTE
You will learn more about types of input later in this chapter.

In the number-doubling program, the Print calculatedAnswer statement represents output. Within a particular program, this statement could cause the output to appear on the monitor (which might be a flat panel screen or a cathode-ray tube), or the output could go to a printer (which could be a laser or inkjet model), or the output could be written to a disk or CD. The logic of the process called "Print" is the same no matter what hardware device you use.

Besides input, processing, and output, the fourth operation in any computer system is storage. Storage comes in two broad categories. All computers have **internal storage**, probably referred to more often as **memory**, **main memory**, or **primary memory**. This storage is inside the machine and is the type of storage most often discussed in this book.

Computers also use **external storage**, which is persistent (relatively permanent) storage on a device such as a floppy disk, hard disk, flash media, or magnetic tape. In other words, external storage is outside of the main memory, not necessarily outside the computer. Both programs and data are sometimes stored on each of these kinds of media.

To use computer programs, you must first load them into memory. You might type a program into memory from the keyboard, or you might use a program that has already been written and stored on a disk. Either way, a copy of the instructions must be placed in memory before the program can be run.

A computer system needs both internal memory and external storage. Internal memory is needed to run the programs, but internal memory is **volatile**—that is, its contents are lost every time the computer loses power. Therefore, if you are going to use a program more than once, you must store a copy of it, or **save** it, on some nonvolatile medium. A program whose only copy is in main memory is lost forever when the computer is turned off. External storage (for example, a disk or USB drive) provides a nonvolatile medium.

>> **NOTE** Even though a hard disk drive is located inside your computer, the hard disk is not main, internal memory. Internal memory is temporary and volatile; a hard drive is permanent, nonvolatile storage. After one or two "tragedies" of losing several pages of a typed computer program due to a power failure or other hardware problem, most programmers learn to save their programs periodically using a nonvolatile medium, such as a disk.

Once you have a copy of a program in main memory, you want to execute or run the program. To do so, you must also place any data that the program requires into memory. For example, after you place the following program into memory and start to run it, you need to provide an actual inputNumber—for example, 8—that you also place in main memory.

```
Get inputNumber.
Compute calculatedAnswer as inputNumber times 2.
Print calculatedAnswer.
```

The value of inputNumber is placed in memory in a specific memory location, and the program will call that location inputNumber. Then, and only then, can the calculatedAnswer (in this case 16) be calculated and printed.

>> **NOTE** Computer memory consists of millions of numbered locations where data can be stored. The memory location of inputNumber has a specific numeric address—for example, 48604. Your program associates inputNumber with that address. Every time you refer to inputNumber within a program, the computer retrieves the value at the associated memory location. When you write programs, you seldom need to be concerned with the value of the memory address; instead, you simply use the easy-to-remember name you created.

>> **NOTE** Computer programmers often refer to memory addresses using hexadecimal notation, or base 16. Using this system, they might use a value like 42FF01A to refer to a memory address. Despite the use of letters, such an address is still a number. When you use the hexadecimal numbering system, the letters A through F stand for the values 10 through 15.

UNDERSTANDING THE EVOLUTION OF PROGRAMMING TECHNIQUES

People have been writing modern computer programs since the 1940s. The oldest programming languages required programmers to work with memory addresses and to memorize awkward codes associated with machine languages. Newer programming languages look much more like natural language and are easier for programmers to use. Part of the reason it is easier to use newer programming languages is that they allow programmers to give meaningful names to memory locations instead of using awkward memory addresses. Another reason is that newer programming languages allow the creation of self-contained modules or program segments that can be pieced together in a variety of ways. The oldest computer programs were written in one piece, from start to finish; modern programs are rarely written that way—they are created by teams of programmers, each developing reusable and connectable program procedures. Writing several small modules is easier than writing one large program, just as most large tasks are easier when you break the work into units and get other workers to help with the units.

> **»NOTE** Ada Byron Lovelace predicted the development of software in 1843; she is often regarded as the first programmer. However, no modern computers existed then; homes and businesses did not yet have electricity. The basis for most modern software was proposed by Alan Turing in 1935.

»NOTE
You will learn more about program modules in Chapters 6 and 7.

Currently, there are two major techniques for developing programs and their procedures. One technique, called **procedural programming**, focuses on the procedures that programmers create to manipulate data. That is, procedural programmers focus on the actions that are carried out—for example, getting input data for an employee and writing the calculations needed to produce a paycheck from the data. Procedural programmers would approach the job of producing a paycheck by breaking down the process into manageable subtasks.

»NOTE
Programmers use the term *OO*, pronounced "oh oh," as an abbreviation for "object oriented." When discussing object-oriented programming, they use *OOP*, which rhymes with "soup."

The other popular programming technique, called **object-oriented programming** (**OOP**), focuses on objects, or "things." OOP describes these objects' features, or attributes, and their behaviors. The **attributes of an object** are the features it "has"; the values of an object's attributes constitute the object's **state**. For example, an attribute of a paycheck is the monetary value of the check, and the state of one paycheck's monetary value might be $400. The **behaviors of an object** are the things it "does"; for example, a paycheck object can be written and cashed, and it contains calculations that result in the check amount. Object-oriented programmers might design a payroll application by thinking about all the objects needed, such as employees, time cards, and paychecks, and describing their attributes and behaviors.

»NOTE
Object-oriented programming employs a large vocabulary; you can learn much of this terminology in Chapter 6.

With either approach, procedural or object-oriented, you can produce a correct paycheck, and both techniques employ reusable program modules. The major difference lies in the focus the programmer takes during the earliest planning stages of a project. Taking an **object-oriented approach** to a problem means defining the objects needed to accomplish a task and developing the objects so that each maintains its own data and carries out tasks when another object requests them. The object-oriented approach is said to be "natural"—it is more natural to think of a world of objects and the ways they interact than a world of systems, data items, and the logic required to manipulate them.

Originally, object-oriented programming was used most frequently for two major types of applications—computer simulations and graphical user interfaces. A **graphical user interface**, or **GUI** (pronounced "gooey"), allows users to interact with a program in a graphical environment. Thinking about objects in these two types of applications makes sense. For example, a city might want to develop a program that provides a simulation of traffic patterns to better prevent traffic tie-ups. By creating a model with objects such as cars and pedestrians that each contain their own data and rules for behavior, the simulation can be set in motion. For example, each car object has a specific current speed and a procedure for changing that speed. By creating a model of city traffic using objects, a computer can create a simulation of a real city at rush hour.

Creating a GUI environment for users is also a natural use for object orientation. It is easy to think of the components a user manipulates on a computer screen, such as buttons and scroll bars, as similar to real-world objects. Each GUI object contains data—for example, a button on a screen has a specific size and color. Each object also contains behaviors—for example, each button can be clicked and reacts in a specific way when clicked. Some people consider the term *object-oriented programming* to be synonymous with GUI programming, but object-oriented programming means more. Modern businesses use object-oriented design techniques when developing all sorts of business applications.

UNDERSTANDING THE PROGRAMMING PROCESS

When a business develops a system, such as payroll, inventory, or billing, using an object-oriented approach involves three separate tasks:

» Analyzing the system using an object-oriented approach (**object-oriented analysis**, or **OOA**)

» Designing the system using an object-oriented approach (**object-oriented design**, or **OOD**)

» Writing the programs using an object-oriented approach (object-oriented programming, or OOP)

Often a programmer performs all of these tasks; sometimes a systems analyst designs the system and programmers simply write the programs. Although these three tasks are often intertwined, this book focuses on the process of writing programs that have already been designed. Writing programs using an object-oriented approach involves the following steps:

1. UNDERSTANDING THE PROBLEM

Professional computer programmers write programs to satisfy the needs of others. Examples could include a Human Resources Department that needs a printed list of all employees, a Billing Department that wants a list of clients who are 30 or more days overdue on their payments, and an Order Department that needs an interactive Web site to store buyers' purchases in an online shopping cart and collect credit card information when they are ready to make purchases. Because programmers are providing a service to these users, programmers must first understand what the users want. If the program has been designed well, this step might involve only a short meeting with the designer. If it has been designed poorly, this step might take many hours of meetings between designers and users. Thoroughly understanding a problem may be one of the most difficult aspects of programming. On any job, the description of what the user needs may be vague—worse yet, users may not even really know what they want, and users who think they know what they want frequently change their minds after seeing sample output. A programmer often must revise a program many times before a user is satisfied with the outcome.

2. ENVISIONING THE OBJECTS

When object-oriented programmers write programs, they envision the objects they need. For example, one necessary object for an application might be a form on a computer screen in which a user can enter data. The programmer then writes instructions in a programming language to create the objects. Perhaps a user will use a form to enter a number and view its double value (such as in the three instructions in the doubling program in the preceding section). A professional programmer usually does not just sit down at a computer keyboard and start typing the instructions in a programming language. The object-oriented programmer's job consists of several distinct steps. You identify all the objects you want to manipulate and how they relate to each other; this is known as **data modeling**. After you have identified an object, you create a general category for the object; this general category is called a **class**. Very often, you do not have to build a class from scratch because someone has already created it—for example, many object-oriented languages already contain a class you can use to create a form on the screen. However, your form might have a size, contain words, or be a color that is different from any existing form, so you have to write those instructions. Whether you use prewritten classes or need to create some from scratch, you also establish the ways you will communicate with the objects in your program, and how they will communicate with each other.

NOTE You will gain a much more thorough understanding of classes in Chapter 7. The first programs you study in this book will be very simple classes—applications that contain only a few instructions.

3. PLANNING THE LOGIC

The heart of the programming process lies in planning the program's logic. During this phase of the process, the programmer plans the steps of the program, deciding what steps to include and how to order them. You can plan the solution to a problem in many ways. The two most common planning tools are flowcharts and pseudocode. Both tools involve writing the steps of the program in English, much as you would plan a trip on paper before getting into the car, or plan a party theme before shopping for food and favors.

The programmer doesn't worry about the syntax of any particular language at this point, but wants to figure out what sequence of events will lead from the available input to the desired output. Planning the logic includes thinking carefully about all the possible data values a pro-gram might encounter and how you want the program to handle each scenario. The process of walking through a program's logic on paper before you actually write the program is called desk-checking. You will learn more about planning the logic later; in fact, this book focuses on this crucial step almost exclusively.

4. CODING THE PROGRAM

You code the statements you need in a programming language. That is, you write the class definitions, including descriptions of all the data in each class and all the operations that will be performed with the data in each class. Well-known object-oriented programming lan-guages include C++, C#, Java, Visual Basic, SmallTalk, OO COBOL, and Simula. Despite their differences, these programming languages are quite alike—each can handle creating objects and establishing communication between them. The objects a program requires and the logic needed to work with the objects can be executed using any number of languages. Only after a language is chosen must the programmer worry about correct spelling and punctuation—in other words, using the correct *syntax*.

Some very experienced programmers can successfully combine the planning and the actual instruction writing, or **coding** of the program, in one step. This may work for planning and writing a simple program, just as you can plan and write a postcard to a friend using one step. A good term paper or a Hollywood screenplay, however, needs planning before writing, and so do most programs.

Which step is harder, planning the objects and classes or coding them? Right now, it may seem to you that writing in a programming language is a very difficult task, considering all the spelling and grammar rules you must learn. However, the planning step is actually more diffi-cult. Which is more difficult, thinking up memorable characters and how they navigate the tangled plot of a best-selling mystery novel, or translating an already written novel from English to Spanish? And who do you think gets paid more, the writer who creates the charac-ters and plot or the translator? (Try asking friends to name any famous translator!)

5. TRANSLATING THE PROGRAM CODE

Even though there are many programming languages, each computer knows only one language: its machine language, which consists of many 1s and 0s. Computers under-stand machine language because they are made up of thousands of tiny electrical switches, each of which can be set in either the on or off state, which is represented by a 1 or 0, respectively.

Languages like Java or Visual Basic are usable because of translator programs (compilers or interpreters) that change the English-like **high-level programming language** of the programmer into the **low-level machine language** that the computer understands. If you write a programming language statement incorrectly (for example, by misspelling a word, using a word that doesn't exist in the language, or using "illegal" grammar), the translator program doesn't know what to do and issues an error message identifying a **syntax error**, or misuse of a language's grammar rules. You receive the same response when you speak nonsense to a human-language translator. Imagine trying to look up a list of words in a Spanish-English dictionary if some of the listed words are misspelled— you can't complete the task until the words are spelled correctly. Although making errors is never desirable, syntax errors are not a major concern because the compiler or translator catches them all, and the computer will not execute a program that contains them.

A computer program must be free of syntax errors before you can execute it. Typically, a programmer develops objects, writes the code the objects need, compiles the program, and then receives a list of syntax errors. The programmer corrects the syntax errors and compiles the program again. Correcting the first set of errors frequently reveals a new set of errors that originally were not apparent to the compiler. For example, if you could use an English compiler and submit the sentence The grl go to school, the compiler at first would point out only one syntax error to you. The second word, grl, is illegal because it is not part of the English language. Only after you corrected the word girl would the compiler find another syntax error on the third word, go, because it is the wrong verb form for the subject girl. This doesn't mean go is necessarily the wrong word. Maybe girl is wrong; perhaps the subject should be girls, in which case go is right. Compilers don't always know exactly what you mean, nor do they know what the proper correction should be, but they do know when something is wrong with your syntax.

When writing a program, a programmer might need to recompile the code several times. An executable program is created only when the code is free of syntax errors. Figure 1-1 shows a diagram of this entire process.

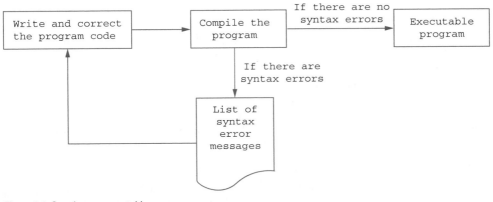

Figure 1-1 Creating an executable program

6. TESTING THE PROGRAM

A program that is free of syntax errors is not necessarily free of **logical errors**. For example, the sentence The girl goes to school, although syntactically perfect, is not logically correct if the girl is a baby or a dropout.

Once a program is free of syntax errors, the programmer can test it—that is, execute it. Many programs require that you enter some sample data to see whether the results are logically correct. Recall the number-doubling program segment from earlier in the chapter:

```
Get inputNumber.
Compute calculatedAnswer as inputNumber times 2.
Print calculatedAnswer.
```

If you write a program containing these statements, execute it, provide the value 2 as input to the program, and the answer 4 prints, you have executed one successful test run of the program.

However, if the answer 40 prints, maybe it's because the program contains a logical error. Maybe the second line of code was mistyped with an extra zero, so that the program reads:

```
Get inputNumber.
Compute calculatedAnswer as inputNumber times 20.
Print calculatedAnswer.
```

Placing 20 instead of 2 in the multiplication statement caused a logical error. Notice that nothing is syntactically wrong with this second program—it is just as reasonable to multiply a number by 20 as by 2—but if the programmer intends only to double inputNumber, then a logical error has occurred.

Programs should be tested with many sets of data. For example, if you write the program to double a number, then enter 2 and get an output value of 4, that doesn't mean you have a correct program. Perhaps you have typed this program by mistake:

```
Get inputNumber.
Compute calculatedAnswer as inputNumber plus 2.
Print calculatedAnswer.
```

An input of 2 results in an answer of 4, but that doesn't mean your program doubles numbers—it actually only adds 2 to them. If you test your program with additional data and get the wrong answer—for example, if you use a 3 and get an answer of 5—you know there is a problem with your code.

Selecting test data is somewhat of an art in itself, and it should be done carefully. If the Human Resources Department wants a list of the names of five-year employees, it would be a mistake to test the program with a small sample file of only long-term employees. If no newer employees are part of the data being used for testing, you don't really know if the program would have eliminated them from the five-year list. Many companies don't know that their software has a problem until an unusual circumstance occurs—for example, the first time an employee has more than nine dependents, the first time a customer orders more than 999 items at a time, or when a new century begins.

7. PUTTING THE PROGRAM INTO PRODUCTION

Once the program is tested adequately, it is ready for the organization to use. Putting the program into production might mean simply running the program once, if it was written to satisfy a user's request for a special list. However, the process might take months if the program will be run on a regular basis, or if it is one of a large system of programs being developed. Perhaps data-entry people must be trained to prepare the input for the new program, users must be trained to understand the output, or existing data in the company must be changed to an entirely new format to accommodate this program. Perhaps the program will be run on an organization's Web site by users who might make choices in unanticipated combinations.

A program that does not work correctly can cause a company to lose thousands or millions of dollars in business, so programs that customers use must be tested very thoroughly. **Conversion**, the entire set of actions an organization must take to switch over to using a new program or set of programs, can sometimes take months or years to accomplish.

8. MAINTAINING THE PROGRAM

After programs are put into production, making required changes is called maintenance. Maintenance is necessary for many reasons: for example, new tax rates are legislated, the format of an input file is altered, or the end user requires additional information not included in the original output specifications.

9. RETIRING THE PROGRAM

You might consider retiring the program as the final step in the programming process. A program is retired when it is no longer needed by an organization—usually when a new program is in the process of being put into production.

USING FLOWCHARTS AND PSEUDOCODE STATEMENTS

When programmers plan the logic for a solution to a programming problem, they often use one of two tools: flowcharts or pseudocode (pronounced "sue-doe-code"). A **flowchart** is a pictorial representation of the logical steps it takes to solve a problem; **pseudocode** is an English-like representation of the same thing. When you create a flowchart, you write program steps in boxes that you connect with arrows, or **flowlines**, to show the order in which steps will be processed. Figure 1-2 shows a flowchart of the number-doubling problem.

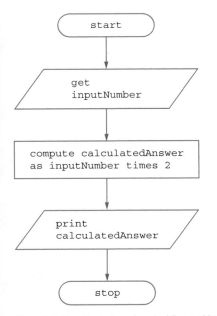

Figure 1-2 Flowchart of number-doubling problem

Figure 1-2 contains an **input symbol** and **output symbol** that contain the input and output statements, respectively. By convention, these symbols are parallelograms. The figure also contains its processing statement in a rectangle, which is the **processing symbol**. Parallelograms and rectangles are conventionally used for these respective purposes by flowchart creators. Additionally, the figure shows the conventional shapes for start and stop symbols; this shape is called a **lozenge**.

Pseudocode provides an alternative to flowcharting. *Pseudo* is a prefix that means "false," and to *code* a program means to put it in a programming language; therefore *pseudocode* simply means "false code," or sentences that appear to have been written in a computer programming language but don't necessarily follow all the syntax rules of any specific language.

You have already seen examples of statements that represent pseudocode earlier in this chapter, and there is nothing mysterious about them. The following statements constitute a pseudocode representation of a number-doubling problem:

```
start
    get inputNumber
    compute calculatedAnswer as inputNumber times 2
    print calculatedAnswer
stop
```

The steps in the pseudocode statement are identical to those between the start and stop symbols in the flowchart shown in Figure 1-2. Using pseudocode simply involves writing down all the steps you will use in a program. Most pseudocode writers do not bother with punctuation, such as periods at the end of pseudocode statements, although it would not be wrong to use them if you prefer that style. Similarly, there is no need to capitalize the first word in a sentence, although you might choose to do so. This book follows the conventions of using lowercase letters for verbs that begin pseudocode statements and omitting periods at the end of statements.

Notice in the pseudocode that the action statements of the program are indented more than `start` and `stop`. Most programmers follow this convention, which helps identify `start` and `stop` as a pair. You will learn more indenting conventions later in this chapter and in the next few chapters.

Some professional programmers prefer writing pseudocode to drawing flowcharts because using pseudocode is more similar to writing the final statements in the programming language. Others prefer drawing flowcharts to represent the logical flow because flowcharts allow programmers to more easily visualize how the program statements will connect. Especially for beginning programmers, flowcharts are an excellent tool to help visualize how the statements in complicated portions of a program are interrelated; you will use flowchart symbols in Chapters 2, 3, and 4 when you learn to write decisions and loops.

CREATING AN APPLICATION CLASS WITH A `main()` METHOD

In purely object-oriented programming languages, such as Java, every statement you make must be part of a class. In other languages, such as C++, you can write programs that contain class objects, yet are not classes themselves. This book will use the "pure view"—that every application is a class. An **application** is a program that accomplishes some task. The pseudocode for every application you create will begin with the word `class` and end with `endClass`. Although no object-oriented programming language uses the term `endClass`, this book will use it to make clear to you where a class ends. In every object-oriented language, all the program actions must take place within a method. A **method** is a set of statements that performs some task or group of tasks. In most object-oriented programming languages, if a class contains only one method that executes, the method is named `main()`. Just about the simplest program you can write is one that prints a message on the screen. Figure 1-3 shows the flowchart and pseudocode for a simple application that prints the word "Hello".

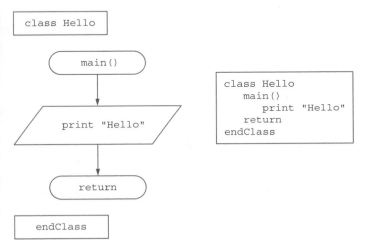

```
class Hello
    main()
        print "Hello"
    return
endClass
```

》NOTE
As a design tool, flowcharts predate object-oriented programming by many years. Therefore, there is no consistent way to express `class` and `endClass`. This book will follow the convention of showing the class stop and start points in two rectangular boxes, as in Figure 1-3.

Figure 1-3 Flowchart and pseudocode for `main()` method that prints "Hello"

In both the flowchart and pseudocode in Figure 1-3, the class begins with the word `class`, followed by the class name. A class name can be any legal identifier you choose. An **identifier** is the name of a programming object—a class, method, or variable.

Every computer programming language has its own set of rules for naming identifiers. Most languages allow both letters and digits within identifiers; all languages prohibit using a digit to begin an identifier. Some languages allow hyphens, underscores, dollar signs, or other special characters in identifiers; others allow foreign-alphabet characters such as π or Ω. You must learn the rules for creating identifiers in each programming language you use.

》NOTE You also can refer to an identifier as a **mnemonic**. In everyday language, a mnemonic is a memory device, like the sentence "Every good boy does fine," which makes it easier to remember the names of the lines on a musical staff. In programming, an identifier makes it easier to remember class and variable names than if you had to remember their memory addresses.

Different languages put different limits on the length of identifiers, although in general, newer languages allow longer names. For example, in some very old versions of BASIC, an identifier could consist of only one or two letters and one or two digits; this caused programmers to create some cryptic identifiers like `hw` or `a3` or `re02`. In other languages, identifiers can be very long; many modern languages allow more than two hundred characters in an identifier, and in the newest versions of C++, C#, and Java, the length of identifiers is virtually unlimited. These languages are case sensitive, so `Hello`, `hello`, and `HELLO` represent three separate classes. Most programmers who use more modern languages employ the format in which class names begin with an uppercase letter. Multiple-word identifiers are run together, and each new word within the identifier begins with an uppercase letter.

> **》NOTE** When an identifier begins with a lowercase letter, but contains uppercase letters within it, as in `studentGrade`, the format is called **camel casing** because such class names have a "hump" in the middle. When the first letter is uppercase, as in `HelloClass`, the format is known as **Pascal casing**. The identifiers in this text are shown using these formats.

Even though every language has its own rules for creating identifiers, you should not concern yourself with the specific syntax of any particular computer language when designing the logic of a program. The logic, after all, works with any language. The identifiers used throughout this book follow only two rules:

1. *Identifier names must be one word.* The name can contain letters, digits, hyphens, underscores, or any other characters you choose, with the exception of *spaces*. Therefore `H` is a legal identifier, as is `Hello`, as is `MyHelloClass`. The identifier `My Hello Class` is not allowed because of the spaces.

2. *Identifiers should have some appropriate meaning.* This is not a rule of any programming language. When you write a class that prints the word "Hello", the computer does not care if you call the class `G`, `U84`, or `Fred`. As long as the correct result appears, the name of the class doesn't really matter. However, it's much easier to keep track of classes that have reasonable names. When you look at an application several months after completing it, you and other programmers working with you will appreciate clear, descriptive identifiers.

The first line on each side of Figure 1-3, `class Hello`, is the **class header**. The `endClass` statement in the last line of Figure 1-3 shows where the class ends. The class header and the `endClass` statement align vertically to show they are a pair—there will always be only one `endClass` statement for each class.

In Figure 1-3, the class contains one method, the `main()` method. The statement `main()` is the **method header**. Programmers who use different languages follow different conventions when naming their methods. By convention, most Java and C++ programmers begin their method names with a lowercase letter, but C# and Visual Basic programmers use an uppercase letter. This book must follow some convention, so method names will begin with a lowercase letter.

Method names are always followed by a set of parentheses. As you learn more about programming, you will discover that sometimes it is necessary to place statements called declarations within these parentheses. Additionally, you frequently will need to add information in front of the `main()` header.

> **》NOTE**
> In C# and Visual Basic, the `main()` method begins with an uppercase M, but in C++ and Java, it begins with a lowercase m.

When a class contains a `main()` method, the class is an application, or executable program. You will learn in Chapter 6 that not all classes contain a `main()` method, but those that do are runnable programs. The first programs you work with in Chapters 2 through 5 of this book will be applications.

In this book, every method will end with a `return` statement. In many programming languages, a `return` statement marks the end of every method. Sometimes you will need to add more information after the `return` statement, but in Figure 1-3, nothing else is needed. In the flowchart representation of the logic, the main() method header and the method's return statement appear in lozenges; in the pseudocode, they vertically align to show they are a pair. They are also indented more than the class and endClass statements, but less than the executable statements in the program. Writing pseudocode with these indentation conventions makes the program easier to understand.

Within the main() method of the Hello class, between the main() method header and the method's return statement, you place all the action (executable) statements of the main() method. In this case, the desired action is to print "Hello".

Figures 1-4 and 1-5 show how the Hello class looks when implemented in Java and C#, respectively. Although each of these programs contains confusing syntax and punctuation not used in the pseudocode, see whether you can discern the pieces of code that correspond to each part of the flowchart and pseudocode in Figure 1-3.

```java
class Hello
{
    public static void main(String[] args)
    {
        System.out.println("Hello");
    }
}
```

Figure 1-4 The Hello class written in the Java programming language

```csharp
public class Hello
{
    public static void Main()
    {
        System.Console.Out.WriteLine("Hello");
    }
}
```

Figure 1-5 The Hello class written in the C# programming language

USING AND NAMING VARIABLES

Programmers commonly refer to the locations in computer memory as variables. **Variables** are memory locations whose contents can vary over time. Although a variable's value can change over time, a variable holds just one value at any given time. Most of the objects you create in programs contain variables that hold the objects' attributes. For example, a GUI form that appears on the screen has a height, and a bank account has a balance. The height of a form and the balance of an account are different at different times. As another example, when you name a memory location inputNumber, as in the last section, sometimes it can hold 2 and calculatedAnswer will hold 4; at other times, inputNumber can hold 6 and calculatedAnswer will hold 12. The ability of memory variables to change in value is what makes computers and programming worthwhile. Because one memory location can be used over and over again with different values, you can write program instructions once and then

»NOTE
When a variable holds data about an object, it is also called a **field**.

use them for thousands of separate calculations. *One* set of payroll instructions at your company produces each employee paycheck, and *one* set of instructions at your electric company produces each household's bill.

The number-doubling example requires two variables, `inputNumber` and `calculatedAnswer`. These variables can just as well be named `userEntry` and `programSolution`, or `inputValue` and `twiceTheValue`. As a programmer, you choose reasonable identifiers for your variables. The language interpreter then associates the names you choose with specific memory addresses.

You use the same rules for naming variables as you do for naming classes. Variable identifiers must be one word without spaces and must have a reasonable meaning. Some programmers have fun with their variable names by naming them after friends or creating puns with them, but such behavior is unprofessional and marks those programmers as amateurs. Table 1-1 lists possible variable names that might be used to hold an employee's last name and provides a rationale for the appropriateness of each one.

» NOTE Another general rule in all programming languages is that variable names may not begin with a digit, although usually they may contain digits. Thus, in most languages `budget2013` is a legal variable name, but `2013Budget` is not.

Suggested Variable Names for Employee's Last Name	Comments
Superior choices	
`employeeLastName`	Good
`employeeLast`	Good—most people would interpret `Last` as meaning last name
`empLast`	Good—`emp` is short for *employee*
Inferior and illegal choices	
`emlstnam`	Legal—but cryptic
`lastNameOfTheEmployeeInQuestion`	Legal—but awkward
`last name`	Not legal—embedded space
`employeelastname`	Legal—but hard to read without camel casing

Table 1-1 Valid and invalid variable names for an employee's last name

ASSIGNING VALUES TO VARIABLES

When you create pseudocode for a program that doubles numbers, you can include the statement `compute calculatedAnswer as inputNumber times 2`. This statement incorporates two actions. First, the computer calculates the arithmetic value of `inputNumber` times 2. Second, the computed value is stored in the `calculatedAnswer` memory location. Most programming languages allow a shorthand expression for **assignment statements**, statements that assign values to variables. For example, `compute calculatedAnswer as inputNumber times 2` is an assignment statement, and the shorthand takes the form calculatedAnswer = inputNumber * 2. The equal sign is the **assignment operator**; it always requires the name of a memory location on its left side—the name of the location where the result will be stored.

>> **NOTE** In Pascal, the expression that assigns a result to calculated Answer is calculatedAnswer := inputNumber * 2. In Pascal, you type a colon followed by an equal sign to create the assignment symbol. Java, C++, C#, Visual Basic, and many other languages all use the equal sign for assignment.

According to the rules of algebra, a statement like calculatedAnswer = inputNumber * 2 should be exactly equivalent to the statement inputNumber * 2 = calculatedAnswer. That's because in algebra, the equal sign always represents equivalency. To most programmers, however, the equal sign represents assignment, and calculatedAnswer = inputNumber * 2 means "multiply inputNumber by 2 and store the result in the variable called calculatedAnswer." Any operation performed to the right of the equal sign results in a value that is placed in the memory location to the left of the equal sign. Therefore, the incorrect statement inputNumber * 2 = calculatedAnswer means to attempt to take the value of calculatedAnswer and store it in a location called inputNumber * 2, but there can't be a location called inputNumber * 2. For one thing, inputNumber * 2 can't be a variable because it has spaces in it. For another, a location can't be multiplied. Its contents can be multiplied, but the location itself cannot be. The backward statement inputNumber * 2 = calculatedAnswer contains a syntax error, no matter what programming language you use; a program with such a statement will not execute.

>> **NOTE** Most programming languages use the asterisk (*) to represent multiplication. When you write pseudocode, you can use an X or a dot for multiplication (as most mathematicians do), but you will be using an unconventional format. This book will always use an asterisk to represent multiplication.

>> **NOTE** When you create an assignment statement, it may help to imagine the word "let" in front of the statement. Thus, you can read the statement calculatedAnswer = inputNumber * 2 as "Let calculatedAnswer equal inputNumber times two." Both the BASIC and Visual Basic programming languages allow you to use the word "let" in such statements. You also might imagine the word "gets" or "receives" in place of the assignment operator. In other words, calculatedAnswer = inputNumber * 2 means calculatedAnswer gets inputNumber * 2.

Computer memory is made up of millions of distinct locations, each of which has an address. Fifty or sixty years ago, programmers had to deal with these addresses and had to remember, for instance, that they stored a salary in location 6428 of their computer. Today, high-level computer languages allow us to pick a reasonable "English" name for a memory address and let the computer keep track of where it is. Just as it is easier for you to remember that the president lives in the White House than at 1600 Pennsylvania Avenue, Washington, D.C., it is also easier for you to remember that your salary is in a variable called mySalary than at memory location 6428104.

Similarly, it does not usually make sense to perform mathematical operations on names given to memory addresses, but it does make sense to perform mathematical operations on the *contents* of memory addresses. If you live in blueSplitLevelOnTheCorner, adding 1 to that would be meaningless, but you certainly can add one person to the number of people already in that house. For our purposes, then, the statement calculatedAnswer = inputNumber * 2 means exactly the same thing as the statement calculate inputNumber * 2 and store the result in the memory location named calculatedAnswer.

>> **NOTE** Many programming languages allow you to create named constants. A **named constant** is a named memory location, similar to a variable, except that its value never changes during the execution of a program. If you are working with a programming language that allows it, you might create a constant for a value like PI = 3.14 or COUNTY_SALES_TAX_RATE = 0.06. Many object-oriented programmers follow the convention of naming constants using all uppercase letters to distinguish constants from variables.

In programming languages, every operator follows **rules of precedence** that dictate the order in which operations are carried out in a statement. For example, multiplication and division always take precedence over addition and subtraction, so in an expression such as a + b * c, the b and c are multiplied first, producing a temporary result before a is added to it. The assignment operator has a very low precedence, meaning that in a statement such as d = e + f + g, the operations to the right of the assignment operator are always performed before the final assignment to the variable on the left.

UNDERSTANDING DATA TYPES

Computers deal with two basic types of data—text and numeric. When you use a specific numeric value such as 43, you write it in a program using the digits and no quotation marks. A specific numeric value is often called a **numeric constant** because it does not change—a 43 always has the value 43. When you use a specific set of characters, or a **string constant**, such as "Chris," you enclose the string within quotation marks. Many programming languages, including C++, C#, Java, and Pascal, use single quotes surrounding a **character constant** (such as 'C') and double quotes for a string (such as "Chris").

Similarly, most computer languages allow at least two distinct types of variables. One type of variable can hold a number, and is often called a **numeric variable**. In the statement calculatedAnswer = inputNumber * 2, both calculatedAnswer and inputNumber are numeric variables; that is, their intended contents are numeric values such as 6 and 3, 150 and 75, or –18 and –9.

Most programming languages have separate types of variables that can hold letters of the alphabet and other special characters such as punctuation marks. Usually, variables that hold a single character are called **character variables**, and those that hold a group of characters are called **string variables**. If a working program contains the statement gradeInTheClass = 'A', then gradeInTheClass is a character variable. If a working program contains the statement lastName = "Lincoln", then lastName is a string variable.

Programmers must distinguish between numeric and character variables because computers handle the two types of data differently. Therefore, means are provided within the syntax rules of computer programming languages to tell the computer which type of data to expect. How this is done is different in every language; some languages have different rules for naming the variables, but with others you must include a simple statement (called a declaration) telling the computer which type of data to expect. A **variable declaration** consists of the data type and the identifier. Optionally, you can provide an initial starting value for the variable—doing so is **initializing** the variable.

Some languages allow for several types of numeric data. All the popular languages, such as C++, C#, Java, and Visual Basic, distinguish between **integer** (whole number) numeric variables and **floating-point** (fractional) numeric variables that contain a decimal point. Thus, in some languages, the numbers 4 and 4.3 would have to be stored in different types of variables.

Some programming languages allow even more specific variable types, but the distinction between character and numeric data is universal. For the programs you develop in this book, assume that each variable is one of three broad types—numeric, character, or string. If a variable called taxRate is supposed to hold a value of 2.5, assume that it is a numeric variable. If a variable called middleInitial is supposed to hold a value of 'M', assume it is a character variable. And, if a variable called `inventoryItem` is supposed to hold a value of "monitor", assume that it is a string variable. You would declare these three variables as follows:

```
numeric taxRate
character middleInitial
string inventoryItem
```

When you declare variables using the preceding statements, you have not provided any initial values. Although some languages provide automatic, or **default values**, for uninitialized variables, this book will assume any uninitialized variable contains an unknown value, sometimes called a **garbage value**.

>> **NOTE** Some compilers will warn you when you attempt to use a variable that has not been provided with a value. Such variables are called **undefined variables**. An undefined variable has been declared—that is, provided with a type and identifier. It just does not contain a usable value. On the other hand, an **undeclared variable** is one that has not been provided with a data type and identifier.

To provide values for the variables `taxRate`, `middleInitial`, and `inventoryItem`, you have two options. First, you can declare the variables and then assign values later, as follows:

```
numeric taxRate
character middleInitial
string inventoryItem
taxRate = 2.5
middleInitial = 'M'
inventoryItem = "monitor"
```

Notice that in the preceding example, the identifier is associated with its data type just once. A declaration such as `numeric taxRate` establishes a memory location named `taxRate`. Later, when you assign a value to it, you do not establish the memory location again.

Alternatively, you can initialize the variables when you declare them, as follows:

```
numeric taxRate = 2.5
character middleInitial = 'M'
string inventoryItem = "monitor"
```

>> **NOTE** Any values can be characters or contained within strings. Besides letters of the alphabet, punctuation marks, spaces, and even digits can be treated as characters. If you intend a variable to be used in arithmetic statements, you declare it to be numeric. However, if a variable is all digits but will not be used in arithmetic statements, such as an ID number or telephone number, you can declare the variable to be a string.

>> **NOTE** Values such as "monitor" and 2.5 are called constants or literal constants because they never change. A variable value *can* change. Thus, `inventoryItem` can hold "monitor" at one moment during the execution of a program, and later you can change its value to "modem".

By convention, this book encloses string data like "monitor" within quotation marks to distinguish the characters from another variable name. Character data, such as 'W', is contained in single quotation marks, following the syntax of Java, C++, and C#. Also by convention, numeric data values are not enclosed within quotation marks. According to these conventions, `taxRate = 2.5` and `inventoryItem = "monitor"` are both valid statements. The statement `inventoryItem = monitor` is a valid statement only if `monitor` is also a string variable. In other words, if `monitor = "color"`, and subsequently `inventoryItem = monitor`, the end result is that the memory address named `inventoryItem` contains the string of characters "color".

Every computer handles text or character data differently from the way it handles numeric data. You may have experienced these differences if you have used application software such as spreadsheets or database programs. For example, in a spreadsheet, you cannot sum a column of words. Similarly, every programming language requires that you distinguish variables by their correct type, and that you use each type of variable appropriately. Identifying your variables correctly as numeric, character, or string is one of the first steps of writing programs in any programming language. Table 1-2 provides a few examples of legal and illegal variable assignment statements.

Assume `lastName` and `firstName` are string variables.

Assume `middleInitial` is a character variable.

Assume `quizScore` and `homeworkScore` are numeric variables.

Examples of Valid Assignments	Examples of Invalid Assignments
lastName = "Parker"	lastName = Parker
firstName = "Laura"	"Parker" = lastName
lastName = firstName	lastName = quizScore
middleInitial = 'P'	middleInitial = P
middleInitial = ' '	middleInitial = lastName
quizScore = 86	homeworkScore = firstName
homeworkScore = quizScore	homeworkScore = "92"
homeworkScore = 92	quizScore = "zero"
quizScore = homeworkScore + 25	firstName = 23
homeworkScore = 3 * 10	100 = homeworkScore

Table 1-2 Some examples of legal and illegal assignments

Figure 1-6 shows a complete `DoubleNumber` class that allows the user to enter a number and see the result when the value is doubled. The class name is `DoubleNumber` and it contains one method, the `main()` method. Two variables, `inputNumber` and `calculatedAnswer`, are declared; there is no need to provide initial values for these variables because one will be provided by a user and the other will be calculated based on the user's input. When you see statements that begin with a data type followed by an identifier, the statements are declarations. When a method contains declarations in this book, they will be the first statements in the method. In Figure 1-6, the three statements that perform the action of the `main()` method follow the variable declarations.

As you work through this book, you will create increasingly complicated classes. However, the format of the flowchart or pseudocode for all your classes will be similar to that shown in Figure 1-6.

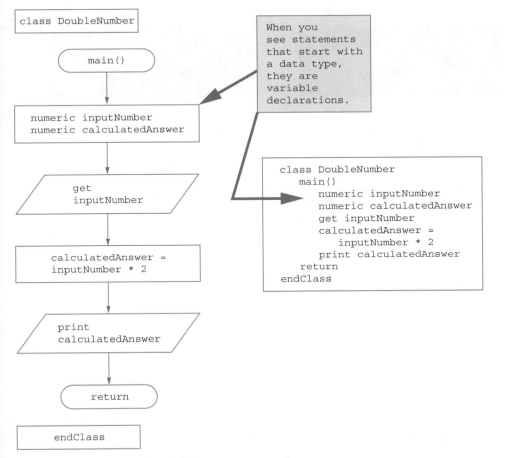

Figure 1-6 Flowchart and pseudocode for the `DoubleNumber` class

UNDERSTANDING VARIOUS FORMS OF INPUT

Some simple programs require simple data. For example, the number-doubling program requires just one value as input. In this type of program, data values are often entered from a keyboard. When users must enter data, they are typically shown a prompt. A **prompt** is a message displayed on a monitor, asking the user for a response. For example, the first screen shown in Figure 1-7 might be displayed while a number-doubling program is running. The second screen shows the result after the user enters a response to the prompt.

The program in Figure 1-7 is executed at the command prompt. Use the **command prompt** on your computer screen to type text that communicates with the computer's operating system. In this case, the user has asked the operating system to run a program named `NumberDoublingProgram`, and then the program has supplied the prompt to the user.

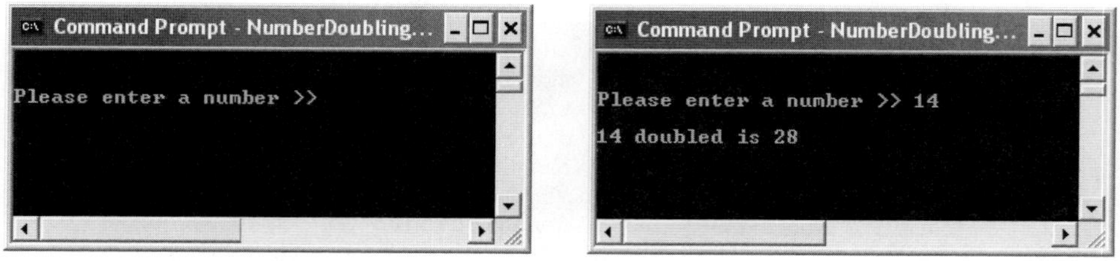

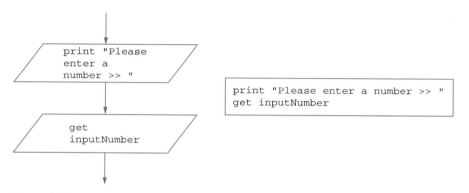

Figure 1-7 A prompt followed by a response and output in a command-line environment

In the type of interactive program shown in Figure 1-7, two program statements are required to represent the `"get"` in the logic `"get inputNumber"`. First, an output statement is required to display the screen prompt. Then the statement that retrieves the data from the keyboard is added. Figure 1-8 shows the flowchart and pseudocode for the two statements that together retrieve the input data for this type of program.

```
print "Please
enter a
number >> "
```

```
get
inputNumber
```

```
print "Please enter a number >> "
get inputNumber
```

Figure 1-8 Flowchart and pseudocode for prompt and response in number-doubling program

A **user interface** is the user's means of interacting with the computer. In Figure 1-7, the user is presented with a text interface. Many programs are not run at the command prompt in a text environment, but are run using a GUI, which typically contains graphical controls such as buttons and text boxes that a user can manipulate with a mouse or other pointing device. Figure 1-9 shows a number-doubling program that performs exactly the same task as the one in Figure 1-7, but this program uses a GUI. The user is presented with a prompt and an empty text box. When the user types a number in the text box, the result appears.

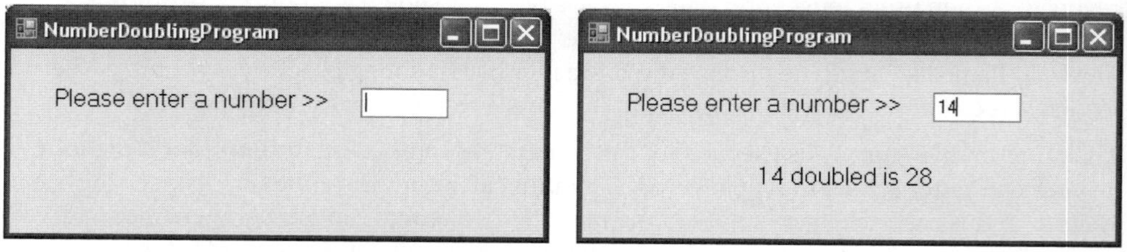

Figure 1-9 A prompt, a response, and output in a GUI environment

22

When you write a program that displays an interactive screen like the one in Figure 1-9, you first design the screen that contains the prompt and the text box. The design details vary depending on the programming language you use, but any language requires statements in your program that accept the user's entry from a text box and store it in the variable you will use. The flowchart and pseudocode for this process might look like Figure 1-10.

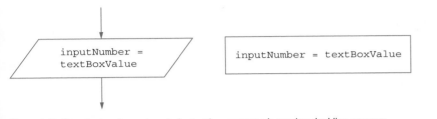

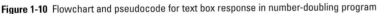

Figure 1-10 Flowchart and pseudocode for text box response in number-doubling program

Although the programs in Figures 1-7 and 1-9 look different when they execute, their logic is the same. Each accepts a user's input, calculates its double, and displays output. The difference in the two is the interface presented to the user.

When you learn to use a programming language, you will create programs like the ones in Figures 1-7 and 1-9. In this book, however, you will be less concerned with the appearance of input and output than with the logic behind those processes.

Whatever format the interface takes, the number-doubling program requires just one value as input. Most business programs, however, use much more data to form records. A record is a collection of data fields. For example, an inventory record might require an item number, description, and price. A personnel or customer record might require an ID number, first and last names, address, phone number, and so on. Additionally, inventory files may contain thousands of item records, and personnel and customer files may contain records for thousands of people.

Whether data has been stored in a flat file or a database, when a program needs all the fields in a record, you can write programming statements to get or input each field in one of several ways. For example, if a program needs an employee's name, address, and salary, most programming languages allow you to write separate statements, such as the following:

NOTE
Related files are often stored in a **database**. When records are stored in a file that is not part of a database, programmers often refer to it as a **flat file**.

```
Get name
Get address
Get salary
```

Most languages also allow you to write a single statement in the following format:

```
Get name, address, salary
```

Additionally, most programming languages provide a way for you to use a group name for record data, as in the following statement:

```
Get EmployeeRecord
```

When you use this format, you need to define the separate fields that compose an `EmployeeRecord`. You will learn to do this when you create classes in Chapter 6. For now, you can take either approach with your programs. For convenience, when multiple input fields are required, this book will usually indicate their retrieval with a statement like the following:

```
Get name, address, salary
```

Keep in mind that the input logic is the same, no matter how the items are grouped or from where they are retrieved.

CHAPTER SUMMARY

» Together, computer hardware (equipment) and software (instructions) accomplish four major operations: input, processing, output, and storage. You write computer instructions in a computer programming language that requires specific syntax; the instructions are translated into machine language by a compiler or interpreter. When both the syntax and logic of a program are correct, you can run, or execute, the program to produce the desired results.

» Procedural programming focuses on the procedures that programmers create to manipulate data. The other popular programming technique, called object-oriented programming (OOP), focuses on objects, or "things." OOP describes these objects' features, or attributes, and their behaviors.

» A programmer's job involves identifying objects and classes, coding the program, translating the program into machine language, testing the program, and putting the program into production.

» When programmers plan the logic for a solution to a programming problem, they often use flowcharts or pseudocode.

» An application is a program that accomplishes some task. In every object-oriented language, all the program actions must take place within a method. A method is a set of statements that performs some task or group of tasks. In most object-oriented programming languages, if a class contains only one method that executes, the method is named `main()`.

» Variables are named memory locations, the contents of which can vary. As a programmer, you choose reasonable names for your variables. Every computer programming language has its own set of rules for naming variables; however, all variable names must be written as one word without embedded spaces, and should have appropriate meaning.

» Most programming languages use the equal sign to assign values to variables. Assignment always takes place from right to left.

» Programmers must distinguish between numeric, character, and string variables because computers handle the types of data differently. A variable declaration tells the computer which type of data to expect.

» Although data can be input by a user in a text or graphical environment, or can come from a file stored alone or as part of a database, the input operation in each of these cases is basically the same.

KEY TERMS

Hardware is the equipment of a computer system.

Software is the set of instructions written by programmers that tell the computer what to do; software is computer programs.

Application software comprises all the programs you apply to a task.

System software comprises the programs that you use to manage your computer, including operating systems such as Windows or UNIX and other utility programs not directly used by end users.

Input devices include keyboards and mice; through these devices, data enters the computer system. Data can also enter a system from storage devices such as magnetic disks and CDs.

Data is a set of facts that are input to a program.

Processing data items may involve organizing them, checking them for accuracy, or performing mathematical operations on them.

The **central processing unit**, or **CPU**, is the hardware component that processes data.

Information is data that has been processed and is ready for output.

An **output device** is hardware (for example, a monitor or printer) that provides information so that people can view, interpret, and work with the results.

Storage devices are hardware, such as magnetic disks, compact discs, or USB drives, on which you can store output information.

Hard copy is printed computer output.

Soft copy is screen output.

Programming languages, such as Visual Basic, C#, C++, Java, Pascal, COBOL, RPG, and Fortran, are used to write programs.

The **syntax** of a language consists of its rules.

Machine language is a computer's on-off circuitry language.

A **compiler** or **interpreter** translates a high-level language into machine language and tells you if you have used a programming language incorrectly.

You develop the **logic** of the computer program when you give instructions to the computer in a specific sequence, without leaving any instructions out or adding extraneous instructions.

Programmers often call logical errors **semantic errors**.

A program is **run** or **executed** when the computer actually uses the written and translated program.

Internal storage is called **memory**, **main memory**, or **primary memory**.

External storage is permanent storage outside the main memory of the machine, on a device such as a floppy disk, hard disk, or magnetic tape.

Internal memory is **volatile**—that is, its contents are lost every time the computer loses power.

You **save** a program by placing a copy on some nonvolatile medium.

Procedural programming focuses on the procedures that programmers create to manipulate data.

Object-oriented programming (OOP) focuses on objects, or "things." OOP describes the objects' features, or attributes, and their behaviors.

The **attributes of an object** are the features it "has."

The values of an object's attributes constitute the object's **state**.

The **behaviors of an object** are the things it "does."

Taking an **object-oriented approach** to a problem means defining the objects needed to accomplish a task and developing the objects so that each maintains its own data and carries out tasks when another object requests them.

A **graphical user interface**, or **GUI** (pronounced "gooey"), allows users to interact with a program in a graphical environment.

Object-oriented analysis, or **OOA**, is analyzing a system using an object-oriented approach.

Object-oriented design, or **OOD**, is designing a system using an object-oriented approach.

Data modeling is the act of identifying all the objects you want to manipulate and how they relate to each other.

A **class** is a general category of objects.

An **algorithm** is the sequence of steps necessary to solve any problem.

Coding a program means writing the statements in a programming language.

High-level programming languages are English-like.

Low-level machine language is the set of statements made up of 1s and 0s that the computer understands.

A **syntax error** is an error in language or grammar.

Logical errors occur when incorrect instructions are performed, or when instructions are performed in the wrong order.

Conversion is the entire set of actions an organization must take to switch over to using a new program or set of programs.

A **flowchart** is a pictorial representation of the logical steps it takes to solve a problem.

Pseudocode is an English-like representation of the logical steps it takes to solve a problem.

Flowlines are the arrows in a flowchart that show the sequence of steps carried out.

An **input symbol** in a flowchart contains an input statement and is represented by a parallelogram.

An **output symbol** in a flowchart contains an output statement and is represented by a parallelogram.

A **processing symbol** in a flowchart contains a processing statement and is represented by a rectangle.

A **lozenge** is a symbol that marks the beginning or end of a flowchart segment, method, or program.

An **application** is a program that accomplishes some task.

A **method** is a set of statements that performs some task or group of tasks.

An **identifier** is the name of a programming object—a class, method, or variable.

A **mnemonic** is a memory device; variable identifiers act as mnemonics for hard-to-remember memory addresses.

Camel casing is the format for naming variables and other program components in which multiple-word variable names are run together, the initial letter is lowercase, and each new word within the variable name begins with an uppercase letter.

Pascal casing is the format for naming variables and other program components in which multiple-word variable names are run together, the initial letter is uppercase, and each new word within the variable name begins with an uppercase letter.

A **class header** contains the word `class` and the class identifier; it is the first line written in a class definition.

A **method header** is the first line in a method.

Variables are memory locations whose contents can vary over time.

When a variable stores data about an object, it can be called a **field**.

An **assignment statement** stores the result of any calculation performed on its right side to the named location on its left side.

The equal sign is the **assignment operator**; it always requires the name of a memory location on its left side.

A **named constant** is a named memory location, similar to a variable, except that its value never changes during the execution of a program.

Rules of precedence dictate the order in which operations in the same statement are carried out.

A **numeric constant** is a specific numeric value.

A **string constant** is a literal set of characters enclosed within quotation marks.

A **character constant** is a single character enclosed in single quotation marks.

Numeric variables hold numeric values.

Character variables hold single character values.

String variables hold a series of characters.

A **variable declaration** is a statement that names a variable and tells the computer which type of data to expect.

Initializing a variable declares it and provides an initial value.

Integer values are whole-number numeric variables.

Floating-point values are fractional numeric variables that contain a decimal point.

Default values are automatically supplied values.

A **garbage value** is an unknown value in an uninitialized variable.

Undefined variables are those that have not been provided with a value before you attempt to use them.

Undeclared variables have not been provided with a data type or identifier.

A **prompt** is a message displayed on a monitor, asking the user for a response.

The **command prompt** is the text-based interface that you can use to communicate with the computer's operating system.

A **user interface** is the user's means of interacting with the computer.

Related files are often stored in a **database**.

When records are stored in a file that is not part of a database, programmers often refer to it as a **flat file**.

REVIEW QUESTIONS

1. The two major components of any computer system are its _____ .

   a. input and output   c. hardware and software

   b. data and programs   d. memory and disk drives

2. The major computer operations include _____ .

   a. hardware and software

   b. input, processing, output, and storage

   c. sequence and looping

   d. spreadsheets, word processing, and data communications

3. Another term meaning "computer instructions" is _____ .

   a. hardware   c. queries

   b. software   d. data

4. Visual Basic, C++, and Java are all examples of computer _____ .

   a. operating systems   c. machine languages

   b. hardware   d. programming languages

5. A programming language's rules are its _____ .

   a. syntax   c. format

   b. logic   d. options

6. The most important task of a compiler or interpreter is to _____ .

   a. create the rules for a programming language

   b. translate English statements into a language such as Java

   c. translate programming language statements into machine language

   d. execute machine language programs to perform useful tasks

7. Which of the following is not associated with internal storage?

   a. main memory   c. primary memory

   b. hard disk   d. volatile storage

8. Object-oriented programming focuses on _____ .

   a. data   c. procedures

   b. objects   d. all of the above

9. The attributes of an object are the things that it _____ .

   a. has   c. influences

   b. does   d. understands

10. In object-oriented programming, each object _____ .

    a. maintains its own data

    b. carries out tasks when another object requests them

    c. both of these

    d. none of these

11. Originally, object-oriented programming was used most frequently for two major types of applications. These were _____ .

    a. payroll and inventory

    b. input and storage

    c. computer simulations and graphical user interfaces

    d. public and private applications

12. Using an object-oriented approach involves all of the following except _____ .

    a. analyzing the system using object-oriented analysis, or OOA

    b. designing the system using object-oriented design, or OOD

    c. writing the programs using object-oriented programming, or OOP

    d. testing the programs using object-oriented testing, or OOT

13. Identifying all the objects you want to manipulate and how they relate to each other is known as _____ .

    a. object orienting

    b. data modeling

    c. method manipulation

    d. relating

14. The two most commonly used tools for planning a program's logic are _____ .

    a. flowcharts and pseudocode

    b. ASCII and EBCDIC

    c. Java and Visual Basic

    d. word processors and spreadsheets

15. Writing a program in a language such as C++ or Java is known as _____ the program.

    a. translating   c. interpreting

    b. coding   d. compiling

16. A compiler would find all of the following programming errors except _____ .

    a. the misspelled word "prrint" in a language that includes the word "print"

    b. the use of an "X" for multiplication in a language that requires an asterisk

    c. a `newBalanceDue` calculated by adding a `customerPayment` to an `oldBalanceDue` instead of subtracting it

    d. an arithmetic statement written as `regularSales + discountedSales = totalSales`

17. Which of the following is not a legal variable name in any programming language?

    a. `semester grade`

    b. `fall2005_grade`

    c. `GradeInCIS100`

    d. `MY_GRADE`

18. The broadest types of data are _____ .

    a. internal and external

    b. volatile, constant, and temporary

    c. string, character, and numeric

    d. permanent and temporary

19. Assuming `address` is a string variable, which of the following is a legal assignment statement?

    a. `address = "23 Elm"`

    b. `"23 Elm" = address`

    c. `address = 23 Elm`

    d. `address = 23`

20. Assuming `salary` is a numeric variable, which of the following is a legal assignment statement?

    a. `salary = "not enough"`

    b. `salary = "23.45"`

    c. both of these

    d. none of these

EXERCISES

1. Match the definition with the appropriate term.

    1. Computer system equipment   a. compiler

    2. Another word for *programs*   b. syntax

    3. Language rules   c. logic

    4. Order of instructions   d. hardware

    5. Language translator   e. software

2. In your own words, describe the steps to writing a computer program.

3. Lakeview Towers is being constructed as a high-rise apartment building in a downtown urban district. The managers of the building want to create a simulation of daily elevator use to plan for the optimum number of elevators, so that they are neither idle too frequently nor cause more than a one-minute wait for any resident. What sorts of objects should be created for this simulation?

4. Which of the following names seem like good variable names to you? If a name doesn't seem like a good variable name, explain why not.

   a. c

   b. cost

   c. costAmount

   d. cost amount

   e. cstofdngbsns

   f. costOfDoingBusinessThisFiscalYear

   g. cost2004

5. If myAge and yourRate are numeric variables, and departmentCode is a string variable, which of the following statements are valid assignments? If a statement is not valid, explain why not.

   a. myAge = 23

   b. myAge = yourRate

   c. myAge = departmentCode

   d. myAge = "departmentCode"

   e. 42 = myAge

   f. yourRate = 3.5

   g. yourRate = myAge

   h. yourRate = departmentCode

   i. 6.91 = yourRate

   j. departmentCode = Personnel

   k. departmentCode = "Personnel"

   l. departmentCode = 413

   m. departmentCode = "413"

   n. departmentCode = myAge

   o. departmentCode = yourRate

   p. 413 = departmentCode

   q. "413" = departmentCode

6. Draw the flowchart or write the pseudocode for an application that allows a user to enter the price of an item and computes 5 percent sales tax on the item.

7. Draw the flowchart or write the pseudocode for an application that allows a user to enter the number of minutes used on a cell phone and displays the phone bill. The calls cost 10 cents per minute plus 6% tax.

8. Draw the flowchart or write the pseudocode for an application that allows a user to enter the cost of home maintenance in each of the four seasons—summer, fall, winter, and spring—and displays the total.

9. Draw the flowchart or write the pseudocode for an application that allows a student to enter scores for four classroom assignments and displays the numeric average.

10. Draw the flowchart or write the pseudocode for an application that allows a user to enter a credit card balance. Assuming the interest rate is 1 percent per month and that the user makes no payments, display the amount that will be due after one month and after two months.

CASE PROJECT

Cost Is No Object is a car rental service that specializes in lending antique and luxury cars to clients on a short-term basis. A typical customer might rent a vintage convertible for a high school reunion weekend, or a luxury car to transport a wedding party. The service currently has three employees and 10 vehicles that it rents. List the objects needed to write a program that could provide a simulation of one day's business activity.

UP FOR DISCUSSION

1. Use an Internet search engine to find at least three definitions of object-oriented programming. (Try searching with and without the hyphen in *object-oriented*.) Compare the definitions and compile them into one "best" definition.

2. What is the difference between a compiler and an interpreter? What programming languages use each? Under what conditions would you prefer to use one over the other?

3. In this chapter, you learned the term *mnemonic*, which is a memory device like the sentence "Every good boy does fine." Another popular mnemonic is "May I have a large container of coffee?" What is its meaning? Have you learned other mnemonics in your studies? Describe at least five other mnemonics that people use to remember lists of items.

4. What is the image of the computer programmer in popular culture? Is the image different in books than in TV shows and movies? Would you like a programmer's image for yourself, and if so, which one?

UNDERSTANDING STRUCTURE

In this chapter, you will:

Understand why programs need to repeat instructions

Learn how to stop a program from executing infinitely

Learn about unstructured spaghetti code

Learn the three basic structures: sequence, selection, and loop

Build structured methods

Use a priming read

Appreciate the reasons to use structure

Recognize structure

Learn about three special structures—case, `do-while`, and `do-until`

Learn about methods

UNDERSTANDING THE NEED TO REPEAT PROGRAM INSTRUCTIONS

Methods within professional computer programs usually get far more complicated than the `main()` method from the number-doubling application discussed in Chapter 1 (and shown again in Figure 2-1).

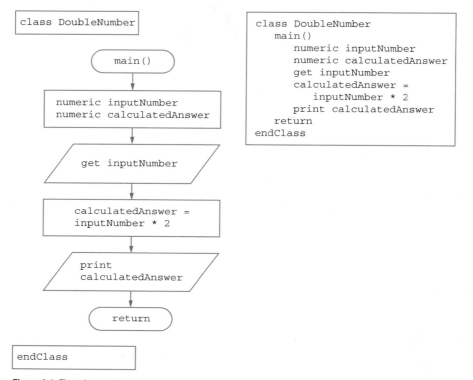

Figure 2-1 Flowchart and pseudocode for the `DoubleNumber` class

> **» NOTE** If you were creating a professional program that uses the logic shown in Figure 2-1, you could replace the numeric constant 2 with a named constant, such as `MULTIPLICATION FACTOR = 2`. Then you would use the named constant in place of the 2 in the arithmetic statement. This technique is used frequently throughout this book, but is left out of this program to keep the example as simple as possible. You learned about named constants in Chapter 1.

After the flowchart or pseudocode has been developed, the programmer only needs to: (1) buy a computer, (2) buy a language compiler, (3) learn a programming language, (4) code the program, (5) attempt to compile it, (6) fix the syntax errors, (7) compile it again, (8) test it with several sets of data, and (9) put it into production.

"Whoa!" you are probably saying to yourself. "This is simply not worth it! All that work to create a flowchart or pseudocode, and *then* all those other steps? For five dollars, I can buy a pocket calculator that will double any number for me instantly!" You are absolutely right. If this were a real computer program, and all it did was double the value of a number, it simply would not be worth all the effort. Writing a computer program would be worth the effort only if you had many—let's say 10,000—numbers to double in a limited amount of time—let's say the next two minutes. Then, it would be worth your while to create a computer program.

Unfortunately, the number-doubling program represented in Figure 2-1 does not double 10,000 numbers; it doubles only one. You could execute the program 10,000 times, of course, but that would require you to sit at the computer and tell it to run the program over and over again. You would be better off with a program that could process 10,000 numbers, one after the other.

One solution is to write the program shown in Figure 2-2 and execute the same steps 10,000 times. Of course, writing this program would be very time-consuming; you might as well buy the calculator.

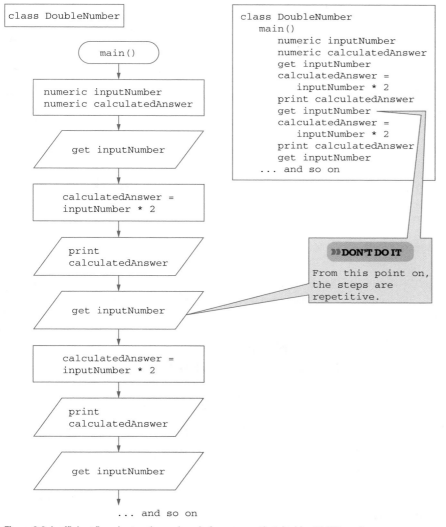

Figure 2-2 Inefficient flowchart and pseudocode for program that doubles 10,000 numbers

A better solution is to have the computer execute the same set of three instructions over and over again, as shown in Figure 2-3. With this approach, the computer gets a number, doubles it, prints the answer, and then starts over with the first instruction. The same spot in memory, called `inputNumber`, is reused for the second number and any subsequent numbers. The spot in memory named `calculatedAnswer` is reused each time to store the result of the multiplication.

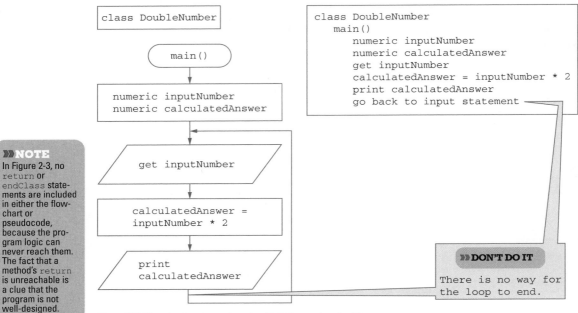

>> NOTE
In Figure 2-3, no `return` or `endClass` statements are included in either the flowchart or pseudocode, because the program logic can never reach them. The fact that a method's `return` is unreachable is a clue that the program is not well-designed.

Figure 2-3 Flowchart and pseudocode of infinite number-doubling program

Unfortunately, the logic in the flowchart and pseudocode shown in Figure 2-3 contains a major problem—the sequence of instructions never ends. You will learn to handle this problem in the next section.

STOPPING A PROGRAM FROM EXECUTING INFINITELY

The problem shown in Figure 2-3 is known as an **infinite loop**—a repeating flow of logic with no end. If, for example, the input numbers are being entered at the keyboard, the program will keep accepting numbers and printing doubles forever. Of course, the user could refuse to type in any more numbers. But the computer is patient, and if you refuse to give it any more numbers, it will wait forever. When you finally type in a number, the program will double it, print the result, and wait for another. The program cannot progress any further while it is waiting for input; meanwhile, the program is occupying computer memory and tying up operating system resources. Refusing to enter any more numbers is not a practical solution. Another way to end the program is simply to turn the computer off. But again, that's neither the best way nor an elegant way to bring the program to an end.

A superior solution is to set a predetermined value for `inputNumber` that means "Stop the program!" For example, the programmer and the user could agree that the user will never need to know the double of 0 (zero), so users could enter 0 when they want to stop. The program could then test any incoming value contained in `inputNumber` and, if it is 0, stop the program. **Testing a value** involves comparing it to another value to make a decision.

You represent a decision in a flowchart by drawing a **decision symbol**, which is shaped like a diamond. The diamond usually contains a question, the answer to which is one of two mutually exclusive options—often yes or no. In a well-written flowchart, one flowline enters the decision symbol and two emerge from it, representing the two possible answers to the question. All good computer questions have only two mutually exclusive answers, such as yes and no or true and false. For example, "What day of the year is your birthday?" is not a good computer question because there are 366 possible answers. But "Is your birthday June 24?" is a good computer question because the answer is always either yes or no.

The question to stop the doubling program should be, "Is the `inputNumber` just entered equal to 0?", or "`inputNumber = 0?`" for short. The flowchart for the complete program will now look like the one shown in Figure 2-4.

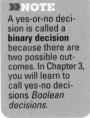

> **» NOTE**
> A yes-or-no decision is called a **binary decision** because there are two possible outcomes. In Chapter 3, you will learn to call yes-no decisions *Boolean decisions*.

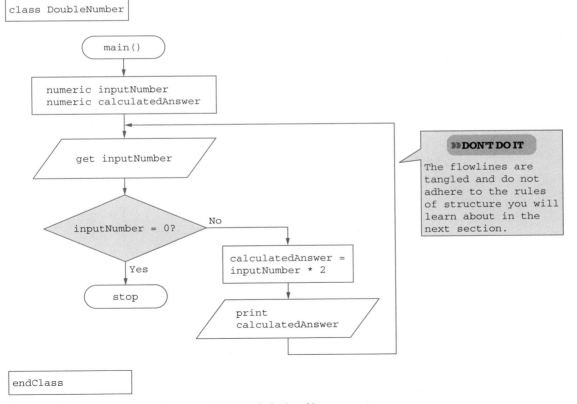

> **» DON'T DO IT**
> The flowlines are tangled and do not adhere to the rules of structure you will learn about in the next section.

Figure 2-4 Flowchart of number-doubling program with sentinel value of 0

One drawback to using 0 to stop a program, of course, is that it won't work if the user needs to find the double of 0. In that case, some other data-entry value that the user never will need, such as 999 or –1, could be selected to signal that the program should end. A preselected value that stops the execution of a program is often called a **dummy value** because it does not represent real data, but just a signal to stop. Sometimes, such a value is called a **sentinel** value because it represents an entry or exit point, like a sentinel who guards a fortress.

Not all programs rely on a user entering data from a keyboard; many programs read data from an input device, such as a disk or flash memory. When organizations store data on a disk or other storage device, they do not commonly use a dummy value to signal the end of the file. For one thing, an input record might have hundreds of fields and be thousands of bytes in length, and if you store a dummy record in every file, you are wasting a large quantity of storage on "non-data." Additionally, it is often difficult to choose sentinel values for fields in a company's data files. Any balanceDue, even a zero or a negative number, can be a legitimate value, and any customerName, even "ZZ", could be someone's name. Fortunately, programming languages can recognize the end of data in a file automatically, through a code that is stored at the end of the data. Many programming languages use the term **eof** (for "end of file") to represent this marker that automatically acts as a sentinel. This book uses eof to indicate the end of data that comes from a stored file, and uses the term generically to indicate the end of any data entry when a specific sentinel value is not relevant to the discussion at hand. Therefore, the flowchart of the number-doubling program can look like the example shown in Figure 2-5.

»NOTE
The flowchart in Figure 2-5 is not yet complete. You will work with the flowchart again later in this chapter.

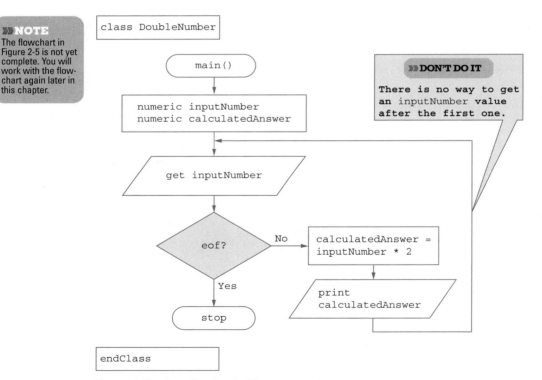

Figure 2-5 Flowchart of number-doubling program using eof

UNDERSTANDING UNSTRUCTURED SPAGHETTI CODE

The `main()` method shown in Figure 2-5 contains only a few statements. Imagine the number of instructions in the computer program that NASA uses to calculate the launch angle of a space shuttle, or in the application the IRS uses to audit your income tax return. Even the program that produces a paycheck for you contains many more instructions. Designing the logic for such an application can be a time-consuming task. When you add several thousand instructions to a program, perhaps including several hundred decisions, it is easy to create a complicated mess. The popular name for snarled program statements is **spaghetti code**. The reason for the name should be obvious—the code is as confusing to read as following one noodle through a plate of spaghetti.

For example, suppose you are in charge of admissions at a college, and you've decided to admit prospective students based on the following criteria:

» You will admit students who score 90 or better on the admissions test your college gives, as long as they are in the upper 75 percent of their high-school graduating class. (These are smart students who score well on the admissions test. Maybe they didn't do so well in high school because it was a tough school, or maybe they have matured.)

» You will admit students who score at least 80 on the admissions test if they also are in the upper 50 percent of their high-school graduating class. (These students score fairly well on the test, and do fairly well in school.)

» You will admit students who score as low as 70 on your test if they are in the top 25 percent of their class. (Maybe these students don't take tests well, but obviously they are achievers.) Table 2-1 summarizes the admission requirements.

Test score	High-school rank (%)
90–100	25–100
80–89	50–100
70–79	75–100

Table 2-1 Admission requirements

The flowchart for the program that determines admission status could look like the one in Figure 2-6.

The kind of flowchart represented in Figure 2-6 is an example of spaghetti code. Many computer programs (especially older ones) bear a striking resemblance to this flowchart. The lines cross each other, and it is difficult to follow a path of logic. Such programs might "work"—that is, they might produce correct results—but they are very difficult to read and maintain, and their logic is difficult to follow. Later in this chapter, the same college admission problem is presented in a structured format, which is easier to follow and less prone to error.

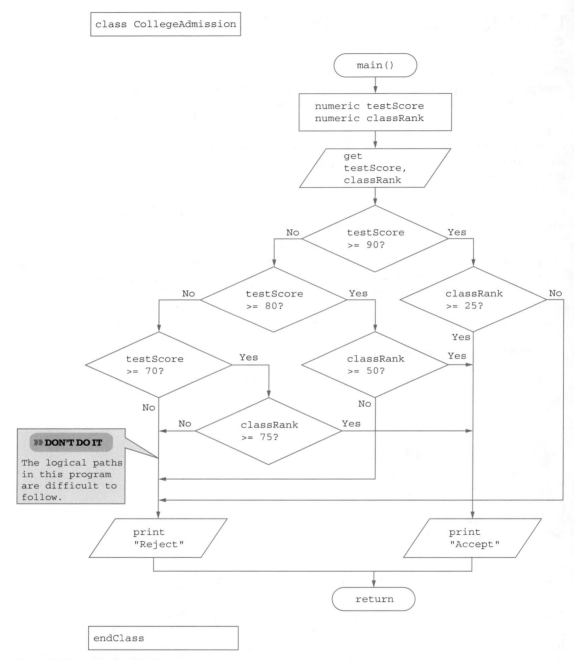

Figure 2-6 Unstructured spaghetti code example

UNDERSTANDING THE THREE BASIC STRUCTURES: SEQUENCE, SELECTION, AND LOOP

In the mid-1960s, mathematicians proved that any program or method within a program or class, no matter how complicated, could be constructed using only three structures. A **structure** is a basic unit of programming logic; each structure is a sequence, selection, or loop. With these three structures alone, you can diagram any event, from doubling a number to performing brain surgery.

THE SEQUENCE STRUCTURE

Figure 2-7 contains a flowchart depicting a sequence structure. With a **sequence structure**, you perform an action or event, and then you perform the next action, in order. A sequence can contain any number of events, but there is no chance to branch off and skip any of the events. Once you start a series of events in a sequence, you must continue step-by-step until the sequence ends.

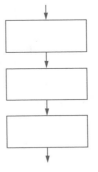

Figure 2-7 Sequence structure

THE SELECTION STRUCTURE

A **selection structure** or **decision structure** appears in Figure 2-8. With this structure, you ask a question, and, depending on the answer, you take one of two courses of action. Then, no matter which path you follow, you continue with the next event.

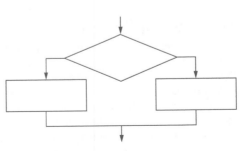

Figure 2-8 Selection structure

Some people call the selection structure an **if-then-else** because it fits the following statement:

```
if someCondition is true then
    do oneProcess
else
    do anotherProcess
```

For example, while cooking you may decide to do the following:

```
if we have brownSugar then
    use brownSugar
else
    use whiteSugar
```

Similarly, a payroll application might include a statement such as:

```
if hoursWorked is more than 40 then
    calculate overtimePay
else
    calculate regularPay
```

The previous examples can also be called **dual-alternative ifs** because they contain two alternatives—the action taken when the tested condition is true, and the action taken when it is false. Note that it is perfectly correct for one branch of the selection to be a "do nothing" branch. For example:

```
if it is raining then
    take anUmbrella
```

or

```
if employee belongs to dentalPlan then
    deduct $40 from employeeGrossPay
```

The previous examples are **single-alternative ifs**, and a diagram of their structure is shown in Figure 2-9. In these cases, you don't take special action if it is not raining or if the employee does not belong to the dental plan. The case in which nothing is done is often called the **null case**.

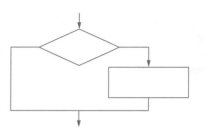

Figure 2-9 Single-alternative selection structure

THE LOOP STRUCTURE

Besides sequence and selection structures, you can use a third structure called a loop, as shown in Figure 2-10. In a **loop structure**, you ask a question; if the answer requires an action, you perform the action and ask the original question again. If the answer requires that the action be taken again, you take the action and then ask the original question again. This continues until the answer requires no further action; then you exit the structure. You may hear programmers refer to looping as **repetition** or **iteration**.

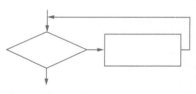

Figure 2-10 Loop structure

Some programmers call the loop structure a **while loop** or a **while-do loop** because it fits the following statement:

```
while testCondition continues to be true
    do someProcess
```

You encounter examples of looping every day, as in the following example:

```
while you continue to beHungry
    take anotherBiteOfFood
```

or

```
while an unreadPage remains in the readingAssignment
    read another unreadPage
```

In a business application, you might write:

```
while quantityInInventory remains low
    continue to orderItems
```

or

```
while there is another retailPrice on which to compute a discount
    compute a discount on a retailPrice
```

BUILDING STRUCTURED METHODS

All logic problems can be solved using the structures of sequence, selection, and looping. Every method you write can be built from just these three structures and combined in an infinite number of ways. For example, you can have a sequence of steps followed by a selection, or a loop followed by a sequence. Attaching structures end-to-end is called **stacking structures**. For example, Figure 2-11 shows a structured flowchart segment achieved by stacking structures, and pseudocode that might follow that flowchart logic.

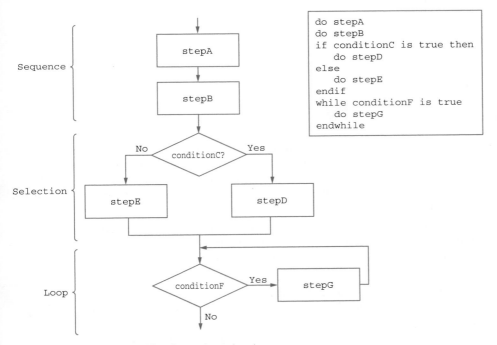

```
do stepA
do stepB
if conditionC is true then
    do stepD
else
    do stepE
endif
while conditionF is true
    do stepG
endwhile
```

Figure 2-11 Stacked, structured flowchart and pseudocode

The pseudocode in Figure 2-11 shows two end-structure statements—endif and endwhile. You can use an endif statement to show clearly where the actions that depend on a decision end. The instruction that follows if occurs when its tested condition is true, the instruction that follows else occurs when the tested condition is false, and the instruction that follows the endif occurs in either case—it is not dependent on the if statement. In other words, statements beyond the endif statement are "outside" the decision structure. Similarly, you use an endwhile statement to show where a loop structure ends. In Figure 2-11, while conditionF continues to be true, stepG continues to execute. If any statements followed the endwhile statement, they would be outside of, and not a part of, the loop.

Besides stacking structures, you can replace any individual steps in a structured flowchart diagram or pseudocode segment with additional structures. In other words, any sequence, selection, or loop can contain other sequences, selections, or loops. For example, you can have a sequence of three steps on one side of a selection, as shown in Figure 2-12. Placing a structure within another structure is called **nesting the structures**.

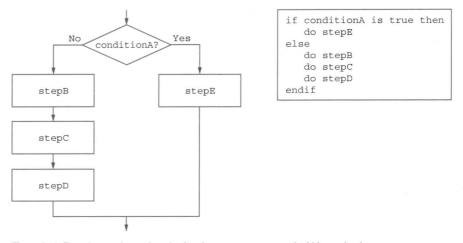

```
if conditionA is true then
    do stepE
else
    do stepB
    do stepC
    do stepD
endif
```

Figure 2-12 Flowchart and pseudocode showing a sequence nested within a selection

When you write the pseudocode for the logic shown in Figure 2-12, the convention is to indent all statements that depend on one branch of the decision, as shown in the pseudocode. The indentation and the endif statement both show that all three statements (do stepB, do stepC, and do stepD) must execute if conditionA is not true. The three statements constitute a **block**, or group of statements that execute as a single unit.

Depending on which tasks this sample program should accomplish, you might need to insert a selection structure in place of a step in the sequence in Figure 2-12. In Figure 2-13, the process named stepC has been replaced with a selection structure that begins with a test of the condition named conditionF.

In the pseudocode shown in Figure 2-13, notice that do stepB, if conditionF is true then, else, and do stepD all align vertically with each other. This shows that they are all "on the same level." If you look at the same problem flowcharted in Figure 2-13, you see that you could draw a vertical line through the symbols containing stepB, conditionF, and stepD. The flowchart and the pseudocode represent exactly the same logic. The stepH and stepG processes are one level "down"; they are dependent on the answer to the conditionF question. Therefore, the do stepH and do stepG statements are indented one additional level in the pseudocode.

Also notice that the pseudocode in Figure 2-13 has two endif statements. Each is aligned to correspond to an if. An endif always partners with the most recent if that does not already have an endif partner, and an endif should always align vertically with its if partner.

In place of do stepH on one side of the new selection in Figure 2-13, you might need to insert a loop structure. This loop, based on conditionI, appears inside the selection within

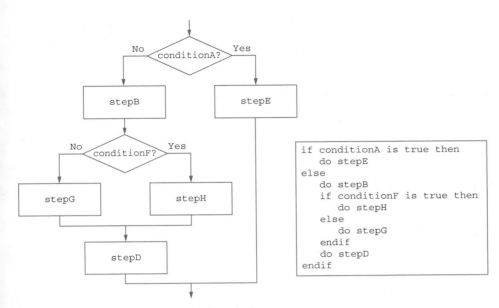

Figure 2-13 Selection within a sequence within a selection

the sequence that constitutes the "no" side of the original conditionA selection. In the pseudocode in Figure 2-14, notice that the while aligns with the endwhile, and that the entire while structure is indented within the true half of the if structure that begins with the decision based on conditionF. The indentation used in the pseudocode reflects the logic laid out graphically in the flowchart.

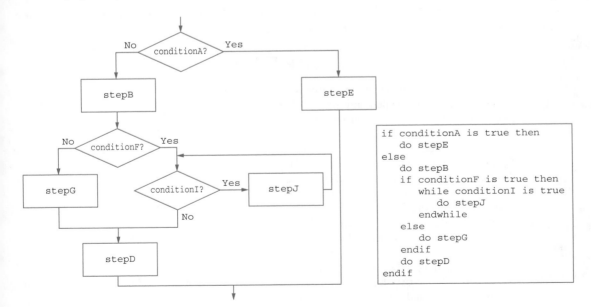

Figure 2-14 Flowchart and pseudocode for a loop within a selection within a sequence within a selection

The combinations are endless, but each of a structured method's segments is a sequence, a selection, or a loop. The three structures are shown together in Figure 2-15. Notice that each structure has one entry and one exit point. One structure can attach to another only at one of these entry or exit points.

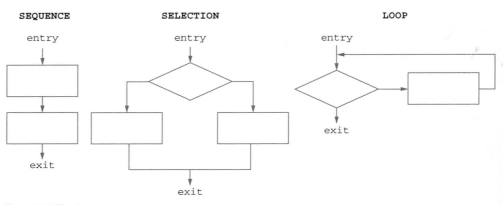

Figure 2-15 The three structures

>> **NOTE** Try to imagine physically picking up any of the three structures using the "handles" marked entry and exit. These are the spots at which you could connect a structure to any of the others. Similarly, any complete structure, from its entry point to its exit point, can be inserted within the process symbol of any other structure.

>> **NOTE**
A structured method is never required to contain examples of all three structures; it might contain only one or two of them. For example, many simple methods contain only a sequence of several events that execute from start to finish without selections or loops.

In summary, a structured method has the following characteristics:

» It includes only combinations of the three structures: sequence, selection, and loop.
» Structures can be stacked or connected to one another only at their entrance or exit points.
» Any structure can be nested within another structure.

USING A PRIMING READ

>> **NOTE**
All programming languages contain a while statement to control loops. Most also contain a for statement that you can use as a shorthand approach to looping tasks. You will learn about the for statement in Chapter 4.

Recall the number-doubling program that was created earlier in this chapter and shown in Figure 2-5. From what you have learned about structure, can you tell whether this program is structured? At first, it might be hard to tell. The flowchart in Figure 2-5 does not look exactly like any of the three allowed structures shown in Figure 2-15. However, because you may stack and nest structures while retaining the overall structure, it might be difficult to determine at first glance whether a flowchart as a whole is structured. It's easiest to analyze the flowchart in Figure 2-5 one step at a time. The beginning of the flowchart looks like Figure 2-16. The first two steps include the declaration of variables and getting the first input value.

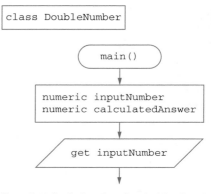

Figure 2-16 Beginning of number-doubling flowchart

Is the portion of the flowchart shown in Figure 2-16 structured? Yes, it's a sequence. When you add the next step, the flowchart looks like Figure 2-17.

In Figure 2-17, the sequence is finished; either a selection or a loop is starting. You might not know which one, but you do know the sequence is not continuing, because sequences can't contain questions. In a sequence, each step must follow without any opportunity to branch off. Therefore, which type of structure starts with the question in Figure 2-17? Is it a selection or a loop?

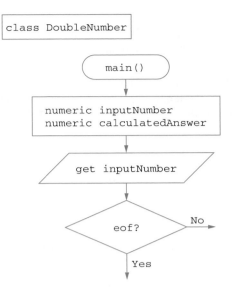

Figure 2-17 Continuation of number-doubling flowchart

In a selection structure, the logic goes in one of two directions after the question, and then the flow comes back together; the question is not asked again. However, if the answer to the question results in a loop being entered so that the loop statements (the **loop's body**) execute, then the logic returns to the question that started the loop. In other words, when the body of a loop executes, the question that controls the loop is always asked again.

Let's return briefly to the original doubling problem in Figure 2-5. If the number the user enters does not represent the end of the data, a calculation is performed, an answer is printed, a new number is obtained, and the eof? question is asked again. While the answer to the question about the user's input value continues to be *no*, eventually the logic returns to the same question. (In other words, while it continues to be true that the end of the data has not yet been entered, the logic keeps returning to the same question.) Therefore, the doubling problem contains a structure beginning with the inputNumber question that is more like the beginning of a loop than a selection.

The doubling problem *does* contain a loop, but it's not a structured loop. In a structured loop, the rules are:

1. You ask a question.

2. If the answer indicates you should perform one or more tasks, you do so.

3. If you perform the tasks, then you must go right back to repeat the question.

The original flowchart in Figure 2-5 asks a question. If the answer is *no* (that is, while it is true that the end of the data has not been reached), the method performs two tasks: it does the arithmetic and it prints the results. Doing two things is acceptable because two steps constitute a sequence, and it is fine to nest a structure within another structure.

However, when the sequence ends, the logic doesn't flow right back to the question. Instead, it goes *above* the question to get another number. For the loop in Figure 2-5 to be a structured loop, the logic must return to the loop-starting question when the sequence ends.

The flowchart in Figure 2-18 shows the flow of logic returning to the question immediately after the sequence. Figure 2-18 shows a structured flowchart segment, but the flowchart has one major flaw—it doesn't do the job of continuously doubling numbers.

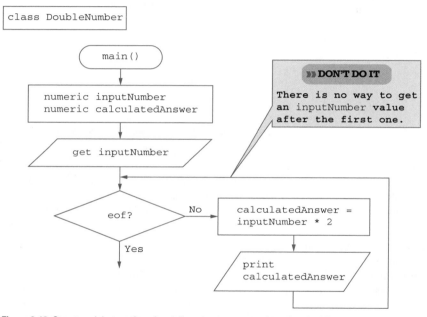

Figure 2-18 Structured, but nonfunctional, flowchart segment of number-doubling problem

Follow the flowchart in Figure 2-18 through a typical execution. Suppose that when the method starts, the user enters a 9 for the value of inputNumber. That's not the end-of-file indicator, so the number doubles, and 18 prints as the value of calculatedAnswer. Then the question eof? is asked again. It can't be a value that has been predetermined to indicate the end of the file, because a new value for inputNumber can't be entered. The logic never returns to the get inputNumber step, so the value of inputNumber never changes. Therefore, 9 doubles again and the answer 18 prints again. It's still not the end of the data, so the same steps are repeated. This goes on *forever*, with the answer 18 printing repeatedly. The logic shown in Figure 2-18 is structured, but it doesn't work; the logic in Figure 2-19 works, but it isn't structured!

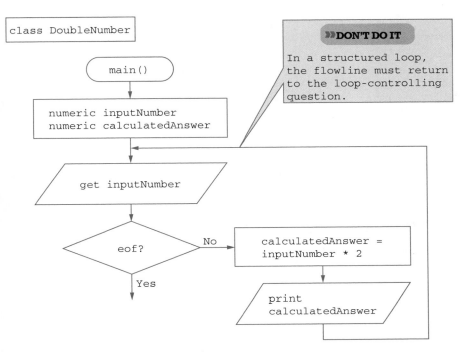

class DoubleNumber

main ()

»DON'T DO IT

In a structured loop, the flowline must return to the loop-controlling question.

numeric inputNumber
numeric calculatedAnswer

get inputNumber

eof?   No   calculatedAnswer = inputNumber * 2

Yes

print calculatedAnswer

Figure 2-19 Functional, but unstructured flowchart segment

The loop in Figure 2-19 is not structured. In a structured loop, the steps execute within the loop, and then the flow of logic must return directly to the loop-controlling question. In Figure 2-19, the logic does not return to the loop-controlling question; instead, it goes "too high", outside the loop to repeat the get inputNumber step.

How can the number-doubling problem become structured and work correctly too? Often, for a method to be structured, you must add something extra. In this case, it's an extra get inputNumber step. Consider the solution in Figure 2-20; it's structured, *and* it does what it's supposed to do. The logic illustrated in Figure 2-20 contains a sequence and a loop. The loop contains another sequence.

The additional get inputNumber step shown in Figure 2-20 is typical in structured methods. The first of the two input steps is the **priming input**, or **priming read**. The term *priming* comes from the fact that the read is first, or *primary* (it gets the process going, as in "priming the pump"). The purpose of the priming read step is to control the upcoming loop that begins with the eof? question. The last element within the structured loop gets the next input values and all subsequent input values. This is also typical in structured loops—the last step executed within the loop alters the condition tested in the question that begins the loop, which in this case is the question that asks whether the user has finished entering data.

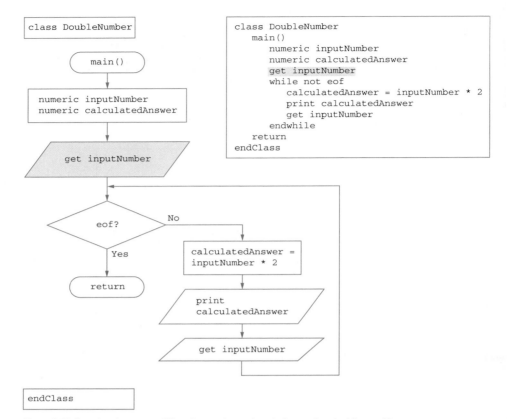

```
class DoubleNumber
    main()
        numeric inputNumber
        numeric calculatedAnswer
        get inputNumber
        while not eof
            calculatedAnswer = inputNumber * 2
            print calculatedAnswer
            get inputNumber
        endwhile
    return
endClass
```

Figure 2-20 Functional, structured flowchart and pseudocode for number-doubling problem

As an additional way to determine whether a flowchart segment is structured, you can try to write pseudocode for it. Examine the original, unstructured flowchart in Figure 2-5 again. To write pseudocode for it, you could write the following:

```
class DoubleNumber
    main()
        numeric inputNumber
        numeric calculatedAnswer
        get inputNumber
        while not eof
            calculatedAnswer = inputNumber * 2
            print calculatedAnswer
            go back to input statement
```

> **» DON'T DO IT**
> In a structured loop, you cannot leave the loop body to go to a statement outside the loop.

The shaded `go back` statement attempts to leave the `while` loop and enter at a spot above where the `while` loop starts. This is not allowed in structured programming. The statements within the `while` loop must be allowed to proceed to the `endwhile` without leaving or "breaking out of" the loop.

Years ago, programmers could avoid using structure by inserting a "go to" statement into their pseudocode like the shaded statement in the preceding example. A "go to" statement would say something like, "After printing the answer, go to the first `get inputNumber` step," and would be the equivalent of drawing an arrow starting after `print calculatedAnswer` and pointing directly to the first `get inputNumber` box in the flowchart. Because "go to" statements cause spaghetti code, they are not allowed in structured programming.

> **» NOTE** A few languages do not always require the priming read. For example, when you write applications in Visual Basic that read data from a file, the language can "look ahead" to determine if the end of the file will be reached on the next input record. However, most programming languages cannot predict the end of the file until an actual read operation is performed, and they require a priming read to properly handle file data. You will learn more about looping to handle data from an input file in Chapter 4.

UNDERSTANDING THE REASONS FOR STRUCTURE

At this point you might be thinking, "I liked the original doubling method just fine. I could follow it. Also, the first method had one less step in it, so it was less work. Who cares if a method is structured?"

Until you have some programming experience, it is difficult to appreciate the reasons for only using the three structures—sequence, selection, and loop. However, staying with these structures is better for the following reasons:

» *Clarity*—The doubling method is small. As methods get bigger, they get more confusing if they're not structured.

» *Professionalism*—All other programmers (and programming teachers) expect your methods to be structured. It is the way things are done professionally.

» *Efficiency*—Most modern computer languages are structured languages with syntax that let you deal efficiently with sequence, selection, and looping. Older languages, such as assembly languages, Common Business-Oriented Language (COBOL), and Report Program Generator (RPG), were developed before the principles of structured programming were discovered. However, even programs that use older languages can be written in a structured form, and many older languages, such as COBOL, have been updated to accommodate structured techniques. Structured methods are expected in professional programming environments today. Newer languages such as C#, C++, and Java enforce structure by their syntax.

» *Maintenance*—You and other programmers will find it easier to modify and maintain structured methods as changes are required in the future.

» *Modularity*—Structured methods can be easily broken into routines that can be assigned to any number of programmers. The routines are then pieced back together like modular furniture at each routine's single entry or exit point. Additionally, a module can often be used by multiple methods, saving development time in the new project. (You will learn more about creating and using methods later in this chapter and in Chapter 6.)

Most programs that you purchase are huge, and contain thousands or millions of statements. If you've worked with a word-processing program or spreadsheet, think of the number of available menu options and keystroke combinations. Such programs are not the work of one programmer. Using object-oriented and structured techniques, the work can more easily be divided among many programmers. The objects created can communicate with each other, the code in their structured methods can be understood and revised more easily, and a large application can be developed much more quickly. Money is often a motivating factor—the more quickly you write a program and make it available for use, the sooner it begins making money for the developer.

Consider the college admissions method that was diagrammed in Figure 2-6 earlier in this chapter. It has been rewritten in structured form in Figure 2-21, and is easier to follow now. Figure 2-21 also shows structured pseudocode for the same problem.

»NOTE
As you examine the flowchart in Figure 2-21, notice that the bottoms of the three testScore decision structures join at the bottom of the diagram. These three joinings correspond to the last three endif statements in the pseudocode. These statements complete each of the three testScore comparisons.

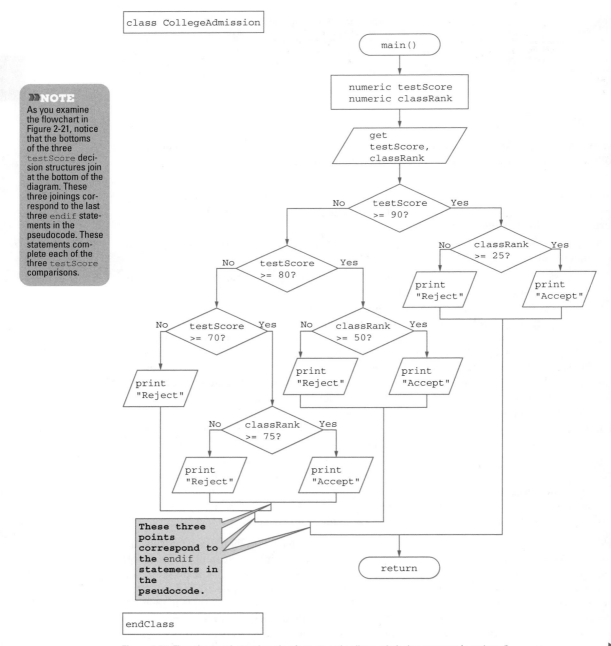

Figure 2-21 Flowchart and pseudocode of structured college admission program (*continued*)

```
class CollegeAdmission
   main()
      numeric testScore
      numeric classRank
      get testScore, classRank
      if testScore >= 90 then
         if classRank >= 25 then
            print "Accept"
         else
            print "Reject"
         endif
      else
         if testScore >= 80 then
            if classRank >= 50 then
               print "Accept"
            else
               print "Reject"
            endif
         else
            if testScore >= 70 then
               if classRank >= 75 then
                  print "Accept"
               else
                  print "Reject"
               endif
            else
               print "Reject"
            endif
         endif
      endif
   return
endClass
```

»NOTE
In Figure 2-21, vertical lines have been inserted to help you see which if, else, and endif statements go together.

Figure 2-21 Flowchart and pseudocode of structured college admission program

RECOGNIZING STRUCTURE

Any set of instructions can be expressed in a structured format. If you can teach someone how to perform any ordinary activity, then you can express it in a structured way. For example, suppose you wanted to teach a child how to play Rock, Paper, Scissors. In this game, two players simultaneously show each other one hand, in one of three positions— clenched in a fist, representing a rock; flat, representing a piece of paper; or with two fingers extended in a V, representing scissors. The goal is to guess which hand your opponent might show, so that you can show the hand that beats it. The rules are that a flat hand beats a fist (because a piece of paper can cover a rock), a fist beats a hand with two extended fingers (because a rock can smash a pair of scissors), and a hand with two extended fingers beats a flat hand (because scissors can cut paper). Figure 2-22 shows the pseudocode for the game.

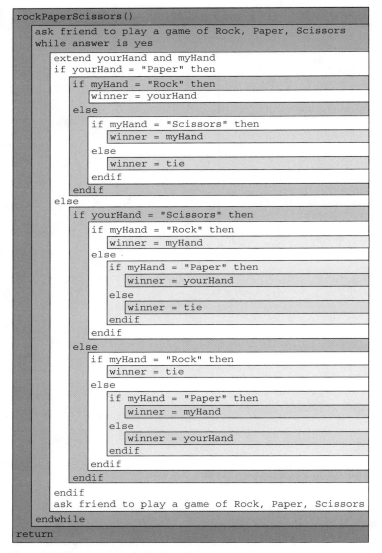

```
rockPaperScissors()
    ask friend to play a game of Rock, Paper, Scissors
    while answer is yes
        extend yourHand and myHand
        if yourHand = "Paper" then
            if myHand = "Rock" then
                winner = yourHand
            else
                if myHand = "Scissors" then
                    winner = myHand
                else
                    winner = tie
                endif
            endif
        else
            if yourHand = "Scissors" then
                if myHand = "Rock" then
                    winner = myHand
                else
                    if myHand = "Paper" then
                        winner = yourHand
                    else
                        winner = tie
                    endif
                endif
            else
                if myHand = "Rock" then
                    winner = tie
                else
                    if myHand = "Paper" then
                        winner = myHand
                    else
                        winner = yourHand
                    endif
                endif
            endif
        endif
        ask friend to play a game of Rock, Paper, Scissors
    endwhile
return
```

Figure 2-22 Pseudocode for Rock, Paper, Scissors game

Figure 2-22 shows a fairly complicated set of statements. Its purpose is not to teach you how to play a game (although you could learn by following the logic), but to convince you that any task to which you can apply rules can be expressed logically using combinations of sequence, selection, and looping. In this example, a game continues while a friend agrees to play, and within that loop, several decisions must be made in order to determine the winner.

When you are just beginning to learn about structured program design, it is difficult to detect whether a flowchart of a method's logic is structured or not. For example, is the flowchart segment in Figure 2-23 structured?

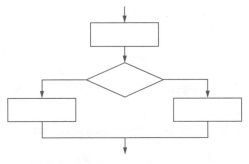

Figure 2-23 Example 1

Yes, it is. It has a sequence and a selection structure.

Is the flowchart segment in Figure 2-24 structured?

Yes, it is. It has a loop, and within the loop is a selection.

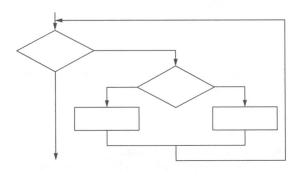

Figure 2-24 Example 2

Is the flowchart segment in Figure 2-25 structured? (The symbols are lettered so you can better follow the discussion.)

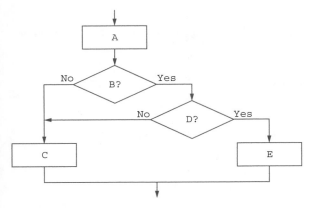

Figure 2-25 Example 3

No, it isn't; it is not constructed from the three basic structures. One way to straighten out an unstructured flowchart segment is to use a "spaghetti bowl" method; that is, picture the flowchart as a bowl of spaghetti that you must untangle. Imagine that you can grab one piece of pasta at the top of the bowl and start pulling. As you "pull" each symbol out of the tangled mess, you can untangle the separate paths until the entire segment is structured. For example, if you start pulling at the top of Figure 2-25, you encounter a procedure box labeled A (see Figure 2-26).

Figure 2-26 Untangling Example 3, first step

A single process like A is part of an acceptable structure—it constitutes at least the beginning of a sequence structure. Imagine that you continue pulling symbols from the tangled segment. The next item in the flowchart is a question that tests a condition labeled B, as you can see in Figure 2-27.

Figure 2-27 Untangling Example 3, second step

At this point, you know the sequence that started with A has ended. Sequences never include decisions, so the sequence is finished; either a selection or a loop is beginning. A loop must return to the question at a later point. You can see from the original logic in Figure 2-25 that whether the answer to B is yes or no, the logic never returns to B. Therefore, B begins a selection structure, not a loop structure.

To continue detangling the logic, you pull up on the flowline that emerges from the left side (the "No" side) of Question B. You encounter C, as shown in Figure 2-28. When you continue beyond C, you reach the end of the flowchart.

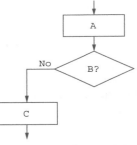

Figure 2-28 Untangling Example 3, third step

Now you can turn your attention to the "Yes" side (the right side) of the condition tested in B. When you pull up on the right side, you encounter Question D (see Figure 2-29).

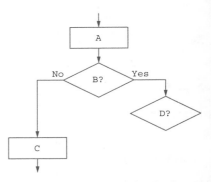

Figure 2-29 Untangling Example 3, fourth step

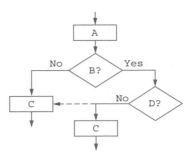

Follow the line on the left side of Question D. If the line is attached somewhere else, as it is (to Step C) in Figure 2-25, just untangle it by repeating the step that is tangled. (In this example, you repeat Step C to untangle it from the other usage of C.) If you continue pulling on the flowline that emerges from Step C, you reach the end of the program segment, as shown in Figure 2-30.

Figure 2-30 Untangling Example 3, fifth step

Now pull on the right side of Question D. Process E pops up, as shown in Figure 2-31; then you reach the end.

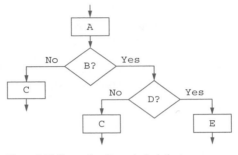

Figure 2-31 Untangling Example 3, sixth step

At this point, the untangled flowchart has three loose ends. The loose ends of Question D can be brought together to form a selection structure, and then the loose ends of Question B can be brought together to form another selection structure. The result is the flowchart shown in Figure 2-32. The entire flowchart segment is structured—it has a sequence (A) followed by a selection inside a selection.

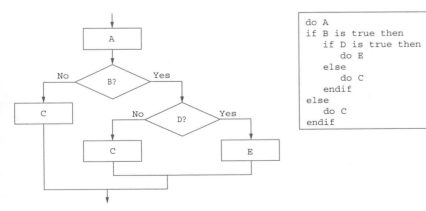

```
do A
if B is true then
    if D is true then
        do E
    else
        do C
    endif
else
    do C
endif
```

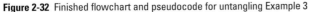

Figure 2-32 Finished flowchart and pseudocode for untangling Example 3

NOTE
If you would like to try structuring a very difficult example of an unstructured application, see Appendix A.

»NOTE
You can skip this section for now without any loss in continuity. Your instructor may prefer to discuss the case structure with Chapter 3 (Making Decisions), and the do-while and do-until loops with Chapter 4 (Looping).

DESCRIBING THREE SPECIAL STRUCTURES—CASE, DO-WHILE, AND DO-UNTIL

You can solve any logic problem you might encounter using only the three structures: sequence, selection, and loop. However, many programming languages allow three more forms of the three basic structures: the case structure, which is an alternative decision-making structure, and the do-while and do-until loops, which are alternatives to the while loop. These structures are never *needed* to solve a problem—you can always use a series of selections instead of the case structure, and you can always use a sequence plus a while loop in place of either of the other loop types. However, these three additional structures are sometimes convenient. Programmers consider them all to be acceptable, legal structures.

THE CASE STRUCTURE

You can use the **case structure** when several possible values exist for a single variable you are testing, and each value requires a different course of action. For example, suppose you work at a school where tuition is $75, $50, $30, or $10 per credit hour, depending on whether a student is a freshman, sophomore, junior, or senior. The structured flowchart in Figure 2-33 shows a series of decisions that assigns the correct tuition to a student.

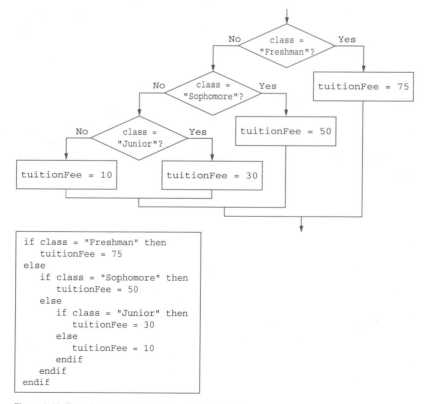

```
if class = "Freshman" then
    tuitionFee = 75
else
    if class = "Sophomore" then
        tuitionFee = 50
    else
        if class = "Junior" then
            tuitionFee = 30
        else
            tuitionFee = 10
        endif
    endif
endif
```

Figure 2-33 Flowchart and pseudocode of tuition decisions

The logic shown in Figure 2-33 is absolutely correct and completely structured. The `class="Junior"` selection structure is contained within the `class="Sophomore"` structure, which is contained within the `class="Freshman"` structure. There is no need to ask if a student is a senior, because if a student is not a freshman, sophomore, or junior, it is assumed that the student is a senior.

Even though the program segments in Figure 2-33 are correct and structured, many programming languages permit using a case structure, as shown in Figure 2-34. When using the case structure, you test a variable against a series of values, taking appropriate action based on the variable's value. To many, such structures seem easier to read, and the case structure is allowed because the same results *could* be achieved with a series of structured selections (thus making the method structured). That is, if the first example is structured and the second one reflects the first one point by point, then the second one must also be structured.

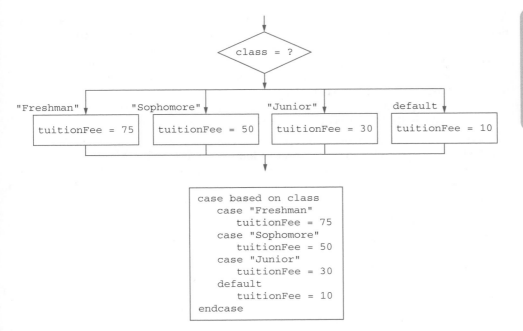

NOTE
The term *default* in Figure 2-34 means "if none of the other cases were true." Each programming language you learn may use a different syntax for the default case.

Figure 2-34 Flowchart and pseudocode of case structure

Even though a programming language permits you to use the case structure, you should understand that it is just a convenience that might make a flowchart, pseudocode, or actual program code easier to understand at first glance. When you write a series of decisions using the case structure, the computer still makes a series of individual decisions, just as though you had used many `if-then-else` combinations. In other words, you might prefer looking at the diagram in Figure 2-34 to understand the tuition fees charged by a school, but a computer actually makes the decisions, as shown in Figure 2-33, one at a time. When you write your own programs, it is always acceptable to express a complicated decision-making process as a series of individual selections.

NOTE
You use the case structure only when a series of decisions is based on different values stored in a single variable. If multiple variables are tested, then you must use a series of decisions.

THE DO-WHILE AND DO-UNTIL LOOPS

Recall that a structured loop (often called a while loop) looks like Figure 2-35. A special loop called a do-while or do-until loop looks like Figure 2-36.

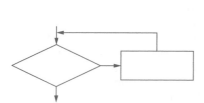

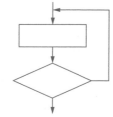

Figure 2-35 The while loop   **Figure 2-36** The do-while or do-until loop

An important difference exists between these two structures. In a while loop, you ask a question and, depending on the answer, you might or might not enter the loop to execute the loop's procedure. Conversely, in either a **do-while** or a **do-until loop**, you ensure that the procedure executes at least once; then, depending on the answer to the controlling question, the loop may or may not execute additional times. In a do-while loop, the loop body continues to execute as long as the answer to the controlling question is yes, or true. In a do-until loop, the loop body continues to execute as long as the answer to the controlling question is no, or false. That is, the body executes *until* the controlling question is yes or true.

In a while loop, the question that controls the loop comes at the beginning, or "top," of the loop body. A while loop is also called a **pretest loop**, because a condition is tested before entering the loop even once. In a do-while or do-until loop, the question that controls the loop comes at the end, or "bottom," of the loop body. Both do-while and do-until loops are **posttest loops**, meaning that a condition is tested after the loop body has executed.

You encounter examples of do-until looping every day. For example:

```
do
     pay a bill
until all bills are paid
```

and

```
do
     wash a dish
until all dishes are washed
```

Similarly, you encounter examples of do-while looping every day. For example:

```
do
     pay a bill
while more bills remain to be paid
```

and

```
do
     wash a dish
while more dishes remain to be washed
```

In these examples, the activity (paying bills or washing dishes) must occur at least one time. With both the `do-while` and `do-until` loops, you ask the question that determines whether you continue only after the activity has been executed at least once. The only difference between these two structures is whether the answer to the bottom loop-controlling question must be false for the loop to continue (as in a `do-until` loop), or true for the loop to continue (as in a `do-while` loop).

You are never required to use a posttest loop. You can duplicate the same series of events in a posttest loop by creating a sequence followed by a standard, pretest `while` loop. For example, just as with the posttest version, the following pseudocode requires you to pay at least one bill. Then, you may or may not have more bills to pay, but the action has occurred at least one time:

```
pay a bill
while there are more bills to pay
    pay a bill
endwhile
```

Consider the flowcharts and pseudocode in Figures 2-37 and 2-38.

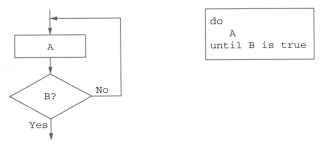

Figure 2-37 Flowchart and pseudocode for a `do-until` loop

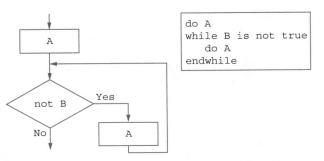

Figure 2-38 Flowchart and pseudocode for a sequence followed by a `while` loop

In Figure 2-37, A is executed, then B is asked. If B is no, then A is executed and B is asked again. In Figure 2-38, A is executed, then B is asked. If B is not yes, then A is executed and B is asked again. In other words, both flowcharts and pseudocode segments do exactly the same thing.

Because programmers understand that a posttest loop can be expressed with a sequence followed by a pretest `while` loop, most languages allow a version of the posttest loop. However, you are never required to use a posttest loop; you can always accomplish the same events with a sequence followed by a `while` loop.

Figure 2-39 shows an unstructured loop. It is not a `while` loop, which begins with a decision and then returns to the decision after an action. Also, the loop is not a `do-until` loop, which begins with an action and ends with a decision that might repeat the action. Instead, it begins like a `do-until` loop, with a process followed by a decision, but one branch of the decision does not repeat the initial process. Instead, it performs an additional new action before repeating the initial process. If you need to use the logic shown in Figure 2-39—performing a task, asking a question, and perhaps performing an additional task before looping back to the first process—then the way to make the logic structured is to repeat the initial process within the loop, at the end of the loop. Figure 2-40 shows the same logic as Figure 2-39, but now it is structured logic, with a sequence of two actions occurring within the loop. Does this diagram look familiar to you? It uses the same technique of repeating a needed step that you saw earlier in this chapter, when you learned the rationale for the priming read.

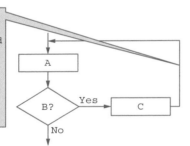

»DON'T DO IT

In a structured loop, you cannot leave the loop body to go to a statement outside the loop.

Figure 2-39 Unstructured loop

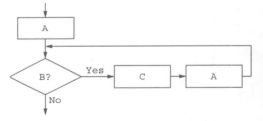

Figure 2-40 A sequence followed by a structured loop that accomplishes the same task as the logic in Figure 2-39

> **»NOTE** It is difficult for beginning programmers to distinguish between `while`, `do-while`, and `do-until` loops. You can think of a `while` loop as one that continues to execute while a condition remains true—for example, while `not end of file` is true, process records, or while `hungry` is true, eat food. The answer to the question might never be true and the loop body might never execute. A `while` loop is the only type of loop you ever need in order to solve a problem because the loop body is optional. You can also think of a `do-while` loop as one that continues to execute while a condition remains true—for example, process records while `not end of file` is true, or eat food while `hungry` is true. On the other hand, a `do-until` loop continues while a condition is false—in other words, you continue until the condition becomes true. For example, address envelopes until there are no more envelopes, or eat food until you are full. When you use a `do-while` or a `do-until` loop, the action always occurs at least once.

INTRODUCTION TO METHODS

> **»NOTE**
> In object-oriented programming languages, every executable statement resides within a method—either the `main()` method or another method.

One of the advantages of structured programming is the ability to break programs into reusable modules, or methods. A **method** is a self-contained program module that contains a series of statements that carry out a task. To execute a method, you **invoke** it or **call** it from another method; the **calling method** invokes the **called method**. Any class can contain an unlimited number of methods, and each method can be called any number of times. Within a class, the simplest methods you can invoke don't require data items to be sent to them, nor do they send data back to you. You will learn about methods that receive and return data in Chapter 6.

For example, consider the `main()` method logic in Figure 2-41. Its generic steps might represent any actions, but you should be able to tell that the steps are structured. The sequence, A, is followed by a selection, represented by B. The condition, B, starts a selection structure with a sequence followed by a selection when B is true, and a sequence when B is false. The second selection, represented by G, is nested within the B selection, and it contains a sequence.

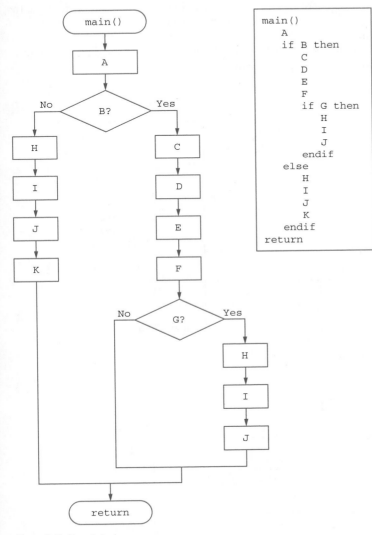

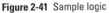

Figure 2-41 Sample logic

In Figure 2-41, you can see that the sequence represented by H, I, and J occurs in two locations. It is perfectly acceptable to have the same tasks performed in different program locations under different conditions, but when the same tasks are repeated in different places, it can be convenient to create a method that is called at each location where it should execute.

Figure 2-42 shows the same logic as Figure 2-41, but the three statements H, I, and J have been contained, or **encapsulated**, into a method named `methodHtoJ()`. The method has its own header (see shading) and `return` statement, and it contains a sequence composed of the three actions. When the logic in the original segment is ready to execute the three statements, it calls the method. (See the two shaded calls in the figure.) In the flowchart, the method calls are represented by process symbols that contain a stripe across the top. When you see the stripe, you understand that the symbol represents a module that might contain many steps. In the pseudocode, the method call is indicated by using the method's name when you want to call it. (Remember, you can tell it is a method because it is followed by parentheses.) In the program in Figure 2-42, the individual steps H, I, and J need only be written once, and they can be called as a unit from multiple program locations.

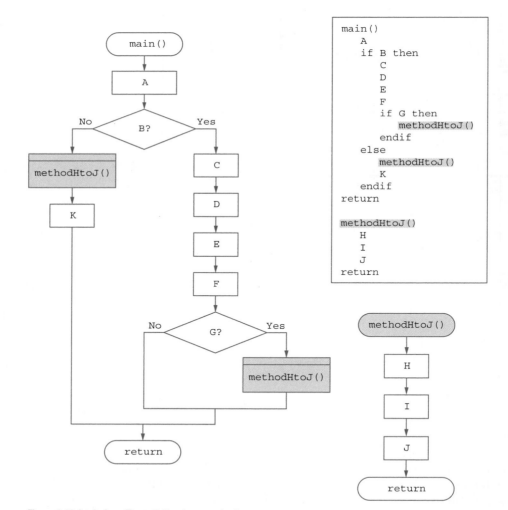

Figure 2-42 Logic from Figure 2-41 using a method

>>NOTE Some programmers use a rectangle with stripes down each side to represent any method in a flowchart. This book uses the convention that if a method is external to a program, a rectangle with side stripes is used. A method that is external to a program might come packaged with a language. For example, many languages contain built-in methods that perform common mathematical functions. Other external methods might be part of another class that is already developed and in use within an organization. In this book, methods that are internal to a program are represented by a rectangle with a single stripe across the top. In the examples in this chapter, all the methods are internal.

In Figure 2-43, the same logic has been modularized even further. The steps C, D, E, and F have been placed into their own method. This approach serves only to group the steps, not to prevent repeating them (because they are not repeated in the program). Just as it is more convenient to say "Bake a cake" than it is to say "Get out a mixing bowl, get a cup of sugar, get

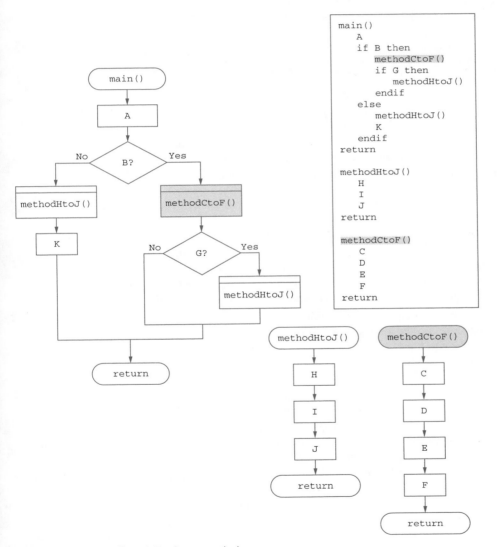

Figure 2-43 Logic from Figure 2-41 using two methods

3 eggs," and so on, it can be clearer and more convenient to call a method name and have the specific directions listed elsewhere. Creating submethods makes the calling method's logic more concise, easier to read, and somewhat easier to identify as structured. You would not want to place steps C through F in their own method without a good reason or if they were unrelated, but you would use a method if the steps were closely related, and especially if they represented steps to a process that might be needed by another program in the future.

Deciding which steps to place in their own methods is an art, and two programmers might disagree on which steps to modularize in any given program. However, creating methods makes large programs easier to manage, and in very large programs, it allows the work to be split more easily among multiple programmers. However, no matter how many methods a program contains, each one must be structured, each must only contain some combination of sequence, selection, and loop structures, and each must be called as part of a larger program that is also structured.

>> **NOTE** Methods are crucial to object-oriented programming. You will learn much more about their construction later in this book. For now, as you work through the sample programs in the next few chapters, try to envision how they might logically be divided into smaller, more concise modules.

CHAPTER SUMMARY

» Most computer programs execute the same set of instructions over and over again because it is efficient to use the same set of variables to hold series of values.

» You can end a program by testing input for a predetermined sentinel value. You represent a test of a condition in a flowchart by drawing a decision symbol, which is shaped like a diamond. Many programming languages use the term `eof` (for "end of file") to represent a marker that automatically acts as an input sentinel.

» The popular name for unstructured, snarled program statements is spaghetti code.

» Clear programs can be constructed using one or more of the three basic structures: sequence, selection, and loop. These three structures can be combined in an infinite number of ways by stacking and nesting. Each structure has one entry and one exit point; one structure can attach to another only at an entry or exit point.

» A priming read or priming input is the first read or data input statement prior to beginning a structured loop. The last step within the loop gets the next input value and all subsequent input values.

» You use structured techniques to promote clarity, professionalism, efficiency, and modularity.

» One way to straighten an unstructured flowchart segment is to imagine the flowchart as a bowl of spaghetti that you must untangle.

» Although you can solve any problem using only sequence, selection, and loop structures, there are three other generally recognized structures. You can use a case structure when several possible values exist for a variable you are testing. You can use a `do-while` or `do-until` loop to test a loop's condition after a loop's process has executed at least once.

» A method is a self-contained program module that contains a series of statements that carry out a task. To execute a method, you invoke it or call it from another method; the calling method invokes the called method. Any class can contain an unlimited number of methods, and each method can be called an unlimited number of times. Every method must be structured.

KEY TERMS

An **infinite loop** is a repeating flow of logic with no end.

Testing a value involves comparing it to another value to make a decision.

A **decision symbol** in a flowchart is shaped like a diamond and contains a question.

A **binary decision** is one with two possible outcomes.

A **dummy value** is a value that does not represent real data; it is just a signal to stop processing.

A **sentinel** value is a dummy value that is an entry or exit point in a program.

Eof (for "end of file") is a marker that automatically acts as a sentinel.

Spaghetti code is the name for snarled, unstructured program statements.

A **structure** is a basic unit of programming logic; each structure is a sequence, selection, or loop. Each structure has a single entry and exit point.

With a **sequence structure**, you perform an action or event, and then you perform the next action, in order. A sequence can contain any number of events, but there is no chance to branch off and skip any of the events.

With a **selection structure** or **decision structure**, you ask a question, and, depending on the answer, you take one of two courses of action. Then, no matter which path you follow, you continue with the next event.

An **if-then-else** is another name for a selection structure.

Dual-alternative ifs define one action to be taken when the tested condition is true, and another action to be taken when it is false.

Single-alternative ifs take action on just one branch of the decision.

The **null case** is the branch of a decision in which no action is taken.

In a **loop structure**, you ask a question; if the answer requires an action, you perform the action and ask the original question again.

Repetition and **iteration** are alternate names for a loop structure.

In a **while loop** or a **while-do loop**, a process continues while some condition continues to be true.

Stacking structures occurs when structures are attached end-to-end.

Nesting structures occurs when a structure is placed within another structure.

A **block** is a group of statements that execute as a single unit.

A **loop's body** is composed of the statements within the loop.

A **priming read** or **priming input** is the first read or data input statement that occurs before and outside of the loop that performs the rest of the input statements.

Go-to-less programming is written without "go to" statements; structured programs are written without "go to" statements.

You can use the **case structure** when several possible values exist for a single variable you are testing, and each requires a different course of action.

A **do-until loop** is a posttest loop in which you ensure that a procedure executes at least once; then, as long as the answer to the controlling question is false, the loop continues to execute additional times.

A **do-while loop** is a posttest loop in which you ensure that a procedure executes at least once; then, as long as the answer to the controlling question is true, the loop continues to execute additional times.

A **pretest loop** is one in which a condition is tested before entering the loop body even once. A while loop is a pretest loop.

A **posttest loop** is one in which a condition is tested after the loop body has executed once. Both do-while and do-until loops are posttest loops.

A **method** is a self-contained program module that contains a series of statements that carry out a task.

To execute a method, you **invoke** it or **call** it from another method.

A **calling method** invokes another method.

A **called method** is a method that is invoked by another method.

Encapsulated means contained.

REVIEW QUESTIONS

1. A repeating flow of logic with no end is a(n) _____ .
   a. structured module
   b. infinite loop
   c. boundless structure
   d. selection

2. Snarled program logic is called _____ code.
   a. snake
   b. spaghetti
   c. string
   d. gnarly

3. A sequence structure can contain _____ .
   a. only one event
   b. exactly three events
   c. no more than three events
   d. any number of events

4. Which of the following is *not* another term for a selection structure?
   a. decision structure
   b. if-then-else structure
   c. loop structure
   d. dual-alternative if structure

5. In one type of logical structure, you ask a question, and, depending on the answer, you take some action and then ask the question again. This structure can be called all of the following except _____ .

a. `if-then-else`

b. loop

c. repetition

d. iteration

6. Placing a structure within another structure is called _____ the structures.

a. stacking

b. nesting

c. building

d. untangling

7. Attaching structures end-to-end is called _____ them.

a. stacking

b. nesting

c. building

d. untangling

8. The statement `if age >= 65 then seniorDiscount = "yes"` is an example of a _____ .

a. single-alternative `if`

b. loop

c. dual-alternative `if`

d. sequence

9. The statement `while temperature remains below 60 F, leave the furnace on` is an example of a _____ .

a. single-alternative `if`

b. loop

c. dual-alternative `if`

d. sequence

10. The statement `if age < 13 then movieTicket = 4.00 else movieTicket = 8.50` is an example of a _____ .

a. single-alternative `if`

b. loop

c. dual-alternative `if`

d. sequence

11. Which of the following attributes do all three basic structures share?

a. Their flowcharts all contain exactly three processing symbols.

b. They all contain a decision.

c. They all begin with a process.

d. They all have one entry and one exit point.

12. The first input statement in an application or method that occurs outside and before the loop that performs the rest of the input _____ .

    a. is called a priming input

    b. must be included in its own method

    c. is the only part of a program allowed to be unstructured

    d. executes hundreds or even thousands of times in most business programs

13. A group of statements that execute as a unit is a _____ .

    a. cohort

    b. family

    c. sequence

    d. block

14. Which of the following is acceptable in a structured program?

    a. placing a sequence within the true half of a dual-alternative decision

    b. placing a decision within a loop

    c. placing a loop within one of the steps in a sequence

    d. all of the above

15. Which of the following is *not* a reason for enforcing structure rules in computer programs?

    a. Structured programs are clearer than unstructured ones.

    b. Other professional programmers will expect programs to be structured.

    c. Structured programs can be broken into modules easily.

    d. Structured programs usually are shorter than unstructured ones.

16. Which of the following is *not* a benefit of modularizing programs?

    a. Modular programs are easier to read and understand than nonmodular ones.

    b. Modular components are reusable in other programs.

    c. If you use modules, you can ignore the rules of structure.

    d. Multiple programmers can work on different modules at the same time.

17. Which of the following is true of structured logic?

    a. Any task can be described using the three structures.

    b. You can use structured logic with newer programming languages like Java and C#, but not with older ones.

    c. Structured programs require that you break the code into easy-to-handle modules or they will not compile.

    d. all of the above

18. The structure that you can use when you must make a decision with several possible outcomes, depending on the value of a single variable, is the _____ .

    a. multiple-alternative `if` structure

    b. case structure

    c. `while` structure

    d. `do-until` structure

19. The loop's body might never execute with _____ .

    a. a `do-until` loop   c. a `do-over` loop

    b. a `do-while` loop   d. a `while` loop

20. A `do-until` loop can always be converted to _____ .

    a. a `while` loop followed by a sequence

    b. a sequence followed by a `while` loop

    c. a case structure

    d. a selection followed by a `do-while` loop

EXERCISES

1. Match the term with the structure diagram in Figure 2-44. (Because the structures go by more than one name, there are more terms than diagrams.)

    1. sequence   5. decision

    2. selection   6. `if-then-else`

    3. loop   7. iteration

    4. `while`

a.   b.   c.

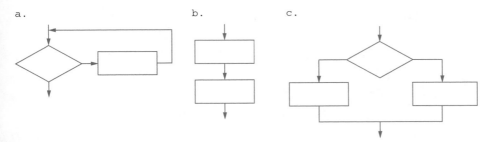

Figure 2-44 Structure diagrams

2. Match the term with the pseudocode segment. (Because the structures go by more than one name, there are more terms than pseudocode segments.)

    1. sequence   4. decision

    2. selection   5. `if-then-else`

    3. loop   6. iteration

```
a. while userNumber not = 0
       print theAnswer
   endwhile
b. if inventoryQuantity > 0 then
       do fillOrderProcess
   else
       do backOrderNotification
   endif
c. do localTaxCalculation
   do stateTaxCalculation
   do federalTaxCalculation
```

3. Is each of the following segments structured, or unstructured? If a segment is unstructured, redraw it so that it does the same thing but is structured.

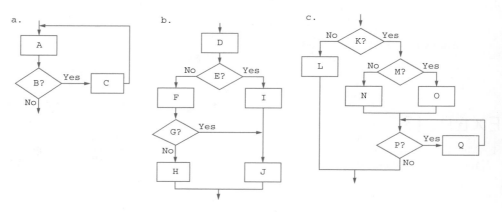

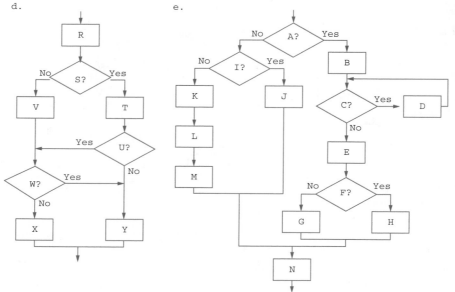

Figure 2-45 Are the segments structured or unstructured?

4. Write pseudocode for each example (a through e) in Exercise 3.

5. Assume you have created a mechanical arm that can hold a pen. The arm can perform the following tasks:

   » Lower the pen to a piece of paper.
   » Raise the pen from the paper.
   » Move the pen one inch along a straight line. (If the pen is lowered, it draws a one-inch line from left to right. If the pen is raised, it is repositioned one inch to the right.)
   » Turn 90 degrees to the right.
   » Draw a circle that is one inch in diameter.

   Draw a structured flowchart or write pseudocode to describe the logic that would cause the arm to create the following. When you are done, have a fellow student act as the mechanical arm that carries out your instructions.

   a. a one-inch square
   b. a two-inch by one-inch rectangle
   c. a string of three beads
   d. a short word; for example, "cat". (Because the mechanical arm cannot draw curved lines, some of your letters will look very simplistic.) Do not reveal the word to your mechanical-arm partner before the partner attempts to carry out your instructions.

6. Assume you have created a mechanical robot that can perform the following tasks:

   » Stand up.
   » Sit down.
   » Turn left 90 degrees.
   » Turn right 90 degrees.
   » Take a step.

   Additionally, the robot can determine the answer to one test condition:

   » Am I touching something?

   Place two chairs 20 feet apart, directly facing each other. Draw a structured flowchart or write pseudocode to describe the logic that would allow the robot to start from a sitting position in one chair, cross the room, and end up sitting in the other chair.

   Have a fellow student act as the robot and carry out your instructions.

7. Looking up a word in a dictionary can be a complicated process. For example, assume you want to look up "object." You might proceed by opening the dictionary to a random page and seeing "kitchen." You know that the word comes alphabetically before "object," so you flip forward and see "nose." That is still not far enough, so you flip forward and see "ostrich." You have gone too far, so you flip back, and so on. Draw a structured flowchart or write structured pseudocode that describes the process of looking up a word in a dictionary. Pick a word at random and have a fellow student attempt to carry out your instructions.

8. Draw a structured flowchart or write structured pseudocode describing your preparation to go to work or school in the morning. Include at least two decisions and two loops.

9. Draw a structured flowchart or write structured pseudocode describing your preparation to go to bed at night. Include at least two decisions and two loops.

10. Choose a simple children's game and describe its logic, using a structured flowchart or pseudocode. For example, you might try to explain Musical Chairs; Duck, Duck, Goose; the card game, War; or the elimination game, Eenie, Meenie, Minie, Moe.

11. Draw a structured flowchart or write structured pseudocode describing how your paycheck is calculated. Include at least two decisions.

12. Draw a structured flowchart or write structured pseudocode describing the steps a retail store employee should follow to process a customer purchase. Include at least two decisions.

CASE PROJECT

In Chapter 1, you thought about the objects needed for Cost Is No Object—a car rental service that specializes in lending antique and luxury cars to clients on a short-term basis. Draw a structured flowchart or write structured pseudocode to describe the process a clerk could use to rent an automobile to a customer. Include at least three decisions and two loops in your logic. Your flowchart or pseudocode should at least check the renter's driving record and credit worthiness, and explain the rental agreement.

UP FOR DISCUSSION

1. In this chapter, you learned what spaghetti code is. What is "ravioli code"?

2. Who was Edsger Dijkstra? Who were Bohm and Jacopini? What contributions did each make to programming?

3. Every logical problem can be solved using only three structures (sequence, selection, and loop), but this does not mean that other useful structures cannot exist. For example, the case, do-while, and do-until structures are never required, but they exist in many programming languages and can be quite useful. Try to design a new structure of your own and explain situations in which it would be useful.

MAKING DECISIONS

In this chapter, you will:

Evaluate Boolean expressions to make comparisons
Use the relational comparison operators
Learn about AND logic
Learn about OR logic
Make selections within ranges
Learn about precedence when combining AND and
    OR selections
Learn more about the case structure
Use a decision table

EVALUATING BOOLEAN EXPRESSIONS TO MAKE COMPARISONS

The reason people frequently think computers are smart lies in the computer program's ability to make decisions. A medical diagnosis program that can decide if your symptoms fit various disease profiles seems quite intelligent, as does a program that can offer different potential vacation routes based on your destination.

The selection structure (sometimes called a decision structure) involved in such programs is not new to you—it's one of the basic structures you learned about in Chapter 2. See Figures 3-1 and 3-2.

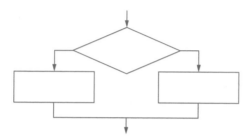

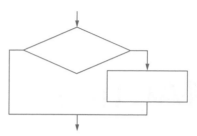

Figure 3-1 Flowchart of the dual-alternative selection structure

Figure 3-2 Flowchart of the single-alternative selection structure

In Chapter 2, you learned that you can refer to the structure in Figure 3-1 as a dual-alternative, or binary, selection because an action is associated with each of two possible outcomes: depending on the answer to the question represented by the diamond, the logical flow proceeds either to the left branch of the structure or to the right. The choices are mutually exclusive; that is, the logic can flow only to one of the two alternatives, never to both. This selection structure is also called an `if-then-else` structure.

The flowchart segment in Figure 3-2 represents a single-alternative selection where action is required for only one outcome of the question. You call this form of the `if-then-else` structure an `if-then`, because no alternative or "`else`" action is necessary.

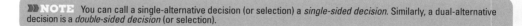

▶▶ NOTE You can call a single-alternative decision (or selection) a *single-sided decision*. Similarly, a dual-alternative decision is a *double-sided decision* (or selection).

Figure 3-3 shows the flowchart and pseudocode for a program that contains a typical `if-then-else` decision in a business program. Many organizations pay employees time and a half (one and one-half times their usual hourly rate) for hours worked in excess of 40 per week.

In the program in Figure 3-3, several variables and constants are declared. The variables include those that will be retrieved from input (`name`, which is a string, and `hoursWorked` and `rate`, which are numbers) and one that will be calculated from the input values

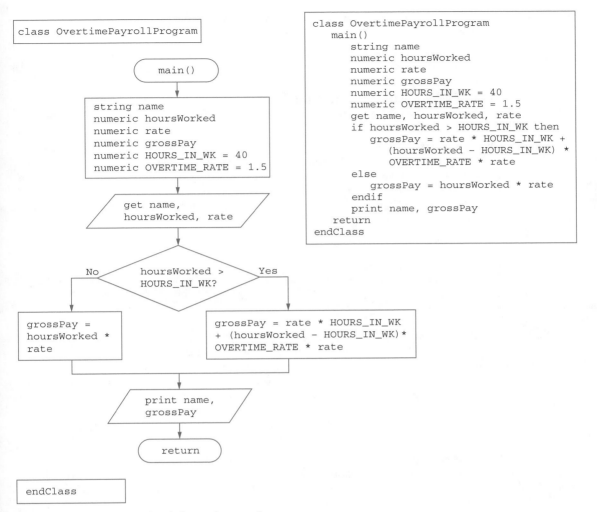

Figure 3-3 Flowchart and pseudocode for overtime payroll program

(grossPay, which is a number). The program in Figure 3-3 also uses two named constants: HOURS_IN_WK, which represents the number of hours in a standard workweek, and OVERTIME_RATE, which represents a multiplication factor for the premium rate at which an employee is paid after working the standard number of hours in a week. The program would work just as well if the numeric constants 40 and 1.5 were used within the program

»NOTE Throughout this book, you will see many examples presented in both flowchart and pseudocode form. When you first analyze a solution, you might find it easier to concentrate on just one of the two design tools at first. When you understand how the program works using one tool (for example, a flowchart), you can proceed to confirm that the solution is identical using the other tool (for example, pseudocode).

to represent these values, but creating named constants for them provides several benefits:

» The constant names provide clarity and a type of internal documentation for the program, so there is less chance that someone reading the program will misunderstand what the values represent.

» If the value of either a standard workweek's hours or the premium pay rate changes in the future, the values will be easy to locate and modify because they are listed at the beginning of the program.

» Using the named constants helps prevent typographical errors. When the program is written in a programming language and compiled, the translation software will issue an error statement if either HOURS_IN_WK or OVERTIME_RATE is misspelled in the program. If the programmer uses constant numeric values instead and mistakenly types 30 instead of 40, for example, the compiler would not recognize an error, and incorrect gross pay amounts would be calculated for many employees.

> **NOTE** When programmers use unnamed constants, they are said to be using **magic numbers**. Just as a trick by a magician is beyond explanation, such numbers are not explained. Using magic numbers is considered a poor programming practice, and you should almost always provide named constants instead.

> **NOTE** In Chapter 2, you learned that named constants conventionally are created using all uppercase letters.

After the input data is retrieved in the program in Figure 3-3, a decision is made about the value of hoursWorked. The longer calculation that adds a time-and-a-half factor to an employee's gross pay executes only when the expression hoursWorked > HOURS_IN_WK is true. The long calculation exists in the **if clause** of the decision—the part of the decision that holds the action or actions that execute when the tested condition in the decision is true. The shorter calculation, which produces grossPay by multiplying hoursWorked by rate, constitutes the **else clause** of the decision—the part that executes only when the tested condition in the decision is false.

Suppose an employee's paycheck should be reduced if the employee participates in the company dental plan and that no action is taken if the employee is not a dental plan participant. Figure 3-4 shows how this decision might be added to the payroll program. The additions from Figure 3-3 are shaded.

The expressions hoursWorked > HOURS_IN_WK and dentalPlanParticipant = "Y" in Figures 3-3 and 3-4 are Boolean expressions. A **Boolean expression** is one that represents only one of two states, usually expressed as true or false. Every decision you make in a computer program involves evaluating a Boolean expression. True/false evaluation is "natural" from a computer's standpoint, because computer circuitry consists of two-state on-off switches, often represented by 1 or 0. Every computer decision yields a true-or-false, yes-or-no, 1-or-0 result.

> **NOTE** George Boole was a mathematician who lived from 1815 to 1864. He approached logic more simply than his predecessors did, by expressing logical selections with common algebraic symbols. He is considered the founder of mathematical logic, and Boolean (true/false) expressions are named for him.

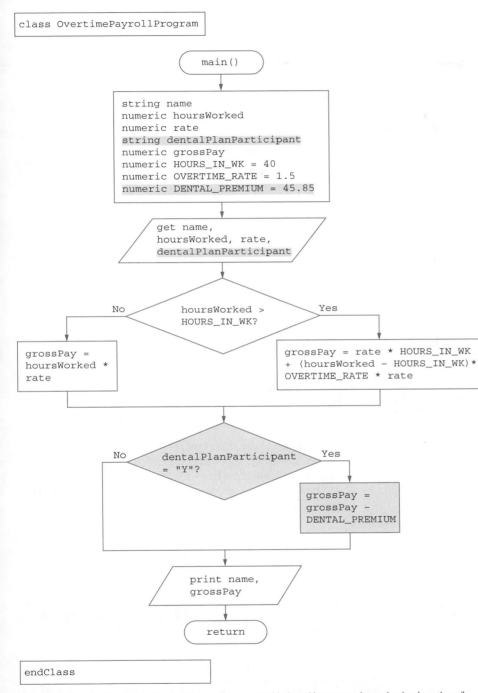

Figure 3-4 Flowchart and pseudocode for payroll program with dental insurance determination (*continued*) ▶

```
class OvertimePayrollProgram
    main()
        string name
        numeric hoursWorked
        numeric rate
        string dentalPlanParticipant
        numeric grossPay
        numeric HOURS_IN_WK = 40
        numeric OVERTIME_RATE = 1.5
        numeric DENTAL_PREMIUM = 45.85
        get name, hoursWorked, rate, dentalPlanParticipant
        if hoursWorked > HOURS_IN_WK then
            grossPay = rate * HOURS_IN_WK +
                (hoursWorked - HOURS_IN_WK *
                OVERTIME_RATE * rate
        else
            grossPay = hoursWorked * rate
        endif
        if dentalPlanParticipant = "Y" then
            grossPay = grossPay - DENTAL_PREMIUM
        endif
        print name, grossPay
    return
endClass
```

Figure 3-4 Flowchart and pseudocode for payroll program with dental insurance determination

USING THE RELATIONAL COMPARISON OPERATORS

Usually, you can compare only values that are of the same type; that is, you can compare numeric values to other numeric values, character values to other characters, and strings to other strings. You can ask every programming question by using one of only three types of comparison operators in a Boolean expression. For any two values that are the same type, you can decide whether:

» The two values are equal.
» The first value is greater than the second value.
» The first value is less than the second value.

》NOTE Many programming languages provide a built-in process to convert a string variable to all uppercase or all lowercase characters. For example, in Visual Basic, if a variable named `firstName` holds "Jim", then an expression such as `name.ToUpper() = "JIM"` would be evaluated as true, as would the expression `name.ToLower() = "jim"`.

》NOTE Some programming languages allow you to compare a character to a number. If you do, then a single character's numeric code value is used in the comparison. For example, many computers use the American Standard Code for Information Interchange (ASCII) coding system or the Unicode system. In both coding schemes, an uppercase "A" is represented numerically as a 65, an uppercase "B" is a 66, and so on.

In any Boolean expression, the two values compared can be either variables or constants. For example, the expression `currentTotal = 100?` compares a variable, `currentTotal`, to a numeric constant, 100. Depending on the `currentTotal` value, the expression's value is true or false. In the expression `currentTotal = previousTotal?`, both values are variables, and the result is also true or false depending on the values stored in each of the two variables. Although it's legal to do so, you would never use expressions in which you compare two constants—for example, `20 = 20?` or `30 = 40?`. Such expressions are considered **trivial** because each will always evaluate to the same result: true for `20 = 20?` and false for `30 = 40?`.

Each programming language supports its own set of **relational comparison operators**, or comparison symbols, that express these Boolean tests. For example, many languages, such as Visual Basic and Pascal, use the equal sign (=) to express testing for equivalency, so `balanceDue = 0?` compares `balanceDue` to zero. COBOL programmers can use the equal sign, but they also can spell out the expression, as in `balanceDue equal to 0?`. Report Program Generator (RPG) programmers use the two-letter operator `EQ` in place of a symbol. C#, C++, and Java programmers use two equal signs to test for equivalency, so they write `balanceDue == 0?` to compare the two values. Although each programming language supports its own syntax for comparing values' equivalency, all languages provide for the same logical concept of equivalency.

> **» NOTE** The reason some languages use two equal signs for comparisons is to avoid confusion with assignment statements such as `balanceDue = 0`. In C++, C#, or Java, this statement only assigns the value 0 to `balanceDue`; it does not compare `balanceDue` to zero.

Most languages allow you to use the algebraic signs for greater than (>) and less than (<) to make the corresponding comparisons. In addition to the three basic comparisons of equal to, greater than, and less than, most programming languages provide three others. For any two values that are the same type, you can decide whether:

» The first is greater than or equal to the second.
» The first is less than or equal to the second.
» The two are not equal.

Most programming languages allow you to express "greater than or equal to" by typing a greater-than sign immediately followed by an equal sign (>=). When you are drawing a flowchart or writing pseudocode, you might prefer a greater-than sign with a line under it (≥) because mathematicians use that symbol to mean "greater than or equal to." However, when you write a program, you type >= as two separate characters, because no single key on the keyboard expresses this concept and no programming language has been designed to understand it. Similarly, "less than or equal to" is written with two symbols, < immediately followed by =.

> **» NOTE** The operators >= and <= are always treated as a single unit; no spaces separate the two parts of the operator. Also, the equal sign always appears second. No programming language allows => or =< as a comparison operator.

Any relational situation can be expressed using just three types of comparisons: equal, greater than, and less than. You never need the three additional comparisons (greater than or equal, less than or equal, or not equal), but using them often makes decisions more convenient. For example, assume you need to issue a 10 percent discount to any customer whose age is 65 or greater, and charge full price to other customers. You can use the greater-than-or-equal-to symbol to write the logic as follows:

```
if customerAge >= 65 then
    discount = 0.10
else
    discount = 0
endif
```

As an alternative, if you want to use the < operator instead of the >= operator, you can express the same logic by writing:

```
if customerAge < 65 then
    discount = 0
else
    discount = 0.10
endif
```

In any decision for which a >= b is true, then a < b is false. Conversely, if a >= b is false, then a < b is true. By rephrasing the question and swapping the actions taken based on the outcome, you can make the same decision in multiple ways. The clearest route is often to ask a question so the positive or true outcome results in the action that is your motivation for making the test. When your company policy is to "provide a discount for those who are 65 and older," the phrase "greater than or equal to" comes to mind, so it is the most natural to use. Conversely, if your policy is to "provide no discount for those under 65," then it is more natural to use the "less than" syntax. Either way, the same people receive a discount.

Comparing two amounts to decide if they are *not* equal to each other is the most confusing of all the comparisons. Using "not equal to" in decisions involves thinking in double negatives, which makes you prone to include logical errors in your programs. For example, consider the flowchart segment in Figure 3-5.

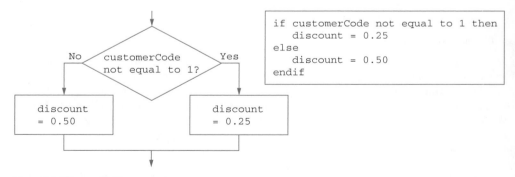

Figure 3-5 Using a negative comparison

In Figure 3-5, if the value of customerCode *is* equal to 1, the logical flow follows the false branch of the selection. If customerCode not equal to 1 is true, the discount is 0.25; if customerCode not equal to 1 is not true, it means customerCode *is* 1, and the discount is 0.50. Even using the phrase customerCode not equal to 1 is not true is awkward.

Figure 3-6 shows the same decision, this time asked in the positive. Making the decision `if customerCode` *is* `1 then discount = 0.50` is clearer than trying to determine what `customerCode` is *not*.

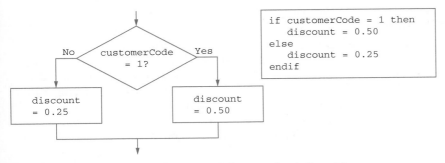

```
if customerCode = 1 then
    discount = 0.50
else
    discount = 0.25
endif
```

Figure 3-6 Using the positive equivalent of the negative comparison in Figure 3-5

Besides being awkward to use, the "not equal to" comparison operator is the one most likely to be different in various programming languages. Visual Basic and Pascal use a less-than sign followed immediately by a greater-than sign (<>); C#, C++, C, and Java use an exclamation point followed by an equal sign (!=). In a flowchart or in pseudocode, you can use the symbol that mathematicians use to mean "not equal," an equal sign with a slash through it (≠). When you program, you will not be able to use this symbol, because no single key on the keyboard produces it. When you draw a flowchart or write pseudocode in which you must use a negative decision, writing "not" is also quite acceptable.

>> **NOTE** Although NOT comparisons can be awkward to use, your meaning is sometimes clearest if you use one. Frequently, this occurs when you use an `if` without an `else`, taking action only when some comparison is false. An example would be: `if customerZipCode is not equal to localZipCode then add deliveryCharge to total`.

Table 3-1 summarizes the six comparison operators and contrasts trivial (both true and false) examples with typical examples of their use.

Comparison	Trivial True Example	Trivial False Example	Typical Example
Equal to	`7 = 7?`	`7 = 4?`	`amtOrdered = 12?`
Greater than	`12 > 3?`	`4 > 9?`	`hoursWorked > 40?`
Less than	`1 < 8?`	`13 < 10?`	`hourlyWage < 5.65?`
Greater than or equal to	`5 >= 5?`	`3 >= 9?`	`customerAge >= 65?`
Less than or equal to	`4 <= 4?`	`8 <= 2?`	`daysOverdue <= 60?`
Not equal to	`16 <> 3?`	`18 <> 18?`	`customerBalance <> 0?`

Table 3-1 Relational comparisons

UNDERSTANDING and LOGIC

Often, you need more than one selection structure to determine whether an action should take place. When you need to ask multiple questions before an outcome is determined, you must create a **compound condition**. One type of compound condition is needed when the results of at least two decisions must be true for some action to take place.

For example, suppose you have salespeople for whom you calculate bonus payments based on sales performance. A salesperson receives a $50 bonus only if the salesperson sells more than three items that total at least $1,000 in value. This type of situation is known as an **AND decision** because the salesperson's data must pass two tests—a minimum number of items sold *and* a minimum value—before the salesperson receives the bonus. A compound, or AND, decision can be constructed using a **nested decision**, or a **nested if**—that is, a decision "inside of" another decision. The flowchart and pseudocode for the program are shown in Figure 3-7.

»NOTE
You first learned about nesting structures in Chapter 2. You can always stack and nest any of the basic structures.

»NOTE
A series of nested if statements can also be called a **cascading** if **statement**.

»NOTE
In Figure 3-7, notice that bonusGiven is initialized to 0. That way, if the result of either decision is false and no new value is assigned to bonusGiven, it still will have a usable value. If you chose not to initialize bonusGiven, you could add statements to assign 0 to it if either decision's result was false.

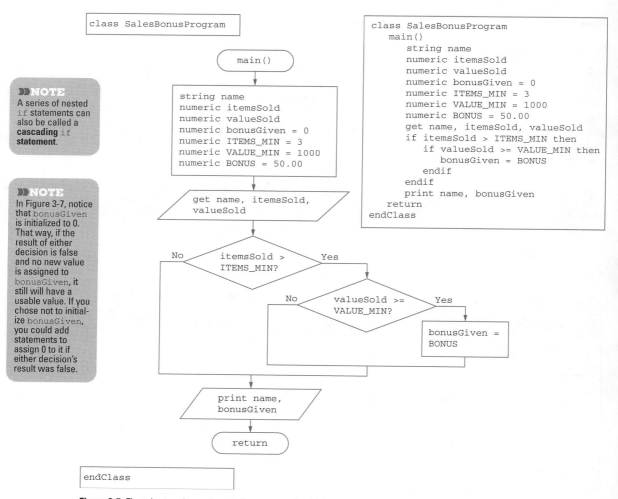

Figure 3-7 Flowchart and pseudocode for program in which salesperson must meet two criteria to get a bonus

In Figure 3-7, variables are declared to hold a salesperson's name, the number of items the salesperson has sold, and the value of the items sold. Constants are declared to hold the minimums needed to receive a bonus and for the value of the bonus itself. In the nested `if` structure in Figure 3-7, the expression `itemsSold > ITEMS_MIN` is evaluated first. If this expression is `true`, then and only then is the second Boolean expression (`valueSold >= VALUE_MIN`) evaluated. If that expression is also `true`, then the bonus assignment executes and the nested `if` structure ends.

When you use nested `if` statements, you must pay careful attention to the placement of any `else` clauses and the `endif` statements in your pseudocode. For example, suppose you want to distribute bonuses on a revised schedule, as follows:

» If the salesperson does not sell at least three items, you want to give a $10 bonus.

» If the salesperson sells at least three items, the bonus is $25 if the value of the items is under $1,000, or $50 if the value is $1,000 or more.

Figure 3-8 shows the section of logic that assigns the bonuses. In the flowchart, you can see that the shaded, second selection structure is contained entirely within one side of the first structure. When one `if` statement follows another in pseudocode, the first `else` clause encountered is paired with the last `if` encountered. The complete nested `if-else` structure that is shaded fits entirely within the `if` portion of the outer `if-else` statement. No matter how many levels of `if-else` statements are needed to produce a solution, the `else` statements always are associated with their `if`s on a "first in-last out" basis.

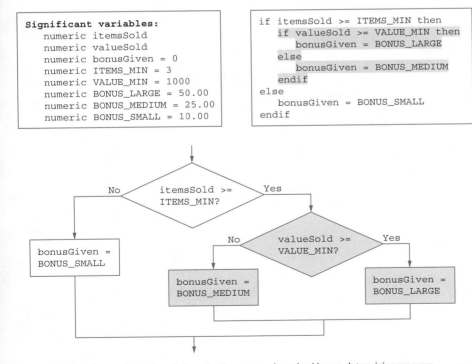

Figure 3-8 Flowchart and pseudocode for selection process in revised bonus-determining program

NESTING AND DECISIONS FOR EFFICIENCY

When you nest decisions because the resulting action requires that two conditions be true, you must decide which of the two decisions to make first. Logically, either selection in an AND decision can come first. However, when there are two selections, you can often improve your program's performance by correctly choosing which selection to make first.

For example, Figure 3-9 shows two ways to design the nested decision structure that assigns a $50 bonus to salespeople who sell more than three items valued at $1,000 or more. If you

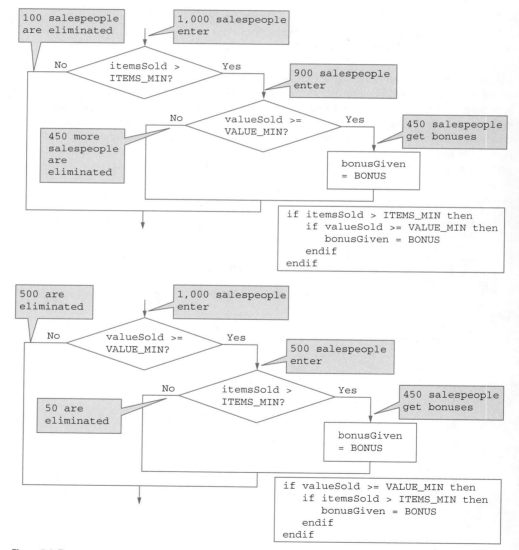

Figure 3-9 Two ways to select bonus recipients using identical criteria

want to assign this bonus, you can ask about the items sold first, eliminate those salespeople who do not qualify, and ask about the value of the items sold only for salespeople who "pass" the number of items test. Or, you could ask about the value of the items first, eliminate those who do not qualify, and ask about the number of items only for those salespeople who "pass" the value test. Either way, only salespeople who pass both tests receive the $50 bonus. Does it make a difference which question is asked first? As far as the result goes, no. Either way, the same salespeople receive the bonus—those who qualify on the basis of both criteria. As far as program efficiency goes, however, it *might* make a difference which question is asked first.

Assume you know that out of 1,000 salespeople in your company, about 90 percent, or 900, sell more than three items in a pay period. Assume you also know that because many of the items are relatively low-priced, only about half the 1,000 salespeople, or 500, sell items valued at $1,000 or more.

If you use the logic shown first in Figure 3-9, and you need to determine bonuses for 1,000 salespeople, the first question, `itemsSold > ITEMS_MIN?`, will execute 1,000 times. For approximately 90 percent of the salespeople, or 900, the answer is `true`, so 100 salespeople are eliminated from the bonus assignment, and 900 proceed to the next question about the value of the items sold. Only about half the salespeople sell at least $1,000 worth of merchandise, so 450 of the 900 receive the bonus.

Using the alternate logic in Figure 3-9, the first question, `valueSold >= VALUE_MIN?`, will also be asked 1,000 times—once for each salesperson. Because only about half the company's salespeople sell at this higher dollar level, only 500 will "pass" this test and proceed to the question for number of items sold. Then about 90 percent of the 500, or 450 salespeople, will pass this second test and receive the bonus.

Whether you use the first or second decision order in Figure 3-9, the same 450 employees who surpass both sales criteria receive the bonus. The difference is that when you ask about the items sold first, the program must ask 1,900 questions to assign the correct bonuses—the first question tests the data for all 1,000 salespeople, and 900 continue to the second question. If you use the alternate logic, asking about `valueSold` first, the program asks only 1,500 questions—all 1,000 records are tested with the first question, but only 500 proceed to the second question. By asking about the dollar value of the goods first, you "save" 400 decisions.

The 400-question difference between the first and second set of decisions doesn't take much time on most computers. But it does take *some* time, and if a corporation has hundreds of thousands of salespeople instead of only 1,000, or if many such decisions have to be made within a program, performance time can be significantly improved by asking questions in the proper order.

In many AND decisions, you have no idea which of two events is more likely to occur; in that case, you can legitimately ask either question first. In addition, even though you might know the probability of each of two conditions, the two events might not be mutually exclusive; that is, one might depend on the other. For example, salespeople who sell more items are also likely to have surpassed a requisite dollar value. Depending on the relationship between these questions, the order in which you ask them might matter less or not matter at all. However, if you do know the probabilities of the conditions, or can make a reasonable guess, the general rule is: *In an* AND *decision, first ask the question that is less likely to be true.* This eliminates as many instances of the second decision as possible, which speeds up processing time.

COMBINING DECISIONS IN AN AND SELECTION

Most programming languages allow you to ask two or more questions in a single comparison by using a **conditional AND operator**, or more simply, an **AND operator**. For example, if you want to provide a bonus for salespeople who sell more than ITEM_MINS items and at least VALUE_MIN in value, you can use nested ifs, or you can include both decisions in a single statement by writing itemsSold > ITEMS_MIN AND valueSold >= VALUE_MIN?. When you use one or more AND operators to combine two or more Boolean expressions, each Boolean expression must be true for the entire expression to be evaluated as true. For example, if you ask, "Are you at least 18, and are you a registered voter, and did you vote in the last election?", the answer to all three parts of the question must be "yes" before the response can be a single, summarizing "yes". If any part of the expression is false, then the entire expression is false.

One tool that can help you understand the AND operator is a truth table. **Truth tables** are diagrams used in mathematics and logic to help describe the truth of an entire expression based on the truth of its parts. Table 3-2 shows a truth table that lists all the possibilities with an AND decision. As the table shows, for any two expressions x and y, the expression x AND y is true only if both x and y are individually true. If either x or y alone is false, or if both are false, then the expression x AND y is false.

NOTE
The conditional AND operator in Java, C++, and C# consists of two ampersands, with no spaces between them (&&). In Visual Basic, you use the word And.

x	y	x AND y
True	True	True
True	False	False
False	True	False
False	False	False

Table 3-2 Truth table for the AND operator

NOTE
You never are required to use the AND operator because using nested if statements can always achieve the same result, but using the AND operator often makes your code more concise, less error-prone, and easier to understand.

If the programming language you use allows an AND operator, you must realize that the question you place first is the one that will be asked first, and cases that are eliminated based on the first question will not proceed to the second question. In other words, each part of an expression that uses an AND operator is evaluated only as far as necessary to determine whether the entire expression is true or false. This feature is called **short-circuit evaluation**. The computer can ask only one question at a time; even when your pseudocode looks like the first example in Figure 3-10, the computer will execute the logic shown in the second example.

NOTE
Some languages provide an additional type of AND statement that does not employ short circuitry.

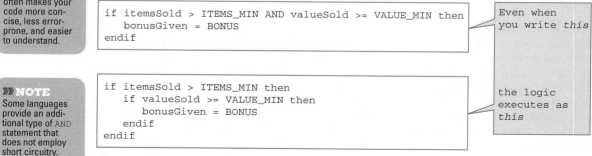

```
if itemsSold > ITEMS_MIN AND valueSold >= VALUE_MIN then
    bonusGiven = BONUS
endif
```
Even when you write *this*

```
if itemsSold > ITEMS_MIN then
    if valueSold >= VALUE_MIN then
        bonusGiven = BONUS
    endif
endif
```
the logic executes as *this*

Figure 3-10 Using an AND operator and the logic behind it

AVOIDING COMMON ERRORS IN AN AND SELECTION

When you must satisfy two or more criteria to initiate an event in a program, you must make sure that the second decision is made entirely within the first decision. For example, if a program's objective is to assign a $50 bonus to salespeople who sell more than ITEMS_MIN items with a value of at least VALUE_MIN, then the program segment shown in Figure 3-11 contains three different types of logic errors.

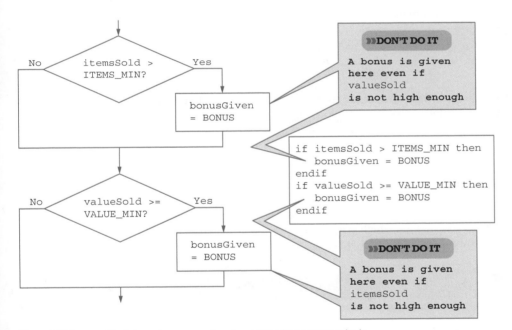

Figure 3-11 Incorrect logic to assign bonuses to salespeople who meet two criteria

The logic in Figure 3-11 shows that a salesperson who sells more than the minimum required items receives a $50 bonus. This salesperson should not necessarily receive the bonus—the dollar value might not be high enough, and it has not yet been tested. In addition, a salesperson who has not sold the minimum number of items is not eliminated from the second question. Instead, all salespeople endure the dollar value question, and some are assigned the bonus even though they might not have passed the criterion for number of items sold. Additionally, any salesperson who passes both tests has a bonus assigned twice. This does not result in an error, because the second $50 assignment replaces the first one, but processing time is wasted. For many reasons, the logic shown in Figure 3-11 is *not* correct for this problem.

Beginning programmers often make another type of error when they must make two comparisons on the same variable while using a logical AND operator. For example, suppose you want to assign a $75 bonus to those who have sold between 5 and 10 items inclusive. When you make this type of decision, you are basing it on a **range of values**—every value between low and high limits. For example, you want to select salespeople whose `itemsSold` value is greater than or equal to 5 `AND` whose `itemsSold` value is less than or equal to 10; therefore, you need to make two comparisons on the same variable. Without the logical `AND` operator, the comparison is:

```
numeric MIN_FOR_BONUS = 5
numeric MAX_FOR_BONUS = 10
numeric BONUS = 75
if itemsSold >= MIN_FOR_BONUS then
    if itemsSold <= MAX_FOR_BONUS then
        bonusGiven = BONUS
    endif
endif
```

The correct way to make this comparison with the `AND` operator is as follows:

> **» DON'T DO IT**
>
> This Boolean expression is missing an operand.

```
if itemsSold >= MIN_FOR_BONUS AND itemsSold <= MAX_FOR_BONUS then
    bonusGiven = BONUS
endif
```

You substitute the `AND` operator for the phrase `then if`. However, some programmers might try to make the comparison as follows:

```
if itemsSold >= MIN_FOR_BONUS AND <= MAX_FOR_BONUS then
    bonusGiven = BONUS
endif
```

In most programming languages, the phrase `itemsSold >= MIN_FOR_BONUS AND <= MAX_FOR_BONUS` is incorrect. The logical `AND` is usually a binary operator that requires a complete Boolean expression on each side. The expression to the right of the `AND` operator is `<= MAX_FOR_BONUS`, which is not a complete Boolean expression; you must indicate *what* is being compared to `MAX_FOR_BONUS`.

> **» NOTE** In some programming languages, such as COBOL and RPG, you can write the equivalent of `itemsSold >= MIN_FOR_BONUS AND <= MAX_FOR_BONUS?`, and the `itemsSold` variable is implied for both comparisons. Still, it is clearer, and therefore preferable, to use the two full Boolean expressions.

> **» NOTE** For clarity, many programmers prefer to surround each Boolean expression in a compound Boolean expression with its own set of parentheses. For example:
>
> ```
> if((itemsSold >= MIN_FOR_BONUS) AND (itemsSold <= MAX_FOR_BONUS))
>     bonusGiven = BONUS
> endif
> ```
>
> Use this format if it is clearer to you.

UNDERSTANDING OR LOGIC

Sometimes you want to take action when one *or* the other of two conditions is true. This is called an **OR decision** because either one condition must be met *or* some other condition must be met in order for an event to take place. If someone asks, "Are you free Friday or Saturday?", only one of the two conditions has to be true for the answer to the whole question to be "yes"; only if the answers to both halves of the question are false is the value of the entire expression false.

For example, suppose you want to assign a $300 bonus to salespeople when they have achieved one of two goals—selling at least five items, or selling at least $2,000 worth of merchandise. Figure 3-12 shows a program that accomplishes this objective.

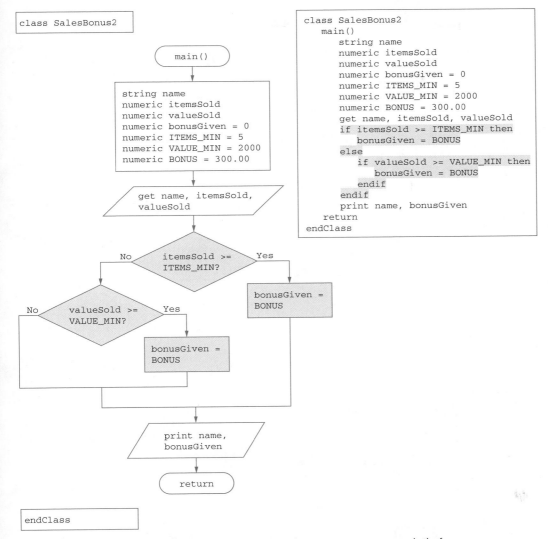

```
class SalesBonus2
    main()
        string name
        numeric itemsSold
        numeric valueSold
        numeric bonusGiven = 0
        numeric ITEMS_MIN = 5
        numeric VALUE_MIN = 2000
        numeric BONUS = 300.00
        get name, itemsSold, valueSold
        if itemsSold >= ITEMS_MIN then
            bonusGiven = BONUS
        else
            if valueSold >= VALUE_MIN then
                bonusGiven = BONUS
            endif
        endif
        print name, bonusGiven
    return
endClass
```

Figure 3-12 Flowchart and pseudocode for program in which a salesperson must meet one or both of two criteria to get a bonus

After a salesperson's data is input in the program in Figure 3-12, you ask the question `itemsSold >= ITEMS_MIN?`, and if the result is true, you assign the $300 bonus. Because selling `ITEMS_MIN` items is enough to qualify for the bonus, there is no need for further questioning. If the salesperson has not sold enough items, only then do you need to ask if `valueSold >= VALUE_MIN?`. If the employee did not sell `ITEMS_MIN` items, but did sell a high dollar value nonetheless, the salesperson receives the bonus.

WRITING OR DECISIONS FOR EFFICIENCY

As with an AND selection, when you use an OR selection, you can choose to ask either question first. For example, you can assign a bonus to salespeople who meet one or the other of two criteria using the logic in either part of Figure 3-13.

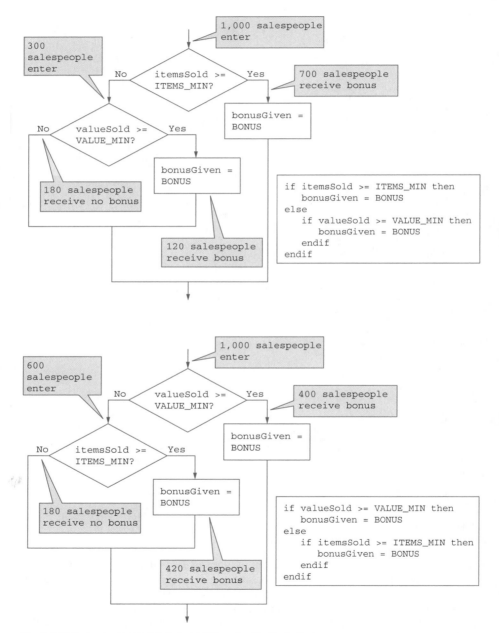

Figure 3-13 Two ways to select bonus recipients using identical criteria

You might have guessed that one of these selections is superior when you have some background information about the relative likelihood of each condition you are testing. For example, assume you know that out of 1,000 employees in your company, about 70 percent, or 700, sell at least ITEMS_MIN items during a given period of time, and that only 40 percent, or 400, sell VALUE_MIN worth of goods or more.

When you use the logic shown in the first half of Figure 3-13 to assign bonuses, you first ask about the number of items sold. For 700 salespeople the answer is true, and you assign the bonus. Only about 300 records continue to the next question regarding the dollar amount sold, where about 40 percent of the 300, or 120, fulfill the bonus requirement. In the end, you made 1,300 decisions to correctly assign bonuses to 820 employees (700 plus 120).

If you use the OR logic in the second half of Figure 3-13, you ask about the dollar value sold first—1,000 times, once each for 1,000 salespeople. The result is true for 40 percent, or 400 employees, who receive a bonus. For 600 salespeople, you ask whether itemsSold is at least the minimum required. For 70 percent of the 600, the result is true, so bonuses are assigned to 420 additional people. In the end, the same 820 salespeople (400 plus 420) receive a bonus, but after executing 1,600 decisions—300 more decisions than when using the first decision logic.

The general rule is: *In an OR decision, first ask the question that is more likely to be true.* In the preceding example, a salesperson qualifies for a bonus as soon as the person's data passes one test. Asking the question that is more likely true first eliminates as many repetitions as possible of the second decision, and the time it takes to process all the salespeople is decreased. As with the AND situation, you might not always know which question is more likely to be true, but when you can make a reasonable guess, it is more efficient to eliminate as many extra decisions as possible.

COMBINING DECISIONS IN AN OR SELECTION

When you need to take action when either one or the other of two conditions is met, you can use two separate, nested selection structures, as in the previous examples. However, most programming languages allow you to ask two or more questions in a single comparison by using a **conditional OR operator** (or simply the **OR operator**)—for example, valueSold >= VALUE_MIN OR itemsSold >= ITEMS_MIN. When you use the logical OR operator, only one of the listed conditions must be met for the resulting action to take place. Table 3-3 shows the truth table for the OR operator. As you can see in the table, the entire expression x OR y is false only when x and y both are false individually.

x	y	x OR y
True	True	True
True	False	True
False	True	True
False	False	False

Table 3-3 Truth table for the OR operator

If the programming language you use supports the OR operator, you still must realize that the question you place first is the question that will be asked first, and cases that pass the test of the first question will not proceed to the second question. (As with the AND operator, this feature is called short-circuiting.) The computer can ask only one question at a time; even when you write code as shown at the top of Figure 3-14, the computer will execute the logic shown at the bottom.

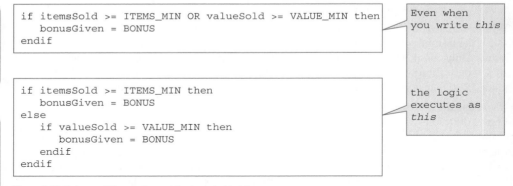

```
if itemsSold >= ITEMS_MIN OR valueSold >= VALUE_MIN then
    bonusGiven = BONUS
endif
```

Even when you write *this*

```
if itemsSold >= ITEMS_MIN then
    bonusGiven = BONUS
else
    if valueSold >= VALUE_MIN then
        bonusGiven = BONUS
    endif
endif
```

the logic executes as *this*

Figure 3-14 Using an OR operator and the logic behind it

»NOTE A common use of the OR operator is to decide to take action whether a character variable is uppercase or lowercase. For example, assume that selection has been declared as a character variable and that the user has entered a value for selection. Using the following decision, any subsequent action occurs whether the selection variable holds an uppercase or lowercase 'A':

```
if selection == 'A' OR selection == 'a' then...
```

AVOIDING COMMON ERRORS IN AN OR SELECTION

You might have noticed that the assignment statement bonusGiven = BONUS appears twice in the decision-making processes in Figures 3-12 and 3-13. When you create a flowchart, the temptation is to draw the logic to look like Figure 3-15. Logically, you can argue that the flowchart in Figure 3-15 is correct because the correct salespeople receive

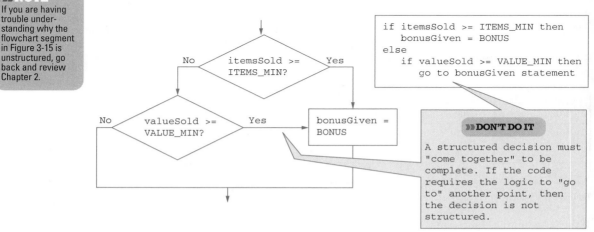

Figure 3-15 Unstructured flowchart for determining bonuses

bonuses. However, this flowchart is not allowed because it is not structured. The second question is not a self-contained structure with one entry and exit point; instead, the flow-line "breaks out" of the inner selection structure to join the true side of the outer selection structure.

An additional source of error that is specific to the OR selection stems from a problem with language and the way people use it more casually than computers do. When a sales manager wants to assign bonuses to salespeople who have sold three or more items or who have achieved $2,000 in sales, she is likely to say, "Give a bonus to anyone who has sold at least three items and to anyone who has achieved $2,000 in sales." Her request contains the word "and" between two types of people—those who sold three items and those who sold $2,000 worth—placing the emphasis on the people. However, each decision you make is about a bonus for a single salesperson who has surpassed one goal OR the other OR both. The logical situation requires an OR decision. Instead of the manager's previous statement, it would be clearer if she said, "Give a bonus to anyone who has sold at least three items or has achieved $2,000 in sales." In other words, because you are making each decision about a single salesperson, it is more correct to put the "or" conjunction between the achieved sales goals than between types of people, but bosses and other human beings often do not speak like computers. As a programmer, you have the job of clarifying what really is being requested. Often, a request for A *and* B means a request for A *or* B.

The way we casually use English can cause another type of error when you are required to find whether a value falls between two other values. For example, a movie theater manager might say, "Provide a discount to patrons who are under 13 years old and those who are over 64 years old; otherwise, charge the full price." Because the manager has used the word "and" in the request, you might be tempted to create the decision shown in Figure 3-16; however,

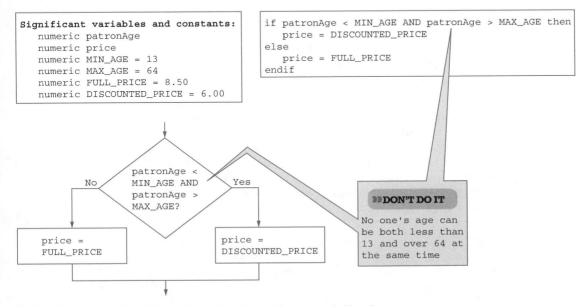

```
Significant variables and constants:
   numeric patronAge
   numeric price
   numeric MIN_AGE = 13
   numeric MAX_AGE = 64
   numeric FULL_PRICE = 8.50
   numeric DISCOUNTED_PRICE = 6.00
```

```
if patronAge < MIN_AGE AND patronAge > MAX_AGE then
   price = DISCOUNTED_PRICE
else
   price = FULL_PRICE
endif
```

No ← patronAge < MIN_AGE AND patronAge > MAX_AGE? → Yes

price = FULL_PRICE

price = DISCOUNTED_PRICE

»DON'T DO IT

No one's age can be both less than 13 and over 64 at the same time

Figure 3-16 Incorrect logic that attempts to provide a discount for young and old movie patrons

this logic will not provide a discounted price for any movie patron. You must remember that every time the decision is made in Figure 3-16, it is made for a single movie patron. If patronAge contains a value lower than 13, it cannot possibly contain a value over 64. Similarly, if it contains a value over 64, there is no way it can contain a lesser value. Therefore, no value could be stored in patronAge for which both parts of the AND question could be true—and the price will never be set to the discounted price for any movie patron. Figure 3-17 shows the correct logic.

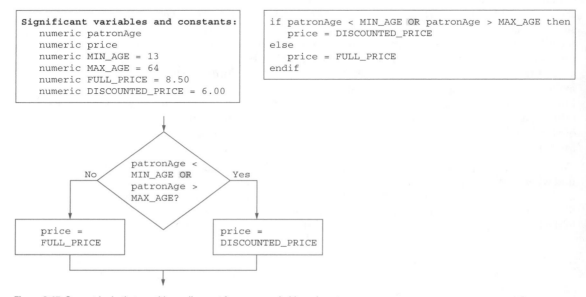

```
Significant variables and constants:
   numeric patronAge
   numeric price
   numeric MIN_AGE = 13
   numeric MAX_AGE = 64
   numeric FULL_PRICE = 8.50
   numeric DISCOUNTED_PRICE = 6.00
```

```
if patronAge < MIN_AGE OR patronAge > MAX_AGE then
    price = DISCOUNTED_PRICE
else
    price = FULL_PRICE
endif
```

Figure 3-17 Correct logic that provides a discount for young and old movie patrons

A similar error can occur in your logic if the theater manager says something like, "Don't give a discount—that is, charge full price—if a patron is over 12 or under 65." Because the word "or" appears in the request, you might plan your logic to resemble Figure 3-18. As in Figure 3-16, no patron ever receives a discount because every patron is either over 12 or under 65. Remember, in an OR decision, only one of the conditions needs to be true for the entire expression to be evaluated as true. So, for example, because a patron who is 10 is under 65, the full price is charged, and because a patron who is 70 is over 12, the full price also is charged. Figure 3-19 shows the correct logic for this decision.

▶▶ NOTE Using an OR operator in a decision that involves multiple conditions does not eliminate your responsibility for determining which condition to test first. Even when you use an OR operator, the computer makes decisions one at a time, and makes them in the order you ask them. If the first question in an OR expression evaluates to true, then the entire expression is true, and the second question is not even tested.

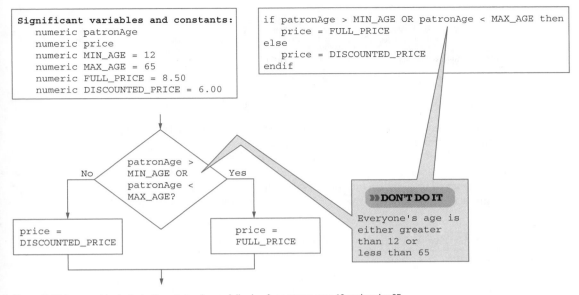

```
Significant variables and constants:
   numeric patronAge
   numeric price
   numeric MIN_AGE = 12
   numeric MAX_AGE = 65
   numeric FULL_PRICE = 8.50
   numeric DISCOUNTED_PRICE = 6.00
```

```
if patronAge > MIN_AGE OR patronAge < MAX_AGE then
   price = FULL_PRICE
else
   price = DISCOUNTED_PRICE
endif
```

▶▶ DON'T DO IT

Everyone's age is either greater than 12 or less than 65

Figure 3-18 Incorrect logic that attempts to charge full price for patrons over 12 and under 65

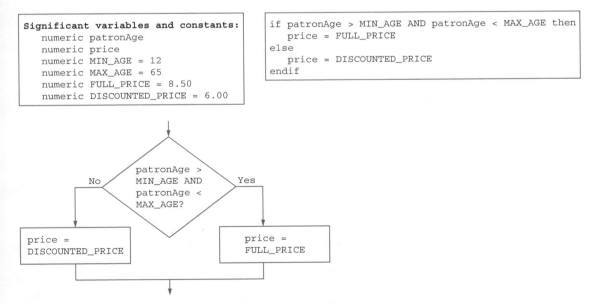

```
Significant variables and constants:
   numeric patronAge
   numeric price
   numeric MIN_AGE = 12
   numeric MAX_AGE = 65
   numeric FULL_PRICE = 8.50
   numeric DISCOUNTED_PRICE = 6.00
```

```
if patronAge > MIN_AGE AND patronAge < MAX_AGE then
   price = FULL_PRICE
else
   price = DISCOUNTED_PRICE
endif
```

Figure 3-19 Correct logic that charges full price for patrons over 12 and under 65

> **»NOTE** Besides AND and OR, most languages support a NOT operator. You use the **logical NOT operator** to reverse the meaning of a Boolean expression. For example, the statement if NOT (age < 21) print "OK" prints "OK" when age is greater than or equal to 21. The NOT operator is unary instead of binary—that is, you do not use it between two expressions, but you use it in front of a single expression. In C++, Java, and C#, the exclamation point is the symbol used for the NOT operator. In Visual Basic, the operator is Not.

MAKING SELECTIONS WITHIN RANGES

You often need to make selections based on a variable falling within a range of values. For example, suppose a company president wants to meet with every department next week to discuss an impending merger, and wants to print a series of memos to notify employees of their department's meeting day and time. Figure 3-20 shows the meeting schedule, which has been arranged by department numbers so that each meeting group is a manageable size. Figure 3-21 shows a typical memo—the shaded portions will change for each employee.

Meeting Day and Time	Departments
Monday at 9 a.m.	1 through 4
Monday at 1 p.m.	5 through 9
Tuesday at 1 p.m.	10 through 17
Wednesday at 9 a.m.	18 through 20

Figure 3-20 Proposed meeting schedule

```
To: Allison Darnell
From: Walter Braxton
Re: Pending merger

Your department will meet with me on Monday at 9 a.m. in the Blue
Conference Room where we will address questions about the upcoming
merger.
```

Figure 3-21 Typical meeting memo

When you write the program that reads an employee's name and department number, you could make 20 decisions before printing each employee's memo, such as department = 1?, department = 2?, and so on. However, it is more convenient to find the meeting day and time by using a range check.

When you use a **range check**, you compare a variable to a series of values that mark the limiting ends of ranges. To perform a range check, make comparisons using either the lowest or highest value in each range of values. For example, to find each employee's meeting day and time as listed in Figure 3-20, either use the values 1, 5, 10, and 18, which represent the low ends of each meeting's department range, or use the values 4, 9, 17, and 20, which represent the high ends.

Figure 3-22 shows the flowchart and pseudocode that represent the logic for a program that chooses a meeting time by using the high end of each range of values for department numbers. Constants have been declared for the meeting times and the high ends of each

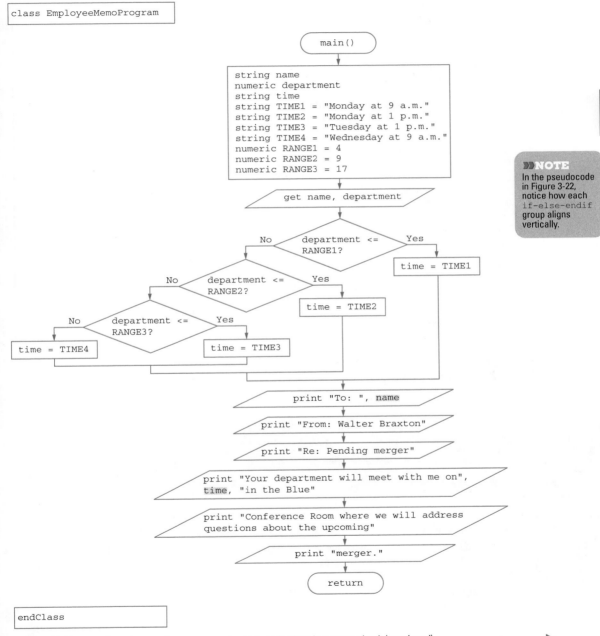

>> NOTE
In the pseudocode in Figure 3-22, notice how each `if-else-endif` group aligns vertically.

Figure 3-22 Program that prints employee memo using high-end values in a range check (*continued*)

```
class EmployeeMemoProgram
   main()
      string name
      numeric department
      string time
      string TIME1 = "Monday at 9 a.m."
      string TIME2 = "Monday at 1 p.m."
      string TIME3 = "Tuesday at 1 p.m."
      string TIME4 = "Wednesday at 9 a.m."
      numeric RANGE1 = 4
      numeric RANGE2 = 9
      numeric RANGE3 = 17
      get name, department
      if department <= RANGE1 then
         time = TIME1
      else
         if department <= RANGE2 then
            time = TIME2
         else
            if department <= RANGE3 then
               time = TIME3
            else
               time = TIME4
            endif
         endif
      endif
      print "To: ", name
      print "From: Walter Braxton"
      print "Re: Pending merger"
      print "Your department will meet with me on ", time, " in the Blue"
      print "Conference Room where we will address questions about the upcoming"
      print "merger."
   return
endClass
```

Figure 3-22 Program that prints employee memo using high-end values in a range check

» NOTE Using the logic in Figure 3-22, the 9 a.m. Wednesday time is set even if department is a high invalid value like 21, 22, or even 300. The example is intended to be simple, using only three decisions. However, in a business application, you might consider amending the logic so an additional, fourth decision is made that compares department to 20. Then, you could assign the Wednesday meeting time when department is less than or equal to 20, and issue an error message otherwise. You might also want to insert a similar decision at the beginning of the selection process to make sure department is not less than 1.

range of department numbers. In Figure 3-22, the employee's department value is compared to the high end of the lowest-range group (RANGE1, or 4). If department is less than or equal to that value, then you know the meeting time, and can store it in the time string variable; if not, you continue checking. If department is less than or equal to the high end of the next range (RANGE2), then the time is TIME2; if not, you continue checking, and time eventually is set to TIME3 or TIME4.

After the decision-making process is complete, the memo is printed one line at a time, with the employee's name and time (see shaded variables) inserted into the text of the memo.

For example, consider four employees who work in different departments, and compare how they would be handled by the set of decisions in Figure 3-22.

» First, assume that the value of `department` for an employee is 2. Using the logic in Figure 3-22, the value of the Boolean expression `department <= RANGE1` is true, the `time` is set to "Monday at 9 a.m.", and the `if` structure ends. In this case, the second decision, `department <= RANGE2`, is never made, because the `else` half of `department <= RANGE1` never executes.

» Next, assume that the value of `department` is 7 for another employee. Then, `department <= RANGE1` evaluates as false, so the `else` clause of the decision executes. There, `department <= RANGE2` is evaluated and found to be `true`, so `time` becomes "Monday at 1 p.m.".

» Next, assume `department` is 17. The expression `department <= RANGE1` evaluates as false, so the `else` clause of the decision executes. There, `department <= RANGE2` also evaluates to `false`, so its `else` clause executes. The expression `department <= RANGE3` is true, so `time` becomes "Tuesday at 1 p.m.".

» Finally, assume that the value of `department` is 19. The first decision, `department <= RANGE1`, is `false`, so the `else` clause executes. The second decision, `department <= RANGE2`, also evaluates as `false`, so the `else` clause of the second decision executes. The expression `department <= RANGE3` is also false, so the `else` clause of this decision executes, and the `time` becomes "Wednesday at 9 a.m.". In this example, the 9 a.m. Wednesday meeting represents a default value, because if none of the decision expressions is true, the last meeting time is selected by default. A **default value** is assigned after a series of selections all are false.

You could just as easily choose a meeting time using the reverse of this method, by comparing the employee department to the low end of the range values that represent each meeting. For example, you could first compare `department` to the low end (18) of the highest range (18 to 20). If the `Employee`'s `department` falls in the range, the meeting day and time are known (`TIME4`); otherwise, you check the next lower group. If `department` is greater than or equal to 10, you use the next meeting time (`TIME3`). If `department` does not fall in that range but is greater than or equal to 5, then the time is `TIME2`. In this example, "Monday at 9 a.m." becomes the default value. That is, if the department number is not greater than or equal to 18, and it is also not greater than or equal to 10, and it also is not greater than or equal to 5, then the meeting is Monday morning by default.

UNDERSTANDING COMMON ERRORS USING RANGE CHECKS

The two common errors that occur when programmers perform range checks both entail more work than is necessary. Figure 3-23 shows a program segment that contains a range check in which the programmer has asked one question too many. If you know that all `department` values are positive numbers, then if `department` is not greater than or equal to 18, and it is also not greater than or equal to 10, and it is also not greater than or equal to 5, by default it must be greater than or equal to 1. Asking whether `department` is greater than or equal to 1 (the shaded question in Figure 3-23) is a waste of time; no employee record can ever travel the logical path on the far left. You might say that the path that can never be traveled is a **dead** or **unreachable path**, and that the statements written there constitute dead or unreachable code. Although a program that contains such logic will execute and assign the correct meeting times to employees, providing such a path is always a logical error.

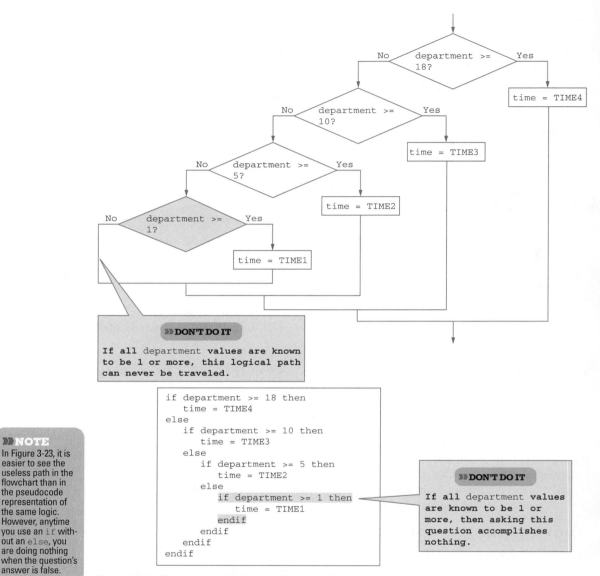

Figure 3-23 Inefficient range selection including unreachable path

》NOTE
In Figure 3-23, it is easier to see the useless path in the flowchart than in the pseudocode representation of the same logic. However, anytime you use an `if` without an `else`, you are doing nothing when the question's answer is false.

The flowchart contains the following elements:

- **department >= 18?** — No → continues down; Yes → time = TIME4
- **department >= 10?** — No → continues down; Yes → time = TIME3
- **department >= 5?** — No → continues down; Yes → time = TIME2
- **department >= 1?** — No → (DON'T DO IT); Yes → time = TIME1

》DON'T DO IT
If all `department` values are known to be 1 or more, this logical path can never be traveled.

```
if department >= 18 then
    time = TIME4
else
    if department >= 10 then
        time = TIME3
    else
        if department >= 5 then
            time = TIME2
        else
            if department >= 1 then
                time = TIME1
            endif
        endif
    endif
endif
```

》DON'T DO IT
If all `department` values are known to be 1 or more, then asking this question accomplishes nothing.

》NOTE When you ask questions of human beings, you sometimes ask a question to which you already know the answer. For example, a good trial lawyer seldom asks a question in court if the answer will be a surprise. With computer logic, however, such questions are an inefficient waste of time.

Another error that programmers make when writing the logic to perform a range check also involves asking unnecessary questions. You should never ask a question if there is only one possible answer or outcome. Figure 3-24 shows an inefficient range selection that asks two

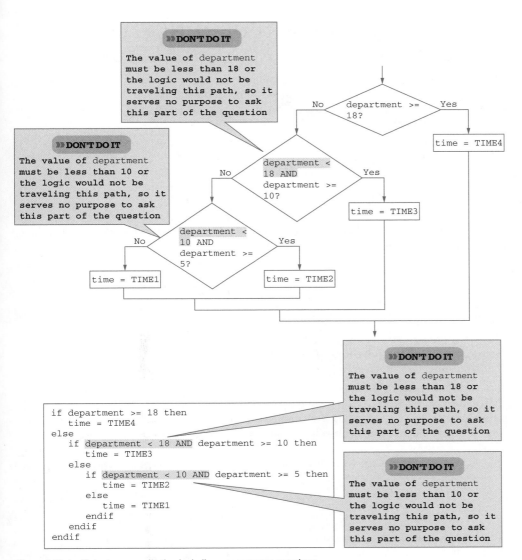

DON'T DO IT

The value of department must be less than 18 or the logic would not be traveling this path, so it serves no purpose to ask this part of the question

DON'T DO IT

The value of department must be less than 10 or the logic would not be traveling this path, so it serves no purpose to ask this part of the question

DON'T DO IT

The value of department must be less than 18 or the logic would not be traveling this path, so it serves no purpose to ask this part of the question

DON'T DO IT

The value of department must be less than 10 or the logic would not be traveling this path, so it serves no purpose to ask this part of the question

```
if department >= 18 then
    time = TIME4
else
    if department < 18 AND department >= 10 then
        time = TIME3
    else
        if department < 10 AND department >= 5 then
            time = TIME2
        else
            time = TIME1
        endif
    endif
endif
```

Figure 3-24 Inefficient range selection including unnecessary questions

unneeded questions. In the figure, if department is greater than or equal to 18, "Wednesday at 9 a.m." is the scheduled meeting. If department is not greater than or equal to 18, then it must be less than 18, so the next question (shaded in the figure) does not have to check for less than 18. The computer logic will never execute the second decision unless department is already less than 18—that is, unless it follows the false branch of the first selection. If you use the logic in Figure 3-24, you are wasting computer time asking a question that has previously been answered. Similarly, if department is not greater than or equal to 18 and it is also not greater than or equal to 10, then it must be less than 10. Therefore, there is no reason to compare department to 10 in the last decision.

NOTE
Beginning programmers sometimes justify their use of unnecessary questions as "just making really sure." Such caution is unnecessary when writing computer logic.

UNDERSTANDING PRECEDENCE WHEN COMBINING AND AND OR SELECTIONS

Most programming languages allow you to combine as many AND and OR operators in an expression as you need. For example, assume you need to score at least 75 on each of three tests to pass a course. You can declare a constant MIN_SCORE equal to 75 and test the multiple conditions with a statement like the following:

```
if score1 >= MIN_SCORE AND score2 >= MIN_SCORE AND score3 >=
        MIN_SCORE then
    classGrade = "Pass"
else
    classGrade = "Fail"
endif
```

On the other hand, if you are enrolled in a course in which you need to pass only one of three tests to pass the course, then the logic is as follows:

```
if score1 >= MIN_SCORE OR score2 >= MIN_SCORE OR score3 >= MIN_SCORE then
    classGrade = "Pass"
else
    classGrade = "Fail"
endif
```

»NOTE
In Chapter 1, you learned that every operator follows rules of precedence. For example, in an arithmetic expression, you learned that multiplication and division are performed before addition and subtraction.

The logic becomes more complicated when you combine AND and OR operators within the same statement. When you combine AND and OR operators, the AND operators take precedence, meaning their Boolean values are evaluated first.

For example, consider a program that determines whether a movie theater patron can purchase a discounted ticket. Assume discounts are allowed for children (age 12 and under) and senior citizens (age 65 and older) who attend "G"-rated movies. The following code looks reasonable but produces incorrect results, because the AND operator evaluates before the OR.

```
if age <= 12 OR age >= 65 AND rating = "G" then
    print "Discount applies"
endif
```

»DON'T DO IT
The AND evaluates first, which is not the intention.

For example, assume a movie patron is 10 years old and the movie rating is "R". The patron should not receive a discount (or be allowed to see the movie!). However, within the if statement, the part of the expression that contains the AND, age >= 65 AND rating = "G", is evaluated first. For a 10-year-old and an "R" rated movie, the question is false (on both counts), so the entire if statement becomes the equivalent of the following:

```
if age <= 12 OR aFalseExpression
    print "Discount applies"
endif
```

Because the patron is 10, age <= 12 is true, so the original if statement becomes the equivalent of:

```
if aTrueExpression OR aFalseExpression
    print "Discount applies"
endif
```

The combination `true OR false` evaluates as true. Therefore, the statement "Discount applies" prints when it should not.

Many programming languages allow you to use parentheses to correct the logic and force the expression `age <= 12 OR age >= 65` to evaluate first, as shown in the following pseudocode.

```
if (age <= 12 OR age >= 65) AND rating = "G" then
    print "Discount applies"
endif
```

With the added parentheses, if the patron's age is 12 or under OR 65 or over, the expression is evaluated as:

```
if aTrueExpression AND rating = "G"
    print "Discount applies"
endif
```

When the `age` value qualifies a patron for a discount, then the `rating` value must also be acceptable before the discount applies. This was the original intention of the statement.

You can always avoid the confusion of mixing `AND` and `OR` decisions by nesting `if` statements instead. With the flowchart and pseudocode shown in Figure 3-25, it is clear which movie patrons receive the discount. In the flowchart, you can see that the `OR` is nested entirely within the Yes branch of the `rating = "G"`? selection. Similarly, in the pseudocode in Figure 3-25, you can see by the alignment that if `rating` is not "G", the logic proceeds directly to the last `endif` statement, bypassing any checking of the age.

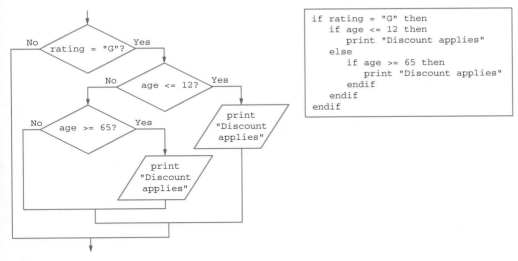

```
if rating = "G" then
    if age <= 12 then
        print "Discount applies"
    else
        if age >= 65 then
            print "Discount applies"
        endif
    endif
endif
```

Figure 3-25 Nested decisions that determine movie patron discount

NOTE In every programming language, multiplication has precedence over addition in an arithmetic statement. That is, the value of 2 + 3 * 4 is 14 because the multiplication occurs before the addition. Similarly, in every programming language, `AND` has precedence over `OR`. That's because computer circuitry treats the `AND` operator as multiplication and the `OR` operator as addition. In every programming language, 1 represents true and 0 represents false. So, for example, `aTrueExpression AND aTrueExpression` results in true, because 1 * 1 is 1, and `aTrueExpression AND aFalseExpression` is false, because 1 * 0 is 0. Similarly, `aFalseExpression OR aFalseExpression AND aTrueExpression` evaluates to false because 0 + 0 * 1 is 0, while `aFalseExpression AND aFalseExpression OR aTrueExpression` evaluates to true because 0 * 0 + 1 evaluates to 1.

UNDERSTANDING THE CASE STRUCTURE

When you have a series of decisions based on the value stored in the same variable, most languages allow you to use a case structure. You first learned about the case structure in Chapter 2. There you learned that you can solve any programming problem using only the three basic structures—sequence, selection, and loop. You are never required to use a case structure—you can always substitute a series of selections. The case structure simply provides a convenient alternative to using a series of decisions when you must make choices based on the value stored in a single variable.

For example, suppose you work for a real estate developer who is selling houses that have one of three different model numbers, each with a unique price. The logic segment of a program that determines the base price of the house might look like the logic shown in Figure 3-26.

NOTE
The syntax used to implement the case structure varies among languages. For example, Visual Basic uses `select case`, and C#, C++, and Java use `switch`.

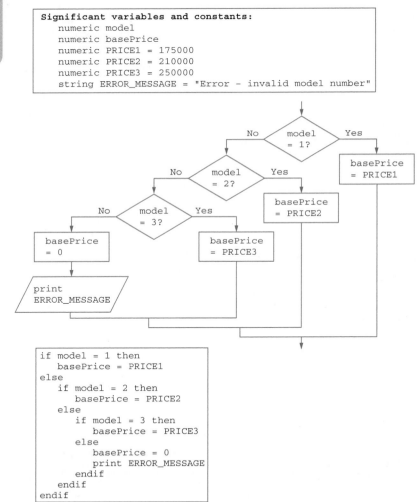

```
Significant variables and constants:
    numeric model
    numeric basePrice
    numeric PRICE1 = 175000
    numeric PRICE2 = 210000
    numeric PRICE3 = 250000
    string ERROR_MESSAGE = "Error - invalid model number"
```

```
if model = 1 then
    basePrice = PRICE1
else
    if model = 2 then
        basePrice = PRICE2
    else
        if model = 3 then
            basePrice = PRICE3
        else
            basePrice = 0
            print ERROR_MESSAGE
        endif
    endif
endif
```

Figure 3-26 Flowchart and pseudocode that determines base price for house based on model number and using nested decision structures

The logic shown in Figure 3-26 is completely structured. However, rewriting the logic using a case structure, as shown in Figure 3-27, might make it easier to understand. When using the case structure, you test a variable against a series of values, taking appropriate action based on the variable's value.

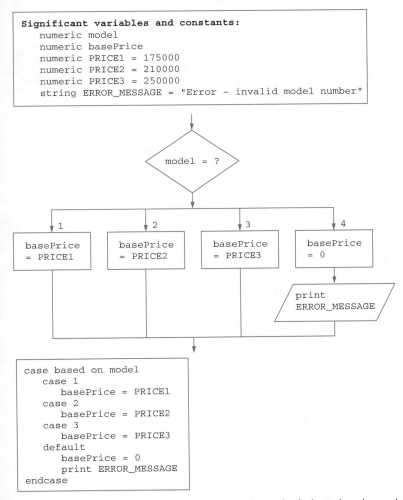

```
Significant variables and constants:
    numeric model
    numeric basePrice
    numeric PRICE1 = 175000
    numeric PRICE2 = 210000
    numeric PRICE3 = 250000
    string ERROR_MESSAGE = "Error - invalid model number"
```

```
case based on model
    case 1
        basePrice = PRICE1
    case 2
        basePrice = PRICE2
    case 3
        basePrice = PRICE3
    default
        basePrice = 0
        print ERROR_MESSAGE
endcase
```

Figure 3-27 Flowchart and pseudocode that determines base price for house based on model number and using the case structure

NOTE
In Visual Basic, the default indicator is `Case Else`. C++, C#, and Java all use `default`.

In Figure 3-27, the model variable is compared in turn with 1, 2, and 3, and an appropriate `basePrice` value is set. The default case is the case that executes in the event no other cases execute. The logic shown in Figure 3-27 is identical to that shown in Figure 3-26; your choice of method to use in seting the housing model prices is entirely a matter of preference.

>>**NOTE** When a nested `if-else` structure contains an outer and inner selection, and the inner nested `if` is within the `if` clause of the outer `if`, the program segment is a candidate for AND logic. On the other hand, if the inner `if` is within the `else` clause of the outer `if`, the program segment might be a candidate for the case structure.

>>**NOTE** Some languages require a `break` statement at the end of each case selection segment. In those languages, once a case is true, all the following cases execute until a `break` statement is encountered. When you study a specific programming language, you will learn how to use `break` statements if they are required in that language.

USING DECISION TABLES

Some applications require multiple decisions to produce useful results. Managing all the possible outcomes of multiple decisions can be a difficult task, so programmers sometimes use a tool called a decision table to help organize the possible combinations of decision outcomes.

A **decision table** is a problem-analysis tool that consists of four parts:

» Conditions
» Possible combinations of Boolean values for the conditions
» Possible actions based on the outcomes
» The specific action that corresponds to each Boolean value of each condition

For example, suppose a college collects input data from students, including an ID number, first and last names, age, and a variable that indicates whether the student has requested a residence hall that enforces quiet study hours. The `quietRequest` variable holds either a "Y" or an "N", indicating whether each student has requested a residence hall with quiet hours. Assume that the director of student housing makes residence hall assignments based on the following rules:

» Students who are under 21 years old and request a residence hall with quiet study hours are assigned to Addams Hall.
» Students who are under 21 years old and who do not request a residence hall with quiet study hours are assigned to Grant Hall.
» Students who are 21 years old or more and request a residence hall with quiet study hours are assigned to Lincoln Hall.
» Students who are 21 years old and over who do not request a residence hall with quiet study hours are also assigned to Lincoln Hall, because it is the only residence hall for students who are at least 21.

You want to write an application that accepts student data and assigns the student to the appropriate residence hall. Before you draw the flowchart or write the pseudocode, you can create a decision table to help you manage the decisions. You can begin the table by listing all the possible conditions that affect the outcome:

» Student's age is under 21, or not

» Student's quietRequest is "Y", or not

Next, you determine all the possible Boolean value combinations that exist for the conditions. In this case, there are four possible combinations, as shown in Table 3-4.

Condition	Outcome			
age < 21	T	T	F	F
quietRequest = "Y"	T	F	T	F

Table 3-4 Conditions and possible values for residence hall determination

Next, add rows to the decision table to list the possible outcome actions. A Student might be assigned to Addams, Grant, or Lincoln Hall. There are no other possibilities, so three possible action or outcome rows are added to the decision table. Table 3-5 shows the expanded table that includes the possible outcomes.

Condition	Outcome			
age < 21	T	T	F	F
quietRequest = "Y"	T	F	T	F
assignedHall = "Addams"				
assignedHall = "Grant"				
assignedHall = "Lincoln"				

Table 3-5 Conditions, possible values, and possible actions for residence hall determination

To complete the decision table, you choose one outcome for each possible combination of conditions. As shown in Table 3-6, you place an "X" (or any other symbol you prefer) in the Addams Hall row when a student's age is less than 21 and the Student has requested quiet study hours. You place an "X" in the Grant Hall row when the Student is under 21 and has not requested study hours. Finally, you place an "X" in the Lincoln Hall row whenever a

Condition	Outcome			
age < 21	T	T	F	F
quietRequest = "Y"	T	F	T	F
assignedHall = "Addams"	X			
assignedHall = "Grant"		X		
assignedHall = "Lincoln"			X	X

Table 3-6 Completed decision table for residence hall selection

Student is not under 21 years old. In this case, the request for quiet study hours is irrelevant because all Students who are 21 and older are assigned to Lincoln Hall.

In Table 3-6, the decision table is complete. There are four possible outcomes, and there is one "X" for each. Now you can begin to design the logic that achieves the correct results. You can begin to write pseudocode for the decision-making process by writing a selection statement for the first condition as follows:

```
if age < 21 then
```

Whether this expression is true or false, you do not know the final residence hall assignment—in the decision table, two columns are affected when the expression is true, and results are marked with an "X" in two different rows. Therefore, you need to insert another question, and the code becomes:

```
if age < 21 then
    if quietRequest = "Y" then
        assignedHall = "Addams"
```

At this point, you have written pseudocode that describes the first column of the decision table. The second column of the table describes the situation when the first decision is true, but the second decision is false. To include the information in the second column, the code becomes:

```
if age < 21 then
    if quietRequest = "Y" then
        assignedHall = "Addams"
    else
        assignedHall = "Grant"
    endif
```

If the student's age is not less than 21, then a second set of decisions applies as follows:

```
if age < 21 then
    if quietRequest = "Y" then
        assignedHall = "Addams"
    else
        assignedHall = "Grant"
    endif
else
    if quietRequest = "Y" then
        assignedHall = "Lincoln"
    else
        assignedHall = "Lincoln"
    endif
endif
```

Now the code matches the decision table exactly. However, you might notice that if the student's age is not under 21, the quietRequest really does not matter—the student is assigned to Lincoln Hall no matter what the study request was. Whenever both the true and false outcomes of a Boolean selection result in the same action, there is no need to make the selection. Figure 3-28 shows a completed program that gets a student's data and executes an abbreviated selection logic for residence hall assignments.

Perhaps you could have created all the decisions in the final residence hall program without creating the decision table first. If so, you need not use the decision table. Decision tables are more useful to the programmer when the decision-making process becomes more complicated.

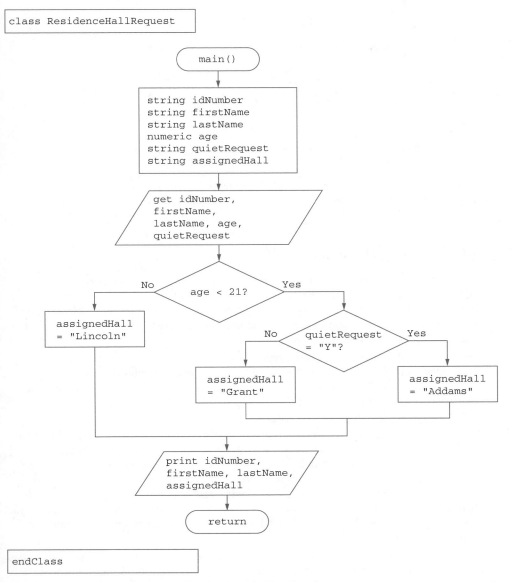

Figure 3-28 Program that assigns a student to a residence hall (*continued*)

```
class ResidenceHallRequest
    main()
        string idNumber
        string firstName
        string lastName
        numeric age
        string quietRequest
        string assignedHall
        get idNumber, firstName, lastName, age, quietRequest
        if age < 21 then
            if quietRequest = "Y" then
                assignedHall = "Addams"
            else
                assignedHall = "Grant"
            endif
        else
            assignedHall = "Lincoln"
        endif
        print idNumber, firstName, lastName, assignedHall
    return
endclass
```

Figure 3-28 Program that assigns a student to a residence hall

Additionally, they frequently serve as a useful graphic tool when you want to explain a program's decision-making process to a user who is not familiar with flowcharting symbols or the format of pseudocode statements.

CHAPTER SUMMARY

» Every decision you make in a computer program involves evaluating a Boolean expression. You can use `if-then-else` or `if-then` structures to choose between two possible outcomes. You can use `if-then-else` structures when action is required whether the selection is true or false, and `if-then` structures when there is only one outcome for the question for which action is required.

» For any two values that are the same type, you can use relational comparison operators to decide whether the two values are equal, the first value is greater than the second value, or the first value is less than the second value. The two values used in a Boolean expression can be either variables or constants.

» An `AND` decision occurs when two conditions must be true in order for a resulting action to take place. An `AND` decision requires a nested decision or a nested `if`. In an `AND` decision, first ask the question that is less likely to be true. This eliminates as many records as possible from the number that have to go through the second decision, which speeds up processing time. Most programming languages allow you to ask two or more questions in a single comparison by using a logical `AND` operator. When you must satisfy two or more criteria to initiate an event in a program, you must make sure that the second decision is made entirely within the first decision, and that you use a complete Boolean expression on both sides of the `AND`.

» An `OR` decision occurs when you want to take action when one or the other of two conditions is true. Errors occur in `OR` decisions when programmers do not maintain structure. An additional source of errors that is particular to the `OR` selection stems from people using the word `AND` to express `OR` requirements. In an `OR` decision, first ask the question that is more likely to be true. Most programming languages allow you to ask two or more questions in a single comparison by using a logical OR operator.

» To perform a range check, make comparisons with either the lowest or highest value in each range of values you are using. Common errors that occur when programmers perform range checks include asking unnecessary and previously answered questions.

» The case structure provides a convenient alternative to using a series of decisions when you must make choices based on the value stored in a single variable.

» A decision table is a problem-analysis tool that lists conditions and combinations of outcomes when those conditions are tested. It helps you identify the conditions under which each possible outcome occurs.

KEY TERMS

An **if-then** structure is a single-alternative selection.

Magic numbers are unnamed numeric constants.

An **if clause** of a decision holds the action that results when a Boolean expression in the decision is true.

The **else clause** of a decision holds the action or actions that execute only when the Boolean expression in the decision is false.

A **Boolean expression** is one that represents only one of two states, usually expressed as true or false.

A **trivial** Boolean expression is one that always evaluates to the same result.

Relational comparison operators are the symbols that express Boolean comparisons. Examples include =, >, <, >=, <=, and <>. These operators can be more simply called **relational operators** or **comparison operators**.

A **compound condition** is constructed when you need to ask multiple questions before determining an outcome.

With an **AND decision**, two conditions must both be true for an action to take place.

A **nested decision**, or a **nested if**, is a decision "inside of" another decision.

A series of nested if statements can also be called a **cascading if statement**.

A **conditional AND operator** (or more simply, an **AND operator**) is a symbol that you use to combine decisions so that two or more conditions must be true for an action to occur.

Truth tables are diagrams used in mathematics and logic to help describe the truth of an entire expression based on the truth of its parts.

Short-circuit evaluation is a logical feature in which each part of a larger expression is evaluated only as far as necessary to determine the final outcome.

A **range of values** encompasses every value between a high and low limit.

An **OR decision** contains two or more decisions; if at least one condition is met, the resulting action takes place.

A **conditional OR operator** (or more simply, an **OR operator**) is a symbol that you use to combine decisions when any one condition can be true for an action to occur.

The **logical NOT operator** is a symbol that reverses the meaning of a Boolean expression.

When you use a **range check**, you compare a variable to a series of values that mark the limiting ends of ranges.

A **default value** is one that is assigned after all test conditions are found to be false.

A **dead** or **unreachable path** is a logical path that can never be traveled.

A **decision table** is a problem-analysis tool that lists conditions, Boolean outcomes when those conditions are tested, and possible actions based on the outcomes.

REVIEW QUESTIONS

1. The selection statement `if quantity > 100 then discountRate = RATE` is an example of a _____ .

    a. single-alternative selection

    b. dual-alternative selection

    c. binary selection

    d. all of these

2. The selection statement `if dayOfWeek = "Sunday" then price = LOWER_PRICE else price = HIGHER_PRICE` is an example of a _____ .

    a. unary selection

    b. single-alternative selection

    c. binary selection

    d. all of the above

3. All selection statements must have _____ .

    a. an `if` clause   c. both of these

    b. an `else` clause   d. none of these

4. An expression like `amount < 10` is a _____ expression.

    a. Gregorian   c. Machiavellian

    b. Boolean   d. Edwardian

5. Usually, you compare only variables that have the same _____ .

    a. value   c. name

    b. size   d. type

6. Symbols like > and < are known as _____ operators.

   a. arithmetic

   b. relational comparison

   c. sequential

   d. scripting accuracy

7. If you could use only three relational comparison operators, you could get by with _____ .

   a. greater than, less than, and greater than or equal to

   b. less than, less than or equal to, and not equal to

   c. equal to, less than, and greater than

   d. equal to, not equal to, and less than

8. If a > b is false, then which of the following is always true?

   a. a < b   c. a = b

   b. a <= b   d. a >= b

9. Usually, the most difficult comparison operator to work with is _____ .

   a. equal to   c. less than

   b. greater than   d. not equal to

10. Which of the lettered choices is equivalent to the following decision?

```
if x > 10 then
    if y > 10 then
        print "X"
    endif
endif
```

   a. if x > 10 AND y > 10 then print "X"

   b. if x > 10 OR y > 10 then print "X"

   c. if x > 10 AND x > y then print "X"

   d. if y > x then print "X"

11. The Acme Computer Company operates in all 50 of the United States. The Midwest Sales region consists of five states—Illinois, Indiana, Iowa, Missouri, and Wisconsin. Suppose you have input records containing Acme customer data, including state of residence. To most efficiently select and display all customers who live in the Midwest Sales region, you would use _____ .

   a. five completely separate unnested if statements

   b. nested if statements using AND logic

   c. nested if statements using OR logic

   d. Not enough information is given.

12. The Midwest Sales region of Acme Computer Company consists of five states—Illinois, Indiana, Iowa, Missouri, and Wisconsin. About 50 percent of the regional customers reside in Illinois, 20 percent in Indiana, and 10 percent in each of the other three states. Suppose you have input records containing Acme customer data, including state of residence. To most efficiently select and display all customers who live in the Midwest Sales region, you would ask first about residency in _____ .

a. Illinois

b. Indiana

c. either Iowa, Missouri, or Wisconsin—it does not matter which one of these three is first

d. any of the five states; it does not matter which one is first

13. The Boffo Balloon Company makes helium balloons. Large balloons cost $13.00 a dozen, medium-sized balloons cost $11.00 a dozen, and small balloons cost $8.60 a dozen. About 60 percent of the company's sales are the smallest balloons, 30 percent are the medium, and large balloons constitute only 10 percent of sales. Customer order records include customer information, quantity ordered, and size. For the most efficient decision when you write a program to determine price based on size, you should ask first whether the size is _____ .

a. large	c. small
b. medium	d. It does not matter.

14. The Boffo Balloon Company makes helium balloons in three sizes, 12 colors, and with a choice of 40 imprinted sayings. As a promotion, the company is offering a 25-percent discount on orders of large, red "Happy Valentine's Day" balloons. To most efficiently select the orders to which a discount applies, you would use _____ .

a. three completely separate unnested `if` statements

b. nested `if` statements using AND logic

c. nested `if` statements using OR logic

d. Not enough information is given.

15. Radio station FM 99 keeps a record of every song played on the air in a week. Each record contains the day, hour, and minute the song started, and the title and artist of the song. The station manager wants a list of every title played during the important 8 a.m. commute hour on the two busiest traffic days, Monday and Friday. Which logic would select the correct titles?

a.
```
if day = "Monday" OR day = "Friday" OR hour = 8 then
     print title
 endif
```

b.
```
if day = "Monday" then
     if hour = 8 then
        print title
     else
         if day = "Friday" then
```

```
            print title
        endif
      endif
  endif
```

c.
```
if hour = 8 AND day = "Monday" OR day = "Friday" then
    print title
endif
```

d.
```
if hour = 8 then
    if day = "Monday" OR day = "Friday" then
        print title
    endif
endif
```

16. In the following pseudocode, what percentage raise will an employee in Department 5 receive?

```
if department < 3 then
    raise = SMALL_RAISE
else
    if department < 5 then
        raise = MEDIUM_RAISE
    else
        raise = BIG_RAISE
    endif
endif
```

a. SMALL_RAISE

b. MEDIUM_RAISE

c. BIG_RAISE

d. impossible to tell

17. In the following pseudocode, what percentage raise will an employee in Department 8 receive?

```
if department < 5 then
    raise = SMALL_RAISE
else
    if department < 14 then
        raise = MEDIUM_RAISE
    else
        if department < 9 then
            raise = BIG_RAISE
        endif
    endif
endif
```

a. SMALL_RAISE

b. MEDIUM_RAISE

c. BIG_RAISE

d. impossible to tell

18. In the following pseudocode, what percentage raise will an employee in Department 10 receive?

```
if department < 2 then
    raise = SMALL_RAISE
else
    if department < 6 then
        raise = MEDIUM_RAISE
    else
        if department < 10 then
            raise = BIG_RAISE
        endif
    endif
endif
```

a. SMALL_RAISE

b. MEDIUM_RAISE

c. BIG_RAISE

d. impossible to tell

19. When you use a range check, you compare a variable to the _____ value in the range.

a. lowest

c. highest

b. middle

d. lowest or highest

20. Which of the following can be used as an alternative to a series of `if` statements based on the same variable?

a. a sequence structure

b. a loop structure

c. an action structure

d. a case structure

EXERCISES

1. Assume the following variables contain the values shown:

numberRed = 100   numberBlue = 200   numberGreen = 300

wordRed = "Wagon"   wordBlue = "Sky"   wordGreen = "Grass"

For each of the following Boolean expressions, decide whether the statement is true, false, or illegal.

a. numberRed = numberBlue?

b. numberBlue > numberGreen?

c. numberGreen < numberRed?

d. numberBlue = wordBlue?

e. `numberGreen = "Green"?`

f. `wordRed = "Red"?`

g. `wordBlue = "Blue"?`

h. `numberRed <= numberGreen?`

i. `numberBlue >= 200?`

j. `numberGreen >= numberRed + numberBlue?`

2. Chocolate Delights Candy Company manufactures several types of candy. Design a flow-chart or pseudocode for the following:

   a. A program that accepts a candy name (for example, "chocolate-covered blueberries"), price per pound, and number of pounds sold in the average month, and displays the item's data values only if it is a best-selling item. Best-selling items are those that sell more than 2,000 pounds per month.

   b. A program that accepts candy data and produces a list of high-priced, best-selling items. Best-selling items are those that sell more than 2,000 pounds per month. High-priced items are those that sell for $10 per pound or more.

3. Pastoral College is a small college in the Midwest. Design a flowchart or pseudocode for the following:

   a. A program that accepts student data: an ID number, first and last names, major field of study, and grade point average. Display a student's data if the student's grade point average is below 2.0.

   b. A program for the Literary Honor Society that displays all students with an English major and a grade point average of 3.5 or higher.

4. The Summerville Telephone Company charges 10 cents per minute for all calls outside the customer's area code that last over 20 minutes. All other calls are 13 cents per minute. Design a flowchart or pseudocode for the following:

   a. A program that accepts data about one phone call: customer area code (three digits), customer phone number (seven digits), called area code (three digits), called number (seven digits), and call time in minutes (four digits). Display the calling number, called number, and price for the call.

   b. A program that accepts data about a phone call and displays all the details only about calls that cost over $10.

   c. A program that accepts data about a phone call and displays details only about calls placed from the 212 area code to the 704 area code that last over 20 minutes.

   d. A program that accepts data about a phone call and prompts the user for a three-digit area code, then displays the data for any phone call to or from the specified area code.

5. Equinox Nursery maintains records about all the plants it has in stock. Design a flow-chart or pseudocode for the following:

   a. A program that accepts a plant's name, price, and light and soil preferences. The light variable might contain a description such as "sunny," "partial sun," or "shady." The soil variable might contain a description such as "clay" or "sandy." Display the details for a plant if it is appropriate for a shady, sandy yard.

b. A program that accepts a plant's data and displays the results for a plant if it is appropriate for a shady or partially sunny yard with clay soil.

6. The Drive-Rite Insurance Company provides automobile insurance policies for drivers. Design a flowchart or pseudocode for the following:

a. A program that accepts insurance policyholder data, including a policy number, customer last name, customer first name, age, premium due month, day, and year, and the number of accidents in which the driver has been involved in the last three years. If a policy number entered is not between 1000 and 9999 inclusive, then set the policy number to 0. If the month is not between 1 and 12 inclusive, or the day is not correct for the month (that is, between 1 and 31 for January, 1 and 29 for February, and so on), then set the month, day, and year to 0. Display the policyholder data after any revisions have been made.

b. A program that accepts a policyholder's data and displays the data for any policyholder who is more than 35 years old.

c. A program that accepts a policyholder's data and displays the data for any policyholder who is at least 21 years old.

d. A program that accepts a policyholder's data and displays the data for any policyholder who is no more than 30 years old.

e. A program that accepts a policyholder's data and displays the data for any policyholder whose premium is due no later than March 15 any year.

f. A program that accepts a policyholder's data and displays the data for any policyholder whose premium is due on or before January 1, 2010.

g. A program that accepts a policyholder's data and displays the data for any policyholder whose premium is due by April 27, 2009.

h. A program that accepts a policyholder's data and displays the data for any policyholder who has a policy number between 1000 and 4000 inclusive, whose policy comes due in April or May of any year, and has had fewer than three accidents.

7. The Barking Lot is a dog day care center. Design a flowchart or pseudocode for a program that accepts data for an ID number of a dog's owner, and the name, breed, age, and weight of the dog.

Display a bill containing all the input data as well as the weekly day care fee, which is $55 for dogs under 15 pounds, $75 for dogs that weigh at least 15 pounds but no more than 30 pounds, $105 for dogs over 30 pounds but no more than 80 pounds, and $125 for dogs over 80 pounds.

8. Rick Hammer is a carpenter who wants an application to compute the price of any desk a customer orders, based on the following: desk length and width in inches, type of wood, and number of drawers. The price is computed as follows:

» The charge for all desks is a minimum $200.

» If the surface (length * width) is over 750 square inches, add $50.

» If the wood is mahogany, add $150; for oak, add $125. No charge is added for pine.

» For every drawer in the desk, there is an additional $30 charge.

Design a flowchart or pseudocode for the following:

a. A program that accepts data for an order number, customer name, length and width of the desk ordered, type of wood, and number of drawers. Display all the entered data and the final price for the desk.

b. A program that accepts desk order data and displays all the relevant information for oak desks that are over 36 inches long and have at least one drawer.

9. Black Dot Printing is attempting to organize carpools to save energy. Each input record contains an employee's name and town of residence. Ten percent of the company's employees live in Wonder Lake. Thirty percent of the employees live in Woodstock. Because these towns are both north of the company, the company wants to encourage employees who live in either town to drive to work together. Design a flowchart or pseudocode for a program that accepts an employee's data and displays it with a message that indicates whether the employee is a candidate for the carpool.

10. Diana Lee is a supervisor in a manufacturing company. She wants to know which employees have increased their production this year over last year, so that she can issue them certificates of commendation and bonuses. Design a flowchart or pseudocode for the following:

a. A program that accepts a worker's first and last names, this year's number of units produced, and last year's number of units produced. Display each employee with a message indicating whether the employee's production has increased over last year's production.

b. A program that accepts a worker's data and displays the name and a bonus amount. Bonuses will be issued only to workers whose production this year exceeds last year's production. The bonuses will be distributed as follows:

If this year's production has improved over last year's, and if this year's production is:

» 1,000 units or fewer, the bonus is $25
» 1,001 to 3,000 units, the bonus is $50
» 3,001 to 6,000 units, the bonus is $100
» 6,001 units and up, the bonus is $200

c. Modify Exercise 10b to reflect the following new facts, and have the program execute as efficiently as possible:

» Thirty percent of the employees have increased production this year.
» Sixty percent of employees produce over 6,000 units per year; 20 percent produce 3,001 to 6,000; 15 percent produce 1,001 to 3,000; and only 5 percent produce fewer than 1,001.

11. The Richmond Riding Club wants to assign the title of Master or Novice to each of its members. A member earns the title of Master by accomplishing two or more of the following:

» Participating in at least eight horse shows
» Winning a first or second place ribbon in at least two horse shows, no matter how many shows the member has participated in
» Winning a first, second, third, or fourth place ribbon in at least four horse shows, no matter how many shows the member has participated in

Design a flowchart or pseudocode for a program that accepts a rider's last name and first name, number of shows in which the rider has participated, and number of first, second, third, and fourth place ribbons the rider has received. If the sum of the first, second, third, and fourth place ribbons exceeds the number of shows, then set all the ribbon values to 0 and display the rider's name and an error message. Otherwise, display the rider's name and either "Master" or "Novice".

12. The Dorian Gray Portrait Studio charges its customers based on the number of subjects who pose for a portrait. The fee schedule is as follows:

Subjects in Portrait	Base Price
1	$100
2	$130
3	$150
4	$165
5	$175
6	$180
7 or more	$185

Portrait sittings on Saturday or Sunday cost 20 percent more than the base price.

Design a flowchart or pseudocode for the following:

a. A program that accepts the following data: the last name of the family sitting for the portrait, the number of subjects in the portrait, the scheduled day of the week, and the scheduled time of day. Display all the input data as well as the calculated sitting fee.

b. A program that accepts the customer data and displays data only for sittings scheduled on Thursday after 1 p.m. or Friday before noon.

CASE PROJECT

In Chapters 1 and 2, you thought about processes needed for Cost Is No Object—a car rental service that specializes in lending antique and luxury cars to clients on a short-term basis. Design a flowchart or pseudocode for a program that accepts rental contract data and displays a completed rental contract ready for a customer's signature.

Accept the following as input:

» Contract number
» Customer's first and last names
» Automobile's vehicle identification number
» Starting date for the rental agreement stored as three separate variables—month, day, and year
» Length, in days, of the rental agreement
» Indicator of whether the customer bought the optional insurance policy

Display output as follows:

» If the contract number is not between 10000 and 99999 inclusive, issue an error message and end the program.

» If the customer ID number is not between 100 and 999 inclusive, issue an error message and end the program.

» If the starting date for the rental agreement is invalid, issue an error message and end the program. (In other words, make sure the month is between 1 and 12, inclusive. If the month is 1, 3, 5, 7, 8, 10, or 12, the day must be between 1 and 31, inclusive. If the month is 2, the day must be between 1 and 28, inclusive. You do not need to check for leap years. If the month is 4, 6, 9, or 11, the day must be between 1 and 30, inclusive.)

» If the length of the rental agreement is not between 1 and 30 days inclusive, issue an error message and end the program. Otherwise, calculate the ending month, day, and year based on the starting date and length of the agreement.

» The insurance indicator must be "Y" or "N" (for "Yes" or "No"); otherwise, display an error message.

» If all the entered data is valid, display it along with the fee for the rental, which is calculated as follows:

  » $25 per day for 10 days or fewer

  » $18 per day for each day over 10 days

  » $2.50 per day for insurance, regardless of the number of days in the contract

UP FOR DISCUSSION

1. Computer programs can be used to make decisions about your insurability as well as the rates you will be charged for health and life insurance policies. For example, certain pre-existing conditions may raise your insurance premiums considerably. Is it ethical for insurance companies to access your health records and then make insurance decisions about you?

2. Job applications are sometimes screened by software that makes decisions about a candidate's suitability based on keywords in the applications. Is such screening fair to applicants?

3. Medical facilities often have more patients waiting for organ transplants than there are available organs. Suppose you have been asked to write a computer program that selects which of several candidates should receive an available organ. What data would you want on file to be able to use in your program, and what decisions would you make based on the data? What data do you think others might use that you would choose not to use?

LOOPING

In this chapter, you will:

Learn about the advantages of looping
Control loops with counters and sentinel values
Use nested loops
Learn to avoid common loop mistakes
Use a `for` loop
Use posttest loops
Recognize the characteristics shared by all loops
Learn about common loop applications

UNDERSTANDING THE ADVANTAGES OF LOOPING

While making decisions is what makes computers seem intelligent, it's looping that makes computer programming both efficient and worthwhile. When you use a loop within a computer program, you can write one set of instructions that operates on multiple, separate sets of data. Consider the following set of tasks required for each employee in a typical payroll program:

» Determine regular pay.

» Determine overtime pay, if any.

» Determine federal withholding tax based on gross wages and number of dependents.

» Determine state withholding tax based on gross wages, number of dependents, and state of residence.

» Determine insurance deduction based on insurance code.

» Determine Social Security deduction based on gross pay.

» Subtract federal tax, state tax, Social Security, and insurance from gross pay.

In reality, this list is too short—companies deduct stock option plans, charitable contributions, union dues, and other items from checks in addition to the items mentioned in this list. Also, they might pay bonuses and commissions and provide sick days and vacation days that must be taken into account and handled appropriately. As you can see, payroll programs are complicated.

> **» NOTE**
> In Chapter 2, you learned that looping is called repetition or iteration.

The advantage of having a computer perform payroll calculations is that all of the deduction instructions need to be written only once and can be repeated over and over again for each paycheck, using a loop, the structure that repeats actions while some condition continues.

CONTROLLING LOOPS WITH COUNTERS AND SENTINEL VALUES

> **» NOTE**
> You first learned about infinite loops in Chapter 2. In that chapter, you also learned how sentinel values control loops.

Recall the loop, or `while` structure, that you learned about in Chapter 2. There you learned about loops that look like Figure 4-1. As long as a Boolean expression remains true, a `while` loop's body executes. When you write a loop, you must control the number of repetitions it performs; if you do not, you run the risk of creating an infinite loop. Commonly, you control a loop's repetitions by using either a counter or a sentinel value.

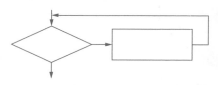

Figure 4-1 The `while` loop

USING A DEFINITE WHILE LOOP WITH A COUNTER

You can use a `while` loop to execute a body of statements continuously as long as some condition continues to be true. To make a `while` loop end correctly, three separate actions should occur:

» A variable, the **loop control variable**, is initialized (before entering the loop).

» The loop control variable is tested, and if the result is true, the loop body is entered.

» The body of the loop must take some action that alters the value of the loop control variable (so that the `while` expression eventually evaluates as false).

> **»NOTE** The decision that controls every loop is always based on a Boolean comparison. In Chapter 3, you learned about six comparison operators that you can use in a selection. You can use any of the same six operators to control a loop: are equal to, greater than, less than, greater than or equal to, less than or equal to, and not equal to.

For example, the code in Figure 4-2 shows a loop that displays "Hello" four times. The variable `count` is the loop control variable, and it is initialized to 0. Then the shaded `while` expression compares `count` to 4, finds it is less than 4, and so the loop body executes. The loop body shown in Figure 4-2 consists of two statements. The first statement prints "Hello" and the second statement adds 1 to `count`. The next time `count` is evaluated, its value is 1, which is still less than 4, so the loop body executes again. "Hello" prints a third time and `count` becomes 3, then "Hello" prints a fourth time and `count` becomes 4. Now when the expression `count < 4` evaluates, it is `false`, so the loop ends.

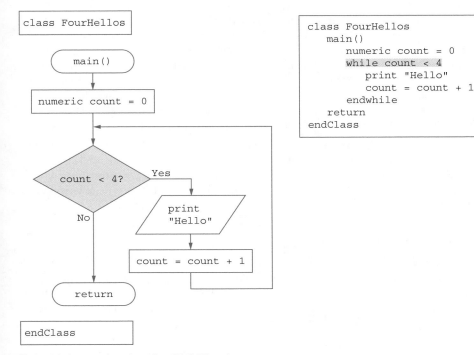

```
class FourHellos
    main()
        numeric count = 0
        while count < 4
            print "Hello"
            count = count + 1
        endwhile
    return
endClass
```

Figure 4-2 A `while` loop that prints "Hello" four times

>> NOTE To an algebra student, a statement such as `count = count + 1` looks wrong—a value can never be one more than itself. In programming languages, however, the expression isn't a mathematical equation; rather, it is a statement that takes the value of `count`, adds 1 to it, and assigns the new value back into `count`.

Within a correctly functioning loop's body, you can change the value of the loop control variable in a number of ways. Many loop control variable values are altered by **incrementing**, or adding to them, as in Figure 4-2. Other loops are controlled by reducing, or **decrementing**, a variable and testing whether the value remains greater than some benchmark value. For example, the loop in Figure 4-2 could be rewritten so that `count` is initialized to 4, and reduced by 1 on each pass through the loop. The loop should then continue while `count` remains greater than 0.

>> NOTE Because you so frequently need to increment a variable, many programming languages contain a shortcut operator for incrementing. For example, in C++, Java, and C#, you can replace the statement `rep = rep + 1` with `++rep` or `rep++`. You pronounce these statements "plus plus rep" and "rep plus plus". Both statements increase the value of `rep` by 1. There is a difference in how these statements operate; you learn the difference when you study a programming language that uses them.

A loop such as the one in Figure 4-2, for which the number of iterations is predetermined, is called a **definite loop** or **counted loop**. The looping logic shown in Figure 4-2 uses a counter. A **counter** is any numeric variable you use to count the number of times an event has occurred. In everyday life, people usually count things starting with 1. Many programmers prefer starting their counted loops with a variable containing a 0 value for two reasons. First, in many computer applications, numbering starts with 0 because of the 0-and-1 nature of computer circuitry. Second, when you learn about arrays in Chapter 5, you will discover that array manipulation naturally lends itself to 0-based loops. However, you are not required to start counting using 0. You could achieve exactly the same results in a program as the one in Figure 4-2 by initializing `count` to 1 and continuing the loop while it remains less than 5. You could even initialize `count` to some arbitrary value such as 23 and continue while it remains less than 27 (which is 4 greater than 23). This last choice is not recommended, because it is confusing; however, the program would work just as well.

Often, the value of a loop control variable is not altered by arithmetic, but instead is altered by user input. For example, perhaps you want to continue performing some task while the user indicates a desire to continue. In that case, you do not know when you write the program whether the loop will be executed two times, 200 times, or not at all. This type of loop is an **indefinite loop**.

USING AN INDEFINITE WHILE LOOP WITH A SENTINEL VALUE

Consider a program that displays a bank balance and asks if the user wants to see what the balance will be after one year of interest has accumulated. Each time the user indicates she wants to continue, an increased balance appears. When the user finally indicates she is finished, the program ends. The loop is indefinite because each time the program executes, the loop might be performed a different number of times. The program appears in Figure 4-3.

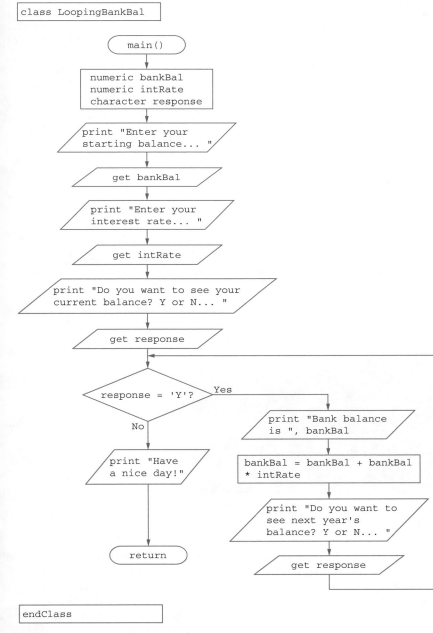

Figure 4-3 LoopingBankBal program (*continued*)

» **NOTE**
The first get response statement in the application in Figure 4-3 is a priming input statement. You learned about the priming input statement in Chapter 2.

》NOTE
The program shown in Figure 4-3 continues to display bank balances while response is *Y*. It could also be written to display while response is not *N*. In Chapter 2, you learned that a value such as 'Y' or 'N' that a user must supply to stop a loop is called a sentinel value.

```
class LoopingBankBal
   main()
      numeric bankBal
      numeric intRate
      character response
      print "Enter your starting balance... "
      get bankBal
      print "Enter your interest rate... "
      get intRate
      print "Do you want to see your current balance? Y or N... "
      get response
      while response = 'Y'
         print "Bank balance is ", bankBal
         bankBal = bankBal + bankBal * intRate
         print "Do you want to see next year's balance? Y or N... "
         get response
      endwhile
      print "Have a nice day!"
   return
endClass
```

Figure 4-3 LoopingBankBal program

》NOTE The body of a loop might contain any number of statements, including method calls, decisions, and other loops. Once your logic enters the body of a structured loop, the entire loop body must execute. Your program can leave a structured loop only at the comparison that tests the loop control variable.

Figure 4-4 shows how this program might be executed when written as a command-line interactive program.

```
Command Prompt                                              _ □ ×

Enter your starting balance ... 1000.00
Enter your interest rate ... 0.03
Do you want to see your current balance? Y or N ...Y
Bank balance is $1,000.00
Do you want to see next year's balance? Y or N ...Y
Bank balance is $1,030.00
Do you want to see next year's balance? Y or N ...Y
Bank balance is $1,060.90
Do you want to see next year's balance? Y or N ...Y
Bank balance is $1,092.73
Do you want to see next year's balance? Y or N ...N
Have a nice day!
```

Figure 4-4 Typical execution of the LoopingBankBal program

The program shown in Figure 4-3 contains three variables that are involved in the looping process: a bank balance, an interest rate, and a response. The variable named response is the loop control variable. It is initialized when the program asks the user, "Do you want to see your current balance?" and reads the response. The loop control variable is tested with the question response = 'Y'?. If the user has entered any response other than *Y*, then the test expression is false, and the loop body never executes; instead, the next statement to execute is to display "Have a nice day!". However, if the user enters *Y*, then the test expression is true and all four statements within the loop body execute. Within the loop body, the current balance is displayed, and the program increases the balance by the interest rate; this value will not be displayed unless the user requests another loop repetition. Within the loop, the program prompts the user and reads in a new value for `response`. This input statement is the one that potentially alters the loop control variable. The loop body ends when program control returns to the top of the loop, where the Boolean expression in the `while` statement is tested again. If the user typed *Y* at the last prompt, then the loop is entered and the increased `bankBal` value that was calculated during the last loop cycle is finally displayed.

The flowchart and pseudocode segments in Figure 4-3 contain three steps that must occur in every loop. These crucial steps are shaded in Figure 4-5.

> **»NOTE**
> In most program-ming languages, character data is case sensitive. If a program tests `response = 'Y'`, a user response of *y* will result in a `false` evaluation.

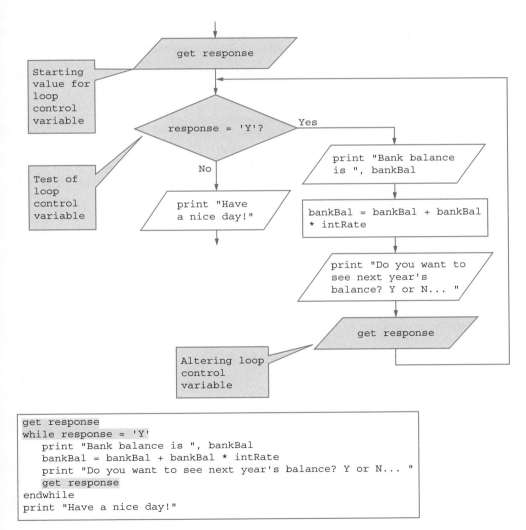

```
get response
while response = 'Y'
    print "Bank balance is ", bankBal
    bankBal = bankBal + bankBal * intRate
    print "Do you want to see next year's balance? Y or N... "
    get response
endwhile
print "Have a nice day!"
```

Figure 4-5 Crucial steps needed in every loop

1. You must provide a starting value that will control the loop. In this case, the starting value is provided by the first request for a user's response.
2. You must make a comparison using the value that controls whether the loop continues or stops. In this case, you compare the user's response with the character `'Y'`.
3. Within the loop, you must alter the value that controls the loop. In this case, you alter the loop control variable by asking the user for a new response.

On each pass through the loop, the value in the `response` variable determines whether the loop will continue. Therefore, `response` is the loop control variable.

USING NESTED LOOPS

Program logic gets more complicated when you must use loops within loops, or **nested loops**. When one loop appears inside another, the loop that contains the other loop is called the **outer loop**, and the loop that is contained is called the **inner loop**. You need to create nested loops when the values of two (or more) variables repeat to produce every combination of values.

For example, suppose you want to write a program that produces a quiz answer sheet like the one shown in Figure 4-6. The quiz has five parts, there are three questions in each part, and you want a fill-in-the-blank line for each question. You could write a program that uses 20 separate print statements to produce the sheet, but it is more efficient to use nested loops.

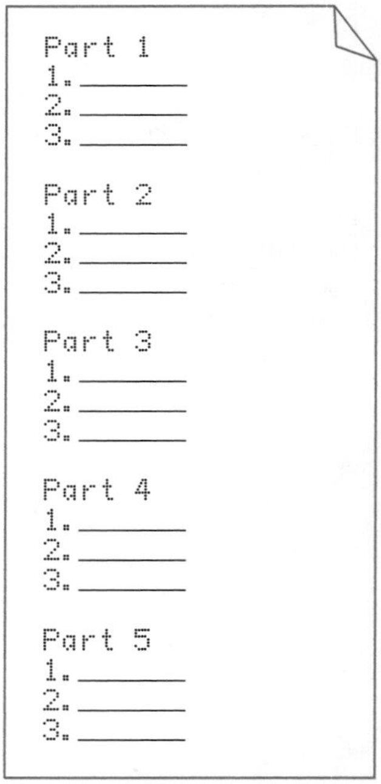

Figure 4-6 A quiz answer sheet

Figure 4-7 shows the logic of the program that produces the answer sheet. Two variables, named `partCounter` and `questionCounter`, are declared to keep track of the answer sheet parts and questions, respectively. Four named constants are also declared to hold the number of parts and questions in each, and to hold the text that will be printed—the word "Part" with each part number, and a period, space, and underscores to form a fill-in

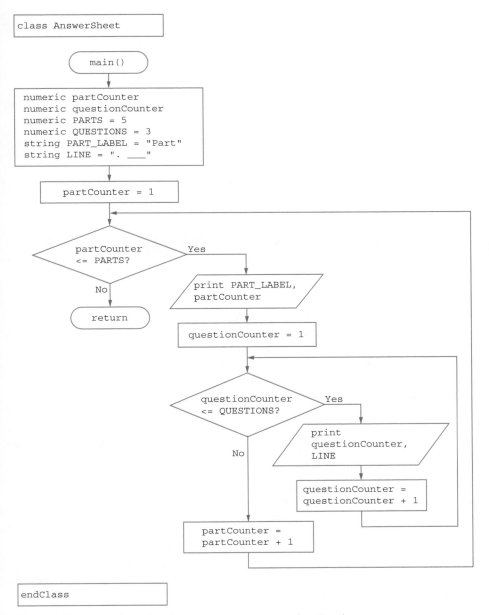

Figure 4-7 Flowchart and pseudocode for `AnswerSheet` program (*continued*)

```
class AnswerSheet
    main()
        numeric partCounter
        numeric questionCounter
        numeric PARTS = 5
        numeric QUESTIONS = 3
        string PART_LABEL = "Part"
        string LINE = ". ___"
        partCounter = 1
        while partCounter <= PARTS
            print PART_LABEL, partCounter
            questionCounter = 1
            while questionCounter <= QUESTIONS
                print questionCounter, LINE
                questionCounter = questionCounter + 1
            endwhile
            partCounter = partCounter + 1
        endwhile
    return
endClass
```

Figure 4-7 Flowchart and pseudocode for `AnswerSheet` program

>> NOTE In the program in Figure 4-7, it is important that `questionCounter` is reset to 1 within the outer loop just before entering the inner loop. If this step was omitted, Part 1 would contain questions 1, 2, and 3, but Part 2 would contain questions 4, 5, and 6, Part 3 would contain questions 7, 8, and 9, and so on.

line for each question. When the program starts, `partCounter` is initialized to 1. The `partCounter` variable is the loop control variable for the outer loop in this program. The outer loop continues while `partCounter` is less than or equal to `PARTS`. The last statement in the outer loop adds 1 to `partCounter`. In other words, the outer loop will execute when `partCounter` is 1, 2, 3, 4 and 5.

In the outer loop in Figure 4-7, the word "Part" and the current `partCounter` value are printed. Then `questionCounter` is set to 1. The variable `questionCounter` is the loop control variable for the inner loop in the nested loop pair. The inner loop-controlling question compares `questionCounter` to `QUESTIONS`, and while it does not exceed `QUESTIONS`, `questionCounter` is printed, followed by a period and a fill-in-the-blank line. Then 1 is added to `questionCounter` and the `questionCounter` comparison is made again. In other words, when `partCounter` is 1, lines print for questions 1, 2, and 3. Then `partCounter` becomes 2, the part heading prints, and lines print for new questions 1, 2, and 3.

MIXING CONSTANT AND VARIABLE SENTINEL VALUES

The number of times a loop executes can depend on a constant or on a value that varies. Suppose you own a factory and have decided to place a label on every product you manufacture. The label contains the words "Made for you personally by", followed by the first name of one of your employees. Assume that for one week's production, you need 100 personalized labels for each employee.

Figure 4-8 shows the application that creates 100 labels for each employee entered. At the start of the main() method, the user is prompted for an employee's name, and while the user does not type the QUIT value ("ZZZ"), the program continues. The labelCounter variable is set to 0 and a label that contains the employee's name is printed. Then the loop control variable, labelCounter, is incremented. Its value is tested again, and if it is not equal to LABELS (100), another label is printed. When the value of labelCounter reaches 100, the user is prompted for a new employee name.

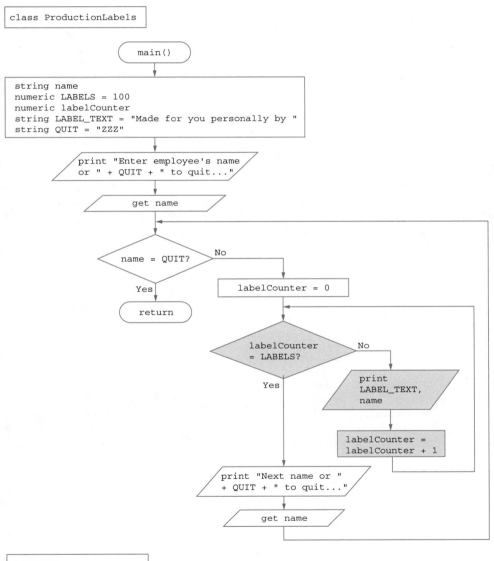

Figure 4-8 Program that produces 100 labels for every employee (*continued*)

```
class ProductionLabels
    main()
        string name
        numeric LABELS = 100
        numeric labelCounter
        string LABEL_TEXT = "Made for you personally by "
        string QUIT = "ZZZ"
        print "Enter employee's name or " + QUIT + " to quit..."
        get name
        while name not equal to QUIT
            labelCounter = 0
            while labelCounter not equal to LABELS
                print LABEL_TEXT, name
                labelCounter = labelCounter + 1
            endwhile
            print "Next name or " + QUIT + " to quit..."
            get name
        endwhile
    return
endClass
```

Figure 4-8 Program that produces 100 labels for every employee

> **NOTE** In the pseudocode in Figure 4-8, you can see that the label-making loop continues while name is not QUIT. In the flowchart, instead of the question name = QUIT?, you might prefer to use the question name not = QUIT?. If you used this version, you would reverse the positions of Yes and No that emerge from the question.

The main() method in Figure 4-8 contains an indefinite outer loop that is controlled by the value of the name the user enters, and a definite inner loop that executes exactly 100 times. Look at the inner loop, which is shaded in Figure 4-8. While the counter, named labelCounter, continues to be less than 100, a label is printed and counter is increased. When 100 labels have printed, control returns to the outer loop, where the next employee name is retrieved.

> **NOTE** Setting labelCounter to 0 within the outer loop is important. After labelCounter reaches 100 for the first employee entered, a second employee is entered and you need to start counting from 0 again. If labelCounter is never reset after the first employee, no labels will print for any subsequent employees. Although some languages initialize a newly declared variable to 0 for you, some do not, and either way, your intentions are clearer if you explicitly assign 0 to labelCounter.

Sometimes you don't want to be forced to repeat every pass through a loop the same number of times. For example, instead of printing 100 labels for each employee, you might want to vary the number of labels based on how many items a worker actually produces. That way, high-achieving workers won't run out of labels, and less productive workers won't have too many. Instead of printing the same, constant number of labels for every employee, a more sophisticated program prints a different number of labels for each employee, depending on that employee's usual production level.

Figure 4-9 shows a slightly modified version of the label-producing program. The changes from Figure 4-8 are shaded. In this version, after the user enters a valid name for an employee, the user is prompted for a production level. The Boolean expression used in the `while` statement in the inner loop compares `labelCounter` to `production`, instead of to a constant, fixed value. Some employees might get 100 labels, but some might get more or fewer.

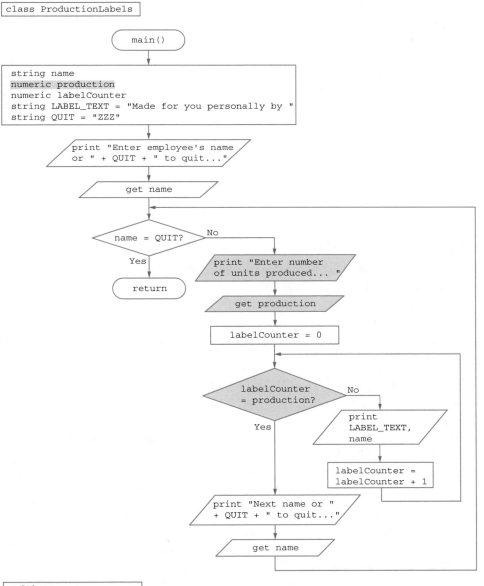

Figure 4-9 Program that produces a variable number of labels for every employee (*continued*)

```
class ProductionLabels
    main()
        string name
        numeric production
        numeric labelCounter
        string LABEL_TEXT = "Made for you personally by "
        string QUIT = "ZZZ"
        print "Enter employee's name or " + QUIT + " to quit..."
        get name
        while name not equal to QUIT
            print "Enter number of units produced... "
            get production
            labelCounter = 0
            while labelCounter not equal to production
                print LABEL_TEXT, name
                labelCounter = labelCounter + 1
            endwhile
            print "Next name or " + QUIT + " to quit..."
            get name
        endwhile
    return
endClass
```

Figure 4-9 Program that produces a variable number of labels for every employee

AVOIDING COMMON LOOP MISTAKES

The mistakes programmers make most often with loops are:

» Neglecting to initialize the loop control variable

» Neglecting to alter the loop control variable

» Using the wrong comparison with the loop control variable

» Including statements inside the loop that belong outside the loop

MISTAKE: NEGLECTING TO INITIALIZE THE LOOP CONTROL VARIABLE

It is always a mistake to fail to initialize a loop's control variable. For example, assume you remove either or both of the loop initialization statements that appeared in the label production program in Figure 4-8; Figure 4-10 shows the results.

If the get name statement is removed, as shown in the first shaded statement in Figure 4-10, then when name is tested at the start of the outer loop, its value is unknown, or garbage. Is name equal to the value of QUIT? Maybe it is, by accident; more likely, it is not. If it is, the program ends before any labels can be printed. If it is not, the inner loop is entered, and 100 labels are printed with an invalid name (QUIT).

If the labelCounter = 0 statement is removed, as shown in the second shaded statement in Figure 4-10, then in many languages, the value of labelCounter is unpredictable. It might or might not be equal to LABELS, and the loop might or might not execute. In a language in which numeric variables are automatically initialized to 0, the first employee's labels will

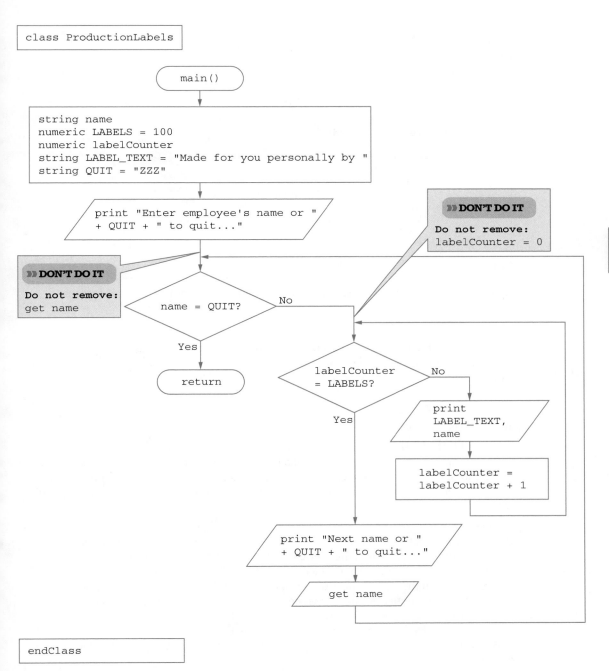

Figure 4-10 Incorrect logic when loop control variable initializations are removed from label-making program (*continued*)

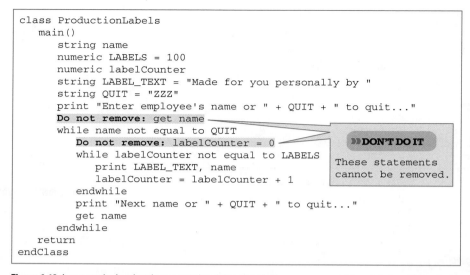

```
class ProductionLabels
    main()
        string name
        numeric LABELS = 100
        numeric labelCounter
        string LABEL_TEXT = "Made for you personally by "
        string QUIT = "ZZZ"
        print "Enter employee's name or " + QUIT + " to quit..."
        Do not remove: get name
        while name not equal to QUIT
            Do not remove: labelCounter = 0
            while labelCounter not equal to LABELS
                print LABEL_TEXT, name
                labelCounter = labelCounter + 1
            endwhile
            print "Next name or " + QUIT + " to quit..."
            get name
        endwhile
    return
endClass
```

⏵⏵**DON'T DO IT**

These statements cannot be removed.

Figure 4-10 Incorrect logic when loop control variable initializations are removed from label-making program

print correctly, but no labels will print for subsequent employees because `labelCounter` will never be altered and will remain equal to `LABELS` for the rest of the program's execution. Either way, a logical error has occurred.

MISTAKE: NEGLECTING TO ALTER THE LOOP CONTROL VARIABLE

Different sorts of errors will occur if you fail to alter a loop control variable within the loop. You create such an error if you remove either of the statements that alter the loop control variables from the original label-making program in Figure 4-8. Figure 4-11 shows the resulting logic.

If you remove the `get name` instruction from the outer loop in the program in Figure 4-11, the user never has the opportunity to enter a name after the first one. For example, assume that when the program starts, the user enters "Fred". The name will be compared to the QUIT value, and the inner loop will be entered. After labels print for Fred, no new name is entered, so when the logic returns to the `name = QUIT?` question, the answer will still be *No*. So, labels containing "Made for you personally by" and the same worker's name will continue to print infinitely. Similarly, if you remove the statement that increments `labelCounter` from the inner loop in the program, then `labelCounter` never can equal `LABELS` and the inner loop executes infinitely. It is always incorrect to create a loop that cannot terminate.

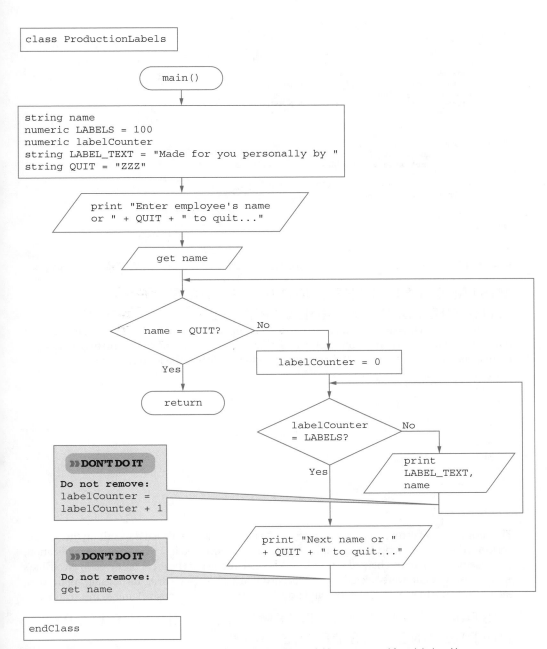

Figure 4-11 Incorrect logic when statements that alter loop control variable are removed from label-making program (*continued*)

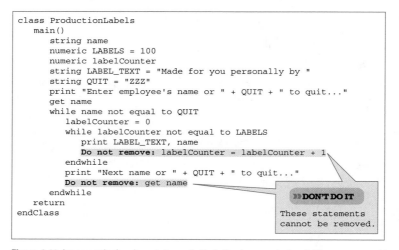

```
class ProductionLabels
    main()
        string name
        numeric LABELS = 100
        numeric labelCounter
        string LABEL_TEXT = "Made for you personally by "
        string QUIT = "ZZZ"
        print "Enter employee's name or " + QUIT + " to quit..."
        get name
        while name not equal to QUIT
            labelCounter = 0
            while labelCounter not equal to LABELS
                print LABEL_TEXT, name
                Do not remove: labelCounter = labelCounter + 1
            endwhile
            print "Next name or " + QUIT + " to quit..."
            Do not remove: get name
        endwhile
    return
endClass
```

» DON'T DO IT

These statements
cannot be removed.

Figure 4-11 Incorrect logic when statements that alter loop control variable are removed from label-making program

MISTAKE: USING THE WRONG COMPARISON WITH THE LOOP CONTROL VARIABLE

Programmers must be careful to use the correct comparison in the statement that controls a loop. Although there is only a one-keystroke difference between the following two code segments, one performs the loop 10 times and the other performs the loop 11 times.

```
counter = 0
while counter < 10
        print "Hello"
        counter = counter + 1
endwhile

counter = 0
while counter <= 10
        print "Hello"
        counter = counter + 1
endwhile
```

The seriousness of erroneously using <= or >= when only < or > is needed depends on the actions performed within the loop. For example, if such an error occurred in a loan company application, each customer might be charged a month's additional interest. If the error occurred in an airline's application, it might overbook a flight. If it occurred in a pharmacy's drug-dispensing application, each patient might receive one extra (and possibly harmful and expensive) unit of medication.

MISTAKE: INCLUDING STATEMENTS INSIDE THE LOOP THAT BELONG OUTSIDE THE LOOP

Consider a program like the one in Figure 4-12. It calculates a user's projected weekly pay raise based on raise rates ranging from half a percent to 10 percent. The user enters an hourly pay rate and the number of hours he works per week. Then the rate of the raise is set to a starting value of 0.005 (half a percent). While the raise rate is not greater than the maximum the program allows, the user's weekly pay is calculated, and then the raise as a percentage of the weekly amount. The results are displayed, and before the loop ends, the loop control

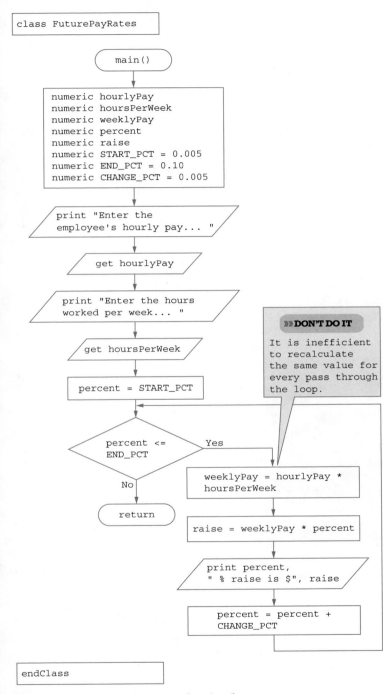

Figure 4-12 Pay rate projection program (*continued*)

```
class FuturePayRates
    main()
        numeric hourlyPay
        numeric hoursPerWeek
        numeric weeklyPay
        numeric percent
        numeric raise
        numeric START_PCT = 0.005
        numeric END_PCT = 0.10
        numeric CHANGE_PCT = 0.005
        print "Enter the employee's hourly pay... "
        get hourlyPay
        print "Enter the hours worked per week... "
        get hoursPerWeek
        percent = START_PCT
        while percent <= END_PCT
            weeklyPay = hourlyPay * hoursPerWeek
            raise = weeklyPay * percent
            print percent, " % raise is $", raise
            percent = percent + CHANGE_PCT
        endwhile
    return
endClass
```

▶▶▶ **DON'T DO IT**

It is inefficient to recalculate the same value for every pass through the loop.

Figure 4-12 Pay rate projection program

variable, `percent`, is increased by half a percent. Figure 4-13 shows a typical execution if the program is in a command-line environment.

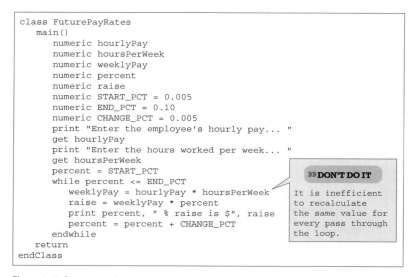

Figure 4-13 Typical execution of pay rate projection program

The program in Figure 4-12 works correctly. However, it is a little inefficient. The user enters his pay rate and hours worked once at the beginning of the program. At that point, the weekly pay could be calculated. However, the weekly pay calculation does not occur until the loop is entered, so in this program, the same calculation is made 20 times. Of course, it does not take a computer very long to perform 20 multiplications, but if the calculation were more complicated and performed for thousands of employees, the program performance would suffer.

Figure 4-14 shows the same program in which the weekly pay rate calculation has been moved to a better place. (See the shaded statement.) The programs in Figures 4-12 and 4-14

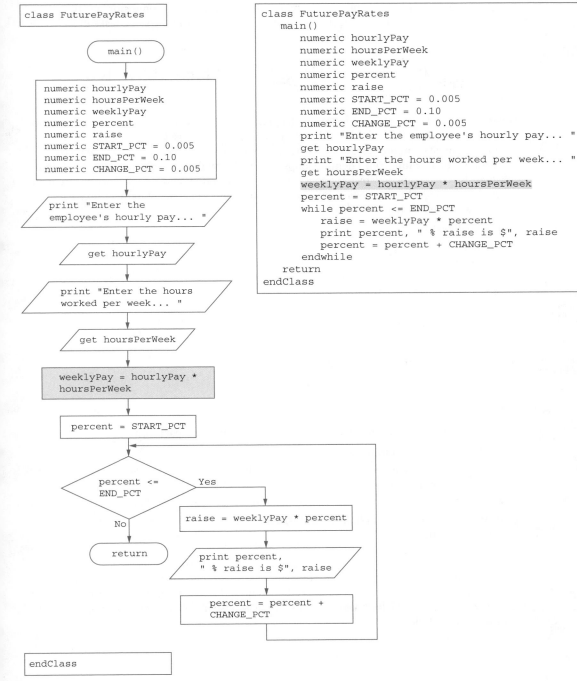

```
class FuturePayRates

                main()

    numeric hourlyPay
    numeric hoursPerWeek
    numeric weeklyPay
    numeric percent
    numeric raise
    numeric START_PCT = 0.005
    numeric END_PCT = 0.10
    numeric CHANGE_PCT = 0.005

    print "Enter the
    employee's hourly pay... "

        get hourlyPay

    print "Enter the hours
    worked per week... "

        get hoursPerWeek

    weeklyPay = hourlyPay *
    hoursPerWeek

    percent = START_PCT

         percent <=        Yes
         END_PCT

             No              raise = weeklyPay * percent

          return             print percent,
                             " % raise is $", raise

                             percent = percent +
                             CHANGE_PCT

endClass
```

```
class FuturePayRates
    main()
        numeric hourlyPay
        numeric hoursPerWeek
        numeric weeklyPay
        numeric percent
        numeric raise
        numeric START_PCT = 0.005
        numeric END_PCT = 0.10
        numeric CHANGE_PCT = 0.005
        print "Enter the employee's hourly pay... "
        get hourlyPay
        print "Enter the hours worked per week... "
        get hoursPerWeek
        weeklyPay = hourlyPay * hoursPerWeek
        percent = START_PCT
        while percent <= END_PCT
            raise = weeklyPay * percent
            print percent, " % raise is $", raise
            percent = percent + CHANGE_PCT
        endwhile
    return
endClass
```

Figure 4-14 Improved pay rate projection program

do the same thing. However, one does it more efficiently. As you become more proficient at programming, you will recognize many opportunities to perform the same tasks in alternate, more elegant, and more efficient ways.

USING A FOR LOOP: COUNTER-CONTROLLED REPETITION

Every high-level computer programming language contains a `while` statement that you can use to code any loop, including both indefinite and definite loops. In addition to the `while` statement, most computer languages also support a `for` statement. You can use the **for statement**, or **for loop**, with definite loops—those that will loop a specific number of times—frequently when you know exactly how many times the loop will repeat. The `for` statement provides you with three actions in one compact statement. The `for` statement uses a loop control variable that it automatically:

» Initializes
» Evaluates
» Increments

The `for` statement takes the form:

```
for initialValue to finalValue
    do something
endfor
```

For example, to print 100 labels you can write:

```
for count = 0 to 99
    print LABEL_TEXT, name
endfor
```

This `for` statement accomplishes several tasks at once in a compact form:

» The `for` statement initializes `count` to 0.
» The `for` statement checks `count` against the limit value 99 and makes sure that `count` is less than or equal to that value.
» If the evaluation is true, the `for` statement body that prints the label executes.
» After the `for` statement body executes, the value of `count` increases by 1, and the comparison to the limit value is made again.

As an alternative to using the loop `for count = 0 to 99`, you can use `for count = 1 to 100`. To achieve the same results, you can use any combination of values, as long as there are 100 whole number values between (and including) the two limits. Of course, the superior option would be to avoid the "magic number," using a constant defined as numeric `LIMIT = 99` and writing the following:

```
for count = 0 to LIMIT
    print LABEL_TEXT, name
endfor
```

You are never required to use a `for` statement; the label-creating loop executes correctly using a `while` statement. However, when a loop's execution is based on a loop control variable progressing from a known starting value to a known ending value in equal increments, the `for` loop provides you with a convenient shorthand that is easy for others to read. Additionally, because the loop control variable's initialization, testing, and alteration are all performed in one location, you are less likely to leave out one of these crucial elements.

USING POSTTEST LOOPS

When you use either a `while` or a `for` loop, the body of the loop may never execute. For example, in the following pseudocode segment, it's possible that the loop never executes because `initialValue` might be greater than `finalValue` at the start:

```
for initialValue to finalValue
    do something
endfor
```

When you want to ensure that a loop's body executes at least one time, you can use a posttest loop. In Chapter 2, you learned that two types of posttest loops exist—the `do-until` loop, which executes until a condition becomes true, and a `do-while` loop, which executes while a condition remains true (that is, until it becomes false). In either type of posttest loop, the loop body always executes at least one time.

For example, suppose you want to create a program that produces employee "Made for you personally by . . . " labels like the one discussed earlier in this chapter (see Figure 4-9). The way the program was originally written, the inner loop was a `while` loop, shown in Figure 4-15. For each employee, `labelCounter` was initialized to 0, and then while `labelCounter` was not equal to the employee's production figure, a label was printed. With this version of the program, if an employee's `production` was 0 (perhaps for a new employee), then no labels were printed.

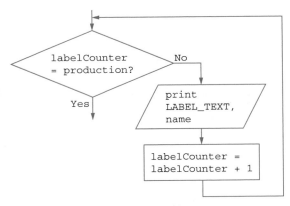

Figure 4-15 Inner loop from label production program in Figure 4-6

Suppose you wanted to guarantee that at least one label is printed for every employee, even if the employee's `production` value is 0. You could simply add one label-printing statement as soon as you entered the `while` loop, before checking `production`, or you could use a posttest loop that would require the loop body to execute at least one time. Figure 4-16 shows this

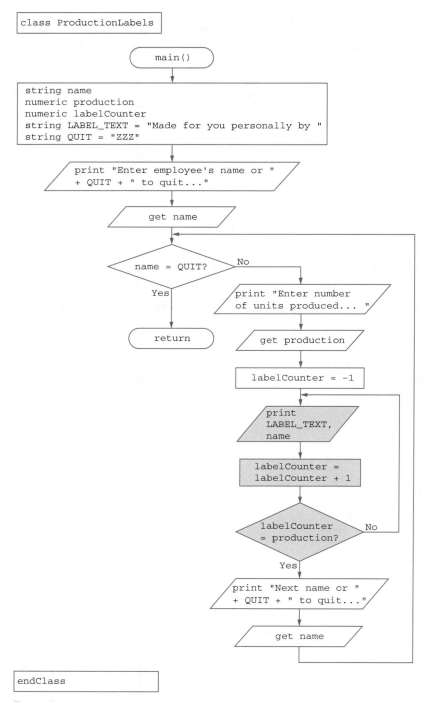

Figure 4-16 Label production program using a do-until loop (*continued*)

```
class ProductionLabels
    main()
        string name
        numeric production
        numeric labelCounter
        string LABEL_TEXT = "Made for you personally by "
        string QUIT = "ZZZ"
        print "Enter employee's name or " + QUIT + " to quit..."
        get name
        while name not = QUIT
            print "Enter number of units produced... "
            get production
            labelCounter = -1
            do
                print LABEL_TEXT, name
                labelCounter = labelCounter + 1
            until labelCounter = production
            print "Next name or " + QUIT + " to quit"
            get name
        endwhile
    return
endClass
```

Figure 4-16 Label production program using a `do-until` loop

approach using a `do-until` loop. In this program, `labelCounter` starts at –1 for each employee. Then, in the shaded inner loop, a label is printed and counted. Then, and only then, is the `labelCounter` variable tested. If it is equal to `production`, the inner loop ends.

The `do-until` loop in Figure 4-16 could be replaced with a one-time label-printing statement followed by a `do-while` loop. There is almost always more than one way to solve the same programming problem. As you learned in Chapter 2, a posttest loop can always be replaced by pairing a sequence followed by a `while` loop. Which method you choose depends on your (or your instructor's or supervisor's) preferences.

RECOGNIZING THE CHARACTERISTICS SHARED BY ALL LOOPS

In this chapter, you have seen both pretest and posttest loops. You have learned the differences between `while`, `for`, `do-until`, and `do-while` loops. You could solve every logical problem using only the `while` loop—the other forms are conveniences for special situations.

As you examine Figures 4-15 and 4-16, notice that with the `while` loop, the loop-controlling question is placed at the beginning of the steps that repeat. With the `do-until` loop, the loop-controlling question is placed at the end of the sequence of the steps that repeat.

All structured loops, both pretest and posttest, share these two characteristics:

» The loop-controlling question must provide either entry to or exit from the repeating structure.
» The loop-controlling question provides the *only* entry to or exit from the repeating structure.

» NOTE
If you can express the logic you want to perform by saying "while a is true, keep doing b," you probably want to use a `while` loop. If what you want to accomplish seems to fit the statement "do a until b is true," you can probably use a `do-until` loop.

In other words, there is exactly one loop-controlling value, and it provides either the only entrance to or the only exit from the loop. You should also notice the difference between unstructured loops and the structured `do-until` and `while` loops. Figure 4-17 diagrams the outline of two unstructured loops. In each case, the decision labeled X breaks out of the loop prematurely. The loop control variable (labeled LC) does not provide the only entry to or exit from either loop.

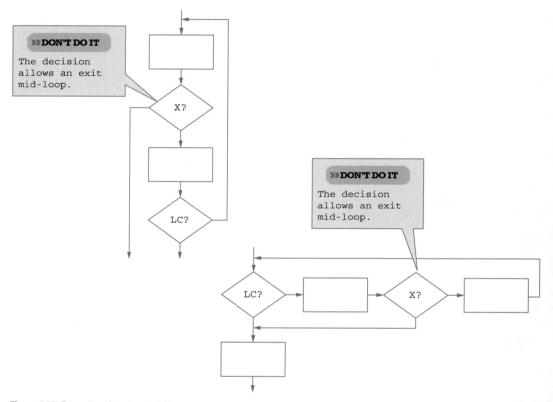

Figure 4-17 Examples of unstructured loops

COMMON LOOP APPLICATIONS

Although every computer program is different, many techniques are common to a variety of applications. Loops, for example, are frequently used to accumulate totals and to validate data.

USING A LOOP TO ACCUMULATE TOTALS

Business reports often include totals. The supervisor requesting a list of employees who participate in the company dental plan is often as interested in how many such employees there are as in who they are. When you receive your telephone bill at the end of the month, you are usually more interested in the total than in the charges for the individual calls.

For example, a real estate broker might want to see a list of all properties sold in the last month, as well as the total value of all the properties. A program might read sales data including the street address of the property sold and its selling price. The data records might be entered by a clerk as each sale is made, stored in a file until the end of the month, and then used in the month-end report. Figure 4-18 shows an example of such a report.

```
MONTH-END SALES REPORT

Address              Price

287 Acorn St        150,000
12 Maple Ave        310,000
8723 Marie Ln        65,500
222 Acorn St        127,000
29 Bahama Way       450,000

Total             1,102,500
```

Figure 4-18 Month-end real estate sales report

» NOTE
Unlike the report shown in Figure 4-18, some business reports list no individual detail records, just totals. Such reports are called **summary reports**.

To calculate the total value of all properties when you read and print a real estate listing record, you must add its value to an accumulator. An **accumulator** is a variable that you use to gather or accumulate values. An accumulator is very similar to a counter that you use to count loop iterations. The difference lies in the value that you add to the variable; usually you add just one to a counter, whereas you add some other value to an accumulator. If the real estate broker wants to know how many listings the company holds, you count them. When she wants to know the total real estate value, you accumulate it.

To accumulate total real estate prices, you declare a numeric variable at the beginning of the application, as shown in Figure 4-19. You must initialize the accumulator, accumValue, to 0. As you read each real estate transaction's data record, you print it and add its value to the accumulator accumValue, as shown in the shaded statement. Then you can read the next record.

» NOTE Some programming languages assign 0 to a variable you fail to initialize explicitly. Some programming languages issue an error message if you don't initialize a variable but then use it for accumulating. Other languages let you accumulate using an uninitialized variable, but the results are worthless because you start with garbage. The safest and clearest course of action is to assign the value 0 to accumulators before using them.

After the last record is read in the program in Figure 4-19, the eof indicator is reached, and loop execution is done. At that point, the accumulator will hold the grand total of all the real estate values. The program prints the word "Total" and the accumulated value, accumValue. Then the program ends.

New programmers often want to reset accumValue to 0 after printing it. Although you can take this step without harming the execution of the program, it does not serve any useful purpose. You cannot set accumValue to 0 in anticipation of having it ready for the next program, or even for the next time you execute this program. Variables exist only for the life of the application, and even if a future application happens to contain a variable named accumValue, the variable will not necessarily occupy the same memory location as this one. Even if you run the same application a second time, the variables might occupy different physical memory locations from the ones they occupied during the first run. At the beginning of any method, it is the programmer's responsibility to initialize all variables that must start with a specific value. There is no benefit to changing a variable's value when it will never be used again during the current execution.

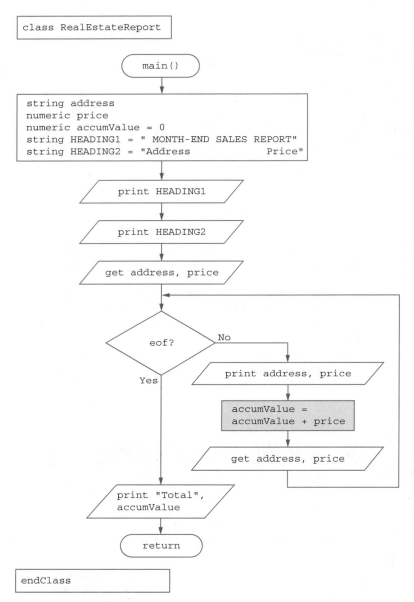

Figure 4-19 Flowchart and pseudocode for real estate sales report program (*continued*)

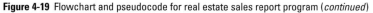

```
class RealEstateReport
   main()
      string address
      numeric price
      numeric accumValue = 0
      string HEADING1 = " MONTH-END SALES REPORT"
      string HEADING2 = "Address             Price"
      print HEADING1
      print HEADING2
      get address, price
      while not eof
         print address, price
         accumValue = accumValue + price
         get address, price
      endwhile
      print "Total", accumValue
   return
endClass
```

Figure 4-19 Flowchart and pseudocode for real estate sales report program

>> **NOTE** You could revise the program in Figure 4-19 so that it creates only a summary report that contains the total of the sale prices, but no individual transaction details. To create such a report, you could simply remove the first statement in the loop—the one that prints each address and price.

USING A LOOP TO VALIDATE DATA

When you ask a user to enter data into a computer program, you have no assurance that the data will be accurate. Loops are frequently used to **validate data**; that is, to make sure it falls within an acceptable range. For example, suppose part of a program you are writing asks a user to enter a number that represents his or her birth month. If the user types a number lower than 1 or greater than 12, you must take some sort of action. For example:

» You could display an error message and stop the program.

» You could choose to assign a default value for the month (for example, 1) before proceeding.

» You could reprompt the user for valid input.

If you chose the last course of action, you could then take at least two approaches. You could use a selection, and if the month is invalid, you could ask the user to reenter a number, as shown in Figure 4-20.

The problem with the logic in Figure 4-20 is that the user still might not enter valid data on the second attempt. So, you could add a third decision. Of course, you still couldn't control what the user enters.

>> **NOTE** Most languages provide a built-in way to check whether entered data is numeric. When you rely on user input, you frequently accept each piece of input data as a string and then attempt to convert it to a number. The procedure for accomplishing numeric checks is slightly different in different programming languages.

>> **NOTE** Object-oriented programmers frequently use a technique called exception handling to manage erroneous data. You will learn about this technique in Chapter 10.

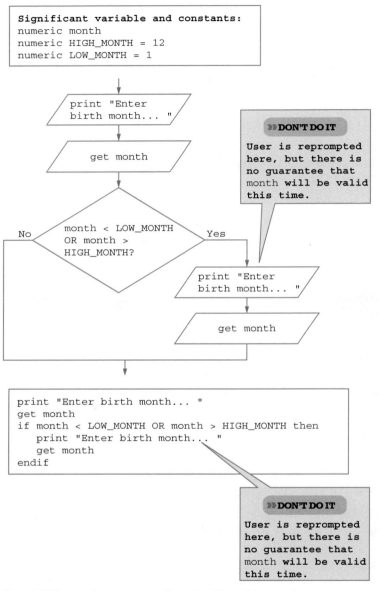

Significant variable and constants:
```
numeric month
numeric HIGH_MONTH = 12
numeric LOW_MONTH = 1
```

print "Enter birth month... "

get month

month < LOW_MONTH OR month > HIGH_MONTH?

No   Yes

▶▶ DON'T DO IT

User is reprompted here, but there is no guarantee that month will be valid this time.

print "Enter birth month... "

get month

```
print "Enter birth month... "
get month
if month < LOW_MONTH OR month > HIGH_MONTH then
    print "Enter birth month... "
    get month
endif
```

▶▶ DON'T DO IT

User is reprompted here, but there is no guarantee that month will be valid this time.

Figure 4-20 Reprompting a user once after an invalid month is entered

▶▶ NOTE Just because a data item is valid does not mean it is correct. For example, a program can determine that 5 is a valid birth month, but not that your birthday actually falls in month 5.

The superior solution is to use a loop to prompt a user for a month continuously until the user enters it correctly. Figure 4-21 shows this approach.

```
Significant variable and constants:
numeric month
numeric HIGH_MONTH = 12
numeric LOW_MONTH = 1
```

```
print "Enter birth month... "
get month
while month < LOW_MONTH OR month > HIGH_MONTH
    print "Enter birth month... "
    get month
endwhile
```

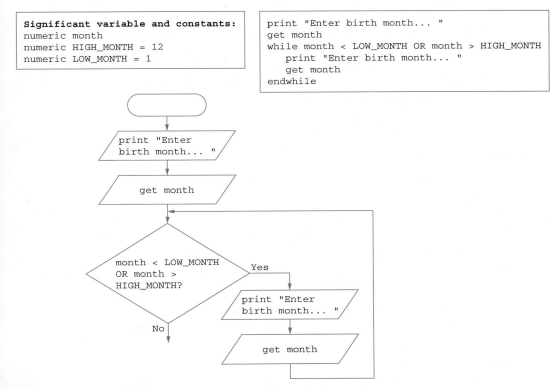

Figure 4-21 Reprompting a user continuously after an invalid month is entered

CHAPTER SUMMARY

» When you use a loop within a computer program, you can write one set of instructions that operates on multiple, separate sets of data.

» Three steps must occur in every loop: You must initialize a loop control variable, compare the variable to some value that controls whether the loop continues or stops, and alter the variable that controls the loop.

» When you must use loops within loops, you use nested loops. When nesting loops, you must maintain two loop control variables and alter each at the appropriate time.

» Common mistakes that programmers make when writing loops include neglecting to initialize the loop control variable, neglecting to alter the loop control variable, using the wrong comparison with the loop control variable, and including statements inside the loop that belong outside the loop.

» Most computer languages support a `for` statement or `for` loop that you can use with definite loops when you know how many times a loop will repeat. The `for` statement uses a loop control variable that it automatically initializes, evaluates, and increments.

» When you want to ensure that a loop's body executes at least one time, you can use a posttest loop in which the loop control variable is evaluated after the loop body executes.

» All structured loops share two characteristics: The loop-controlling question provides either entry to or exit from the repeating structure, and the loop-controlling question provides the *only* entry to or exit from the repeating structure.

» Loops are used in many applications. For example, business reports often include totals. Summary reports list no detail records—only totals. An accumulator is a variable that you use to gather or accumulate values. Loops also are used to ensure that user data is valid by continuously reprompting the user.

KEY TERMS

A **loop control variable** is a variable that determines whether a loop will continue.

Incrementing a variable is adding a constant value to it, frequently 1.

Decrementing a variable is decreasing it by a constant value, frequently 1.

A **definite loop** or **counted loop** is one for which the number of repetitions is a fixed value.

A **counter** is any numeric variable you use to count the number of times an event has occurred.

An **indefinite loop** is one for which you cannot predetermine the number of executions.

Nested loops occur when a loop structure exists within another loop structure; nested loops are loops within loops.

When loops are nested, the loop that contains the other loop is the **outer loop**.

When loops are nested, the loop that is contained within the other is the **inner loop**.

A **for statement**, or **for loop**, can be used to code definite loops. It contains a loop control variable that it automatically initializes, evaluates, and increments.

A **step value** is a number you use to increase a loop control variable on each pass through a loop.

A **summary report** lists only totals, without individual detail records.

An **accumulator** is a variable that you use to gather or accumulate values.

When you **validate data**, you make sure it falls within an acceptable range.

REVIEW QUESTIONS

1. The structure that allows you to write one set of instructions that operates on multiple, separate sets of data is the _____ .

    a. sequence   c. loop

    b. selection   d. case

2. Which of the following is not a step that must occur in every loop?

    a. Initialize a loop control variable.

    b. Compare the loop control value to a sentinel.

    c. Set the loop control value equal to a sentinel.

    d. Alter the loop control variable.

3. The statements executed within a loop are known collectively as the _____ .

a. sentinels   c. sequences

b. loop controls   d. loop body

4. A counter keeps track of _____ .

a. the number of times an event has occurred

b. the number of machine cycles required by a segment of a program

c. the number of loop structures within a program

d. the number of times a program has been converted to machine language

5. Adding 1 to a variable is also called _____ it.

a. digesting

b. incrementing

c. decrementing

d. resetting

6. In the following pseudocode, what is printed?

```
a = 1
b = 2
c = 5
while a < c
a = a + 1
b = b + c
endwhile
print a, b, c
```

a. 1 2 5

b. 5 22 5

c. 5 6 5

d. 6 22 9

7. In the following pseudocode, what is printed?

```
d = 4
e = 6
f = 7
while d > f
d = d + 1
e = e - 1
endwhile
print d, e, f
```

a. 7 3 7

b. 8 2 8

c. 4 6 7

d. 5 5 7

8. When you decrement a variable, you _____ .

   a. set it to 0

   b. reduce it by one-tenth

   c. subtract 1 from it

   d. remove it from a program

9. In the following pseudocode, what is printed?

```
g = 4
h = 6
while g < h
g = g + 1
endwhile
print g, h
```

   a. nothing   c. 5 6

   b. 4 6   d. 6 6

10. Most programmers use a `for` loop _____ .

    a. for every loop they write

    b. when they know the exact number of times a loop will repeat

    c. when they do not know the exact number of times a loop will repeat

    d. when a loop will not repeat

11. Unlike a pretest loop, you use a posttest loop when _____ .

    a. you can predict the exact number of loop repetitions

    b. the loop body might never execute

    c. the loop body must execute exactly one time

    d. the loop body must execute at least one time

12. Which of the following is a characteristic shared by `while` loops and `do-until` loops?

    a. Both have one entry and one exit.

    b. Both have a body that executes at least once.

    c. Both compare a loop control variable at the top of the loop.

    d. all of the above

13. A comparison with a loop control variable provides _____ .

    a. the only entry to a `while` loop

    b. the only exit from a `do-until` loop

    c. both of the above

    d. none of the above

14. When two loops are nested, the loop that is contained by the other is the _____ loop.

    a. inner

    b. outer

    c. unstructured

    d. captive

15. In the following pseudocode, how many times is "Hello" printed?

```
j = 2
k = 5
m = 6
n = 9
while j < k
while m < n
print "Hello"
m = m + 1
endwhile
j = j + 1
endwhile
```

    a. zero

    b. three

    c. six

    d. nine

16. In the following pseudocode, how many times is "Hola" printed?

```
j = 2
k = 5
n = 9
while j < k
m = 6
while m < n
print "Hola"
m = m + 1
endwhile
j = j + 1
endwhile
```

    a. zero

    b. three

    c. six

    d. nine

17. In the following pseudocode, how many times is "Bonjour" printed?

```
p = 2
q = 4
while p < q
print "Bonjour"
r = 1
while r < q
print "Bonjour"
r = r + 1
endwhile
p = p + 1
endwhile
```

   a. zero   c. six

   b. four   d. eight

18. A report that lists no details about individual records, but totals only, is a(n) _____ report.

   a. accumulator

   b. final

   c. summary

   d. detailless

19. Typically, the value added to a counter variable is _____ .

   a. 0   c. 10

   b. 1   d. 100

20. Typically, the value added to an accumulator variable is _____ .

   a. 0

   b. 1

   c. smaller than a value added to a counter variable

   d. larger than a value added to a counter variable

EXERCISES

1. Design the logic for a program that prints every number from 1 through 10.

2. Design the logic for a program that prints every number from 1 through 10 along with its square and cube.

3. Design the logic for a program that prints every even number from 2 through 30.

4. Design the logic for a program that prints numbers in reverse order from 10 down to 1.

5. The No Interest Credit Company provides zero-interest loans to customers. (They make a profit by selling advertising space in their monthly statements and selling their customer lists.) Design an application that gets customer account data, including an account number, customer name, and balance due. For each customer, print the account number and name; then print the customer's projected balance each month for the next 10 months. Assume that there is no finance charge on this account, that the customer makes no new purchases, and that the customer pays off the balance with equal monthly payments, which are 10 percent of the original bill.

6. The Some Interest Credit Company provides loans to customers, at 1.5 percent interest per month. Design an application that gets customer account data, including an account number, customer name, and balance due. For each customer, print the account number and name; then print the customer's projected balance each month for the next 10 months. Assume that when the balance reaches $10 or less, the customer can pay off the account. At the beginning of every month, 1.5 percent interest is added to the balance, and then the customer makes a payment equal to 5 percent of the current balance. Assume the customer makes no new purchases.

7. The Howell Bank provides savings accounts that compound interest on a yearly basis. In other words, if you deposit $100 for two years at 4 percent interest, at the end of one year you will have $104. At the end of two years, you will have the $104 plus 4 percent of that, or $108.16. Design a program that accepts an account number, the account owner's first and last names, and a balance. Print the projected running total balance for each of the next 20 years.

8. Henry Clay Community College wants to print name tags for each student and teacher to wear at the first meeting of each class this semester. A typical tag looks like the one in Figure 4-22.

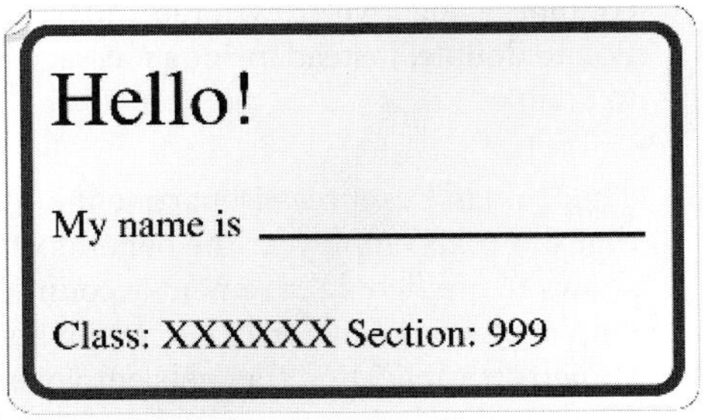

Hello!

My name is _____

Class: XXXXXX Section: 999

Figure 4-22 Name tag

The name tag border is preprinted, but you must design the program to print all the text you see on the sticker. Design a program that reads in course information that includes the class code (for example, CIS111), the three-digit section number (for example, 101), the teacher's last name (for example, "Zaplatynsky"), the number of students enrolled in the section (for example, 25), and the room in which the class meets (for example, "A213"). Print as many name tags as a section needs to provide one for each enrolled student, plus one for the teacher. Each name tag leaves a blank for the student's (or teacher's) name—each recipient writes in his or her name with a pen because the student names are not part of the input.

9. The Vernon Hills Mail-Order Company often sends multiple packages per order. For each customer order, print enough mailing labels to use on each of the separate boxes that will be mailed. The mailing labels contain the customer's complete name and address, along with a box number in the form "Box 9 of 9". For example, an order that requires three boxes produces three labels: "Box 1 of 3", "Box 2 of 3", and "Box 3 of 3". Design an application that continuously accepts a customer's title (for example "Mrs."), a first name, last name, street address, city, state, zip code, and number of boxes in the order until an appropriate sentinel value is entered. Produce enough mailing labels for each order.

10. Secondhand Rose Resale Shop is having a seven-day sale during which the price of any unsold item drops 10 percent each day. The inventory file includes an item number, description, and original price on day one. For example, an item that costs $10.00 on the first day costs 10 percent less, or $9.00, on the second day. On the third day, the same item is 10 percent less than $9.00, or $8.10. Design an application that reads inventory records and produces a report that shows the price of every item on each day, one through seven.

11. The state of Florida maintains a census file in which each record contains the name of a county, its current population, and the rate at which population is increasing per year. For example, one record might contain Miami-Dade County, 2,253,000, and 2%. The governor wants a report listing each county and the number of years it will take for the population of the county to double, assuming the present rate of growth remains constant. Design an application that reads records from an input file and prints the county's name and the number of years it will take for the population to double. If a county's record contains a negative growth rate, do not print the number of years needed for the population to double; instead, print a message indicating that the population is never expected to double.

12. The Human Resources Department of Apex Manufacturing Company wants a report that shows its employees the benefits of saving for retirement. Produce a report that shows 12 predicted retirement account values for each employee—the values if the employee saves 5, 10, or 15 percent of his or her annual salary for 10, 20, 30, or 40 years. Design an application that gets employee names and salaries and prints a report for each employee, including using the employee's name in a heading line. Assume that savings grow at a rate of 8 percent per year.

13. Mr. Roper owns 20 apartment buildings. Each building contains 15 units that he rents for $800 per month each. Design the application that would print 12 payment coupons for each of the 15 apartments in each of the 20 buildings. Each coupon should contain the building number (1 through 20), the apartment number (1 through 15), the month (1 through 12), and the amount of rent due.

14. Mr. Furly owns 20 apartment buildings. Each building contains 15 units that he rents. The usual monthly rent for apartments numbered 1 through 9 in each building is $700; the monthly rent is $850 for apartments numbered 10 through 15. The usual rent is

due every month except July and December; in those months Mr. Furly gives his renters a 50 percent credit, so they owe only half the usual amount. Design the application that would print 12 payment coupons for each of the 15 apartments in each of the 20 buildings. Each coupon should contain the building number (1 through 20), the apartment number (1 through 15), the month (1 through 12), and the amount of rent due.

CASE PROJECT

In earlier chapters, you developed classes needed for Cost Is No Object—a car rental service that specializes in lending antique and luxury cars to clients on a short-term basis. The rental service produces computerized paychecks for its employees every week. Write a program that gets data for each of the following:

» An employee ID number
» A first name
» A last name
» A street address
» A zip code
» An hourly pay rate
» Number of hours worked this week
» An insurance plan code

Create an application that prompts the user for employee data; the application continues to accept data for new employees until the user enters 0 for an ID number to indicate the desire to quit. While the ID number is not zero, prompt the user for a value for each field in turn. Any time the user enters an invalid value, continue to reprompt the user for the same data. Continue with the next data item only when the previous item is valid, as follows:

» An employee ID must be between 100 and 999 inclusive.
» A zip code must not be greater than 99999.
» An hourly pay rate must be between $6.00 and $25.00 inclusive.
» An insurance plan code must be 1 or 2.

When all the needed data has been entered correctly for an employee, display a copy of all the data fields for the employee as well as the following:

» Gross pay, calculated as hours worked times pay rate
» Income tax, which is calculated as 15% of the gross pay if the gross pay is $400 or less; otherwise, it is 20% of the gross pay
» Insurance premium, which is $60 for insurance plan code 1 and $100 for insurance plan code 2
» Net pay, which is calculated as gross pay minus income tax, minus insurance premium; if the net pay is negative (the employee did not earn enough to cover the tax and insurance), then the net pay should be $0

UP FOR DISCUSSION

1. If programs could only make decisions or loops, but not both, which structure would you prefer to retain?

2. Suppose you wrote a program that you suspect is in an infinite loop because it keeps running for several minutes with no output and without ending. What would you add to your program to help you discover the origin of the problem?

3. Suppose you know that every employee in your organization has a seven-digit ID number used for logging on to the computer system to retrieve sensitive information about their own customers. A loop would be useful to guess every combination of seven digits in an ID. Are there any circumstances in which you should try to guess another employee's ID number?

ARRAYS

In this chapter, you will:

Understand arrays and how they occupy computer memory

Manipulate an array to replace nested decisions

Use a named constant to refer to an array's size

Declare and initialize an array

Understand the difference between variable and constant arrays

Search an array for an exact match

Use parallel arrays

Search an array for a range match

Learn about remaining within array bounds

Use a `for` loop to process arrays

UNDERSTANDING ARRAYS AND HOW THEY OCCUPY COMPUTER MEMORY

An **array** is a series or list of variables in computer memory, all of which have the same name and data type but are differentiated with special numbers called subscripts. Usually, all the values in an array have something in common; for example, they might represent a list of employee ID numbers or a list of prices for items a store sells. A **subscript**, also called an **index**, is a number that indicates the position of a particular item within an array. Whenever you require multiple storage locations for objects, you are using a real-life counterpart of a programming array. For example, if you store important papers in a series of file folders and label each folder with a consecutive letter of the alphabet, then you are using the equivalent of an array. If you store mementos in a series of stacked shoeboxes, each labeled with a year, or if you sort mail into slots, each labeled with a name, then you are also using a real-life equivalent of a programming array.

When you look down the left side of a tax table to find your income level before looking to the right to find your income tax obligation, you are using an array. Similarly, if you look down the left side of a train schedule to find your station before looking to the right to find the train's arrival time, you also are using an array.

> **NOTE**
> Some programmers refer to an array as a *table* or a *matrix*.

Each of these real-life arrays helps you organize real-life objects. You *could* store all your papers or mementos in one huge cardboard box, or find your tax rate or train's arrival time if both were printed randomly in one large book. However, using an organized storage and display system makes your life easier in each case. Using a programming array will accomplish the same results for your data.

HOW ARRAYS OCCUPY COMPUTER MEMORY

When you declare an array, you declare a structure that contains multiple variables. Each variable within an array has the same name and the same data type; each separate array variable is one **element** of the array. Each array element occupies an area in memory next to, or contiguous to, the others, as shown in Figure 5-1. You can indicate the number of elements an array will hold—the **size of the array**—when you declare the array along with your other variables.

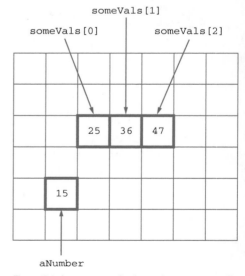

Figure 5-1 Appearance of a three-element array and a single variable in computer memory

All array elements have the same group name, but each individual element also has a unique subscript indicating how far away it is from the first element. Therefore, any array's subscripts are always a sequence of integers such as 0 through 4 or 0 through 9.

Depending on the syntax rules of the programming language you use, you place the subscript within parentheses or square brackets following the group name. This text will use square brackets to hold array element subscripts so that you don't mistake array names for method names, and because most object-oriented programming (OOP) languages such as C++, Java, and C# use the bracket notation. For example, Figure 5-1 shows how a single variable and an array are stored in computer memory. The single variable named aNumber holds the value 15. The array named someVals contains three elements, so the elements are someVals[0], someVals[1], and someVals[2]. The value stored in someVals[0] is 25; someVals[1] holds 36, and someVals[2] holds 47. The element someVals[0] is zero numbers away from the beginning of the array—in other words, it is located at the same memory address as the array. The element someVals[1] is one number away from the beginning of the array and someVals[2] is two numbers away.

> **NOTE** You can picture the memory address of someVals[0] as the address of the someVals array plus zero more numbers. Similarly, you can picture the memory address of someVals[1] as the memory address of the someVals array plus one more number.

> **NOTE** You never are required to use arrays within your programs, but learning to use arrays correctly can make many programming tasks far more efficient and professional. When you understand how to use arrays, you will be able to provide elegant solutions to problems that otherwise would require tedious programming steps.

MANIPULATING AN ARRAY TO REPLACE NESTED DECISIONS

Consider an application requested by a Human Resources Department to produce statistics on employees' claimed dependents. The department wants a report that lists the number of Employees who have claimed 0, 1, 2, 3, 4, or 5 dependents. (Assume you know that no employees have more than five dependents.) Figure 5-2 shows a typical report.

```
          Dependents Report

  Dependents              Count
      0                     34
      1                     62
      2                     71
      3                     42
      4                     28
      5                      7
```

Figure 5-2 The Dependents report

Without using an array, you could write the application that produces counts for the six categories of dependents (for each number of dependents, 0 through 5) by using a series of decisions. Figure 5-3 shows the pseudocode and flowchart for the decision-making part of

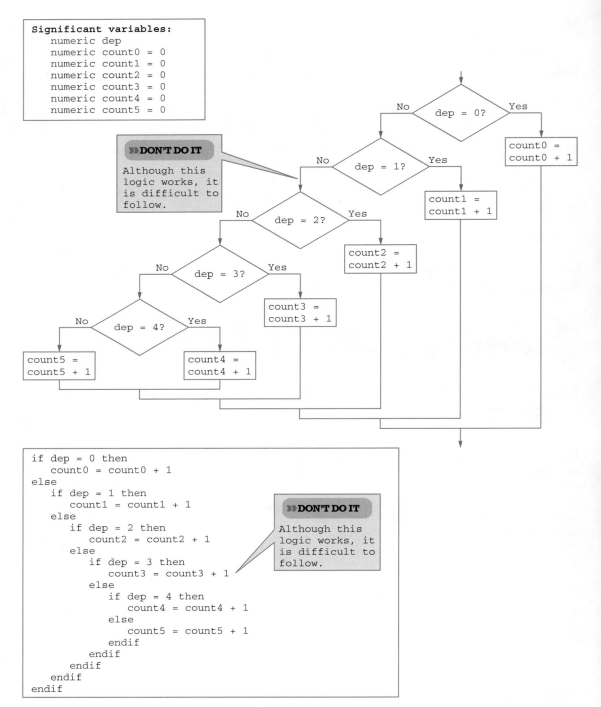

```
Significant variables:
   numeric dep
   numeric count0 = 0
   numeric count1 = 0
   numeric count2 = 0
   numeric count3 = 0
   numeric count4 = 0
   numeric count5 = 0
```

▶▶ DON'T DO IT

Although this logic works, it is difficult to follow.

```
if dep = 0 then
   count0 = count0 + 1
else
   if dep = 1 then
      count1 = count1 + 1
   else
      if dep = 2 then
         count2 = count2 + 1
      else
         if dep = 3 then
            count3 = count3 + 1
         else
            if dep = 4 then
               count4 = count4 + 1
            else
               count5 = count5 + 1
            endif
         endif
      endif
   endif
endif
```

▶▶ DON'T DO IT

Although this logic works, it is difficult to follow.

Figure 5-3 Flowchart and pseudocode of decision-making process using a series of decisions—the hard way

an application that counts dependents in each of six different categories. Although this program works, its length and complexity are unnecessary once you understand how to use an array.

In Figure 5-3, the variable dep is compared to 0. If it is 0, 1 is added to count0. If it is not 0, then dep is compared to 1. It is either added to count1, or compared to 2, and so on. Each time the application executes this decision-making process, 1 is added to one of the five variables that acts as a counter for one of the possible numbers of dependents. The decision-making process in Figure 5-3 accomplishes its purpose, and nothing is wrong with its logic, but it is cumbersome. Follow its logic here so that you understand how the application works.

The dependent-counting application in Figure 5-3 works, but even with only six categories of dependents, the decision-making process is unwieldy. What if the number of dependents might be any value from 0 to 10, or 0 to 20? With either of these scenarios, the basic logic of the program would remain the same; however, you would need to declare many additional accumulator variables and you would need many additional decisions.

Using an array provides an alternate approach to this programming problem, which greatly reduces the number of statements you need. When you declare an array, you provide a group name for a number of associated variables in memory. For example, the six dependent count accumulators can be redefined as a single array named count. The individual elements become count[0] , count[1] , count[2] , count[3] , count[4] , and count[5] , as shown in the revised decision-making process in Figure 5-4.

The shaded statement in Figure 5-4 shows that when dep is 0, 1 is added to count[0] . You can see similar statements for the rest of the count elements; when dep is 1, 1 is added to count[1] , when dep is 2, 1 is added to count[2] , and so on. When the dep value is 5, it means it was not 1, 2, 3, or 4, so 1 is added to count[5] . In other words, 1 is added to one of the elements of the count array instead of to an individual variable named count0, count1, count2, count3, count4, or count5. Is this version a big improvement over the original in Figure 5-3? Of course it isn't. You still have not taken advantage of the benefits of using the array in this application.

The true benefit of using an array lies in your ability to use a variable as a subscript to the array, instead of using a constant such as 0 or 5. Notice in the logic in Figure 5-4 that within each decision, the value you are comparing to dep and the constant you are using as a subscript in the resulting "Yes" process are always identical. That is, when dep is 0, the subscript used to add 1 to the count array is 0; when dep is 1, the subscript used for the count array is 1, and so on. Therefore, you can just use dep as a subscript to the array. You can rewrite the decision-making process as shown in Figure 5-5.

Of course, the code segment in Figure 5-5 looks no more efficient than the one in Figure 5-4. However, notice that in Figure 5-5 the shaded statements are all the same—in other words, the process that occurs after each decision is exactly the same. In each case, no matter what

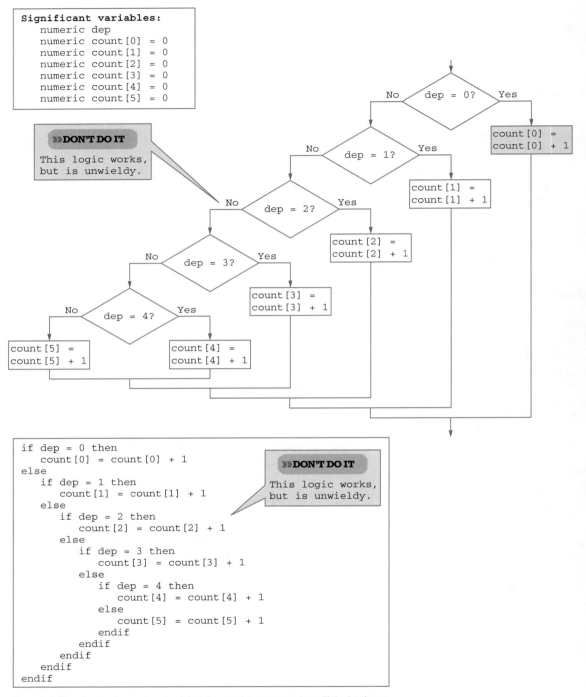

```
Significant variables:
   numeric dep
   numeric count[0] = 0
   numeric count[1] = 0
   numeric count[2] = 0
   numeric count[3] = 0
   numeric count[4] = 0
   numeric count[5] = 0
```

▶▶DON'T DO IT

This logic works, but is unwieldy.

▶▶DON'T DO IT

This logic works, but is unwieldy.

```
if dep = 0 then
   count[0] = count[0] + 1
else
   if dep = 1 then
      count[1] = count[1] + 1
   else
      if dep = 2 then
         count[2] = count[2] + 1
      else
         if dep = 3 then
            count[3] = count[3] + 1
         else
            if dep = 4 then
               count[4] = count[4] + 1
            else
               count[5] = count[5] + 1
            endif
         endif
      endif
   endif
endif
```

Figure 5-4 Flowchart and pseudocode of decision-making process—but still the hard way

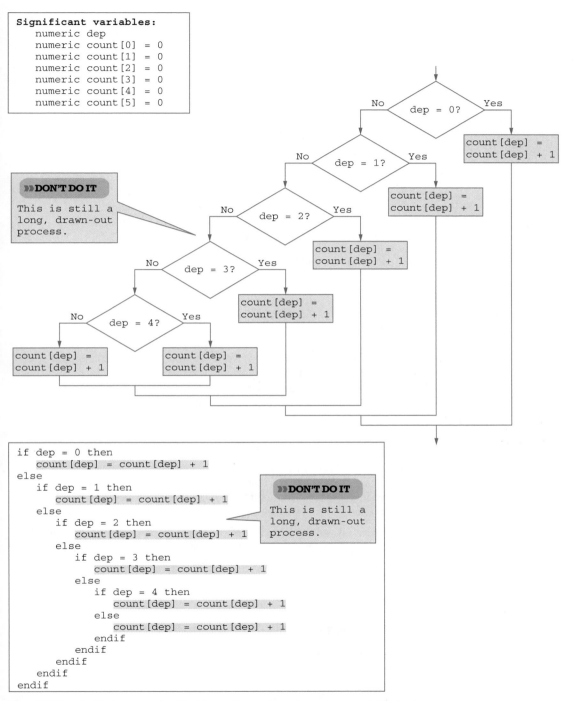

```
Significant variables:
   numeric dep
   numeric count[0] = 0
   numeric count[1] = 0
   numeric count[2] = 0
   numeric count[3] = 0
   numeric count[4] = 0
   numeric count[5] = 0
```

»DON'T DO IT

This is still a long, drawn-out process.

```
if dep = 0 then
   count[dep] = count[dep] + 1
else
   if dep = 1 then
      count[dep] = count[dep] + 1
   else
      if dep = 2 then
         count[dep] = count[dep] + 1
      else
         if dep = 3 then
            count[dep] = count[dep] + 1
         else
            if dep = 4 then
               count[dep] = count[dep] + 1
            else
               count[dep] = count[dep] + 1
            endif
         endif
      endif
   endif
endif
```

»DON'T DO IT

This is still a long, drawn-out process.

Figure 5-5 Flowchart and pseudocode of decision-making process using an array—but still a hard way

the value of dep is, you always add 1 to count[dep] . If you always take the same action no matter what the answer is, why ask the question? Instead, you can rewrite the decision-making process as shown in Figure 5-6.

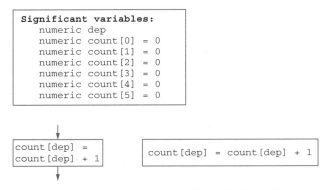

```
Significant variables:
    numeric dep
    numeric count[0] = 0
    numeric count[1] = 0
    numeric count[2] = 0
    numeric count[3] = 0
    numeric count[4] = 0
    numeric count[5] = 0
```

```
count[dep] =
count[dep] + 1
```

```
count[dep] = count[dep] + 1
```

Figure 5-6 Flowchart and pseudocode of efficient decision-making process using an array

The single statement in Figure 5-6 eliminates the *entire* decision-making process that was the original highlighted section in Figure 5-5! When dep is 2, 1 is added to count[2] ; when dep is 4, 1 is added to count[4] , and so on. *Now* you have a big improvement to the original process. What's more, this process does not change whether there are 20, 30, or any other number of possible categories. To use more than five accumulators, you would declare additional count elements in the array, but the categorizing logic would remain the same as it is in Figure 5-6. Figure 5-7 shows an entire application that takes advantage of the array to produce the report that shows counts for dependent categories.

In the program in Figure 5-7, variables and constants are declared and a first value for dep is read into the program. If it is not the end of the file, then 1 is added to the appropriate element of the count array and the next record is read. When data entry is complete and the end of the file is reached, the report can finally be printed. After printing the report headers, you can set dep to 0, then print dep and count[dep] . The first line that prints contains 0 (as the number of dependents) and the value stored in count[0] . Then, add 1 to dep and use the same set of instructions again. You can use dep as a loop control variable to print the six individual count array values.

When you print the final count values at the end of the program, naming the loop control variable dep makes sense because it represents a number of dependents. However, this variable could be named dependents, sub, index, or any other legal identifier and used as a subscript to the array as long as it is:

» Numeric with no decimal places

» Initialized to 0

» Incremented by 1 each time the logic passes through the loop

In other words, nothing is linking the name dep to the count array per se; when you cycle through the array to print the report, you are welcome to use a different variable name than you use when accumulating counts earlier in the program.

The dependent-counting application *worked* when it contained a long series of decisions and print statements, but the application is easier to write when you employ arrays. Additionally,

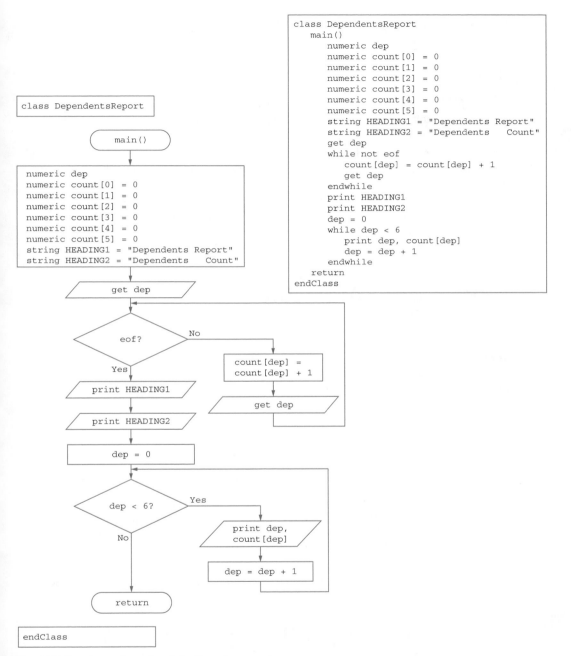

```
class DependentsReport
    main()
        numeric dep
        numeric count[0] = 0
        numeric count[1] = 0
        numeric count[2] = 0
        numeric count[3] = 0
        numeric count[4] = 0
        numeric count[5] = 0
        string HEADING1 = "Dependents Report"
        string HEADING2 = "Dependents    Count"
        get dep
        while not eof
            count[dep] = count[dep] + 1
            get dep
        endwhile
        print HEADING1
        print HEADING2
        dep = 0
        while dep < 6
            print dep, count[dep]
            dep = dep + 1
        endwhile
    return
endClass
```

Figure 5-7 Flowchart and pseudocode for Dependents report program

the application is more efficient, easier for other programmers to understand, and easier to maintain. Arrays are never mandatory, but often they can drastically cut down on your programming time and make your logic easier to understand.

USING A NAMED CONSTANT TO REFER TO AN ARRAY'S SIZE

The program in Figure 5-7 still contains one minor flaw. Throughout this book you have learned to avoid "magic numbers"—that is, unnamed constants. When the report-printing part of the program in Figure 5-7 executes, the array subscript is compared to the constant 6. The program can be improved if you use a named constant instead. In most programming languages you can take one of two approaches:

» You can declare a named numeric constant such as ARRAY_SIZE = 6. Then you can use this constant every time you access the array, always making sure any subscript you use remains less than the constant value.

» When you declare an array in many languages, a constant that represents the array size is automatically created for you. For example, in Java, after you declare an array named count, its size is stored in a field named count.length. In both C# and Visual Basic, the array size is count.Length. (The difference is the "L" in Length.)

ARRAY DECLARATION AND INITIALIZATION

In the completed dependent-counting application in Figure 5-7, the six count array elements were declared and initialized to 0s at the start of the class. They need to be initialized to 0 so you can add to them during the course of the program. In Figure 5-7, the initialization is provided using six separate statements:

```
numeric count[0] = 0
numeric count[1] = 0
numeric count[2] = 0
numeric count[3] = 0
numeric count[4] = 0
numeric count[5] = 0
```

Separately declaring and initializing each count element is acceptable only if there are a small number of counts. If the dependent-counting application were updated to keep track of employees with up to 20 dependents, you would have to initialize 20 separate variables; it would be tedious to write 20 separate declaration statements.

Programming languages do not require the programmer to name each count element count[0], count[1], and so on. Instead, you can make a declaration such as one of those in Table 5-1.

Programming Language	Declaration of a 20-Element Array
Visual Basic	`Dim Count[20] As Integer`
C#, C++	`int count[20]`
Java	`int[] count = new int[20]`

Table 5-1 Declaring a 20-element array named count in several common languages

»NOTE C, C#, C++, and Java programmers typically create variable names that start with a lowercase letter. Visual Basic programmers are likely to begin variable names with an uppercase letter. (All these languages typically use an uppercase letter for second and subsequent words in an identifier.) In Chapter 1, you learned that these styles are called camel casing and Pascal casing, respectively. Table 5-1 uses these conventions.

All the declarations in Table 5-1 have two things in common: They name the `count` array and indicate that there will be 20 separate numeric elements. For flowcharting or pseudocode purposes, a statement such as `numeric count[20]` indicates the same thing.

Declaring a numeric array does not necessarily set its individual elements to 0, although it does in some programming languages, such as Visual Basic and Java. Most programming languages allow a statement similar to the following:

```
numeric count[20]  =  0
```

You should use a statement like this when you want to initialize an array in your flowcharts or pseudocode.

When an array is declared and you want to set all the elements in the array to different values, you can always make individual assignments, as in the following:

```
count[0]  =  5
count[1]  =  12
count[2]  =  24
```

As an alternative to defining the values of `count[0]` , `count[1]` , and so on separately, most programming languages allow a more concise version to initialize an array. It takes the general form:

```
numeric count[3]  =  5,  12,  24
```

When you use this form of array initialization, the first value you list is assigned to the first array element, and the subsequent values are assigned in order. Most programming languages allow you to assign fewer values than there are array elements declared, but no language allows you to assign more values.

»NOTE Many languages allow you to declare an array with a statement similar to the following:

```
numeric count[ ]  =  5,  12,  24
```

In this case, the array is **implicitly sized**, or automatically given a size (3) based on the list of provided values.

»NOTE Many programming languages require that you know an array's size (that is, its number of elements) when you write the program. Some languages allow you to alter an array's size during program execution. Arrays whose size can be altered are **dynamic arrays**, or **dynamically allocated** arrays.

»NOTE
Providing array values is also called **populating the array.**

Alternately, to start all array elements with the same initial value, you can use an initialization loop. An **initialization loop** is a loop structure that provides initial values for every element in any array. To create an initialization loop, you must use a numeric variable as a subscript. For example, if you declare a numeric variable named sub, and initialize sub to 0, then you can use a loop like the one shown in Figure 5-8 to set all the array elements to 0.

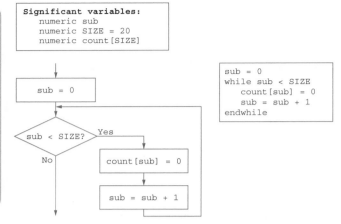

```
Significant variables:
    numeric sub
    numeric SIZE = 20
    numeric count[SIZE]
```

```
sub = 0
while sub < SIZE
    count[sub] = 0
    sub = sub + 1
endwhile
```

Figure 5-8 A loop that sets values for every element in an array

VARIABLE AND CONSTANT ARRAYS

The array that you used to accumulate dependent counts in the application that produces the Dependents report is a **variable array** because the values in it change during program execution. The values that you want to use—the final dependent counts—are created during an actual run, or execution, of the application. In other words, if there will be 200 employees with 0 dependents, you don't know that fact at the beginning of the program. Instead, that value is accumulated during the execution of the application and not known until the end.

Sometimes you can use an array that is a **constant array**. That is, the array can be assigned its permanent and final values when you write the program code. For example, let's say you own an apartment building with apartments in the basement as well as on three other floors. The floors are numbered 0 (for the basement), 1, 2, or 3. Every month you print a rent bill for each tenant. Your rent charges are based on the floor of the building, as shown in Figure 5-9.

Floor	Rent in $
0 (basement)	350
1	400
2	600
3 (penthouse)	1000

Figure 5-9 Rents by floor

Suppose you want to create an application that accepts each tenant's name and floor number and prints a letter to each tenant showing the amount of rent due, similar to the letter shown in Figure 5-10. To determine the correct rent for each tenant, you could use a series of decisions

```
Dear Rosa Martinez,
    Reminder — the rent for your apartment on floor 2
is due on the first of the month. The rent is $600.

Sincerely,
The Management
```

Figure 5-10 Typical letter to a tenant

concerning the floor number. However, it is more efficient to use an array to hold the four rent figures. The array is initialized with values that are **hard-coded** into the array; that is, they are explicitly assigned to the array elements.

The application in Figure 5-11 assigns the correct rent to every tenant. When you declare variables at the start of the application, you also create a constant array for the four rent figures and assign the correct rent to each.

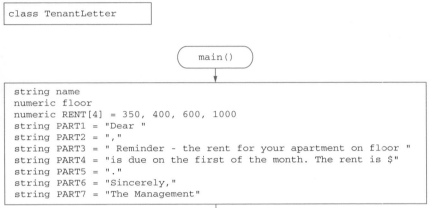

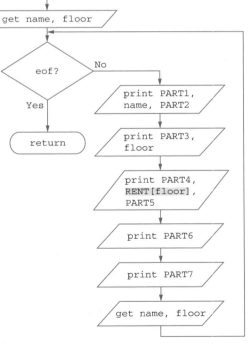

Figure 5-11 Program that produces tenant letters (*continued*)

```
class TenantLetter
   main()
      string name
      numeric floor
      numeric RENT[4] = 350, 400, 600, 1000
      string PART1 = "Dear "
      string PART2 = ","
      string PART3 = " Reminder - the rent for your apartment on floor "
      string PART4 = "is due on the first of the month. The rent is $"
      string PART5 = "."
      string PART6 = "Sincerely,"
      string PART7 = "The Management"
      get name, floor
      while not eof
         print PART1, name, PART2
         print PART3, floor
         print PART4, RENT[floor], PART5
         print PART6
         print PART7
         get name, floor
      endwhile
   return
endClass
```

Figure 5-11 Program that produces tenant letters

After you get the first tenant's name and floor number in the application in Figure 5-11, and as long as the end-of-file (eof) condition is not met, you print 10 separate items spread over five lines:

» The string "Dear "

» The tenant's name, retrieved from input

» A string containing a comma to follow the name

» A string that contains " Reminder - the rent for your apartment on floor "

» The floor number, from input

» A string that contains "is due on the first of the month. The rent is $"

» The rent amount, retrieved from the array with RENT[floor]

» A string that contains the period that follows the rent amount

» A string that contains "Sincerely,"

» A string that contains "The Management"

Instead of making a series of selections such as if floor = 0 then print RENT[0] and if floor = 1 then print RENT[1], you take advantage of the rent array by using floor as a subscript to access the correct RENT array element. (See the shaded statement in Figure 5-11.) When deciding what variable to use as a subscript with an array, ask yourself, "Of all the values available in the array, what does the correct selection depend on?" When printing a RENT value, the rent you use depends on the floor on which the tenant lives, so the correct action is print RENT[floor].

Without a RENT array, the program that prints the tenant's letters would have to contain three decisions and four different resulting actions. With the RENT array, there are no decisions.

Each tenant's rent is simply based on the RENT element that corresponds to the tenant's floor number. In other words, the floor number indicates the positional value of the corresponding rent. Arrays can really lighten the workload required to write a program.

SEARCHING AN ARRAY FOR AN EXACT MATCH

In both the dependent-counting application and the rent-determining application that you've seen in this chapter, the values that the arrays depend on conveniently hold small whole numbers. The number of dependents allowed in the first application was 0 through 5, and the number of a tenant's floor in the second application was 0 through 3. Unfortunately, real life doesn't always happen in small integers. Sometimes you don't have a variable that conveniently holds an array position; sometimes you have to search through an array to find a value you need.

Consider a mail-order business in which orders come in with a customer name, address, item number ordered, and quantity ordered. Assume the item numbers from which a customer can choose are three-digit numbers, but perhaps they are not consecutive 001 through 999. Instead, over the years, items have been deleted and new items have been added to the inventory. For example, there might no longer be an item with number 105 or 129. Sometimes there might be a hundred-number gap or more between items. For example, let's say that this season you are down to offering the six items shown in Figure 5-12.

Item Number	Item Price in $
106	0.59
108	0.99
307	4.50
405	15.99
457	17.50
688	35.00

Figure 5-12 Available items in mail-order company

When a customer orders an item, you want to determine whether the item number is valid. You could use a series of six decisions to determine whether the ordered item is valid by comparing, in turn, each customer order's item number to each of the six allowed values. However, a superior approach is to create an array that holds the list of valid item numbers. Then you can search through the array for an exact match to the ordered item. If you search through the entire array without finding a match for the item the customer ordered, you can print an error message—for example, "Item not found."

Suppose you create an array named VALID_ITEM that contains six elements, and that you set each to a valid item number. If an office has no computer and a customer orders item 307, a clerical worker can tell whether it is valid by looking down the list and verifying that 307 is a member of the list. In a similar fashion, you can use a loop in a computer program to test each VALID_ITEM against the ordered item number.

The technique for verifying that an item number exists involves setting a subscript to 0 and setting a flag variable to indicate that you have not yet determined whether the customer's order is valid. A **flag** is a variable that you set to indicate whether some event has occurred; frequently it holds a true or false value. For example, you can initialize a string variable named `foundIt` to "N", indicating "No." (See the first shaded statement in Figure 5-13.) Then you compare the customer's ordered item number to the first item in the array. If the customer-ordered item matches the first item in the array, you can set the flag variable to "Y", or

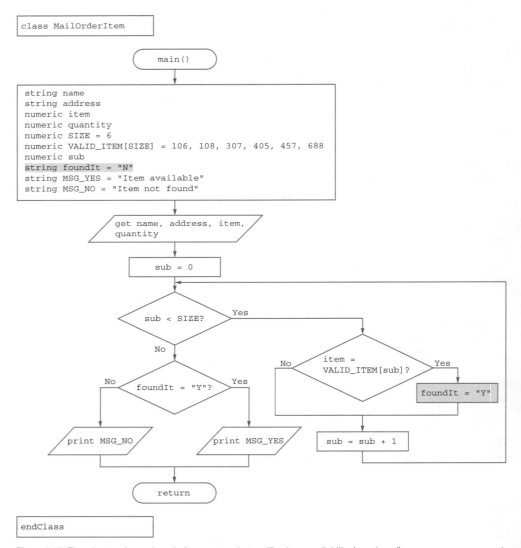

```
class MailOrderItem
```

main()

```
string name
string address
numeric item
numeric quantity
numeric SIZE = 6
numeric VALID_ITEM[SIZE] = 106, 108, 307, 405, 457, 688
numeric sub
string foundIt = "N"
string MSG_YES = "Item available"
string MSG_NO = "Item not found"
```

get name, address, item, quantity

sub = 0

sub < SIZE?

No · Yes

foundIt = "Y"?

No · Yes

item = VALID_ITEM[sub]?

No · Yes

foundIt = "Y"

print MSG_NO

print MSG_YES

sub = sub + 1

return

```
endClass
```

Figure 5-13 Flowchart and pseudocode for program that verifies item availability (*continued*)

```
class MailOrderItem
    main()
        string name
        string address
        numeric item
        numeric quantity
        numeric SIZE = 6
        numeric VALID_ITEM[SIZE] = 106, 108, 307, 405, 457, 688
        numeric sub
        string foundIt = "N"
        string MSG_YES = "Item available"
        string MSG_NO = "Item not found"
        get name, address, item, quantity
        sub = 0
        while sub < SIZE
            if item = VALID_ITEM[sub] then
                foundIt = "Y"
            endif
            sub = sub + 1
        endwhile
        if foundIt = "Y"
            print MSG_YES
        else
            print MSG_NO
        endif
    return
endClass
```

Figure 5-13 Flowchart and pseudocode for program that verifies item availability

» NOTE
Instead of the string `foundIt` variable in the method in Figure 5-13, you might prefer to use a numeric variable that you set to 1 or 0. Most programming languages also support a Boolean data type that you can use for `foundIt`; when you declare a variable to be Boolean, you can set its value to true or false.

any other value that is not "N". (See the second shaded statement in Figure 5-13.) If the items do not match, you increase the subscript and continue to look down the list of numbers stored in the array. If you check all six valid item numbers and the customer item matches none of them, then the flag variable `foundIt` still holds the value "N". If the flag variable is "N" after you have looked through the entire list, you can issue an error message indicating that no match was ever found. Figure 5-13 shows a program that accepts customer order data and accomplishes the item verification.

USING PARALLEL ARRAYS

When you read a customer's order in a mail-order company program, you usually want to accomplish more than simply verifying the item's existence. For example, you might want to determine the price of the ordered item, multiply that price by the quantity ordered, and print a bill. Using the prices listed in Figure 5-12, you *could* write a program in which you read a customer order record and then use the order's item number as a subscript to pull a price from an array. To use this method, you would need an array with at least 689 elements (because the lowest subscript is 0 and the highest item number is 688). If, for example, a customer ordered item 405, the price would be found at `PRICE[item]`, which is `PRICE[405]`, or the 406th element of the array. Because you sell only six items, you would waste 683 of the reserved memory positions. Instead of reserving a large quantity of memory that remains unused, you can set up this program to use two much smaller arrays.

Consider the `FindPrice` application in Figure 5-14. Two arrays are set up—one contains six elements named `VALID_ITEM`; all six elements are valid item numbers. The other array, highlighted in the figure, also has six elements. The array is named `VALID_ITEM_PRICE`; all six elements are prices. Each price in this `VALID_ITEM_PRICE` array is conveniently and purposely in the same position as the corresponding item number in the other `VALID_ITEM` array. Two corresponding arrays such as these are **parallel arrays** because each element in one array is associated with the element in the same relative position in the other array.

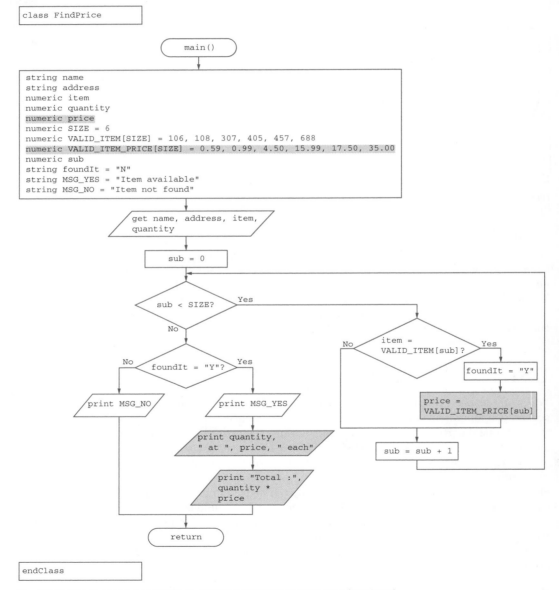

Figure 5-14 Flowchart and pseudocode of application that finds an item's price (*continued*)

```
class FindPrice
   main()
      string name
      string address
      numeric item
      numeric quantity
      numeric price
      numeric SIZE = 6
      numeric VALID_ITEM[SIZE] = 106, 108, 307, 405, 457, 688
      numeric VALID_ITEM_PRICE[SIZE] = 0.59, 0.99, 4.50, 15.99, 17.50, 35.00
      numeric sub
      string foundIt = "N"
      string MSG_YES = "Item available"
      string MSG_NO = "Item not found"
      get name, address, item, quantity
      sub = 0
      while sub < SIZE
         if item = VALID_ITEM[sub] then
            foundIt = "Y"
            price = VALID_ITEM_PRICE[sub]
         endif
         sub = sub + 1
      endwhile
      if foundIt = "Y"
         print MSG_YES
         print quantity, " at ", price, " each"
         print "Total :", quantity * price
      else
         print MSG_NO
      endif
   return
endClass
```

Figure 5-14 Flowchart and pseudocode of application that finds an item's price

As the application in Figure 5-14 receives each customer's order data, you look through each of the VALID_ITEM values separately by varying the subscript sub from 0 to the number of items available. When a match for the item number is found, you pull the corresponding parallel price out of the list of VALID_ITEM_PRICE values and store it in the price variable. (See the shaded statements in Figure 5-14.)

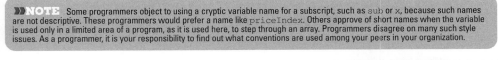

NOTE Some programmers object to using a cryptic variable name for a subscript, such as sub or x, because such names are not descriptive. These programmers would prefer a name like priceIndex. Others approve of short names when the variable is used only in a limited area of a program, as it is used here, to step through an array. Programmers disagree on many such style issues. As a programmer, it is your responsibility to find out what conventions are used among your peers in your organization.

Once you find a match for the ordered item number in the VALID_ITEM array, you know that the price of that item is in the same position in the other array, VALID_ITEM_PRICE. When VALID_ITEM[sub] is the correct item, VALID_ITEM_PRICE[sub] must be the correct price. You can then print the price and multiply it by the quantity ordered to produce a total, as shown in the last shaded statements in Figure 5-14.

Suppose that a customer orders item 457. If the program is written in a GUI environment, the results might look like Figure 5-15. Walk through the logic yourself to see if you come up with the correct price per item: $17.50.

Mail Order

Name	Madison Harper
Address	22 Pine
Item	457
Quantity	3

```
Item available
3 at 17.50 each
Total: 52.50
```

Figure 5-15 Typical execution of application that finds an item's price

IMPROVING SEARCH EFFICIENCY USING AN EARLY EXIT

The mail-order program in Figure 5-14 is still a little inefficient. The problem is that if lots of customers order item 106 or 108, their price is found on the first or second pass through the loop. The application continues searching through the item array, however, until sub reaches the value SIZE. One way to stop the search when the item has been found and foundIt is set to "Y" is to force (that is, explicitly assign) sub to the value of SIZE immediately. Then, when the program loops back to check whether sub is still less than SIZE, the loop will be exited and the program won't bother checking any of the higher item numbers. Leaving a loop as soon as a match is found is called an **early exit**; it improves the program's efficiency. The larger the array, the more beneficial it becomes to exit the searching loop as soon as you find what you're looking for.

Figure 5-16 shows the improved version of the loop that finds an item's price. Notice the shaded improvement. You search the VALID_ITEM array, element by element. If an item number is not

>> **NOTE**
Instead of forcing sub to SIZE when an item number is found, you could change the comparison that controls the while loop to continue while sub < SIZE AND foundIt = "N". If you use this approach, the loop exits as soon as an item is found and foundIt becomes "Y", even though sub is still less than SIZE. Many programmers prefer this approach to the one shown in Figure 5-16.

>> **NOTE**
Notice that the price-finding application is most efficient when the most frequently ordered items are stored at the beginning of the array. When you use this technique, only the seldom-ordered items require many cycles through the searching loop before finding a match.

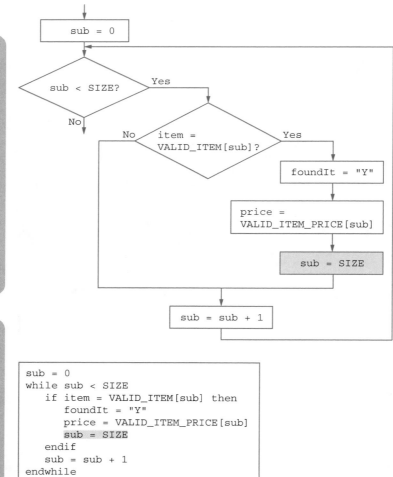

```
sub = 0
while sub < SIZE
    if item = VALID_ITEM[sub] then
        foundIt = "Y"
        price = VALID_ITEM_PRICE[sub]
        sub = SIZE
    endif
    sub = sub + 1
endwhile
```

Figure 5-16 Flowchart and pseudocode of the loop that finds an item's price, exiting the loop as soon as it is found

> **» NOTE** In the shaded portion of the logic in Figure 5-16, `sub` could be set to any value of 5 or over. At the end of the loop, 1 is added to `sub`; as long as the result is 6 or more, the loop will not continue. It is convenient to use the named constant `SIZE` because it makes your intentions clear. Also, if the program is modified at some future point when a different number of items is needed, you can change the value of `SIZE` just once where it is declared, and the rest of the program will automatically work correctly.

matched in a given location, the subscript is increased and the next location is checked. As soon as an item number is located in the array, you store the price, turn on the flag, and force the subscript to a high number (6) so the program will not check the item number array any further.

SEARCHING AN ARRAY FOR A RANGE MATCH

Customer order item numbers need to match available item numbers exactly in order to determine the correct price of an item. Sometimes, however, programmers want to work with ranges of values in arrays. In Chapter 3, you learned that a range of values is any series of values—for example, 1 through 5, or 20 through 30. Consider the mail order item-pricing program discussed in the previous section. Suppose the company decides to offer quantity discounts, as shown in Figure 5-17.

Quantity	Discount %
0–8	0
9–12	10
13–25	15
26 or more	20

Figure 5-17 Discounts on orders by quantity

You want to be able to read customer order data and determine a discount percentage based on the value in the `quantity` variable. For example, if a customer has ordered 20 items, you want to be able to print "Your discount is 15 percent". One ill-advised approach might be to set up an array with as many elements as any customer might ever order, and store the appropriate discount for each possible number, as shown in Figure 5-18. This

```
numeric DISCOUNT[76]
 = 0, 0, 0, 0, 0, 0, 0, 0, 0,
   0.10, 0.10, 0.10, 0.10,
   0.15, 0.15, 0.15, 0.15, 0.15,
   0.15, 0.15, 0.15, 0.15, 0.15,
   0.15, 0.15, 0.15,
   0.20, 0.20, 0.20, 0.20, 0.20,
   0.20, 0.20, 0.20, 0.20, 0.20,
   0.20, 0.20, 0.20, 0.20, 0.20,
   0.20, 0.20, 0.20, 0.20, 0.20,
   0.20, 0.20, 0.20, 0.20, 0.20,
   0.20, 0.20, 0.20, 0.20, 0.20,
   0.20, 0.20, 0.20, 0.20, 0.20,
   0.20, 0.20, 0.20, 0.20, 0.20,
   0.20, 0.20, 0.20, 0.20, 0.20,
   0.20, 0.20, 0.20, 0.20, 0.20
```

» DON'T DO IT

Although this array is usable, it is repetitious, prone to error, and difficult to use.

Figure 5-18 Usable but inefficient discount array

array is set up to contain the discount for 0 items, 1 item, 2 items, and so on. This approach has at least three drawbacks:

» It requires a very large array that uses a lot of memory.

» You must store the same value repeatedly. For example, each of the first nine elements receives the same value, 0, and each of the next four elements receives the same value, 10.

» How do you know you have enough array elements? Is a customer order quantity of 75 items enough? What if a customer orders 100 or 1,000 items? No matter how many elements you place in the array, there's always a chance that a customer will order more.

A better approach is to create just four discount array elements, one for each of the possible discount rates, as shown in Figure 5-19. The four-element array holds each possible discount, with no repetition.

```
numeric DISCOUNT[4]
   = 0, 0.10, 0.15, 0.20
```

Figure 5-19 Superior discount array

With the new four-element DISCOUNT array, you need a parallel array to search for the appropriate discount level. At first, beginning programmers might consider creating an array of constants named DISCOUNT_RANGE similar to the following, and then testing whether the quantity ordered equals one of the four stored values.

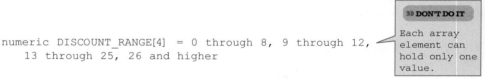

```
numeric DISCOUNT_RANGE[4]  = 0 through 8,  9 through 12,
    13 through 25,  26 and higher
```

»» DON'T DO IT
Each array element can hold only one value.

However, you cannot create an array like this one. Each element in any array is simply a single variable. A simple variable like age or payRate can hold 6 or 12, but it can't hold every value 6 *through* 12. Similarly, the DISCOUNT_RANGE[0] variable can hold a 0, 1, 8, or any other single value, but it can't hold 0 *through* 8; there is no such numeric value.

One solution to determine discount ranges is to create a usable array that holds only the low-end value of each range, as Figure 5-20 shows.

```
numeric DISCOUNT_RANGE[4]
   = 0, 9, 13, 26
```

Figure 5-20 The DISCOUNT_RANGE array using the low end of each range

To find the correct discount for any customer's ordered quantity, you can start with the *last* range limit (DISCOUNT_RANGE[3]). If the quantity ordered is at least that value, 26, the loop is never entered and the customer gets the highest discount rate (DISCOUNT[3] , or 20 percent). If the quantity ordered is not at least DISCOUNT_RANGE[3] —that is, if it is less than 26—then you reduce the subscript and check to see if the quantity is at least

DISCOUNT_RANGE[2] , or 13. If so, the customer receives DISCOUNT[2] , or 15 percent, and so on. Figure 5-21 shows a program that accepts a customer's quantity ordered and determines the appropriate discount rate.

When using an array to store range limits, you use a loop to make a series of comparisons that would otherwise require many separate decisions. The program that determines customer

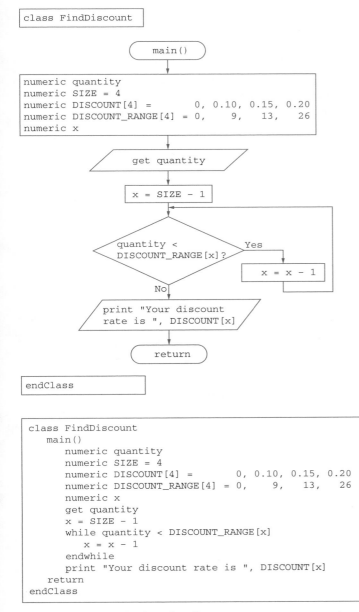

```
class FindDiscount
    main()
        numeric quantity
        numeric SIZE = 4
        numeric DISCOUNT[4] =        0, 0.10, 0.15, 0.20
        numeric DISCOUNT_RANGE[4] = 0,    9,   13,   26
        numeric x
        get quantity
        x = SIZE - 1
        while quantity < DISCOUNT_RANGE[x]
            x = x - 1
        endwhile
        print "Your discount rate is ", DISCOUNT[x]
    return
endClass
```

Figure 5-21 Application that determines discount rate

discount rates is written using fewer instructions than would be required if you did not use an array, and modifications to your method will be easier to make in the future.

REMAINING WITHIN ARRAY BOUNDS

Every array has a finite size. You can think of an array's size in one of two ways—either by the number of elements in the array or by the number of bytes in the array. Arrays are always composed of elements of the same data type, and elements of the same data type always occupy the same number of bytes of memory, so the number of bytes in an array is always a multiple of the number of elements in an array. For example, in Java, integers occupy four bytes of memory, so an array of 10 integers occupies exactly 40 bytes.

In every programming language, when you access data stored in an array, it is important to use a subscript containing a value that accesses memory occupied by the array. For example, examine the `PrintMonthName` program in Figure 5-22. The method accepts a numeric `month` and displays the name associated with that month.

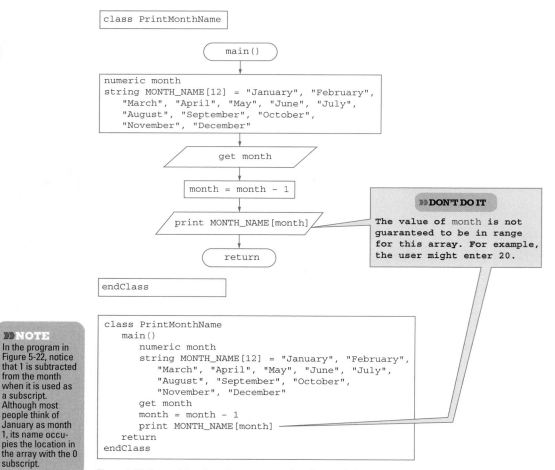

▶▶NOTE
In the program in Figure 5-22, notice that 1 is subtracted from the month when it is used as a subscript. Although most people think of January as month 1, its name occupies the location in the array with the 0 subscript.

Figure 5-22 Determining the string representation of a month from a user's numeric entry

The logic makes a dangerous assumption: that every number entered by the user is a valid month number. If the user enters a number that is too small or too large, one of two things will happen depending on the programming language you use. When you use a subscript value that is negative or higher than the number of elements in an array:

» Some programming languages will stop execution of the program and issue an error message.

» Other programming languages will not issue an error message but will access a value in a memory location that is outside the area occupied by the array. That area might contain garbage, or worse, it accidentally might contain the name of an incorrect month.

»» NOTE
Besides entering an invalid number, a user might not enter a number at all. You will handle this type of error in Chapter 12.

Either way, a logical error occurs. When you use a subscript that is not within the range of acceptable subscripts, your subscript is said to be **out of bounds**. Users enter incorrect data frequently; a good program should be able to handle the mistake and not allow the subscript to be out of bounds.

You can improve the program in Figure 5-22 by adding a test that ensures the subscript used to access the array is within the array bounds. Figure 5-23 shows one method that ensures that the subscript used with the array is appropriate; it tests the subscript and displays an error message if the subscript is not valid. Figure 5-24 shows another approach. This program repeatedly prompts for a month until the user enters a valid value. Which technique you use depends on the requirements of your application.

Every time you use an array, you should keep its size and boundaries in mind. For example, when a user's input value is used to access an array, you should always test the size of the value to make sure it is within bounds before using the value. If the value of the variable used as a subscript is too low (below 0) or too high (the size of the array or larger), you should either not access the array or force the value to a usable value with an assignment statement.

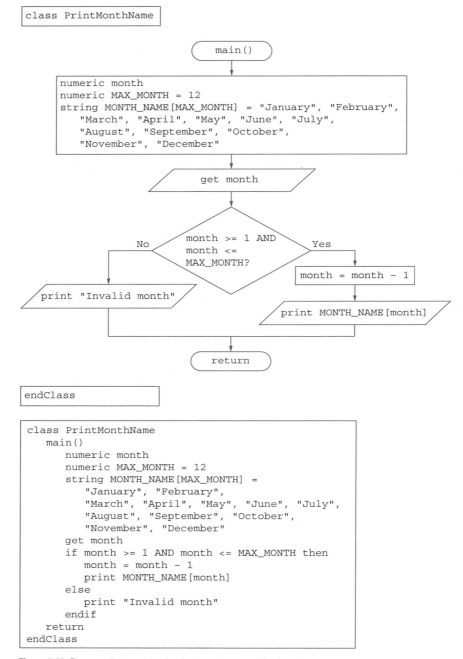

```
class PrintMonthName
   main()
      numeric month
      numeric MAX_MONTH = 12
      string MONTH_NAME[MAX_MONTH] =
         "January", "February",
         "March", "April", "May", "June", "July",
         "August", "September", "October",
         "November", "December"
      get month
      if month >= 1 AND month <= MAX_MONTH then
         month = month - 1
         print MONTH_NAME[month]
      else
         print "Invalid month"
      endif
   return
endClass
```

Figure 5-23 Program that uses a selection to ensure a valid subscript

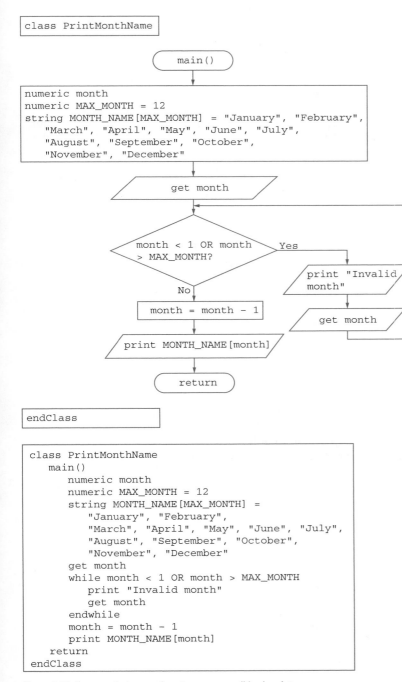

```
class PrintMonthName
    main()
        numeric month
        numeric MAX_MONTH = 12
        string MONTH_NAME[MAX_MONTH] =
            "January", "February",
            "March", "April", "May", "June", "July",
            "August", "September", "October",
            "November", "December"
        get month
        while month < 1 OR month > MAX_MONTH
            print "Invalid month"
            get month
        endwhile
        month = month - 1
        print MONTH_NAME[month]
    return
endClass
```

Figure 5-24 Program that uses a loop to ensure a valid subscript

USING A FOR LOOP TO PROCESS ARRAYS

In Chapter 4, you learned about the `for` loop—a loop that, in a single statement, initializes a loop control variable, compares it to a limit, and alters it. The `for` loop is a particularly convenient tool when working with arrays because you frequently need to process every element of an array from beginning to end. As with a `while` loop, when you use a `for` loop, you must be careful to stay within array bounds, remembering that the highest usable array subscript is one less than the size of the array. Figure 5-25 shows a `for` loop that correctly prints all the month names in the MONTH_NAME array. Notice that `month` is incremented through one less than the number of months because with a 12-item array, the subscripts you can use are 0 through 11.

```
class PrintMonthNames
    main()
        numeric month
        numeric MAX_MONTH = 12
        string MONTH_NAME[MAX_MONTH] =
            "January", "February",
            "March", "April", "May", "June", "July",
            "August", "September", "October",
            "November", "December"
        for month 0 to MAX_MONTH - 1
            print MONTH_NAME[month]
        endfor
    return
endClass
```

Figure 5-25 Pseudocode that demonstrates using a `for` loop to print month names

The loop in Figure 5-25 is slightly inefficient because, as it executes 12 times, the subtraction operation that deducts 1 from MAX_MONTH occurs each time. Twelve subtraction operations do not consume much computer power or time, but in a loop that processes thousands or millions of array elements, the program's efficiency would be compromised. Figure 5-26 shows a superior solution. A new constant, ARRAY_LIMIT, is calculated once, then used repeatedly in the comparison operation to determine when to stop cycling through the array.

```
class PrintMonthNames
    main()
        numeric month
        numeric MAX_MONTH = 12
        numeric ARRAY_LIMIT = MAX_MONTH - 1
        string MONTH_NAME[MAX_MONTH] =
            "January", "February",
            "March", "April", "May", "June", "July",
            "August", "September", "October",
            "November", "December"
        for month 0 to ARRAY_LIMIT
            print MONTH_NAME[month]
        endfor
    return
endClass
```

Figure 5-26 Using a more efficient `for` loop to print month names

>> **NOTE** In Java, C++, and C#, the `for` loop looks the same. To control a loop in which `month` varies from 0 to one less than `MAX_MONTH`, you can write the following:

```
for(month = 0; month < MAX_MONTH; month++)
```

The keyword `for` is followed by parentheses. The parentheses contain three sections, separated with semicolons. The first section sets `month` to a starting value. The middle section makes a comparison; the `for` loop continues to execute while this expression is true. The last section executes when the body of the loop is complete; usually it alters the loop control variable. In Java, C++, and C#, `month++` means "add one to `month`".

>> **NOTE** You will learn more about arrays in Chapter 12.

CHAPTER SUMMARY

» An array is a series or list of variables in computer memory, all of which have the same name and data type but are differentiated with special numbers called subscripts.

» You can often use a variable as a subscript to an array, which allows you to replace multiple nested decisions with many fewer statements.

» Using a named constant for an array's size makes the code easier to understand and less likely to contain an error.

» You can declare and initialize all of the elements in an array using a single statement that provides a type, a name, and a quantity of elements for the array. You can also initialize array values within an initialization loop.

» Some arrays contain values that are determined during the execution of a program; other arrays are more useful when their final desired values are hard-coded when you write the program.

» Searching through an array to find a value you need involves initializing a subscript, using a loop to test each array element, and setting a flag when a match is found.

» With parallel arrays, each element in one array is associated with the element in the same relative position in the other array.

» When you need to compare a value to a range of values in an array, you can store either the low- or high-end value of each range for comparison.

» When you access data stored in an array, it is important to use a subscript containing a value that accesses memory occupied by the array. When you use a subscript that is not within the defined range of acceptable subscripts, your subscript is said to be out of bounds.

» The `for` loop is a particularly convenient tool when working with arrays because you frequently need to process every element of an array from beginning to end.

KEY TERMS

An **array** is a series or list of variables in computer memory, all of which have the same name and data type but are differentiated with special numbers called subscripts.

A **subscript**, also called an **index**, is a number that indicates the position of a particular item within an array.

Each separate array variable is one **element** of the array.

The **size of the array** is the number of elements it can hold.

An **implicitly sized** array is automatically given a size based on a list of provided values.

Arrays whose size can be altered are **dynamic arrays**, or **dynamically allocated** arrays.

An **initialization loop** is a loop structure that provides initial values for every element in any array.

Populating an array is the act of assigning values to the array elements.

A **variable array** is one whose values change during program execution.

A **constant array** is one whose values are assigned permanently when you write the program code.

Hard-coded values are explicitly assigned.

A **flag** is a variable that you set to indicate whether some event has occurred.

Parallel arrays are two or more arrays in which each element in one array is associated with the element in the same relative position in the other array or arrays.

Leaving a loop as soon as a match is found is called an **early exit**.

An array subscript is **out of bounds** when it is not within the range of acceptable subscripts.

REVIEW QUESTIONS

1. A subscript is a(n) _____ .

   a. element in an array

   b. alternate name for an array

   c. number that indicates the position of a particular item within an array

   d. number that represents the highest value stored within an array

2. Each variable in an array must have the same _____ as the others.

   a. subscript   c. value

   b. data type   d. memory location

3. Each variable in an array is called a(n) _____ .

   a. element   c. component

   b. subscript   d. data type

4. The subscripts of any array are always _____ .

   a. characters   c. integers

   b. fractions   d. strings of characters

5. Suppose you have an array named `number`, and two of its elements are `number[1]` and `number[4]` . You know that _____ .

   a. the two elements hold the same value

   b. the two elements are at the same memory location

   c. the array holds exactly four elements

   d. there are exactly two elements between those two elements

6. Suppose you want to write a program that reads customer records and prints a summary of the number of customers who owe more than $1,000 each, in each of 12 sales regions. Customer fields include `name`, `zipCode`, `balanceDue`, and `regionNumber`. At some point during record processing, you would add 1 to an array element whose subscript would be represented by _____ .

   a. `name`   c. `balanceDue`

   b. `zipCode`   d. `regionNumber`

7. Arrays are most useful when you use a _____ as a subscript when accessing their values.

   a. numeric constant

   b. character

   c. variable

   d. filename

8. Suppose you create a program containing a seven-element array that contains the names of the days of the week. At the start of the program, you display the day names using a subscript named `dayNum`. You display the same array values again at the end of the program, where you _____ as a subscript to the array.

   a. must use `dayNum`

   b. can use `dayNum` but can also use another variable

   c. must not use `dayNum`

   d. must use a numeric constant instead of a variable

9. Declaring a numeric array sets its individual elements' values to _____ .

   a. 0 in every programming language

   b. 0 in some programming languages

   c. consecutive digits in every programming language

   d. consecutive digits in some programming languages

10. Filling an array with values during a program's execution is known as _____ the array.

   a. populating

   b. colonizing

   c. executing

   d. declaring

11. A hard-coded array is one whose final desired values are set _____ .

   a. to constant values at the beginning of the program

   b. to variable values during the execution of the program

   c. to values by the end of the program

   d. to 0

12. A _____ is a variable that you set to indicate whether some event has occurred.

   a. subscript

   b. flag

   c. counter

   d. banner

13. What do you call two arrays in which each element in one array is associated with the element in the same relative position in the other array?

   a. cohesive arrays

   b. perpendicular arrays

   c. hidden arrays

   d. parallel arrays

14. In most modern programming languages, the highest subscript you should use with a 10-element array is _____ .

   a. 8   c. 10

   b. 9   d. 11

15. When you perform an early exit from a loop while searching through an array for a match, you _____ .

   a. quit searching as soon as you find a match

   b. quit searching before you find a match

   c. set a flag as soon as you find a match, but keep searching for additional matches

   d. repeat a search only if the first search was unsuccessful

16. Each element in a five-element array can hold _____ value(s) at a time.

   a. one

   b. five

   c. at least five

   d. an unlimited number of

17. After the annual dog show in which the Barkley Dog Training Academy awards points to each participant, the academy assigns a status to each dog based on the following criteria:

Points Earned	Level of Achievement
0–5	Good
6–7	Excellent
8–9	Superior
10	Unbelievable

The academy needs a program that compares a dog's points earned with the grading scale, so that each dog can receive a certificate acknowledging the appropriate level of achievement. Of the following, which set of values would be most useful for the contents of an array used in the program?

a. 0, 6, 9, 10

c. 5, 7, 9, 10

b. 5, 7, 8, 10

d. any of these

18. When you use a subscript value that is negative or higher than the number of elements in an array, ―――――― .

a. execution of the program stops and an error message is issued

b. a value in a memory location that is outside the area occupied by the array will be accessed

c. a value in a memory location that is outside the area occupied by the array will be accessed, but only if the value is the correct data type

d. the resulting action depends on the programming language used

19. In every array, a subscript is out of bounds when it is ―――――― .

a. negative

c. 1

b. 0

d. 999

20. You can access every element of an array using a ―――――― .

a. `while` loop

c. posttest loop

b. `for` loop

d. any of the above

EXERCISES

1. a. The city of Cary is holding a special census. The census takers collect one record for each resident. Each record contains the resident's age, gender, marital status, and voting district. The voting district is a number from 1 through 22. Design a program that accepts data for each resident until all have been entered and then produces a list of all 22 districts and the number of residents in each.

   b. Design a program that accepts resident data and produces a count of the number of residents in each of the following age groups: under 18, 18 through 30, 31 through 45, 46 through 64, and 65 and older.

2. a. The Midville Park District maintains records containing information about players on its soccer teams. Each record contains a player's first name, last name, and team number. The teams are:

Team Number	Team Name
1	Goal Getters
2	The Force
3	Top Guns
4	Shooting Stars
5	Midfield Monsters

Design a program that accepts player data and creates a report that lists each player along with his or her team number and team name.

b. Design an application that produces a count of the number of players registered for each team listed in Exercise 2a.

3. a. Watson Elementary School contains 30 classrooms numbered 1 through 30. Each classroom can contain any number of students up to 35. Each student takes an achievement test at the end of the school year and receives a score from 0 through 100. Write a program that accepts data for each student in the school—student ID, classroom number, and score on the achievement test. The program also should list the total points scored for each of the 30 classrooms.

b. Modify Exercise 3a so that each classroom's average of the test scores prints, rather than each classroom's total.

c. Watson Elementary School maintains a file containing the teacher's name for each classroom. Each record in this file contains a room number 1 through 30, and the last name of the teacher. Modify the program in Exercise 3b so that the correct teacher's name appears on the list with his or her class's average.

4. The Billy Goat Fast-Food restaurant sells the following products:

Product	Price ($)
Cheeseburger	2.49
Pepsi	1.00
Chips	0.59

Design the logic for an application that reads in a customer's item ordered and prints either the correct price or the message "Sorry, we do not carry that" as output.

5. a. Design the logic for an application for a company that wants a report containing a breakdown of payroll by department. Input includes each employee's last name, first name, department number, hourly salary, and number of hours worked. The output is a list of the seven departments in the company (numbered 1 through 7) and the total gross payroll (rate times hours) for each department.

b. Modify Exercise 5a so that the report lists department names as well as numbers. The department names are:

Department Number	Department Name
1	Personnel
2	Marketing
3	Manufacturing
4	Computer Services
5	Sales
6	Accounting
7	Shipping

c. Modify the report created in Exercise 5b so that it prints a line of information for each employee before printing the department summary at the end of the report. Each detail line must contain the employee's name, department number, department name, hourly wage, hours worked, gross pay, and withholding tax.

Withholding taxes are based on the following percentages of gross pay:

Weekly Gross Pay ($)	Withholding Percent (%)
0.00–200.00	10
200.01–350.00	14
350.01–500.00	18
500.01–up	22

6. The Perfect Party Catering Company hosts events for clients. Create an application that accepts an event number, the event host's last name, and numeric month, day, and year values representing the event date. Also accept the number of guests that will attend the event and a numeric meal code that represents the entrée the event hosts will serve. As each client's data is entered, verify that the month, day, year, and meal code are valid; if any of this data is not valid, continue to prompt the user until it is. The valid meal codes are as follows:

Code	Entrée	Price per person ($)
1	Roast beef	24.50
2	Salmon	19.00
3	Linguine	16.50
4	Chicken	18.00

Design the logic for an application that produces a report that lists each event number, host name, validated date, meal code, entrée name, number of guests, gross total price for the party, and price for the party after discount. The gross total price for the party is the price per guest for the meal, times the number of guests. The final price includes a discount based on the following table:

Number of Guests	Discount ($)
1-25	0
26-50	75
51-100	125
101-250	200
251 and over	300

7. a. *Daily Life Magazine* wants an analysis of the demographic characteristics of its readers. The Marketing Department has collected reader survey records containing the age,

gender, marital status, and annual income of readers. Design an application that accepts reader data and produces a count of readers by age groups as follows: under 20, 20–29, 30–39, 40–49, and 50 and older.

b. Create the logic for a program that would produce a count of readers by gender within age group—that is, under 20 females, under 20 males, and so on.

c. Create the logic for a program that would produce a count of readers by income groups as follows: under $20,000, $20,000–$29,999, $30,000–$49,999, $50,000–$69,999, and $70,000 and up.

8. Glen Ross Vacation Property Sales employs seven salespeople as follows:

ID Number	Salesperson Name
103	Darwin
104	Kratz
201	Shulstad
319	Fortune
367	Wickert
388	Miller
435	Vick

When a salesperson makes a sale, a record is created including the date, time, and dollar amount of the sale. The time is expressed in hours and minutes, based on a 24-hour clock. The sale amount is expressed in whole dollars.

Salespeople earn a commission that differs for each sale, based on the following rate schedule:

Sale Amount ($)	Commission Rate (%)
0–50,999	4
51,000–125,999	5
126,000–200,999	6
201,000 and up	7

Design an application that produces each of the following reports:

a. A report listing each salesperson number, name, total sales, and total commissions

b. A report listing each month of the year as both a number and a word (for example, "01 January"), and the total sales for the month for all salespeople

c. A report listing total sales as well as total commissions earned by all salespeople for each of the following time frames, based on hour of the day: 00–05, 06–12, 13–18, and 19–23

CASE PROJECT

In earlier chapters, you developed programs for Cost Is No Object—a car rental service that specializes in lending antique and luxury cars to clients on a short-term basis.

Create an application that continues to prompt the user for employee data and writes a report that contains a line for each employee. The application continues until the user enters 0 for an ID number to indicate the desire to quit. While the ID number is not 0, prompt the user for a value for each employee's first and last names, street address, zip code, and job description code.

Any time the user enters an invalid value, continue to reprompt the user for the same data. Invalid values are:

» An employee ID number that is negative or greater than 999
» A zip code that is not in the list of allowed zip codes
» A job description code that is not between 10 and 19 inclusive

Determine the employee's city and state based on the zip code, as described in Table 5-2. Determine the employee's job title based on the values in Table 5-3. Determine the

Zip Code	City	State
53115	Delavan	WI
53125	Fontana	WI
53147	Lake Geneva	WI
53184	Walworth	WI
53585	Sharon	IL
60001	Alden	IL
60033	Harvard	IL
60034	Hebron	IL
61012	Capron	IL

Table 5-2 Zip codes for Cost Is No Object

Job Code	Title
10	Desk clerk
11	Credit checker
12	Billing
13	Car cleaner
14	Chauffeur
15	Marketer
16	Accountant
17	Mechanic
18	CEO
19	Contract

Table 5-3 Job titles for Cost Is No Object

employee's hourly pay rate based on the values in Table 5-4. (Contract employees have an hourly rate of $0.)

Job Code	Hourly Pay Rate ($)
10–13	9.00
14–15	14.50
16–17	20.00
18	65.00
19	0.00

Table 5-4 Hourly pay rates for Cost Is No Object

When all the needed data has been entered correctly for an employee, print the ID number, first and last names, street address, city, state, zip code, job code, job title, and hourly pay rate for each employee, and prompt the user for the next ID number. At the end of the report, print the following summaries:

» A count of the number of employees in each job code

» A count of the number of employees who live in each zip code

UP FOR DISCUSSION

1. A train schedule is an everyday, real-life example of an array. Think of at least four more.

2. Every element in an array always has the same data type. Why is this necessary?

3. What is a Fibonacci sequence? How do Fibonacci sequences apply to natural phenomena? Why do programmers use an array when working with this mathematical concept?

USING METHODS

In this chapter, you will:

Create a simple method
Use local and global variables and constants
Create a method that requires a single argument
Create a method that requires multiple arguments
Create a method that returns a value
Pass an array to a method
Overload methods
Learn how to avoid ambiguous methods
Use prewritten, built-in methods

CREATING A SIMPLE METHOD

A method is a program module that contains a series of statements that carry out a task. In Chapter 2, you learned that you can invoke or call a method from another method. Any class can contain an unlimited number of methods, and each method can be called an unlimited number of times. Within a class, the simplest methods you can invoke don't require any data items (called **arguments** or **parameters**) to be sent to them, nor do they send any data back to you (called **returning a value**). Consider the simple application in Figure 6-1 that accepts a customer's name and balance due and prints a bill. The company's name and address are displayed on three lines at the top of the bill. You can simply include three print statements in the main() method, as shown in

NOTE
Later in this chapter you will learn that *argument* and *parameter* do not mean the same thing. However, the terms are closely related.

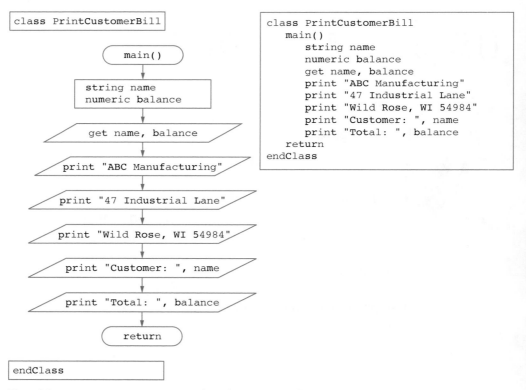

```
class PrintCustomerBill
    main()
        string name
        numeric balance
        get name, balance
        print "ABC Manufacturing"
        print "47 Industrial Lane"
        print "Wild Rose, WI 54984"
        print "Customer: ", name
        print "Total: ", balance
    return
endClass
```

Figure 6-1 PrintCustomerBill program using only a main() method

Figure 6-1, or you can create both a `main()` and a `nameAndAddress()` method, as shown in Figure 6-2.

When the `nameAndAddress()` method is called as shown in Figure 6-2, logic transfers from the `main()` method to the `nameAndAddress()` method. There, each statement within the method executes in turn before logical control is transferred back to the `main()` method. In `main()`, the logic continues with the statement that follows the method call.

» NOTE
When you call a method, the action is similar to putting a VCR or DVD player on pause. You abandon your first action (watching a video), take care of some other task (for example, making a sandwich), and when the secondary task is complete, you return to the main task exactly where you left off.

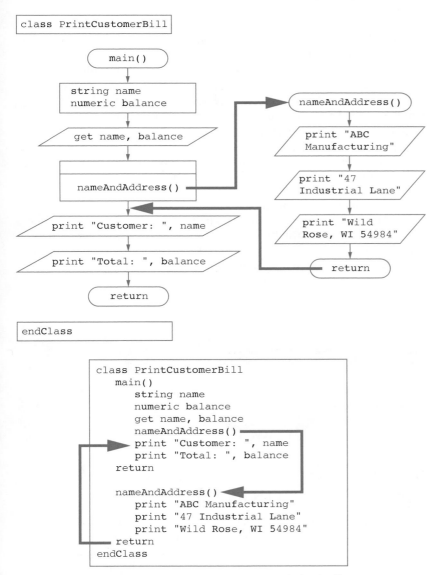

Figure 6-2 `PrintCustomerBill` program using a `main()` method and calling a `nameAndAddress()` method

Two major reasons might compel you to create a separate method to display the three address lines. First, the main() method will remain short and easy to follow because main() will contain just one statement to call the method, rather than three separate print statements to perform the work of the method. Second, and more importantly, a method is easily reusable. After you create the name and address method, you can use it in any application that needs the company's name and address. In other words, you do the work once, and then you can use the method many times.

A method must include the following:

» A **method header** (or **method declaration**). This is the entry point to the method. In some languages, notably C++, a method's declaration and header provide the same basic information but are written separately. In many other languages, the declaration is the header. A method declaration includes its identifier and an optional parameter list, which you will learn about later in this chapter. You will also learn that in many programming languages, a declaration also includes a return type and other accessibility information.

» A **method body**, which consists of the method's statements. When you write the statements that constitute a method's body, you are **implementing the method**, and the statements within a method are called the **method's implementation**.

» A **return statement** that marks the end of the method. In most programming languages, if you do not include a return statement at the end of a method, the method still will return to the spot from which it was called. For clarity, this book follows the convention of explicitly including a return statement with every method.

The full name of the nameAndAddress() method is PrintCustomerBill. nameAndAddress(). The full name includes the class name, a dot, and the method name. When you use the nameAndAddress() method within its own class, you do not need to use the full name (although you can); the method name alone is enough. However, if you want to use the nameAndAddress() method in another class, the compiler will not recognize the method unless you use the full name, writing it as PrintCustomerBill. nameAndAddress(). This format notifies the new class that the method is located in the PrintCustomerBill class.

UNDERSTANDING LOCAL AND GLOBAL VARIABLES AND CONSTANTS

The program in Figure 6-2 contains many print statements that print literal constants. Throughout this book you have been advised that your programs generally will be easier to maintain and modify if you use named constants to hold fixed values. In the programs you have studied up to this point, all the variables have been declared at the beginning of the main() method, so you might decide to modify the program in Figure 6-2 to look like the one in Figure 6-3. You would declare string constants to hold the three company address lines, and then print these constants when you need to print the address. (See the shaded portions of Figure 6-3.) However, this program will not work.

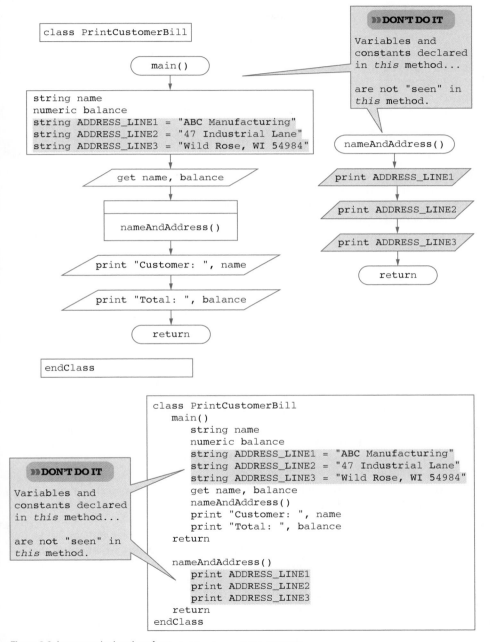

Figure 6-3 Incorrect declarations for PrintCustomerBill program

>> NOTE In Chapter 7, you will create classes from which objects are created. In some programming languages—for example, Java and C#—any method that can be used *without* creating an object requires the keyword modifier static. In these languages, you would place the word static in the method header. The main() method always is such a method. In Figure 6-3, the nameAndAddress() method is another such method. The meaning of static will become clearer to you when you study class creation in Chapter 7, so it is not used in method headers in this chapter.

In every object-oriented programming language, the variables and constants declared in any method are usable only within that method. Programmers say the data items are **visible** or "can be seen" only after they have been declared and within the method in which they are declared. Programmers also say that variables and constants declared within a method are **in scope** only after declaration within that method. Programmers also say that variables and constants are **local** to the method in which they are declared. All this means that when the strings ADDRESS_LINE1, ADDRESS_LINE2, and ADDRESS_LINE3 are declared in the main() method in Figure 6-3, they are not recognized and cannot be used by the nameAndAddress() method.

One of the motivations for creating methods is that separate methods are easily reusable in multiple programs. If the nameAndAddress() method will be used by several programs within the organization, it makes sense that the definitions for the variables and constants the method uses must "come with" it. Therefore, the superior solution for the PrintCustomerBill program is to create it as shown in Figure 6-4. In this version, the data items that are needed by the main() method are defined within that method, and the ones needed by the nameAndAddress() method are defined there. Each method contains its own data and does not "know about" the data in any other methods.

Besides local variables and constants, you can create global variables and constants. **Global** variables and constants are those that are known to an entire class. Figure 6-5 shows how the three address line constants might be declared globally in code for the PrintCustomerBill class. Variables and constants that are declared in a class but outside any method are declared at the **class level**. In general, and in this case, this is not a recommended practice.

On selected occasions, you might consider declaring variables and constants outside of a method:

» Some programmers approve of declaring global variables for constants that will be needed in many methods throughout a class. For example, if a mathematical program contains many methods that require a constant for a value such as pi, or a business program contains many methods that require a standard tax or discount rate, many programmers would allow these to be declared globally.

» When you create a class from which you will derive objects, you can declare the class's data fields at the class level. You will do this in Chapter 7.

In other circumstances, however, you should not declare global variables and constants. When you do, you violate the programming principle of **encapsulation**, which states that a method's instructions and its data should be contained within the same method. If you declare variables and constants within the methods that use them, the methods are more **portable**; that is, they can more easily be reused in multiple programs. Sometimes two or more methods in a program require access to the same data; when this is the case, however, you do not declare global data items. Instead, you **pass the data** from one method to another.

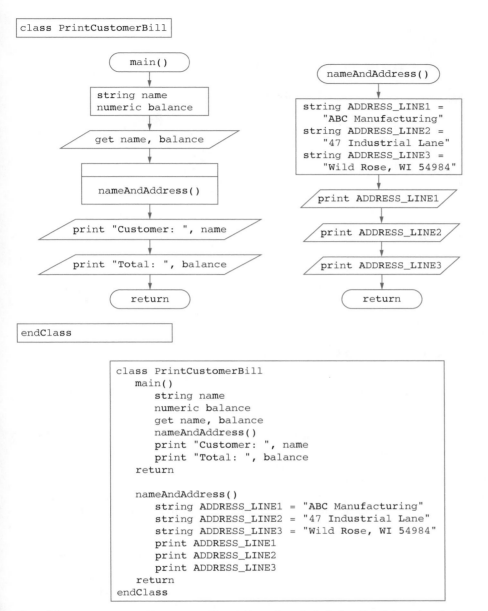

Figure 6-4 `PrintCustomerBill` program with variables and constants declared locally in each method

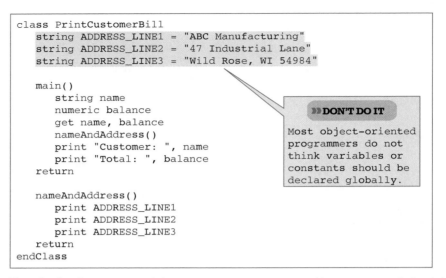

```
class PrintCustomerBill
    string ADDRESS_LINE1 = "ABC Manufacturing"
    string ADDRESS_LINE2 = "47 Industrial Lane"
    string ADDRESS_LINE3 = "Wild Rose, WI 54984"

    main()
        string name
        numeric balance
        get name, balance
        nameAndAddress()
        print "Customer: ", name
        print "Total: ", balance
    return

    nameAndAddress()
        print ADDRESS_LINE1
        print ADDRESS_LINE2
        print ADDRESS_LINE3
    return
endClass
```

DON'T DO IT

Most object-oriented programmers do not think variables or constants should be declared globally.

Figure 6-5 Usually not recommended: `PrintCustomerBill` program with some constants declared globally

CREATING METHODS THAT REQUIRE A SINGLE ARGUMENT

Some methods require information to be sent in from the outside. If a method could not receive your communications, called parameters, then you would have to write an infinite number of methods to cover every possible situation. As a real-life example, when you make a restaurant reservation, you do not need to employ a different method for every date of the year at every possible time of day. Rather, you can supply the date and time as information to the person who carries out the method. The method, recording the reservation, is then carried out in the same manner, no matter what date and time are involved. In a program, if you design a method to square numeric values, it makes sense to design a `square()` method that you can supply with a parameter that represents the value to be squared, rather than having to develop a `square1()` method (that squares the value 1), a `square2()` method (that squares the value 2), and so on. To call a `square()` method that accepts a parameter, you might write a statement like `square(17)` or `square(86)` and let the method use whatever value you send. When you call a method with a value within its parentheses, the value is an argument to the method.

An important principle of object-oriented (OO) programming is the notion of **implementation hiding**, the encapsulation of method details within a class. With implementation hiding, you make a request to a method without knowing the details of how the method works. For example, when you make a real-life restaurant reservation, you do not need to know how the reservation is actually recorded at the restaurant—perhaps it is written in a book, marked on a large chalkboard, or entered into a computerized database. The implementation details don't concern you as a patron, and if the restaurant changes its methods from one year to the next, the change does not affect your use of the reservation method—you still call and provide your name, a date, and a time. With well-written OO methods, using implementation hiding means that a method that calls another must know the name of the called method, what type of information to send it, and what type of `return` data to expect, but the program does not need to know how the method works internally. The calling method needs to understand only the **interface to the method** that is called. In other words, the interface is the only part of a method that the **method's client** (or method's caller) sees or with which it interacts. Additionally, if you substitute a new, improved method implementation, as long as the interface to the method does not change, you won't need to make any changes in any methods that call the altered method.

When you write the method declaration for a method that can receive a parameter, you must include the following items within the method declaration's parentheses:

» The type of the parameter
» A local name for the parameter

For example, Figure 6-6 shows a `computeTax()` method added to the `PrintCustomerBill` application. The method accepts a numeric amount, computes the tax on it assuming a constant rate of 7%, and displays the result. The declaration for the method is

> **»NOTE**
> Programmers refer to hidden implementation details as existing in a **black box**. This means that you can examine what goes in and what comes out, but not the details of how it works inside.

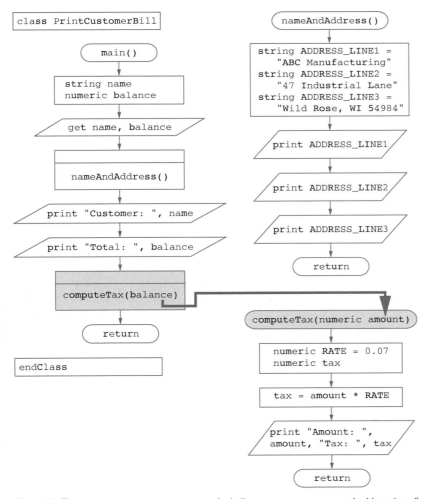

> **»NOTE**
> In Figure 6-6, the constant RATE and the variable tax are local to the computeTax() method.

Figure 6-6 The `PrintCustomerBill` program including a `computeTax()` method (*continued*)

```
class PrintCustomerBill
   main()
      string name
      numeric balance
      get name, balance
      nameAndAddress()
      print "Customer: ", name
      print "Total: ", balance
      computeTax(balance)
   return

   nameAndAddress()
      string ADDRESS_LINE1 = "ABC Manufacturing"
      string ADDRESS_LINE2 = "47 Industrial Lane"
      string ADDRESS_LINE3 = "Wild Rose, WI 54984"
      print ADDRESS_LINE1
      print ADDRESS_LINE2
      print ADDRESS_LINE3
   return

   computeTax(numeric amount)
      numeric RATE = 0.07
      numeric tax
      tax = amount * RATE
      print "Amount: ", amount, " Tax: ", tax
   return
endClass
```

Figure 6-6 The `PrintCustomerBill` program including a `computeTax()` method

> **NOTE**
> In Chapter 7, you will learn that a method's argument can also be a more complex type called a class type.

`computeTax(numeric amount)`. The method call from the `main()` method is `computeTax(balance)`. You can think of the parentheses in a method declaration as a funnel into the method—data arguments listed there are "dropped in" to the method. An argument passed into a method can be any data type, including numeric, character, or string.

In the program in Figure 6-6, the numeric variable `balance` is sent as an argument to the method. The parameter `numeric amount` within the parentheses in the method header indicates that the method will receive a value of type `numeric`, and that within the method, the passed value representing a balance will be known as `amount`.

The `computeTax()` method could be called from the `main()` method any number of times, if needed. It could be called using any numeric variable. For example, if you declare a numeric variable named `myMoney`, you can call `computeTax(myMoney)`. The method also could be called using a literal constant—for example, `computeTax(123.45)`. The only requirement is that each time the `computeTax()` method is called, it must be called using a numeric argument. Within the `computeTax()` method, each of these arguments, whether variable or constant, would become known as `amount`. The identifier `amount` represents a variable that holds any numeric value passed into the method.

It is interesting to note that if the value used as an argument in the method call to `computeTax()` is a variable, it might possess the same identifier as `amount`, or a different

one, such as `myMoney`. For example, the code in Figure 6-7 shows three calls to the
`computeTax()` method, and Figure 6-8 shows the output. One call uses an unnamed constant,
400.00. The other two use variables—one with the same name as `amount`, and the other with a
different name, `myMoney`. Within the `computeTax()` method, the identifier `amount` is simply
a temporary placeholder; it makes no difference what name it "goes by" in the calling method.

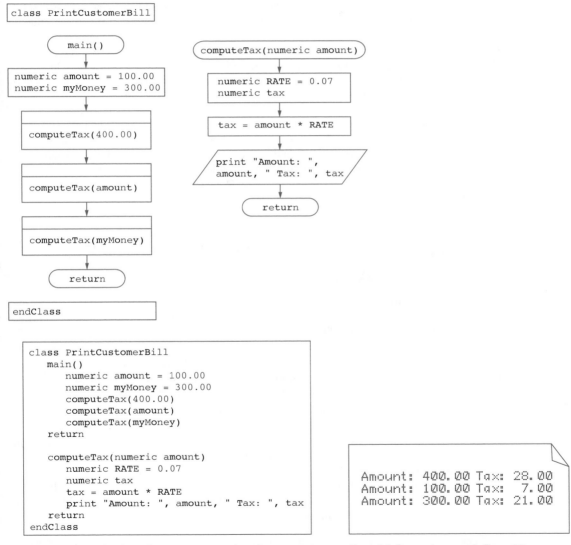

```
class PrintCustomerBill
    main()
        numeric amount = 100.00
        numeric myMoney = 300.00
        computeTax(400.00)
        computeTax(amount)
        computeTax(myMoney)
    return

    computeTax(numeric amount)
        numeric RATE = 0.07
        numeric tax
        tax = amount * RATE
        print "Amount: ", amount, " Tax: ", tax
    return
endClass
```

Figure 6-7 An application that calls `computeTax()` three times

```
Amount: 400.00 Tax: 28.00
Amount: 100.00 Tax:  7.00
Amount: 300.00 Tax: 21.00
```

Figure 6-8 Output of program in Figure 6-7

The variable `amount` is declared in the method header and is a local variable to the `computeTax()` method; in other words, it is known only within the boundaries of the method.

Within the `computeTax()` method in Figure 6-7, if you later decide to change the way in which the 7 percent tax is calculated, no method that uses the `computeTax()` method will ever know the difference. The calling method will pass a value into `computeTax()` and then a correct calculated result will be produced.

Each time the `computeTax()` method in Figure 6-7 executes, an `amount` variable is redeclared—that means a new memory location large enough to hold a numeric value is set up and named `amount`. Within the `computeTax()` method, `amount` holds whatever value is passed into the method by the `main()` method. When the `computeTax()` method ends at the `return` statement, the local `amount` variable ceases to exist. After the tax is calculated in the method, assigning a new value to `amount` would make no difference. For example, if you change the value of `amount` after you have used it in the calculation within `computeTax()`, it affects nothing else. A variable passed into a method is **passed by value**—a copy of its value is sent to the method and stored in a new memory location accessible to the method. The memory location that holds `amount` is released at the end of the method. If you change its value, it does not affect any variable in the calling method. In particular, do not think there would be any change in the variable named `amount` in the `main()` method; that variable, even though it has the same name, is a different variable with its own memory address and is totally distinct from the one in the `computeTax()` method. When a variable ceases to exist at the end of a method, programmers say the variable "goes out of scope."

CREATING METHODS THAT REQUIRE MULTIPLE ARGUMENTS

A method can require more than one argument. You indicate that a method requires multiple arguments by including a comma-separated list of data types and local identifiers within the method header's parentheses. When you call the method, you use a comma-separated list of arguments (but not data types). For example, rather than creating a `computeTax()` method that calculates a 7 percent tax on any value passed into it, you might prefer to create a method to which you can pass two values—the amount to be taxed, as well as a percentage figure by which to tax it. Figure 6-9 shows a method that uses two such arguments.

In Figure 6-9, two parameters (`numeric amount` and `numeric rate`) appear within the parentheses in the method header. Each parameter requires its own declared type (in this case, both are numeric) as well as its own identifier. When values are passed to the method in a statement such as `computeTax(balance, rate)`, the first value passed will be referenced as `amount` within the method, and the second value passed will be referenced as `rate`. Therefore, arguments passed to the method must be passed in the correct order. A call `computeTax(rate, balance)` instead of `computeTax(balance, rate)` would result in incorrect values being displayed in the `print` statement.

> **NOTE** When multiple parameters appear in a method header, they comprise a **parameter list**. If method arguments are the same type—for example, two numeric arguments—passing them to a method in the wrong order results in a logical error. The program will compile and execute, but produce incorrect results. If a method expects arguments of diverse types, then passing arguments in the wrong order constitutes a syntax error, and the program will not compile.

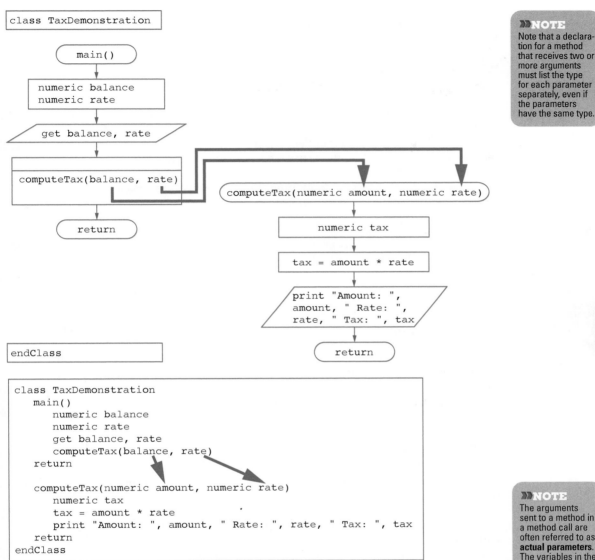

NOTE
Note that a declaration for a method that receives two or more arguments must list the type for each parameter separately, even if the parameters have the same type.

```
class TaxDemonstration
    main()
        numeric balance
        numeric rate
        get balance, rate
        computeTax(balance, rate)
    return

    computeTax(numeric amount, numeric rate)
        numeric tax
        tax = amount * rate
        print "Amount: ", amount, " Rate: ", rate, " Tax: ", tax
    return
endClass
```

Figure 6-9 A program that calls a `computeTax()` method that requires two parameters

NOTE
The arguments sent to a method in a method call are often referred to as **actual parameters**. The variables in the method declaration that accept the values from the actual parameters are the **formal parameters**.

NOTE
A method's name and parameter list constitute the method's **signature**.

You can write a method so that it takes any number of parameters in any order. However, when you call a method, the arguments you send to a method must match in order—both in number and in type—the arguments listed in the method declaration. Thus, a method to compute an automobile salesperson's commission amount might require arguments such as a string for the salesperson's name, a number for the value of a car sold, and a number for the commission rate. The method will execute correctly only when three arguments of the correct types are sent in the correct order.

CREATING METHODS THAT RETURN VALUES

When a variable is declared within a method, it ceases to exist when the method ends—it goes out of scope. When you want to retain a value that exists in a method, you can return the value from the method. That is, you can send the value back to the calling method. When a method returns a value, the method must have a return type. The **return type** for a method can be any type, which includes numeric, character, and string, as well as other more specific types that exist in the programming language you are using. Of course, a method can also return nothing, in which case the return type is usually indicated as void, and the method is a **void method**. (The term *void* means "nothing" or "empty.") A method's return type is known more succinctly as a **method's type**. A method's type is indicated in front of the method name when the method is defined.

>> **NOTE** Along with an identifier and parameter list, a return type is part of a method's declaration. Some programmers claim a method's return type is part of its signature, but this is not the case. Only the method name and parameter list constitute the signature.

For example, a method that returns the number of hours an employee has worked might be numeric getHoursWorked(). This method returns a numeric value, so its type is numeric.

When a method returns a value, you usually want to use it in the calling method (although using it is not required). For example, Figure 6-10 shows how a main() method might use the value returned by the getHoursWorked() method. In Figure 6-10, the main() method declares a variable named hours. When the main() method calls getHoursWorked(), the method call is part of an assignment statement. The logic transfers to the getHoursWorked() method, which contains a variable named workHours. A value is obtained for this variable, and is returned to the main() method. In the main() method, the value is assigned to hours. After the logic returns to main() from the getHoursWorked() method, the local variable workHours no longer exists. However, its value has been stored in main() where, as hours, it can be displayed and used in a calculation.

Notice the return type void that precedes the main() method name in Figure 6-10, and that the main() method return statement includes no return value. Also notice the return type numeric that precedes the method name in the getHoursWorked() method header in Figure 6-10. A numeric value is included in the return statement that is the last statement within the getHoursWorked() method. When you place a value in a return statement, the value is sent from the called method back to the calling method. A method's declared return type must match the type of the value used in the return statement; if it does not, the class will not compile.

You are not required to assign a method's return value to a variable in order to use the value. Instead, you can choose to use a method's returned value directly, without storing it. When you use a method's value, you use it the same way you would use any variable of the same type. For example, you can print a return value in a statement such as the following:

```
print "Hours worked is ", getHoursWorked()
```

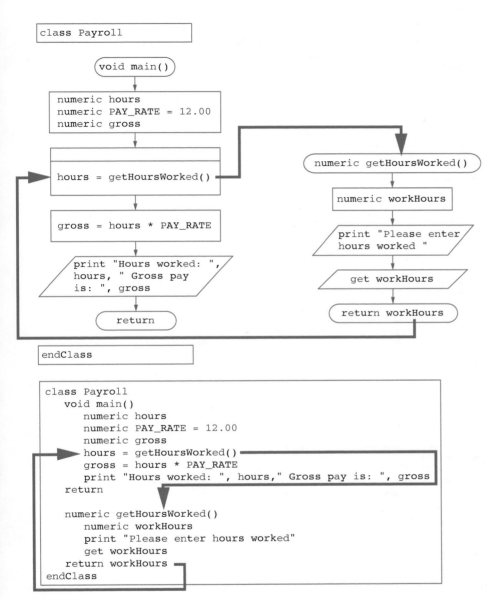

Figure 6-10 The `Payroll` class with a `main()` method that calls a method that returns a value

Because getHoursWorked() returns a numeric value, you can use the method call getHoursWorked() in the same way that you would use any simple numeric value. Figure 6-11 shows an example of a main() method that uses a method's returned value in an arithmetic statement directly without storing it.

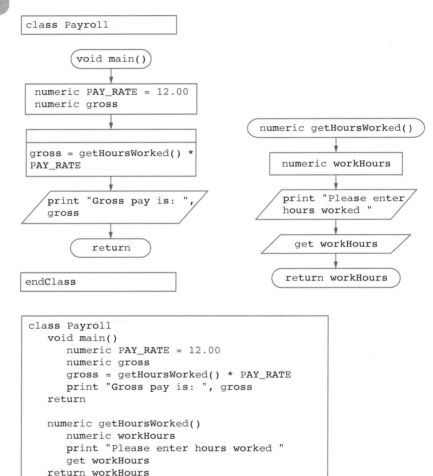

```
class Payroll
   void main()
      numeric PAY_RATE = 12.00
      numeric gross
      gross = getHoursWorked() * PAY_RATE
      print "Gross pay is: ", gross
   return

   numeric getHoursWorked()
      numeric workHours
      print "Please enter hours worked "
      get workHours
   return workHours
endClass
```

Figure 6-11 A program that uses a method's returned value without storing it

In most programming languages, you are allowed to include multiple `return` statements in a method. For example, consider the `findLargest()` method in Figure 6-12. The method accepts three arguments and returns the largest of the values. Although this method works correctly (and you might see this technique used in programs written by others), it is not the recommended way to write the method. In Chapter 2, you learned that structured logic requires each structure to contain one entry point and one exit point. The `return` statements in Figure 6-12 violate this convention by leaving the decision structure before it is complete.

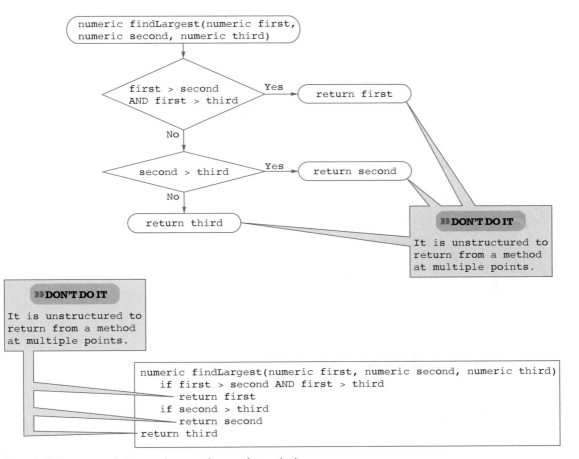

Figure 6-12 Unrecommended approach to returning one of several values

Figure 6-13 shows the superior and recommended way to handle the problem. In Figure 6-13, the largest value is stored in a variable. Then, when the decision structure is complete, the stored value is returned.

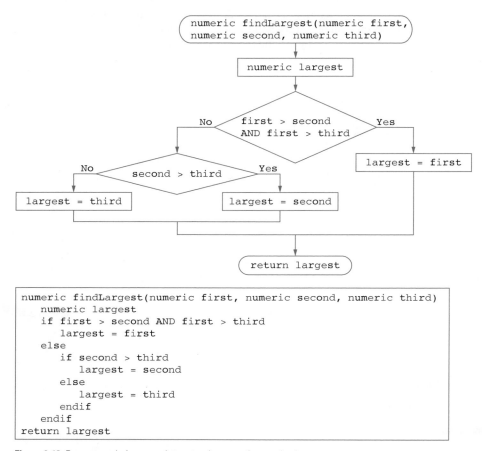

```
numeric findLargest(numeric first, numeric second, numeric third)
   numeric largest
   if first > second AND first > third
      largest = first
   else
      if second > third
         largest = second
      else
         largest = third
      endif
   endif
return largest
```

Figure 6-13 Recommended approach to returning one of several values

PASSING AN ARRAY TO A METHOD

In Chapter 5, you learned that you can declare an array to create a list of elements, and that you can use any individual array element in the same manner as you would use any single variable of the same type. Suppose you declare an numeric array as follows:

```
numeric someNums[12]
```

You can subsequently print someNums[0] or perform arithmetic with someNums[11] , just as you would for any simple variable that is not part of an array. Similarly, you can pass a single array element to a method in exactly the same manner as you would pass a variable or constant.

Consider the program shown in Figure 6-14. This program creates an array of four numeric values and then prints them. Next, the program calls a method named `tripleTheValue()` four times, passing each of the array elements in turn. The method prints the passed value,

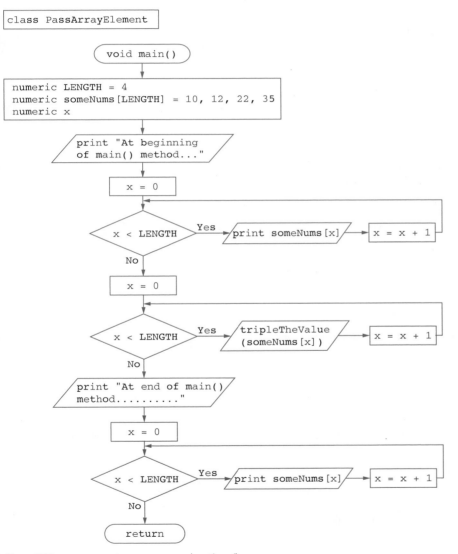

Figure 6-14 `PassArrayElement` program (*continued*)

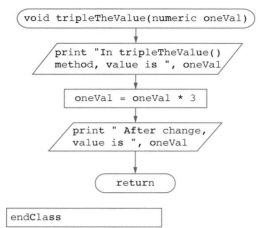

```
endClass
```

```
class PassArrayElement
    void main()
        numeric LENGTH = 4
        numeric someNums[LENGTH] = 10, 12, 22, 35
        numeric x
        print "At beginning of main() method..."
        x = 0
        while x < LENGTH
            print someNums[x]
            x = x + 1
        endwhile
        x = 0
        while x < LENGTH
            tripleTheValue(someNums[x])
            x = x + 1
        endwhile
        print "At end of main() method.........."
        x = 0
        while x < LENGTH
            print someNums[x]
            x = x + 1
        endwhile
    return

    void tripleTheValue(numeric oneVal)
        print "In tripleTheValue() method, value is ", oneVal
        oneVal = oneVal * 3
        print " After change, value is ", oneVal
    return
endClass
```

Figure 6-14 PassArrayElement program

multiplies it by 3, and prints it again. Finally, back in the main() method, the four numbers are printed again. Figure 6-15 shows an execution of this program in a command-line environment.

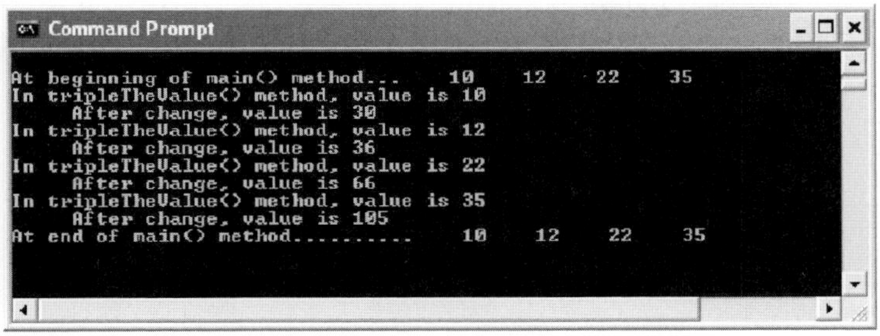

Figure 6-15 Output of PassArrayElement program

As you can see in Figure 6-15, the program displays the four original values, then passes each to the tripleTheValue() method, where it is displayed, multiplied by 3, and displayed again. After the method executes four times, the logic returns to the main() method, where the four values are displayed again, showing that they are unchanged by the new assignments within tripleTheValue(). The oneVal variable is local to the tripleTheValue() method; therefore, any changes to it are not permanent and are not reflected in the array declared in the main() program. Each oneVal variable in the tripleTheValue() method holds only a copy of the array element passed into the method, and the oneVal variable that holds each newly assigned, larger value exists only while the tripleTheValue() method is executing.

Instead of passing a single array element to a method, you can pass an entire array as an argument. You can indicate that a method parameter must be an array by placing square brackets after the data type in the method's parameter list. When you pass an array to a method, changes you make to array elements within the method are permanent; in other words, they are reflected in the original array that was sent to the method. Arrays, unlike simple built-in types, are **passed by reference**; the method receives the actual memory address of the array and has access to the actual values in the array elements.

» NOTE The name of an array represents a memory address, and the subscript used with an array name represents an offset from that address.

» NOTE Simple non-array variables are usually passed to methods by value. Many programming languages provide the means to pass variables by reference as well as by value. The syntax to accomplish this differs among the languages that allow it; you will learn this technique when you study a specific language.

The program shown in Figure 6-16 creates an array of four numeric values. After the numbers are printed, the entire array is passed to a method named `quadrupleTheValues()`. Within the method header, the parameter is declared as an array by using square brackets after the parameter type. Within the method, the numbers are printed, which shows that they retain their values from `main()` upon entering the method; then the array values are multiplied by 4. Even though `quadrupleTheValues()` returns nothing to the `main()` method, all of the values have been changed to their new quadrupled values when the program prints the array

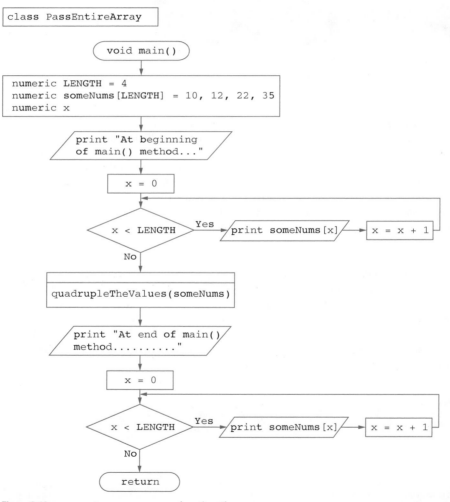

Figure 6-16 `PassEntireArray` program (*continued*)

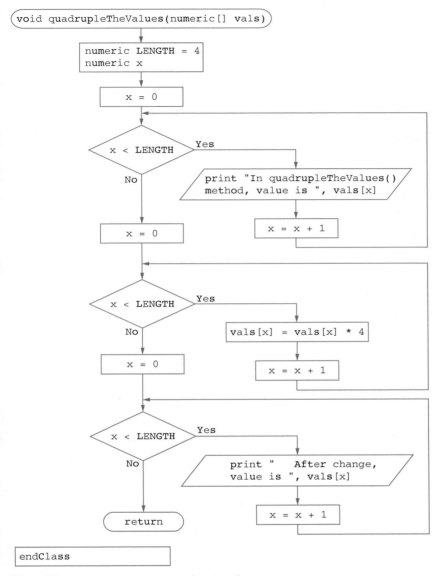

Figure 6-16 PassEntireArray program (*continued*)

▶

```
class PassEntireArray
   void main()
      numeric LENGTH = 4
      numeric someNums[LENGTH] = 10, 12, 22, 35
      numeric x
      print "At beginning of main() method..."
      x = 0
      while x < LENGTH
         print someNums[x]
         x = x + 1
      endwhile
      quadrupleTheValues(someNums)
      print "At end of main() method.........."
      x = 0
      while x < LENGTH
         print someNums[x]
         x = x + 1
      endwhile
   return

   void quadrupleTheValues(numeric[] vals)
      numeric LENGTH = 4
      numeric x
      x = 0
      while x < LENGTH
         print "In quadrupleTheValues() method, value is ", vals[x]
         x = x + 1
      endwhile
      x = 0
      while x < LENGTH
         vals[x] = vals[x] * 4
         x = x + 1
      endwhile
      x = 0
      while x < LENGTH
         print "  After change, value is ", vals[x]
         x = x + 1
      endwhile
   return
endClass
```

Figure 6-16 `PassEntireArray` program

for the second time within the `main()` method. Figure 6-17 shows an execution of the program. Because arrays are passed by reference, the `quadrupleTheValues()` method "knows" the address of the array declared in `main()` and makes its changes directly to the original array that was declared in the `main()` method.

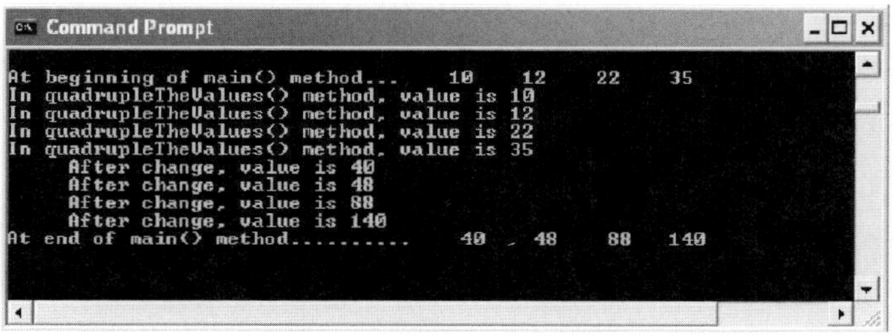

Figure 6-17 Output of the `PassEntireArray` program

OVERLOADING METHODS

In programming, **overloading** involves supplying diverse meanings for a single item. When you use the English language, you frequently overload words. When you say, "break a window," "break bread," "break the bank," and "take a break," you describe four very different actions that use different methods and produce different results. However, anyone who speaks English fluently has no trouble comprehending your meaning because "break" is understood in the context of the words that accompany it. In most programming languages, some operators are overloaded. For example, a + between two values indicates addition, but a single + to the left of a value means the value is positive. The + sign has different meanings based on the arguments used with it.

When you **overload a method**, you write multiple methods with a shared name but different parameter lists. The compiler understands your meaning based on the arguments you use when you call the method. For example, suppose you create a method to print a message and the amount due on a customer bill. The method receives a numeric parameter that represents the customer's balance and prints two lines of output. Figure 6-18 shows the method.

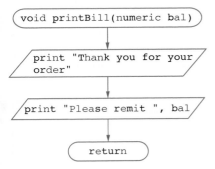

```
void printBill(numeric bal)
   print "Thank you for your order"
   print "Please remit ", bal
return
```

Figure 6-18 The `printBill()` method with a numeric parameter

Assume you need a method that is similar to `printBill()`, except the new method applies a discount to the customer bill. One solution to this problem would be to write a new method with a different name—for example, `printBillWithDiscount()`. A downside to this approach is that a programmer who uses your methods must remember the different names you gave to each slightly different version. It is more natural for your methods' clients to be able to use a single well-designed method name for the task of printing bills, but to be able to provide different arguments as appropriate. In this case, you can overload the `printBill()`

method so that, besides the version that takes a single numeric argument, you can create a version that takes two numeric arguments—one that represents the balance and the other that represents the discount rate. Figure 6-19 shows this version of the method.

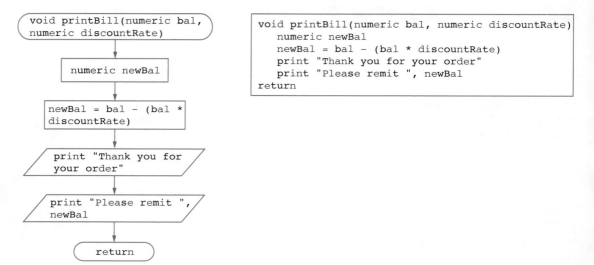

```
void printBill(numeric bal, numeric discountRate)
    numeric newBal
    newBal = bal - (bal * discountRate)
    print "Thank you for your order"
    print "Please remit ", newBal
return
```

Figure 6-19 The `printBill()` method with two numeric parameters

All object-oriented languages allow you to provide multiple methods with the same name in the same class or program; this feature was not allowed in older programming languages that were not object-oriented. If both versions of `printBill()` are included in a program and you call the method using a single numeric argument, as in `printBill(custBalance)`, then the first version of the method shown in Figure 6-18 executes. If you use two numeric arguments in the call, as in `printBill(custBalance, rate)`, then the method shown in Figure 6-19 executes.

If it suited your needs, you could provide more versions of the `printBill()` method, as shown in Figures 6-20 and 6-21. The version in Figure 6-20 accepts a numeric parameter that holds the

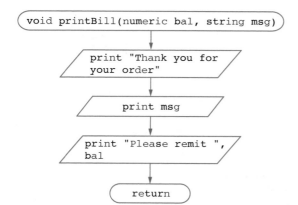

```
void printBill(numeric bal, string msg)
    print "Thank you for your order"
    print msg
    print "Please remit ", bal
return
```

Figure 6-20 The `printBill()` method with a numeric parameter and a string parameter

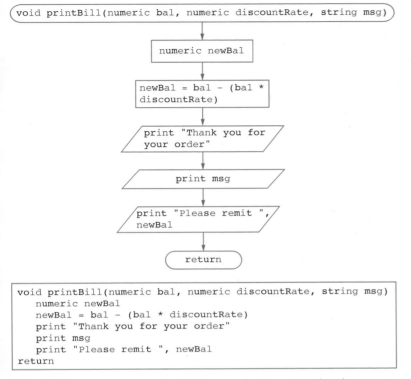

```
void printBill(numeric bal, numeric discountRate, string msg)
   numeric newBal
   newBal = bal - (bal * discountRate)
   print "Thank you for your order"
   print msg
   print "Please remit ", newBal
return
```

Figure 6-21 The printBill() method with two numeric parameters and a string parameter

customer's balance and a string parameter that holds an additional message. This message can be customized for the bill recipient and displayed on the bill. For example, if a program makes a method call such as the following, then the printBill() version in Figure 6-20 will execute:

```
printBill(custBal, "Due in 10 days")
```

In the version in Figure 6-21, printBill() accepts three parameters, providing a balance, discount rate, and customized message. For example, the following method call would use this version of the method:

```
printBill(balanceDue, discountRate, specialMessage)
```

Overloading methods is never required in a program. Instead, you could create multiple methods with unique identifiers such as printBill() and printBillWithDiscountAndMessage(). Overloading methods does not reduce the work you do when creating a class; you still need to write each method individually. The advantage is provided to your class clients; those that use your class need to remember just one appropriate method name for all related tasks.

»NOTE In many programming languages, the print statement is actually an overloaded method that you call. It is convenient that you use a single name, such as print, whether you want to print a number, a string, or any combination of the two.

»NOTE Even though you have written two or more overloaded versions of a method, many program clients will use just one version. For example, suppose you develop a bill-creating class that contains all four versions of the printBill() method just discussed, and then sell it to different companies. Any one organization that adopts your class might only want to use one or two versions of the method. You probably own many devices for which only some of the features are meaningful to you. For example, many people who own microwave ovens only use the Popcorn button or never use Defrost.

AVOIDING AMBIGUOUS METHODS

When you overload a method, you run the risk of creating **ambiguous** methods—a situation in which the compiler cannot determine which method to use. Every time you call a method, the compiler decides whether a suitable method exists; if so, the method executes, and if not, you receive an error message. For example, suppose you write two versions of a printBill() method, as in the program in Figure 6-22. One version of the method is intended to accept a customer balance and a discount rate, and the other is intended to accept a customer balance and a discount amount expressed in dollars.

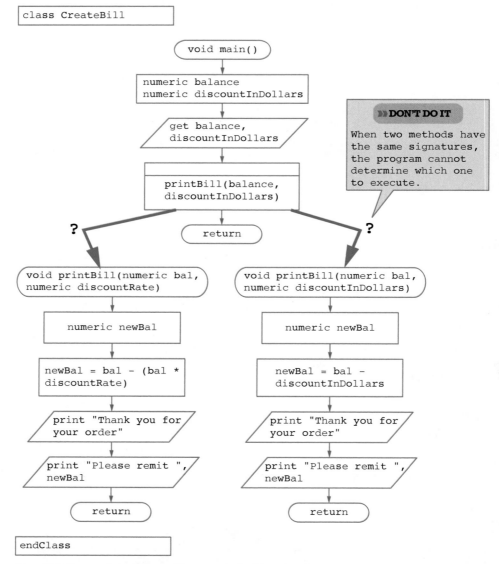

Figure 6-22 Program that contains ambiguous method call (*continued*)

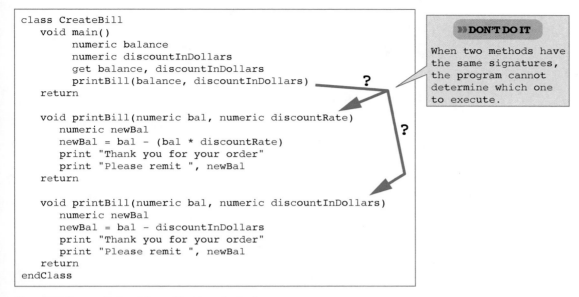

Figure 6-22 Program that contains ambiguous method call

Each of the two versions of printBill() in Figure 6-22 is a valid method on its own. However, when the two versions exist in the same class, a problem arises. When the main() method calls printBill() using two numeric arguments, the compiler cannot determine which version to call. Even though you may think the argument name discountInDollars in main() implies that the second version of the method that uses the same parameter name should be called, the compiler makes no such assumptions. The compiler determines which version of a method to call based on argument data types only, not their identifiers. Because both versions of the method accept two numeric parameters, an error occurs and program execution stops.

>> **NOTE** An overloaded method is not ambiguous on its own—it becomes ambiguous only if you create an ambiguous situation. A program with potentially ambiguous methods will run without problems if you make no ambiguous method calls. For example, if you remove one of the versions of the printBill() method from the program in Figure 6-22, or revise one of the methods to contain a different parameter list, no error occurs.

Methods can be overloaded correctly by providing different parameter lists for methods with the same name. Methods with identical names that have identical parameter lists but different return types are not overloaded—they are illegal. For example, the following two methods cannot coexist within a program.

```
string aMethod(numeric x)
numeric aMethod(numeric y)
```

The compiler determines which of several versions of a method to call based on parameter lists. When the method call aMethod(17) is made, the compiler will not know which of the two methods to execute because both possibilities take a numeric argument.

USING PREWRITTEN, BUILT-IN METHODS

All modern programming languages contain many methods that have already been written for you. Methods are built into a language to save you time and effort. For example, in most languages, printing a message on the screen involves using a built-in method. When you want to display "Hello" on the command prompt screen in C#, you write the following:

```
Console.WriteLine("Hello");
```

In Java, you write:

```
System.out.println("Hello");
```

» NOTE
In C# the convention is to begin method names with an uppercase letter, and in Java the convention is to begin them with a lowercase letter. The `WriteLine()` and `println()` methods follow their respective language's convention.

In these statements, you can recognize `WriteLine()` and `println()` as method names because they are followed by parentheses; the parentheses hold an argument that represents the message that is displayed. If these methods were not written for you, you would have to worry about the low-level details of how to manipulate pixels on a display screen to get the characters to print. Instead, by using the prewritten methods, you can concentrate on the higher-level task of displaying a useful and appropriate message.

» NOTE
In Chapter 7, you will learn more about the first parts of these method names that are separated using dots.

» NOTE The `WriteLine()` and `println()` methods are both overloaded methods. For example, if you pass a string to either method, the version of the method that can display it correctly is called. If you pass a number, another version that can display it correctly is called. Several versions of each method exist.

Most programming languages also contain a variety of mathematical methods, such as those that compute a square root or the absolute value of a number. Other methods perform tasks such as retrieving the current date and time from the operating system or selecting a random number for you to use in a game application. These methods were written as a convenience for you—computing a square root and generating random numbers are complicated tasks, so it is convenient to have methods already written, tested, and available to you when you need them. The names of the methods that perform these functions differ among programming languages, so you need to research the language's documentation before using them. For example, many of a language's methods are described in introductory programming language textbooks, and you can also find language documentation online.

When you want to use a prewritten, built-in method, you need to know only four things:

» What the method does in general—for example, compute a square root.

» The method's name—for example, it might be `sqrt()`.

» The method's required parameters—for example, a square root method might require a single numeric parameter. There might be multiple overloaded versions of the method from which you can choose.

» The method's return type—for example, a square root method most likely returns a numeric value that is the square root of the argument that was passed to the method.

What you do not need to know is how the method is implemented—that is, how the instruction statements are written within it. Built-in methods are usually black boxes to you. You can use built-in methods without worrying about their low-level implementation details.

CHAPTER SUMMARY

» A method is a program module that contains a series of statements that carry out a task. Any class can contain an unlimited number of methods, and each method can be called an unlimited number of times. Within a class, the simplest methods you can invoke don't require any data items (called arguments or parameters) to be sent to them, nor do they send any data back to you (called returning a value). When you create methods, the calling method is easier to follow. Additionally, methods are easily reusable. A method must include a declaration (or header or definition), a body, and a `return` statement that marks the end of the method.

» In every object-oriented programming language, the variables and constants declared in any method are usable only within that method. In other words, data items are local, visible, or in scope only within the method in which they are declared. Besides local variables and constants, you can create global variables and constants that are known to an entire class or declared at the class level. In general, this is not a recommended practice because it violates the programming principle of encapsulation, which states that a method's instructions and its data should be contained in the same method.

» Some methods require information to be passed to them. A calling method sends an argument to a called method. A called method accepts the value as its parameter. Passing arguments supports implementation hiding, which is the encapsulation of method details within a class. When you write the method declaration for a method that can receive a parameter, you must include the parameter type and a local identifier for the parameter within the method declaration's parentheses. A variable passed into a method is passed by value—a copy of its value is sent to the method and stored in a new memory location accessible to the method.

» You indicate that a method requires multiple arguments by listing their data types and local identifiers within the method header's parentheses. You can pass multiple arguments from a calling method to a called method by listing the arguments within the method call and separating them with commas. When you call a method, the arguments you send to a method must match in order—both in number and in type—the arguments listed in the method declaration. A method's name and parameter list constitute the method's signature.

» When a method returns a value, the method must have a return type. A method's return type is known more succinctly as a method's type and is indicated in front of the method name when the method is defined. When a method returns a value, you usually want to use it in the calling method (although using it is not required).

» You can pass a single array element to a method in exactly the same manner as you would pass a variable or constant. Additionally, you can pass an entire array as a method. You can indicate that a method parameter must be an array by placing square brackets after the data type in the method's parameter list. When you pass an array to a method, it is passed by reference; that is, the method receives the actual memory address of the array and has access to the actual values in the array elements.

» When you overload a method, you write multiple methods with a shared name but different parameter lists. The compiler understands your meaning based on the arguments you use when you call the method.

» When you overload a method, you run the risk of creating ambiguous methods—a situation in which the compiler cannot determine which method to use. Every time you call a method, the compiler decides whether a suitable method exists; if so, the method executes, and if not, you receive an error message. Methods can be overloaded correctly by providing different parameter lists for methods with the same name.

» All modern programming languages contain many methods that have already been written for you. Methods are built into a language to save you time and effort.

KEY TERMS

Arguments are the data items sent to methods.

Parameters are the data items received by methods.

Returning a value sends a data value from a called method back to the calling method.

A **method header** is the first line of a method. It is the entry point to a method, and it provides an identifier, parameter list, and frequently other information.

A **method declaration** describes a method. In some languages, it is the first line of the method; in others, it is a separate statement.

A **method body** holds the method's statements.

Implementing a method is the act of writing the statements that constitute its body.

A **method's implementation** is the set of statements within the method.

A **return statement** marks the end of the method; sometimes it includes a value to be returned.

Abstraction is the programming feature that allows you to use a method name to encapsulate a series of statements.

Data items are **visible**, or **in scope**, after they have been declared and within the method in which they are declared.

A **local** variable or constant is known only within the boundaries of a method.

Global variables and constants are known to an entire class.

Variables and constants declared at the **class level** are known to the entire class.

Encapsulation is the feature of methods that provides for their instructions and data to be contained in the method.

Portable program features are those that can more easily be reused in multiple programs.

When you **pass the data** from one method to another, you send arguments to method parameters.

Implementation hiding is a principle of OO programming that describes the encapsulation of method details within a class.

The **interface to a method** includes the method's return type, name, and arguments. It is the part that a client sees and uses.

A **method's client** is a program or other method that uses the method.

Programmers refer to hidden implementation details as existing in a **black box**.

A variable passed into a method is **passed by value**—a copy of its value is sent to the method and stored in a new memory location accessible to the method.

When multiple parameters appear in a method header, they comprise a **parameter list**.

The arguments in a method call are often referred to as **actual parameters**.

The variables in the method declaration that accept the values from the actual parameters are the **formal parameters**.

A method's name and argument list constitute the method's **signature**.

A method's **return type** is the data type for any value it returns.

A **void method** returns no value.

A method's return type is known more succinctly as a **method's type**.

When an item is **passed by reference** to a method, the method receives the actual memory address item. Arrays are passed by reference.

Overloading involves supplying diverse meanings for a single item.

Polymorphism is the ability of a method to act appropriately depending on the context.

When you **overload a method**, you write multiple methods with a shared name but different parameter lists.

If you create **ambiguous** methods, the compiler cannot determine which method to use.

REVIEW QUESTIONS

1. Which of the following is true?

    a. A class can contain, at most, two methods.

    b. A class can contain a method that calls two other methods.

    c. A method can contain two or more other methods.

    d. All of these are true.

2. Which of the following must every method have?

    a. a header   c. a return value

    b. a parameter list   d. all of these

3. Which of the following is most closely related to the concept of *local*?

    a. abstract   c. in scope

    b. object-oriented   d. class level

4. Although the terms *parameter* and *argument* are closely related, the difference between them is that *argument* refers to _____ .

    a. a passed constant

    b. a value in a method call

    c. a formal parameter

    d. a variable that is local to a method

5. The notion of _____ most closely describes the way a calling method is not aware of the statements within a called method.

    a. abstraction

    b. object-oriented

    c. implementation hiding

    d. encapsulation

6. A method's name and parameter list constitute its _____ .

    a. signature

    b. return type

    c. identifier

    d. class

7. Which of the following must be included in a method declaration for a method that receives a parameter?

    a. the name of the argument that will be used to call the method

    b. a local name for the parameter

    c. the return value for the method

    d. all of these

8. When you use a variable name in a method call, it _____ the same name as the variable in the method header.

    a. can have

    b. cannot have

    c. must have

    d. The answer depends on the programming language.

9. Assume you have written a method with the header `void myMethod(numeric a, string b)`. Which of the following is a correct method call?

    a. `myMethod(12)`

    b. `myMethod(12, "Hello")`

    c. `myMethod("Goodbye")`

    d. It is impossible to tell.

10. Assume you have written a method with the header `numeric myMethod(string name, character code)`. The method's type is _____ .

    a. `numeric`

    b. `string`

    c. `character`

    d. `void`

11. Assume you have written a method with the header `string myMethod(numeric score, character grade)`. Also assume you have declared a numeric variable named `test`. Which of the following is a correct method call?

   a. `myMethod()`

   b. `myMethod(test)`

   c. `myMethod(test, test)`

   d. `myMethod(test,'A')`

12. If a method returns a value, then when you call the method, you _____ the returned value.

   a. must use

   b. must not use

   c. usually will want to use

   d. usually will not want to use

13. A `void` method _____ .

   a. returns nothing

   b. accepts no arguments

   c. has an empty body

   d. all of the above

14. When a method receives a copy of the value stored in an argument used in the method call, it means the variable was _____ .

   a. unnamed

   b. passed by value

   c. passed by reference

   d. assigned its original value when it was declared

15. When an array is passed to a method, it is _____ .

   a. passed by reference

   b. passed by value

   c. unnamed in the method

   d. unalterable in the method

16. When you overload a method, you write multiple methods with the same _____ .

   a. name

   b. parameter list

   c. number of parameters

   d. return type

17. A class contains a method with the header `numeric calculateTaxes(numeric amount, string name)`. Which of the following methods can coexist in the same class with no possible ambiguity?

    a. `numeric calculateTaxes(string name, numeric amount)`

    b. `string calculateTaxes(numeric money, string taxpayer)`

    c. `numeric calculateTaxes(numeric annualPay, string taxpayerId)`

    d. All of these can coexist without ambiguity.

18. A class contains a method with the header `void printData(string name, string address)`. Which of the following methods can coexist in the same class with no possible ambiguity?

    a. `string printData(string name, numeric amount)`

    b. `void printData (string name)`

    c. `void printData ()`

    d. All of these can coexist without ambiguity.

19. Methods in the same class with identical names and identical parameter lists are _____ .

    a. overloaded

    b. overworked

    c. overwhelmed

    d. illegal

20. Methods in different classes with identical names and identical parameter lists are _____ .

    a. overloaded

    b. illegal

    c. both of these

    d. none of these

EXERCISES

1. Create the logic for a program that calculates and displays the amount of money you would have if you invested $1,000 at 5 percent interest for one year. Create a separate method to do the calculation and return the result to be displayed.

2. a. Create the logic for a program that prompts the user for the month, day, and year a bill is received. Calculate the day the bill is due to be paid as one month later than the bill is received. Print both dates by passing the month, day, and year in turn to a method that inserts slashes between the parts of the date—for example, 3/14/2009.

   b. Modify the date-displaying method so it displays each date using a word for the month—for example, March 14, 2009.

3. a. Create an application class named `Numbers` whose `main()` method holds two numeric variables. Prompt the user for values for the variables. Pass both variables to methods named `sum()` and `difference()`. Create the logic for the methods `sum()` and `difference()`; they compute the sum of and difference between the values of two arguments, respectively. Each method should perform the appropriate computation and display the results.

   b. Add a method named `product()` to the `Numbers` class. The `product()` method should compute the result when multiplying two numbers, but not display the answer. Instead, it should return the answer to the calling method, which displays the answer.

4. Create the logic for an application class named `Monogram`. Its `main()` method holds three character variables that hold your first, middle, and last initials, respectively. Create a method to which you pass the three initials and that displays the initials twice—once in the order first, middle, last, and a second time in traditional monogram style (first, last, middle).

5. Create the logic for an application that contains a `main()` method that continuously prompts the user for a number of dollars until the user enters 0. Pass the amount to a conversion method that displays the breakdown of the passed amount into the fewest bills; in other words, it calculates the number of 20s, 10s, 5s, and 1s needed.

6. Create the logic for an application that continuously prompts a user for a numeric value until the user enters 0. The application passes the value in turn to a method that squares the number and to a method that cubes the number. The `main()` method prints the results before reprompting the user. Create the two methods that respectively square and cube a number that is passed to them, returning the calculated value.

7. Create the logic for an application that calls a method that computes the final price for a sales transaction. The `main()` method contains variables that hold the price of an item, the salesperson's commission expressed as a percentage, and the customer discount expressed as a percentage. Create a `calculatePrice()` method that determines the final price and returns the value to the calling method. The `calculatePrice()` method requires three arguments: product price, salesperson commission rate, and customer discount rate. A product's final price is the original price plus the commission amount minus the discount amount; the customer discount is taken as a percentage of the total price after the salesperson commission has been added to the original price.

8. Create the logic for a program that prompts the user for two numeric values that represent the sides of a rectangle. Include two overloaded methods that compute a rectangle's area. One method takes two numeric parameters and calculates area by multiplying them. The other takes a single numeric parameter, which is squared to calculate area. Each method displays its calculated result. If the user enters two positive nonzero numbers, call the method version that accepts two parameters. If just one of the values that the user enters is positive and nonzero, call the version of the method that accepts one parameter. If the user enters two values that both are zero or negative, display an error message.

9. Create the logic for an application that computes weekly salary. Include two overloaded methods named `computeWeeklySalary()`. One version accepts an annual salary as a number and calculates weekly salary as 1/52 of the annual amount. The other accepts a number of hours worked per week and an hourly pay rate, and calculates weekly salary as a product of the two. Each returns the weekly salary to the calling method. Create a `main()` method that prompts the user for the type of calculation to perform, and based on the user's response, prompts for appropriate data, calls the correct method, and displays the result.

10. Create the logic for a program whose `main()` method prompts a user for three numbers and stores them in an array. Pass the array to a method that reverses the order of the numbers. In the `main()` method, display the numbers.

11. Create the logic for a program whose `main()` method contains an array of 10 numbers. Prompt the user for a value for each number. Pass the array to a method that calculates the arithmetic average of the numbers and returns the value to the calling program. Display each number and how far it is from the arithmetic average. Continue to prompt the user for additional sets of 10 numbers until the user indicates a desire to quit.

CASE PROJECT

In earlier chapters, you have been developing programs for Cost Is No Object—a car rental service that specializes in lending antique and luxury cars to clients on a short-term basis. Create a class whose `main()` method assigns cars and rental fees to customers for the current day. The program continuously prompts for input data until the user indicates the end of the data has been reached.

Input data includes the following:

» Customer name
» Code for desired car type—A for Antique Car or L for Luxury Car
» Number of days for the rental

In the `main()` method, create four parallel arrays. The first three contain car descriptions, daily rental fees, and the car-type code, as follows:

Description	Daily Fee	Code
1967 Ford Mustang	$ 65	A
1922 Ford Model T	$ 95	A
2008 Lincoln Continental	$135	L
2002 Lexus	$140	L
2007 BMW	$160	L
1910 Mercer Runabout	$165	A
2009 Mercedes Benz	$200	L
1930 Cadillac V-16	$205	A

The fourth array contains an indicator that specifies whether the car is already rented out or not. At the start of the program, none of the cars are rented.

After the user is prompted for the first customer's data, pass the customer's name, car type requested, and the four arrays of data to a method named `fulfillRequest()`. The method finds the first available car of the correct type, displays its description and rental fee, and changes the rental indicator to show the car is no longer available. If no cars are available of the type requested by the customer, display an appropriate message. The method returns the daily rental fee unless no cars of the correct type are available, in which case the method returns 0. The `main()` method displays the daily rental fee.

If a car of the correct type is available, the `main()` method should pass the daily rental fee, the number of days for the rental, and the car type requested to a method named `calculateContractAmount()`. The contract amount is the daily fee times the number of days plus tax. The tax is 6 percent of the rental price for an antique car and 8 percent of the price for a luxury car. The method returns the amount of the contract to the `main()` method, where it is displayed.

Before the user is prompted for data for any customer after the first one, first determine whether any cars are still available for rent. If no more cars are available, display an appropriate message and end the program.

UP FOR DISCUSSION

1. Name any device you use every day. Discuss how implementation hiding is demonstrated in the way this device works. Is it a benefit or a drawback to you that implementation hiding exists for this device?

2. One of the advantages to writing a program that is subdivided into methods is that such a structure allows different programmers to write separate methods, thus dividing the work. Would you prefer to write a large program by yourself, or to work on a team in which each programmer produces one or more modules? Why?

OBJECT-ORIENTED PROGRAMMING CONCEPTS—CLASSES AND OBJECTS

In this chapter, you will:

Understand some basic principles of object-oriented programming
Define classes and create class diagrams
Understand public and private access
Appreciate different ways to organize classes
Understand instance and static, class methods
Understand constructors
Understand how to overload class methods
Learn how to use objects
Understand destructors
Understand composition
Appreciate GUI objects and other advantages of OOP

AN OVERVIEW OF SOME PRINCIPLES OF OBJECT-ORIENTED PROGRAMMING

Much of your understanding of the world comes from your ability to categorize objects and events into classes. As a young child, you learned the concept of "animal" long before you knew the word. Your first encounter with an animal might have been with the family dog, a neighbor's cat, or a goat at a petting zoo. As you developed speech, you might have used the same term for all of these creatures, gleefully shouting "Doggie!" as your parents pointed out cows, horses, and sheep in picture books or along the roadside on drives in the country. As you grew more sophisticated, you learned to distinguish dogs from cows; still later, you learned to distinguish breeds. Your understanding of the class "animal" helps you see the similarities between dogs and cows, and your understanding of the class "dog" helps you see the similarities between a Great Dane and a Chihuahua. Understanding classes gives you a framework for categorizing new experiences. You might not know the term "okapi," but when you learn it's an animal, you begin to develop a concept of what an okapi might be like.

Classes are also the basic building blocks of object-oriented programming. You already understand that applications exist in classes that have a `main()` method, and possibly other methods. When you write object-oriented programs, you also can create classes from which you instantiate objects. While these classes can contain a `main()` method, it is not required.

When you think in an object-oriented manner, everything is an object, and every object is a member of a class. You can think of any inanimate physical item as an object—your desk, your computer, and your house are all called "objects" in everyday conversation. You can think of living things as objects, too—your houseplant, your pet fish, and your sister are objects. Events also are objects—the stock purchase you made, the mortgage closing you attended, and your graduation party are all objects.

> **»NOTE**
> Object-oriented programmers also use the term *is-a* when describing inheritance. You will learn about inheritance in Chapter 9.

Everything is an object, and every object is a member of a more general class. Your desk is a member of the class that includes all desks, and your pet fish is a member of the class that contains all fish. An object-oriented programmer would say that the desk in your office is an **instance**, or one tangible example, of the `Desk` class and your fish is an instance of the `Fish` class. These statements represent **is-a relationships** because you can say, "My oak desk with the scratch on top *is a* `Desk` and my goldfish named Moby *is a* `Fish`." The difference between a class and an object parallels the difference between abstract and concrete. Your goldfish, my guppy, and the zoo's shark each constitute one instance of the `Fish` class.

> **»NOTE**
> Object-oriented programmers sometimes say an object is one **instantiation** of a class; this is just another form of *instance*.

The concept of a class is useful because of its reusability. Objects receive their attributes from classes. For example, if you invite me to a graduation party, I automatically know many things about the object (the party). I assume there will be a starting time, a number of guests, some quantity of food, and some nature of gifts. I understand parties because of my previous knowledge of the `Party` class, of which all parties are members. I don't know the number of guests or the date or time of this particular party, but I understand that because all parties have a date and time, then this one must as well. Similarly, even though every stock purchase is unique, each must have a dollar amount and a number of shares. All objects have predictable attributes because they are members of certain classes.

The data components of a class that belong to every instantiated object are the class's **instance variables**. Also, object attributes are often called **fields** to help distinguish them from other variables you might use. The set of all the values or contents of a class object's instance variables is also known as its **state**. For example, the current state of a particular party is 8 p.m. and Friday; the state of a particular stock purchase is $10 and five shares.

In addition to their attributes, class objects have methods associated with them, and every object that is an instance of a class possesses the same methods. For example, at some point you might want to issue invitations for a party. You might name the method `issueInvitations()`, and it might display some text as well as the values of the party's date and time fields. Your graduation party, then, might possess the identifier `myGraduationParty`. As a member of the `Party` class, it might have data members for the date and time, like all parties, and it might have a method to issue invitations. When you use the method, you might want to be able to send an argument to `issueInvitations()` that indicates how many copies to print. When you think of an object and its methods, it is as though you can send a message to the object to direct it to accomplish some task—you can tell the party object named `myGraduationParty` to print the number of invitations you request. Even though `yourAnniversaryParty` is also a member of the `Party` class, and even though it also has an `issueInvitations()` method, you will send a different argument value to `yourAnniversaryParty`'s `issueInvitations()` method than I send to `myGraduationParty`'s corresponding method. Within any object-oriented program, you continuously make requests to objects' methods, often including arguments as part of those requests.

》NOTE
In grammar, a noun is equivalent to an object and the values of a class's attributes are adjectives—they describe the characteristics of the objects. An object can also have methods, which are equivalent to verbs.

When you program in object-oriented languages, you frequently create classes from which objects will be instantiated. You also write applications to use the objects, along with their data and methods. Often, you will write programs that use classes created by others; other times, you might create a class that other programmers will use to instantiate objects within their own programs. A program or class that instantiates objects of another prewritten class is a **class client** or **class user**. For example, your organization might already have written a class named `Customer` that contains attributes such as `name`, `address`, and `phoneNumber`, and you might create clients that include arrays of thousands of `Customer`s. Similarly, in a graphical user interface (GUI) operating environment, you might write applications that include prewritten components that are members of classes with names like `Window` and `Button`. You expect each component on a GUI screen to have specific, consistent attributes, such as a button being clickable or a window being closeable, because each component gains these attributes as a member of its general class.

Besides classes and objects, three important features of object-oriented languages are:

» Polymorphism
» Inheritance
» Encapsulation

POLYMORPHISM

The real world is full of objects. Consider a door. A door needs to be opened and closed. You open a door with an easy-to-use interface known as a doorknob. Object-oriented programmers would say you are "passing a message" to the door when you "tell" it to open by turning its knob. The same message (turning a knob) has a different result when applied to your radio than when applied to a door. The procedure you use to open something—call it the "open" procedure—works differently on a door to a room than it does on a desk drawer, a bank account, a computer file, or your eyes. However, even though these procedures operate differently using the different objects, you can call all of these procedures "open." In object-oriented programming, procedures are called methods.

With object-oriented programming, you focus on the objects that will be manipulated by the program—for example, a customer invoice, a loan application, or a menu from which the user will select an option. You define the characteristics of those objects and the methods each of the objects will use; you also define the information that must be passed to those methods.

You can create multiple methods with the same name, which will act differently and appropriately when used with different types of objects. In Chapter 6, you learned that this concept is *polymorphism* and you learned to overload methods. For example, you might use a method named `print()` to print a customer invoice, loan application, or envelope. Because you use the same method name, `print()`, to describe the different actions needed to print these diverse objects, you can write statements in object-oriented programming languages that are more like English; you can use the same method name to describe the same type of action, no matter what type of object is being acted upon. Using the method name `print()` is easier than remembering `printInvoice()`, `printLoanApplication()`, and so on. In English, you understand the difference between "running a race," "running a business," and "running a computer program." Object-oriented languages understand verbs in context, just as people do.

As another example of the advantages to using one name for a variety of objects, consider a screen you might design for a user to enter data into an application you are writing. Suppose the screen contains a variety of objects—some forms, buttons, scroll bars, dialog boxes, and so on. Suppose also that you decide to make all the objects blue. Instead of having to memorize the names that these objects use to change color—perhaps `changeFormColor()`, `changeButtonColor()`, and so on—your job would be easier if the creators of all those objects had developed a `setColor()` method that works appropriately with each type of object.

INHERITANCE

Another important concept in object-oriented programming is **inheritance**, which is the process of acquiring the traits of one's predecessors. In the real world, a new door with a stained glass window inherits most of its traits from a standard door. It has the same purpose, it opens and closes in the same way, and it has the same knob and hinges. The door with the stained glass window simply has one additional trait—its window. Even if you have never seen a door with a stained glass window, when you encounter one you know what it is and how to use it because you understand the characteristics of all doors. With object-oriented programming, once you create an object, you can develop new objects that possess all the traits of the original object plus any new traits you desire. If you develop a `CustomerBill` class of objects, there is no need to develop an `OverdueCustomerBill` class from scratch. You can create the new class to contain all the characteristics of the already developed one, and simply add necessary new characteristics. This not only reduces the work involved in creating new objects, it makes them easier to understand because they possess most of the characteristics of already developed objects.

ENCAPSULATION

» NOTE
Information hiding is also called **data hiding**.

Real-world objects often employ encapsulation and information hiding. In Chapter 6, you learned that encapsulation is the process of combining all of an object's attributes and methods into a single package. **Information hiding** is the concept that other classes should not alter an object's attributes—only the methods of an object's own class should have that privilege. Outside classes should only be allowed to make a request that an attribute be altered; then it is up to the class's methods to determine whether the request is appropriate. When using a door, you are usually unconcerned with the latch or hinge construction features, and you do not have access to the interior workings of the knob or know what color of paint might have been used on the inside of the door panel. You only care about the functionality and the interface, the user-friendly boundary between the user and internal mechanisms of the device. Similarly, the detailed workings of objects you create within object-oriented programs can be hidden from outside programs and modules if you want them to be. When the details are hidden, programmers can focus on the functionality and the interface, as people do with real-life objects.

In summary, understanding object-oriented programming means that you must consider five of its integral components: classes, objects, polymorphism, inheritance, and encapsulation. The rest of this chapter concentrates on classes and objects and how their data and methods are encapsulated. You will learn more about inheritance and polymorphism in Chapter 9.

DEFINING CLASSES AND CREATING CLASS DIAGRAMS

A class is a category of things; an object is a specific instance of a class. A **class definition** is a set of program statements that tell you the characteristics of the class's objects and the methods that can be applied to its objects.

A class definition can contain three parts:

» Every class has a name.
» Most classes contain data, although this is not required.
» Most classes contain methods, although this is not required.

For example, you can create a class named `Employee`. Each `Employee` object will represent one employee who works for an organization. Data members, or attributes of the `Employee` class, include fields such as `lastName`, `hourlyWage`, and `weeklyPay`.

The methods of a class include all actions you want to perform with the class. Appropriate methods for an `Employee` class might include `setHourlyWage()`, `getHourlyWage()`, and `calculateWeeklyPay()`. The job of `setHourlyWage()` is to provide values for an `Employee`'s wage data field, the purpose of `getHourlyWage()` is to retrieve the wage value, and the purpose of `calculateWeeklyPay()` is to multiply the `Employee`'s `hourlyWage` by the number of hours in a workweek to calculate a weekly salary. With object-oriented languages, you think of the class name, data, and methods as a single encapsulated unit.

Declaring a class does not create any actual objects. A class is just an abstract description of what an object will be like if any objects are ever actually instantiated. Just as you might understand all the characteristics of an item you intend to manufacture long before the first item rolls off the assembly line, you can create a class with fields and methods long before you instantiate any objects that are members of that class. After an object has been instantiated, its methods can be accessed using the object's identifier, a dot, and a method call. When you

»NOTE
The application classes you have read about and created in the first six chapters of this book have contained methods, but not their own data. The *methods* contained data, but the classes did not contain data at the class level.

declare a simple variable that is a built-in data type, you write a statement such as one of the following:

```
numeric money
string name
```

When you write a program that declares an object that is a class data type, you write a statement such as the following:

```
Employee myAssistant
```

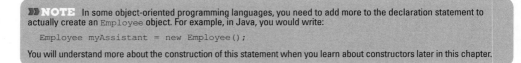

> **NOTE** In some object-oriented programming languages, you need to add more to the declaration statement to actually create an `Employee` object. For example, in Java, you would write:
>
> ```
> Employee myAssistant = new Employee();
> ```
>
> You will understand more about the construction of this statement when you learn about constructors later in this chapter.

When you declare the `myAssistant` object, the object contains all the data fields and has access to all the methods contained within the class. In other words, a larger section of memory is set aside than when you declare a simple variable, because an `Employee` contains several fields. You can use any of an `Employee`'s methods with the `myAssistant` object. The usual syntax is to provide an object name, a dot (period), and a method name. For example, you can write a program that contains statements such as the ones shown in the pseudocode in Figure 7-1.

```
class EmployeeDemo
    main()
        Employee myAssistant
        myAssistant.setLastName("Reynolds")
        myAssistant.setHourlyWage(16.75)
        print "My assistant makes ",
            myAssistant.getHourlyWage(), " per hour"
    return
endClass
```

Figure 7-1 The `EmployeeDemo` application

> **NOTE** Besides referring to `Employee` as a class, many programmers would refer to it as a **user-defined type**; a more accurate term is **programmer-defined type**. Object-oriented programmers typically refer to a class like `Employee` as an **abstract data type** (ADT); this term implies that the type's data can be accessed only through methods.

When you write a statement such as `myAssistant.setHourlyWage(16.75)`, you are making a call to a method that is contained within the `Employee` class. Because `myAssistant` is an `Employee` object, it is allowed to use the `setHourlyWage()` method that is part of its class.

> **NOTE** Some programmers write only client programs, never creating nonclient classes themselves, but using only classes that others have created.

When you write the `EmployeeDemo` application in Figure 7-1, you do not need to know what statements are written within the `Employee` class methods, although you could make an educated guess based on the methods' names. Before you could execute the application in Figure 7-1, someone would have to write appropriate statements within the `Employee` class methods. If you wrote the methods, of course you would know their contents, but if another programmer has already written the methods, then you could use the application without knowing the details contained in the methods. In Chapter 6, you learned that the ability to use methods without knowing the details of their contents (as a "black box") is a feature of encapsulation. The real world is full of many black box devices. For example, you can use your television and microwave oven without knowing how they work internally—all you need to understand is the interface. Similarly, with well-written methods that belong to classes you use, you need not understand how they work internally to be able to use them; you need only understand what the ultimate result will be when you use them.

In the client program segment in Figure 7-1, the focus is on the object—the `Employee` named `myAssistant`—and the methods you can use with that object. This is the essence of object-oriented programming.

>> **NOTE** Of course, the program segment in Figure 7-1 is very short. In a more useful real-life program, you might read employee data from a data file before assigning it to the object's fields, each `Employee` might contain dozens of fields, and your application might create hundreds or thousands of objects.

>> **NOTE** In older object-oriented programming languages, simple numbers and characters are said to be **primitive data types**; this distinguishes them from objects that are class types. In the newest programming languages, every item you name, even one that is a numeric or string type, really is an object that is a member of a class that contains both data and methods.

>> **NOTE** When you instantiate objects, the data fields of each are stored at separate memory locations. However, all members of the same class share one copy of the class's methods. You will learn more about this concept later in this chapter.

CREATING CLASS DIAGRAMS

Programmers often use a class diagram to illustrate class features or to help to plan them. A **class diagram** consists of a rectangle divided into three sections, as shown in Figure 7-2. The top section contains the name of the class, the middle section contains the names and data types of the attributes, and the bottom section contains the methods. This generic class diagram shows two attributes and three methods, but a given class might have any number of either, including none. Figure 7-3 shows the class diagram for the `Employee` class.

>> **NOTE** Class diagrams are a type of Unified Modeling Language (UML) diagram. Chapter 11 covers the UML.

Employee
lastName: string hourlyWage: numeric weeklyPay: numeric
setLastName(name : string) : void setHourlyWage(wage : numeric) : void getLastName() : string getHourlyWage() : numeric getWeeklyPay() : numeric calculateWeeklyPay() : void

>> **DON'T DO IT**

This class diagram does not contain access specifiers. You will learn how to add them later in this chapter.

Class name
Attribute 1:data type Attribute 2:data type
Method 1 Method 2 Method 3

Figure 7-2 Generic class diagram

Figure 7-3 `Employee` class diagram

Figures 7-2 and 7-3 both show that a class diagram is intended to be only an overview of class attributes and methods. A class diagram shows *what* data items and methods the class will use, not the details of the methods nor *when* they will be used. It is a design tool that helps you see the big picture in terms of class requirements. Figure 7-3 shows the `Employee` class containing three data fields that represent an employee's name, hourly pay rate, and weekly pay amount. Every `Employee` object created in any program that uses this class will contain these three data fields. In other words, when you declare an `Employee` object, you declare three fields with one statement and reserve enough memory to hold all three fields.

Figure 7-3 also shows that the `Employee` class contains six methods. For example, the first method is defined as follows:

```
setLastName(name : string) : void
```

This notation means that the method name is `setLastName()`, that it takes a single `string` parameter named `name`, and that it returns nothing.

The `Employee` class diagram shows that two of the six methods take parameters (`setLastName()` and `setHourlyWage()`). The diagram also shows the return type for each method—three void methods, two numeric methods, and one string method. The class diagram does not tell you what takes place inside the method (although you might be able to make an educated guess). Later, when you write the code that actually creates the `Employee` class, you include method implementation details. For example, Figure 7-4 shows some pseudocode you can use to show the details for the methods contained within the `Employee` class.

In Figure 7-4, the `Employee` class attributes or fields are identified with a data type and a field name. In addition to listing the data fields required, Figure 7-4 shows the complete methods for the `Employee` class. The purposes of the methods can be divided into three categories:

» Two of the methods accept values from the outside world; these methods, by convention, start with the prefix *set*. These methods are used to set the data fields in the class.

```
class Employee
   string lastName
   numeric hourlyWage
   numeric weeklyPay

   void setLastName(string name)
      lastName = name
   return

   void setHourlyWage(numeric wage)
      hourlyWage = wage
      calculateWeeklyPay()
   return

   string getLastName()
   return lastName

   numeric getHourlyWage()
   return hourlyWage

   numeric getWeeklyPay()
   return weeklyPay

   void calculateWeeklyPay()
      numeric WORK_WEEK_HOURS = 40
      weeklyPay = hourlyWage * WORK_WEEK_HOURS
   return
endClass
```

Figure 7-4 Pseudocode for Employee class described in the class diagram in Figure 7-3

» Three of the methods send data to the outside world; these methods, by convention, start with the prefix *get*. These methods return field values to a client program.

» One method performs work within the class; this method is named calculateWeeklyPay(). This method does not communicate with the outside; its purpose is to multiply hourlyWage by the number of hours in a week.

THE SET METHODS

In Figure 7-4, two of the methods begin with the word *set*; they are setLastName() and setHourlyWage(). They are known as **set methods** because their purpose is to set the values of data fields within the class. Each accepts data from the outside and assigns it to a field within the class. There is no requirement that such methods start with the prefix *set*; the prefix is merely conventional and makes the intention of the methods clear. The method setLastName() is implemented as follows:

```
void setLastName(string name)
   lastName = name
return
```

In this method, a string `name` is passed in as a parameter and assigned to the field `lastName`. Because `lastName` is contained in the same class as this method, the method has access to the field and can alter it.

Similarly, the method `setHourlyWage()` accepts a numeric parameter and assigns it to the class field `hourlyWage`. This method also calls the `calculateWeeklyPay()` method, which sets `weeklyPay` based on `hourlyWage`. By writing the `setHourlyWage()` method to call the `calculateWeeklyPay()` method automatically, you guarantee that the `weeklyPay` field is updated any time `hourlyWage` changes.

»NOTE
Methods that set values are called **mutator methods**.

When you create an `Employee` object with a statement such as `Employee mySecretary`, then you can use statements such as the following:

```
mySecretary.setLastName("Johnson")
mySecretary.setHourlyWage(15.00)
```

Similarly, you could pass variables or named constants to the methods as long as they were the correct data type. For example, if you write a program in which you make the following declarations, then the assignment in the next statement is valid.

```
numeric PAY_RATE_TO_START = 8.00
mySecretary.setHourlyWage(PAY_RATE_TO_START)
```

»NOTE In some languages—for example, Visual Basic and C#—you can create a **property** instead of creating a set method. Using a property provides a way to set a field value using a simpler syntax. By convention, if a class field is `hourlyWage`, its property would be `HourlyWage`, and in a program you could make a statement similar to `mySecretary.HourlyWage = PAY_RATE_TO_START`. The implementation of the property `HourlyWage` (with an uppercase initial letter) would be written in a format very similar to that of the `setHourlyWage()` method.

Just like any other methods, the methods that manipulate fields within a class can contain any statements you need. For example, a more complicated `setHourlyWage()` method might be written as in Figure 7-5. In this version, the wage passed to the method is tested against minimum and maximum values, and is assigned to the class field `hourlyWage` only if it falls within the prescribed limits. If the wage is too low, the `MINWAGE` value is substituted, and if the wage is too high, the `MAXWAGE` value is substituted.

```
void setHourlyWage(numeric wage)
   numeric MINWAGE = 6.00
   numeric MAXWAGE = 70.00
   if wage < MINWAGE then
      hourlyWage = MINWAGE
   else
      if wage > MAXWAGE then
         hourlyWage = MAXWAGE
      else
         hourlyWage = wage
      endif
   endif
   calculateWeeklyPay()
return
```

Figure 7-5 More complex `setHourlyWage()` method

Similarly, if the set methods in a class required them, the methods could contain print statements, loops, array declarations, or any other legal programming statements. However, if the main purpose of a method is not to set a field value, then the method should not be named with the set prefix.

THE GET METHODS

In the `Employee` class in Figure 7-4, three of the methods begin with the prefix *get*: `getLastName()`, `getHourlyWage()`, and `getWeeklyPay()`. The purpose of a **get method** is to return a value to the world outside the class. The methods are implemented as follows:

```
string getLastName()
return lastName

numeric getHourlyWage()
return hourlyWage

numeric getWeeklyPay()
return weeklyPay
```

Each of these methods simply returns the value in the field implied by the method name. Like set methods, any of these get methods could also contain more complicated statements as needed. For example, in a more complicated class, you might want to return the hourly wage of an employee only if the user had also passed an appropriate access code to the method, or you might want to return the weekly pay value as a string with a dollar sign attached instead of as a numeric value.

> **》NOTE**
> Methods that get values from class fields are known as **accessor methods**.

When you declare an `Employee` object such as `Employee mySecretary`, you can then make statements in a program similar to the following:

```
string employeeName
employeeName = mySecretary.getLastName()
print "Wage is ", mySecretary.getHourlyWage()
print "Pay for half a week is ", mySecretary.getWeeklyPay() * 0.5
```

In other words, the value returned from a get method can be used as any other variable of its type would be used. You can assign the value to another variable, print it, perform arithmetic with it, or make any other statement that works correctly with the returned data type.

> **》NOTE** In some languages—for example, Visual Basic and C#—instead of creating a get method, you can add statements to the property to return a value using simpler syntax. For example, if you create an `HourlyWage` property, you could write a program that makes the statement print `mySecretary.HourlyWage`.

OTHER METHODS

The `Employee` class in Figure 7-4 contains one method that is neither a get nor a set method. This method, `calculateWeeklyPay()`, is a **work method** within the class. It contains a locally named constant that represents the hours in a standard workweek and it computes the `weeklyPay` field value by multiplying `hourlyWage` by the named constant. The method is written as follows:

> **》NOTE**
> Some programmers call work methods **help methods** or **facilitators**.

```
void calculateWeeklyPay()
    numeric WORK_WEEK_HOURS = 40
    weeklyPay = hourlyWage * WORK_WEEK_HOURS
return
```

No values need to be passed into this method, and no value is returned from it because this method does not communicate with the outside world. Instead, this method is called only from within another method in the same class (the `setHourlyWage()` method), and that method is called from the outside world. Any time a program uses the `setHourlyWage()` method to alter an `Employee`'s `hourlyWage` field, then `calculateWeeklyPay()` is called to recalculate the `weeklyPay` field.

> **» NOTE** No `setWeeklyPay()` method is included in this `Employee` class because the intention is that `weeklyPay` is set only each time the `setHourlyWage()` method is used. If you wanted programs to be able to set the `weeklyPay` field directly, you would have to write a method to allow it.

> **» NOTE** Programmers who are new to class creation often want to pass the `hourlyWage` value into the `setWeeklyPay()` method so it can use the value in its calculation. Although this technique would work, it is not required. The `setWeeklyPay()` method has direct access to the `hourlyWage` field by virtue of being a member of the same class.

For example, Figure 7-6 shows a program that declares an `Employee` object and sets the hourly wage value. The program prints the `weeklyPay` value. Then a new value is assigned to `hourlyWage` and `weeklyPay` is printed again. As you can see from the output in Figure 7-7, the `weeklyPay` value has been recalculated even though it was never set directly by the client program.

```
class EmployeeDemo2
    main()
        numeric LOW = 9.00
        numeric HIGH = 14.65
        Employee myGardener
        myGardener.setLastName("Greene")
        myGardener.setHourlyWage(LOW)
        print "My gardener makes ",
            myGardener.getWeeklyPay(), " per week"
        myGardener.setHourlyWage(HIGH)
        print "My gardener makes ",
            myGardener.getWeeklyPay(), " per week"
    return
endClass
```

Figure 7-6 Program that sets and displays `Employee` data two times

Figure 7-7 Execution of program in Figure 7-6

UNDERSTANDING PUBLIC AND PRIVATE ACCESS

When you buy a product with a warranty, one of the conditions of the warranty is usually that the manufacturer must perform all repair work. For example, if your computer has a warranty and something goes wrong with its operation, you cannot open the system unit yourself, remove and replace parts, and then expect to get your money back for a device that does not work properly. Instead, when something goes wrong with your computer, you must take the device to the manufacturer. The manufacturer guarantees that your machine will work properly only if the manufacturer can control how the internal mechanisms of the machine are modified.

Similarly, in object-oriented design, usually you do not want any outside programs or methods to alter your class's data fields unless you have control over the process. For example, you might design a class that performs a complicated statistical analysis on some data and stores the result. You would not want others to be able to alter your carefully crafted result. As another example, you might design a class from which others can create an innovative and useful GUI screen object. In this case you would not want others altering the dimensions of your artistic design. To prevent outsiders from changing your data fields in ways you do not endorse, you force other programs and methods to use a method that is part of the class, such as `setLastName()` and `setHourlyWage()`, to alter data. (Earlier in this chapter, you learned that the principle of keeping data private and inaccessible to outside classes is called information hiding or data hiding.) Object-oriented programmers usually specify that their data fields will have **private access**—that is, the data cannot be accessed by any method that is not part of the class. The methods themselves, like `setHourlyWage()`, support **public access**—which means that other programs and methods may use the methods that control access to the private data. Figure 7-8 shows a complete `Employee` class to which the access

```
class Employee
   private string lastName
   private numeric hourlyWage
   private numeric weeklyPay

   public void setLastName(string name)
      lastName = name
   return

   public void setHourlyWage(numeric wage)
      hourlyWage = wage
      calculateWeeklyPay()
   return

   public string getLastName()
   return lastName

   public numeric getHourlyWage()
   return hourlyWage

   public numeric getWeeklyPay()
   return weeklyPay

   private void calculateWeeklyPay()
      numeric WORK_WEEK_HOURS = 40
      weeklyPay = hourlyWage * WORK_WEEK_HOURS
   return
endClass
```

Figure 7-8 `Employee` class including `public` and `private` access specifiers

NOTE
In many object-oriented programming languages, if you do not declare an access specifier for a data field or method, then it is private by default. This book will follow the convention of explicitly specifying access for every class member.

specifier has been added to describe each attribute and method. An **access specifier** (or **access modifier**) is the adjective that defines the type of access that outside classes will have to the attribute or method (public or private) In the figure, each access specifier is shaded.

In Figure 7-8, each of the data fields is private; that means each field is inaccessible to an object declared in a program. In other words, if a program declares an Employee object, such as Employee myAssistant, then the following statement is illegal:

myAssistant.hourlyWage = 15.00

>> **DON'T DO IT**

The hourlyWage **field**
is not accessible
outside the class.

Instead, hourlyWage can be assigned only through a public method as follows:

myAssistant.setHourlyWage(15.00)

If you made hourlyWage public instead of private, then a direct assignment statement would work, but you would violate important principles of OO programming—those of data hiding using encapsulation. Data fields should usually be private and a client application should be able to access them only through the public interfaces; that is, through the class's public methods. That way, if you have restrictions on the value of hourlyWage, those restrictions will be enforced by the public method that acts as an interface to the private data field. Similarly, a public get method might control how a private value is retrieved. Perhaps you do not want clients to have access to an Employee's hourlyWage if it is more than a specific value, or perhaps you always want to return it to the client as a string with a dollar sign attached. Even when a field has no data value requirements or restrictions, making data private and providing public set and get methods establishes a framework that makes such modifications easier in the future.

In the Employee class in Figure 7-8, only one method is not public; the calculateWeeklyPay() method is private. That means if you write a program and declare an Employee object such as Employee myAssistant, then the following statement is not permitted:

myAssistant.calculateWeeklyPay()

>> **DON'T DO IT**

The calculateWeeklyPay()
method is not accessible
outside the class.

>> NOTE
Many object-oriented languages provide more specific access specifiers than just public and private. In Chapter 9, you will learn about the protected access specifier.

Because it is private, the only way to call the calculateWeeklyPay() method is from within another method that already belongs to the class. In this example, it is called from the setHourlyWage() method. This prevents any client program from setting hourlyWage to one value while setting weeklyPay to some incompatible value. By making the calculateWeeklyPay() method private, you ensure that the class retains full control over when and how it is used. Classes most often contain private data and public methods, but as you have just seen, they can contain private methods; they can contain public data items as well. For example, an Employee class might contain a public constant data field named MINIMUM_WAGE; outside programs then would be able to access that value without using a method. Public data fields are not required to be named constants, but they frequently are.

≫NOTE In some object-oriented programming languages, such as C++, you can label a set of data fields or methods as public or private using the access specifier name just once, then following it with a list of the items in that category. In other languages, such as Java, you use the specifier public or private with each field or method. For clarity, this book will label each field and method as public or private.

Many programmers like to specify in their class diagrams whether each component in a class is public or private. Figure 7-9 shows the conventions that are typically used. A minus sign (−) precedes the items that are private; a plus sign (+) precedes those that are public.

```
Employee

-lastName: string
-hourlyWage: numeric
-weeklyPay: numeric

+setLastName(name : string) : void
+setHourlyWage(wage : numeric) : void
+getLastName() : string
+getHourlyWage() : numeric
+getWeeklyPay() : numeric
-calculateWeeklyPay() : void
```

Figure 7-9 Employee class diagram with public and private access specifiers

≫NOTE When you learn more about inheritance in Chapter 9, you will learn about the protected access specifier. You use an octothorpe, also called a pound sign or number sign (#), to indicate protected access.

≫NOTE When you write an application program that contains a main() method, that method is virtually always defined as public. Therefore, when sample code includes a main() method from this point forward in the book, the public modifier will be used with it.

ORGANIZING CLASSES

The Employee class in Figure 7-9 contains just three data fields and six methods; most classes you create for professional applications will have many more. For example, in addition to requiring a last name and pay information, real employees require an employee number, a first name, address, phone number, hire date, and so on, as well as methods to set and get those fields. As classes grow in complexity, deciding how to organize them becomes increasingly important.

Although there is no requirement to do so, most programmers place data fields in some logical order at the beginning of a class. For example, an ID number is most likely used as a unique identifier for each employee (what database users often call a **primary key**), so it makes sense to list the employee ID number first in the class. An employee's last name and first name "go together," so it makes sense to store these two Employee components adjacently. Despite these common-sense rules, you have a lot of flexibility in how you position your data fields within any class. For example, depending on the class, you might choose to store the data fields alphabetically, or you might choose to group together all the fields that are the same data type. Alternatively, you might choose to store all public data items first, followed by private ones, or vice versa.

≫NOTE A unique identifier is one that should have no duplicates within an application. For example, an organization might have many employees with the last name Johnson or an hourly wage of $10.00, but only one employee will have employee number 12438.

In some languages you can organize a class's data fields and methods in any order within a class. For example, you could place all the methods first, followed by all the data fields, or you could organize the class so that several data fields are followed by methods that use them, and then several more data fields might be followed by the methods that use them. This book will follow the convention of placing all data fields first so that you can see their names and data types before reading the methods that use them. This format also echoes the way data and methods appear in standard class diagrams.

For ease in locating a class's methods, many programmers store them in alphabetical order. Other programmers arrange them in pairs of get and set methods, in the same order as the data fields are defined. Another option is to list all accessor (get) methods together and all mutator (set) methods together. Depending on the class, there might be other orders that result in logically functional groupings. Of course, if your company distributes guidelines for organizing class components, you must follow those rules.

UNDERSTANDING INSTANCE METHODS

Class objects have data and methods associated with them, and every object that is an instance of a class is assumed to possess the same data and have access to the same methods. For example, Figure 7-10 shows a class diagram for a simple Student class that contains just one private data field that holds a student's grade point average. The class also contains get and set methods for the field. Figure 7-11 shows the pseudocode for the Student class.

```
Student

-numeric gradePointAverage

+setGradePointAverage(gpa: numeric) : void
+getGradePointAverage() : numeric
```

Figure 7-10 Class diagram for Student class

```
class Student
    private numeric gradePointAverage

    public numeric setGradePointAverage(numeric gpa)
        gradePointAverage = gpa
    return

    public numeric getGradePointAverage()
    return gradePointAverage
endClass
```

Figure 7-11 Pseudocode for the Student class

This class becomes the model for a new data type named Student; when Student objects are eventually created, each will have its own gradePointAverage field and have access to methods to get and set it.

In the Student class in Figure 7-11, the method setGradePointAverage() takes one argument—a value for the Student's grade point average. The identifier gpa is local to the setGradePointAverage() method, and holds a value that will come into the method from the outside. Within the method, the value in gpa is assigned to gradePointAverage, which is a field within the class. The setGradePointAverage() method assigns a value to the gradePointAverage field for each separate Student object you ever create. Therefore, a method such as setGradePointAverage() is called an **instance method** because it operates correctly yet differently (providing different values) for each separate instance of the Student class. In other words, if you create 100 Students and assign grade point averages to each of them, you need 100 storage locations in computer memory to store each unique grade point average.

Figure 7-12 shows a program that creates three Student objects and assigns values to their gradePointAverage fields. It also shows how the Student objects look in memory after the values have been assigned.

```
class StudentDemo
    public void main()
        Student oneSophomore
        Student oneJunior
        Student oneSenior
        oneSophomore.setGradePointAverage(2.6)
        oneJunior.setGradePointAverage(3.8)
        oneSenior.setGradePointAverage(3.4)
    return
endClass
```

oneSophomore
2.6

oneJunior
3.8

oneSenior
3.4

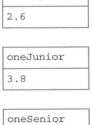

Figure 7-12 StudentDemo program and how Student objects look in memory

It makes sense for each Student object in Figure 7-12 to have its own gradePointAverage field, but it does not make sense for each Student to have its own copy of the methods that get and set gradePointAverage. Any method might have dozens of instructions in it, and to make 100 copies of identical methods would be inefficient. Instead, even though every Student has its own gradePointAverage field, only one copy of each of the methods getGradePointAverage() and setGradePointAverage() is stored in memory, but any instantiated object of the class can use the single copy.

Because only one copy of each instance method is stored, the computer needs a way to determine whose gradePointAverage is being set or retrieved when one of the methods is called. The mechanism that handles this problem is illustrated in Figure 7-13. When a method call such as `oneSophomore.setGradePointAverage(2.6)` is made, the true method call that is invisible and automatically constructed includes the memory address of the `oneSophomore` object. (These invisible and automatically constructed method calls are represented by the three narrow boxes in the center of Figure 7-13.)

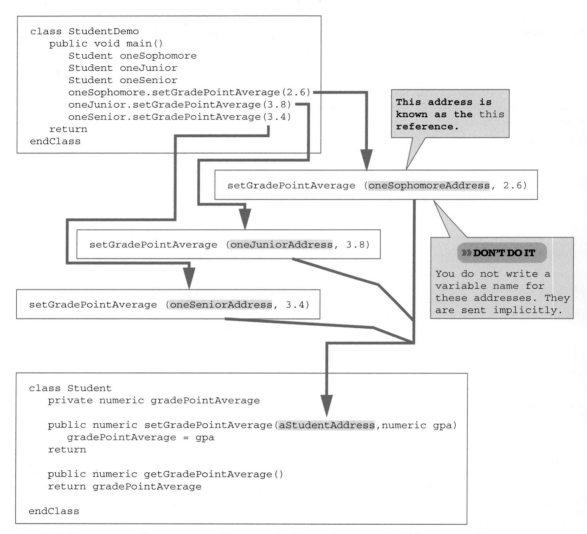

Figure 7-13 How `Student` addresses are passed from an application to an instance method of the `Student` class

Within the `setGradePointAverage()` method in the `Student` class, an invisible and automatically created parameter is added to the list. (For illustration purposes, this parameter is named `aStudentAddress` and is shaded in the `Student` class definition in Figure 7-13. In fact, no parameter is created with that name.) This parameter accepts the address of a `Student` object because the instance method belongs to the Student class; if this method belonged to another class—Employee, for example—then the method would accept an address for that type of object. The shaded addresses in Figure 7-13 are not written as code in any program—they are "secretly" sent and received behind the scenes. The address variable in Figure 7-13 is called a this reference. A **this reference** is an automatically created variable that holds the address of an object and passes it to an instance method whenever the method is called. It is called a this reference because it refers to "this particular object" that is using the method at the moment. In the application in Figure 7-13, when oneSophomore uses the setGradePointAverage() method, the address of the oneSophomore object is contained in the this reference. Later in the program, when the oneJunior object uses the setGradePointAverage() method, the this reference will hold the address of that Student object.

Figure 7-13 shows each place the this reference is used in the Student class. It is implicitly passed as a parameter to each instance method. You never explicitly refer to the this reference when you write the method header for an instance method; Figure 7-13 just shows where it implicitly exists. Within each instance method, the this reference is implied any time you refer to one of the class data fields. For example, when you call setGradePointAverage() using a oneSophomore object, the gradePointAverage that is assigned within the method is the "*this* gradePointAverage", or the one that belongs to the oneSophomore object. The phrase "this gradePointAverage" usually is written as this, followed by a dot, followed by the field name—this.gradePointAverage.

The this reference exists throughout any instance method. You can explicitly use the this reference with data fields as shown in the methods in the Student class in Figure 7-14, but you are not required to do so. Figure 7-14 shows you where the this reference can be used implicitly, but where you can (but do not have to) use it explicitly. When you write an instance method in a class, the following two identifiers within the method always mean exactly the same thing:

» any field name

» this, followed by a dot, followed by the same field name

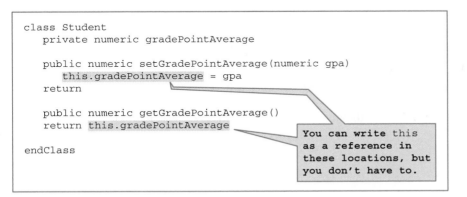

```
class Student
    private numeric gradePointAverage

    public numeric setGradePointAverage(numeric gpa)
        this.gradePointAverage = gpa
    return

    public numeric getGradePointAverage()
    return this.gradePointAverage

endClass
```

You can write this as a reference in these locations, but you don't have to.

Figure 7-14 Explicitly using this in the Student class

>> NOTE
The term *this reference* is used in many object-oriented programming languages, but not all of them. For example, in Lingo, the reference is called *me*.

>> NOTE
In a class method, the this reference can be used only with identifiers that are field names. For example, in Figure 7-14 you could not refer to this.gpa because gpa is not a class field—it is only a local variable.

>> NOTE The syntax for using this differs among programming languages. For example, within a class in C++, you can refer to the Student class gradePointAverage value as this->gradePointAverage or (*this).gradePointAverage, but in Java you refer to it as this.gradePointAverage.

For example, within the `setGradePointAverage()` method, `gradePointAverage` and `this.gradePointAverage` refer to exactly the same memory location.

Usually, you neither want nor need to use the `this` reference explicitly within the methods you write, but the `this` reference is always there, working behind the scenes, so that the data field for the correct object can be accessed.

As an example of an occasion when you might use the `this` reference explicitly, consider the following `setGradePointAverage()` method and compare it to the version in the `Student` class in Figure 7-14.

```
public void setGradePointAverage(numeric gradePointAverage)
   this.gradePointAverage = gradePointAverage
return
```

In this version of the method, the programmer has chosen to use the variable name `gradePointAverage` as the parameter to the method as well as the instance field within the class. This means that `gradePointAverage` is the name of a local variable within the method whose value is received by passing, as well as the name of a class field. To differentiate the two, you explicitly use the `this` reference with the copy of `gradePointAverage` that is a member of the class. Omitting the `this` reference in this case would result in the local parameter `gradePointAverage` being assigned to itself. The class's instance variable would not be set.

> **》 NOTE** Any time a local variable in a method has the same identifier as a class field, the class field is hidden. This applies whether the local variable is a passed parameter or simply one that is declared within the method. In these cases, you must use a `this` reference to refer to the class field.

UNDERSTANDING STATIC, CLASS METHODS

Some methods do not require a `this` reference. For example, the `displayStudentMotto()` method in the `Student` class in Figure 7-15 does not use any data fields from the class, so it does not matter which `Student` object calls it. If you write a program in which you declare 100 `Student` objects, the `displayStudentMotto()` method executes in exactly the same way for each of them; it does not need to know whose motto is displayed and it

```
public static void displayStudentMotto()
   print "Every student is an individual"
   print "in the pursuit of knowledge."
   print "Every student strives to be"
   print "a literate, responsible citizen."
return
```

Figure 7-15 Student class `displayStudentMotto()` method

does not need to access any specific object addresses. As a matter of fact, you might want to display the Student motto without instantiating any Student objects. Therefore, the displayStudentMotto() method can be written as a **class method** instead of an instance method.

When you write a class you can indicate two types of methods:

» **Static methods** are those for which no object needs to exist, like the displayStudentMotto() method in Figure 7-15. Static methods do not receive a this reference as an implicit parameter. Typically, static methods include the word static in the method header, as shown shaded in Figure 7-15.

» **Nonstatic methods** are methods that exist to be used with an object created from a class. These instance methods receive a this reference to a specific object. In most programming languages, you use the word static when you want to declare a static class member and do not use any special word when you want a class member to be nonstatic. In other words, methods in a class are nonstatic instance methods by default.

>> **NOTE** In everyday language, the word *static* means "stationary"; it is the opposite of *dynamic*, which means changing. In other words, static methods are always the same for the class, whereas nonstatic methods act differently depending on the object used to call them.

In most programming languages, you use a static method with the class name, as in the following:

```
Student.displayStudentMotto()
```

In other words, no object is necessary with a static method.

>> **NOTE** In some languages, notably C++, besides using a static method with the class name, you are also allowed to use a static method with any object of the class, as in oneSophomore.displayStudentMotto().

>> **NOTE** When you write an application program with a main() method and other methods it calls, they are static methods—you do not create objects to use them. Now that you understand the meaning of static, this book will use it in any method header that requires it, including all main() methods in application programs.

AN INTRODUCTION TO CONSTRUCTORS

When you use a class such as Employee to instantiate an object with a statement such as Employee chauffeur, you are actually calling a method named Employee() that is provided by default by the compiler of the object-oriented language in which you are working. A constructor method, or more simply, a **constructor**, is a method that establishes an object. A **default constructor** is one that requires no arguments; in OO languages, a default constructor is created automatically by the compiler for every class you write.

When the prewritten, default constructor for the `Employee` class is called (the constructor is the method named `Employee()`), it establishes one `Employee` object with the identifier provided. Depending on the programming language, a default constructor might provide initial values for the object's data fields; for example, a language might set all numeric fields to zero by default. If you do not want an object's fields to hold these default values, or if you want to perform additional tasks when you create an instance of a class, you can write your own constructor. Any constructor you write must have the same name as the class it constructs, and constructor methods cannot have a return type. Normally, you declare constructors to be public so that other classes can instantiate objects that belong to the class.

For example, if you want every `Employee` object to have a starting hourly wage of $10.00 as well as the correct weekly pay for that wage, then you could write the constructor for the `Employee` class that appears in Figure 7-16. Any `Employee` object instantiated will have an

```
class Employee
    private string lastName
    private numeric hourlyWage
    private numeric weeklyPay

    public Employee()
        hourlyWage = 10.00
        calculateWeeklyPay()
    return

    public void setLastName(string name)
        lastName = name
    return

    public void setHourlyWage(numeric wage)
        hourlyWage = wage
        calculateWeeklyPay()
    return

    public string getLastName()
    return lastName

    public numeric getHourlyWage()
    return hourlyWage

    public numeric getWeeklyPay()
    return weeklyPay

    private void calculateWeeklyPay()
        numeric WORK_WEEK_HOURS = 40
        weeklyPay = hourlyWage * WORK_WEEK_HOURS
    return
endClass
```

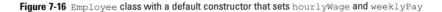

Figure 7-16 `Employee` class with a default constructor that sets `hourlyWage` and `weeklyPay`

hourlyWage field value equal to 10.00, a weeklyPay field equal to $400.00, and a lastName field equal to the default value for strings in the programming language in which this class is implemented.

The Employee constructor in Figure 7-16 calls the calculateWeeklyPay() method. You can write any statement in a constructor you like; it is just a method. Although you usually have no reason to do so, you could print a message from within a constructor, declare local variables, or perform any other task. You can place the constructor anywhere inside the class, outside of any other method. Typically, a constructor will be placed with the other methods. Often, programmers list the constructor first among the methods, because it is the first method used when an object is created.

Figure 7-17 shows a program in which two Employee objects are declared and their hourlyWage values are displayed. In the output in Figure 7-18, you can see that even though the setHourlyWage() method is never used in the program, the Employees possess valid hourly wages as set by their constructors.

```
public class EmployeeDemo3
    public static void main()
        Employee myPersonalTrainer
        Employee myInteriorDecorator
        print "Trainer's wage: ",
            myPersonalTrainer.getHourlyWage()
        print "Decorator's wage: ",
            myInteriorDecorator.getHourlyWage()
    return
endClass
```

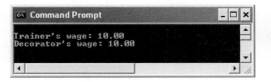

Figure 7-17 Program that declares Employee objects using class in Figure 7-16

Figure 7-18 Output of program in Figure 7-17

NOTE If a class contained it, you could use its setHourlyWage() method to assign values to individual Employee objects after construction. A constructor assigns its values at the time an object is created.

A potentially superior way to write the Employee class constructor that initializes every Employee's hourlyWage field to 10.00 is shown in Figure 7-19. In this version of the

```
public Employee()
    numeric DEFAULT_WAGE = 10.00
    setHourlyWage(DEFAULT_WAGE)
return
```

Figure 7-19 Alternate and efficient version of the Employee class constructor

constructor, a named constant containing 10.00 is passed to `setHourlyWage()`. Using this technique provides a couple of advantages:

» The statement to call `calculateWeeklyPay()` is no longer required in the constructor because the constructor calls `setHourlyWage()`, which calls `calculateWeeklyPay()`.

» In the future, if restrictions are imposed on `hourlyWage`, the code will need to be altered in only one location. For example, if `setHourlyWage()` is modified to disallow rates that are too high and too low, the code will change only in the `setHourlyWage()` method and will not have to be modified in the constructor. This reduces the amount of work required and reduces the possibility for error.

Of course, if different `hourlyWage()` requirements are needed at initialization than are required when the value is set after construction, then different code statements will be written in the constructor than those written in the `setHourlyWage()` method.

CONSTRUCTORS WITH PARAMETERS

Instead of forcing every `Employee` to be constructed with the same initial values, you might choose to create `Employee` objects with values that differ for each employee. For example, to initialize every `Employee` with a unique `hourlyWage`, you can pass a numeric value to the constructor; in other words, you can write constructors that receive arguments. Figure 7-20 shows an `Employee` class constructor that receives an argument. With this constructor, an argument is passed using a statement similar to one of the following:

```
public Employee(numeric rate)
   hourlyWage = rate
   calculateWeeklyPay()
return
```

Figure 7-20 `Employee` constructor that accepts a parameter

```
Employee partTimeWorker(8.81)
Employee partTimeWorker(valueEnteredByUser)
```

When the constructor executes, the numeric value within the method call is passed to `Employee()` as the argument `rate`, which is assigned to the `hourlyWage` within the constructor.

When you create an `Employee` class with a constructor such as the one shown in Figure 7-20, then every `Employee` object you create must use a numeric argument. In other words, with this new version of the class, the declaration statement `Employee partTimeWorker` no longer works. Once you write a constructor for a class, you no longer receive the automatically written default constructor. If a class's only constructor requires an argument, you must provide an argument for every object of that class you create.

OVERLOADING CLASS METHODS

In Chapter 6, you learned that you can overload methods by writing multiple versions of a method with the same name but different argument lists. In the same way, you can overload instance methods and constructors. For example, Figure 7-21 shows a version of the `Employee` class that contains two constructors. One version requires no argument and the other requires a numeric argument.

NOTE
Recall from Chapter 6 that a method's name and parameter list together are its signature.

```
class Employee
   private string lastName
   private numeric hourlyWage
   private numeric weeklyPay

   public Employee()
      hourlyWage = 10.00
      calculateWeeklyPay()
   return

   public Employee(numeric rate)
      hourlyWage = rate
      calculateWeeklyPay()
   return

   public void setLastName(string name)
      lastName = name
   return

   public void setHourlyWage(numeric wage)
      hourlyWage = wage
      calculateWeeklyPay()
   return

   public string getLastName()
   return lastName

   public numeric getHourlyWage()
   return hourlyWage

   public numeric getWeeklyPay()
   return weeklyPay

   private void calculateWeeklyPay()
      numeric WORK_WEEK_HOURS = 40
      weeklyPay = hourlyWage * WORK_WEEK_HOURS
   return
endClass
```

Figure 7-21 `Employee` class with overloaded constructors

When you use Figure 7-21's version of the class, then you can make statements like both of the following:

```
Employee deliveryPerson
Employee myButler(25.85)
```

When you declare an `Employee` using the first of these statements, an `hourlyWage` of 10.00 is automatically set because the statement uses the parameterless version of the constructor. When you declare an `Employee` using the second of these statements, the `hourlyWage` is set to the passed value. Any method or constructor in a class can be overloaded, and you can provide as many versions as you want. For example, you could add a third constructor to the

NOTE You might create an `Employee` class with several constructor versions to provide flexibility for client programs. A particular client program might use only one version, and a different client might use another.

`Employee` class, as shown in Figure 7-22. This version can coexist with the other two because the parameter list is different from either existing version. With this version you can specify the hourly rate for the `Employee` as well as a name. If an application makes a statement similar to the following, then this version would execute:

```
Employee myMaid(22.50, "Parker")
```

```
public Employee(numeric rate, string name)
   lastName = name
   hourlyWage = rate
   calculateWeeklyPay()
return
```

Figure 7-22 A third possible `Employee` class constructor

USING OBJECTS

After you create a class from which you want to instantiate objects, you can use the objects in ways similar to the way you would use any other simpler data type. For example, consider the `InventoryItem` class in Figure 7-23. The class represents items a company manufactures

```
class InventoryItem
   private string inventoryNumber
   private string description
   private numeric price

   public InventoryItem()
      this.inventoryNumber = "XXX"
      this.description = "XXX"
      this.price = 0.0
   return

   public void setInventoryNumber(string number)
      this.inventoryNumber = number
   return

   public void setDescription(string description)
      this.description = description
   return

   public void setPrice(numeric price)
      if(price < 0)
         this.price = 0
      else
         this.price = price
   return

   public string getInventoryNumber()
   return inventoryNumber

   public string getDescription()
   return description

   public numeric getPrice()
   return price

endClass
```

Figure 7-23 `InventoryItem` class

and holds in inventory. Each item has a number, description, and price. The class contains a single constructor that provides default values for InventoryItem objects. The class also contains a get and set method for each of the three fields.

Once you declare an InventoryItem object, you can use it in many of the ways you would use a simple numeric or string variable. For example, you could pass an InventoryItem object to a method or return one from a method. Figure 7-24 shows a program that declares an InventoryItem object and passes it to a method for printing. The InventoryItem is declared in the main() method and assigned values. Then the completed item is passed to a method where it is displayed. Figure 7-25 shows the execution of the program.

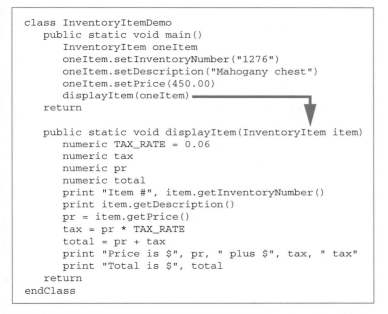

```
class InventoryItemDemo
    public static void main()
        InventoryItem oneItem
        oneItem.setInventoryNumber("1276")
        oneItem.setDescription("Mahogany chest")
        oneItem.setPrice(450.00)
        displayItem(oneItem)
    return

    public static void displayItem(InventoryItem item)
        numeric TAX_RATE = 0.06
        numeric tax
        numeric pr
        numeric total
        print "Item #", item.getInventoryNumber()
        print item.getDescription()
        pr = item.getPrice()
        tax = pr * TAX_RATE
        total = pr + tax
        print "Price is $", pr, " plus $", tax, " tax"
        print "Total is $", total
    return
endClass
```

Figure 7-24 Application program that declares and uses an InventoryItem object

Figure 7-25 Execution of application in Figure 7-24

The InventoryItem declared in the main() method in Figure 7-24 is passed to the displayItem() method in much the same way a numeric or string variable would be. The method receives a copy of the InventoryItem that is known locally by the identifier item. Within the method, the field values of the local item can be retrieved, displayed, and used in arithmetic statements in the same way they could have been in the main() method where the InventoryItem was originally declared.

Figure 7-26 shows a more realistic application that uses `InventoryItem` objects. In the `main()` method of this program, an `InventoryItem` is declared and the user is prompted for a number. As long as the user does not enter the `QUIT` value, a loop is executed in which the entered inventory item number is passed to the `getItemValues()` method. Within that method, a local `InventoryItem` object is declared. This local object is used to gather and hold the user's input values. The user is prompted for a description and price; then the passed item number, as well as the newly obtained description and price, are assigned to the local `InventoryItem` object via its set methods. The completed object is returned to the `main()`

```
class InventoryItemDemo2
   public static void main()
      InventoryItem oneItem
      string itemNum
      string QUIT = "0"
      print "Enter item number or ", QUIT, " to quit... "
      get itemNum
      while itemNum not = QUIT
         oneItem = getItemValues(itemNum)
         displayItem(oneItem)
         print "Enter next item number or ", QUIT, " to quit... "
         get itemNum
      endwhile
   return

   public static InventoryItem getItemValues(string num)
      InventoryItem inItem
      string desc
      numeric price
      print "Enter description... "
      get desc
      print "Enter price... "
      get price
      inItem.setInventoryNumber(num)
      inItem.setDescription(desc)
      inItem.setPrice(price)
   return inItem

   public static void displayItem(InventoryItem item)
      numeric TAX_RATE = 0.06
      numeric tax
      numeric pr
      numeric total
      print "Item #", item.getInventoryNumber()
      print item.getDescription()
      pr = item.getPrice()
      tax = pr * TAX_RATE
      total = pr + tax
      print "Price is $", pr, " plus $", tax, " tax"
      print "Total is $", total
   return
endClass
```

Figure 7-26 Application that uses `InventoryItem` objects

> **NOTE** In Figure 7-26, notice that the return type for the `getItemValues()` method is `InventoryItem`. A method can return only a single value. Therefore, it is convenient that the `getItemValues()` method can encapsulate two strings and a number in a single `InventoryItem` object that it returns to the main program.

method where it is assigned to `main()`'s `InventoryItem` object. That item is then passed to the `displayItem()` method. As in the previous example, the method calculates tax and displays results. Figure 7-27 shows a typical execution.

Enter item number or 0 to quit... 1276
Enter description... Mahogany chest
Enter price... 450.00

Item #1276
Mahogany chest
Price is $450.00 plus $27.00 tax
Total is $477.00

Enter next item number or 0 to quit... 1488
Enter description... Wicker chair
Enter price... 129.98

Item #1488
Wicker chair
Price is $129.98 plus $7.80 tax
Total is $137.78

Enter next item number or 0 to quit... 2215
Enter description... Decorator pillow
Enter price... 40.00

Item #2215
Decorator pillow
Price is $40.00 plus $2.40 tax
Total is $42.40

Enter next item number or 0 to quit... 0

Figure 7-27 Typical execution of program in Figure 7-26

UNDERSTANDING DESTRUCTORS

A **destructor** contains the actions you require when an instance of a class is destroyed. Most often, an instance of a class is destroyed when it goes out of scope. As with constructors, if you do not explicitly create a destructor for a class, one is automatically provided.

The most common way to explicitly declare a destructor is to use an identifier that consists of a tilde (~) followed by the class name. You cannot provide any parameters to a destructor; it must have an empty argument list. As a consequence, destructors cannot be overloaded; a class can have at most one destructor. Like a constructor, a destructor has no return type.

Figure 7-28 shows an `Employee` class that contains only one field (`idNumber`), a constructor, and a shaded destructor. Although it is unusual for a constructor or destructor to print

> **»NOTE**
> The rules for creating and naming destructors vary among programming languages. For example, in Visual Basic.NET classes, the destructor is called `Finalize`.

```
class Employee
    private string idNumber
    public Employee(string empId)
        idNumber = empId
        print "Employee ", idNumber, " is created"
    return
    public ~Employee()
        print "Employee ", idNumber, " is destroyed"
    return
endClass
```

Figure 7-28 `Employee` class with destructor

anything, these print messages so that you can see when the objects are created and destroyed. When you execute the `main()` method in the `DemoEmployeeDestructor` class in Figure 7-29, you instantiate two `Employee` objects, each with its own `idNumber` value. When the `main()` method ends, the two `Employee` objects go out of scope, and the destructor for each object is called automatically. Figure 7-30 shows the output.

```
class DemoEmployeeDestructor
    public static void main()
        Employee aWorker("101")
        Employee anotherWorker("202")
    return
endClass
```

Figure 7-29 `DemoEmployeeDestructor` program

Figure 7-30 Output of `DemoEmployeeDestructor` program

The program in Figure 7-30 never explicitly calls the `Employee` class destructor, yet you can see from the output that the destructor executes twice. Destructors are invoked automatically; you cannot explicitly call one. Interestingly, the last object created is the first object destroyed; the same relationship would hold true no matter how many objects the program instantiated.

> **NOTE** An instance of a class becomes eligible for destruction when it is no longer possible for any code to use it—that is, when it goes out of scope. In many languages, the actual execution of an object's destructor might occur at any time after the object becomes eligible for destruction.

For now, you have little reason to create a destructor except to demonstrate how it is called automatically. Later, when you write more sophisticated programs that work with files, databases, or large quantities of computer memory, you might want to perform specific clean-up or close-down tasks when an object goes out of scope. Then you will place appropriate instructions within a destructor.

UNDERSTANDING COMPOSITION

A class can contain another class's objects as data members. For example, you might create a class named `Date` that contains a month, day, and year, and add two `Date` fields to an `Employee` class to hold the `Employee`'s birth date and hire date. Then you might create a class named `Department` that represents every department in a company, and create each `Department` class member to contain an array of 50 `Employee` objects. Using a class object within another class object is known as **composition**. The relationship created is also called a **has-a relationship** because one class "has an" instance of another.

When your classes contain objects that are members of other classes, your programming job becomes increasingly complex. For example, you sometimes must refer to a method by a very long name. Suppose you create a `Department` class that contains a method named `getHighestPaidEmployee()`, a method that returns an `Employee` object. Suppose the `Employee` class contains a method that returns a `Date` object that is an `Employee`'s hire date.

Further suppose that the Date class contains a method that returns the year portion of the Date. Then an application might contain a statement such as the following:

```
salesDepartment.getHighestPaidEmployee().getHireDate().getYear()
```

Additionally, when classes contain objects that are members of other classes, all the corresponding constructors and destructors execute in a specific order. As you work with object-oriented programming languages, you will learn to manage these complex issues.

ONE EXAMPLE OF USING PREDEFINED CLASSES: CREATING GUI OBJECTS

When you purchase or download an object-oriented programming language compiler, it comes packaged with myriad predefined, built-in classes. The classes are stored in **libraries**—collections of classes that serve related purposes. Some of the most useful are the classes you can use to create GUI objects such as frames, buttons, labels, and text boxes. You place these GUI components within interactive programs so that users can manipulate them using input devices, most frequently a keyboard and a mouse. For example, if you want to place a clickable button on the screen using a language that supports GUI applications, you instantiate an object that belongs to the already created class named Button. In many object-oriented languages, a class with a name similar to Button is already created. It contains private data fields such as text and height and public methods such as setText() and setHeight() that allow you to place instructions on your Button object and to change its vertical size, respectively.

» NOTE
In some languages, such as Java, libraries are also called **packages**.

If no predefined GUI object classes existed, you could create your own. However, there would be several disadvantages:

» It would be a lot of work. Creating graphical objects requires a lot of code and at least a modicum of artistic talent.

» It would be repetitious work. Almost all GUI programs require standard components such as buttons and labels. If each programmer created the classes that represent these components from scratch, a lot of work would be unnecessarily repeated.

» The components would look different in various applications. If each programmer created his or her own component classes, then objects like buttons would look and operate slightly differently in different applications. Users like standardization in their components—title bars on windows that are a uniform height, buttons that appear to be pressed when clicked, frames and windows that contain maximize and minimize buttons in predictable locations, and so on. By using standard component classes, programmers are assured that the GUI components in their programs have the same look and feel as those in other programs.

In programming languages that supply existing GUI classes, you often are provided with a **visual development environment** in which you can create programs by dragging components such as buttons and labels onto a screen and arranging them visually. Then you write programming statements to control the actions that take place when a user manipulates the controls by clicking them using a mouse, for example. Many programmers never create any classes of their own from which they will instantiate objects, but only write classes that are applications that use built-in GUI component classes. Some languages—for example, Visual Basic and C#—lend themselves very well to this type of programming.

» NOTE
In several languages, the visual development environment is known by the acronym **IDE**, which stands for Integrated Development Environment.

In Chapter 8, you will learn more about creating programs that use GUI objects.

REVIEWING THE ADVANTAGES OF OBJECT-ORIENTED PROGRAMMING

Using the features of object-oriented programming languages provides you with many benefits as you develop your programs. Whether you use classes you have created or use those created by others, when you instantiate objects in programs, you save development time because each object automatically includes appropriate, reliable methods and attributes. When using inheritance (which you will learn more about in Chapter 9), you can develop new classes more quickly by extending classes that already exist and work; you need to concentrate only on new features the new class adds. When using existing objects, you need to concentrate only on the interface to those objects, not on the internal instructions that make them work. By using polymorphism, you can use reasonable, easy-to-remember names for methods and concentrate on their purpose rather than on memorizing different method names.

CHAPTER SUMMARY

» Classes are the basic building blocks of object-oriented programming. When you think in an object-oriented manner, everything is an object, and every object is an instance of a class. A class's fields, or instance variables, hold its data, and every object that is an instance of a class possesses the same methods. A program or class that instantiates objects of another prewritten class is a class client or class user. Besides classes and objects, three important features of object-oriented languages are polymorphism, inheritance, and encapsulation.

» A class definition is a set of program statements that tell you the characteristics of the class's objects and the methods that can be applied to its objects. A class definition can contain a name, data, and methods. Programmers often use a class diagram to illustrate class features. The purposes of many methods contained in a class can be divided into three categories: set methods, get methods, and work methods.

» Object-oriented programmers usually specify that their data fields will have private access—that is, the data cannot be accessed by any method that is not part of the class. The methods frequently support public access, which means that other programs and methods may use the methods that control access to the private data. In a class diagram, a minus sign (–) precedes the items that are private; a plus sign (+) precedes those that are public.

» As classes grow in complexity, deciding how to organize them becomes increasingly important. Depending on the class, you might choose to store the data fields by listing a key field first, listing fields alphabetically, or by data type or accessibility. Methods might be stored in alphabetical order or in pairs of get and set methods.

» An instance method operates correctly yet differently for every object instantiated from a class. When an instance method is called, a `this` reference that holds the object's memory address is automatically passed to the method.

» Some methods do not require a `this` reference. When you write a class you can indicate two types of methods: static methods, which are also known as class methods and do not receive a `this` reference as an implicit parameter; and nonstatic methods, which are instance methods and do receive a `this` reference.

» A constructor is a method that establishes an object. A default constructor is one that requires no arguments; in OO languages, a default constructor is created automatically by the compiler for every class you write. If you want to perform specific tasks when you create an instance of a class, then you can write your own constructor. Any constructor you write must have the same name as the class it constructs, and constructor methods cannot have a return type. Once you write a constructor for a class, you no longer receive the automatically written default constructor. If a class's only constructor requires an argument, then you must provide an argument for every object of that class that you create.

» You can overload instance methods and constructors.

» After you create a class from which you want to instantiate objects, you can use the objects in ways similar to the way you would use any other simpler data type.

» A destructor contains the actions you require when an instance of a class is destroyed. Most often, an instance of a class is destroyed when it goes out of scope. As with constructors, if you do not explicitly create a destructor for a class, one is automatically provided. The most common way to explicitly declare a destructor is to use an identifier that consists of a tilde (~) followed by the class name. You cannot provide any parameters to a destructor; it must have an empty argument list. As a consequence, destructors cannot be overloaded; a class can have at most one destructor. Like a constructor, a destructor has no return type.

» A class can contain another class's objects as data members. Using a class object within another class object is known as composition.

» Some of the most useful classes packaged in language libraries are the classes you can use to create graphical user interface (GUI) objects such as frames, buttons, labels, and text boxes. In programming languages that supply existing GUI classes, you are often provided with a visual development environment in which you can create programs by dragging components such as buttons and labels onto a screen and arranging them visually.

» When you instantiate objects in programs, you save development time because each object automatically includes appropriate, reliable methods and attributes. You can develop new classes more quickly by extending classes that already exist and work, and you can use reasonable, easy-to-remember names for methods.

KEY TERMS

An **instance** is one tangible example of a class.

An **is-a relationship** exists between an object and its class.

An **instantiation** of a class is an instance.

A class's **instance variables** are the data components that belong to every instantiated object.

Fields are object attributes or data.

The **state** of an object is the set of all the values or contents of its instance variables.

A **class client** or **class user** is a program or class that instantiates objects of another prewritten class.

Inheritance is the process of acquiring the traits of one's predecessors.

Information hiding (or **data hiding**) is the concept that other classes should not alter an object's attributes—only the methods of an object's own class should have that privilege.

A **class definition** is a set of program statements that tell you the characteristics of the class's objects and the methods that can be applied to its objects.

A **user-defined type**, or **programmer-defined type**, is a class.

An **abstract data type** (ADT) is a programmer-defined type.

Primitive data types are simple numbers and characters that are not class types.

A **class diagram** consists of a rectangle divided into three sections that show a class's name, data, and methods.

A **set method** sets the values of a data field within a class.

Mutator methods are ones that set values in a class.

A **property** provides methods that allow you to get and set a class field value using a simple syntax.

A **get method** returns a value from a class.

Accessor methods get values from class fields.

Work methods perform tasks within a class.

Help methods and **facilitators** are other names for work methods.

Private access, as applied to a class's data or methods, specifies that the data or method cannot be used by any method that is not part of the same class.

Public access, as applied to a class's data or methods, specifies that other programs and methods may use the specified data or methods.

An **access specifier** (or **access modifier**) is the adjective that defines the type of access that outside classes will have to the attribute or method.

A **primary key** is a unique identifier for each object in a database.

An **instance method** operates correctly yet differently for each class object. An instance method is nonstatic and receives a `this` reference.

A **`this` reference** is an automatically created variable that holds the address of an object and passes it to an instance method whenever the method is called.

A **class method** is a static method. Class methods are not instance methods and they do not receive a `this` reference.

Static methods are those for which no object needs to exist. Static methods are not instance methods and they do not receive a `this` reference.

Nonstatic methods are methods that exist to be used with an object created from a class; they are instance methods and they receive a `this` reference.

A **constructor** is an automatically called method that establishes an object.

A **default constructor** is one that requires no arguments.

A **destructor** is an automatically called method that contains the actions you require when an instance of a class is destroyed.

Using a class object within another class object is known as **composition**.

A **has-a relationship** is the type that exists when using composition.

Libraries are stored collections of classes that serve related purposes.

Packages are another name for libraries in some languages.

A **visual development environment** is one in which you can create programs by dragging components such as buttons and labels onto a screen and arranging them visually.

In several languages, the visual development environment is known by the acronym **IDE**, which stands for Integrated Development Environment.

REVIEW QUESTIONS

1. Which of the following means the same as *object*?

   a. class

   b. field

   c. instance

   d. category

2. Which of the following means the same as *instance variable*?

   a. field

   b. instance

   c. category

   d. class

3. A program that instantiates objects of another prewritten class is a(n) _____ .

   a. object

   b. client

   c. instance

   d. GUI

4. The process of acquiring the traits of one's predecessors is _____ .

   a. inheritance

   b. encapsulation

   c. polymorphism

   d. orientation

5. Every class definition must contain _____ .

   a. a name

   b. data

   c. methods

   d. all of the above

6. Assume a working program contains the following statement:

   ```
   myCat.setName("Socks")
   ```

   Which of the following do you know?

   a. `myCat` is an object of a class named `Cat`

   b. `setName()` is a static method

   c. both of these

   d. none of these

7. Assume a working program contains the following statement:

   `myDog.setName("Bowser")`

   Which of the following do you know?

   a. `setName()` is a public method

   b. `setName()` accepts a string parameter

   c. both of these

   d. none of these

8. Which of the following is the most likely scenario for a specific class?

   a. Its data is private and its methods are public.

   b. Its data is public and its methods are private.

   c. Its data and methods are both public.

   d. Its data and methods are both private.

9. Which of the following is true?

   a. Methods can be private.   c. both of these

   b. Methods can be public.   d. none of these

10. An instance method _____ .

    a. is static   c. both of these

    b. receives a `this` reference   d. none of these

11. Assume a working program contains the following statement:

    `myHorse.setAge(4)`

    Which of the following must be true about the `setAge()` method?

    a. The method is static.

    b. The method returns a number.

    c. both of these

    d. none of these

12. Assume you have created a class named `Dog` that contains a data field named `weight` and an instance method named `setWeight()`. Further assume the `setWeight()` method accepts a numeric parameter named `weight`. Which of the following statements correctly sets a `Dog`'s weight within the `setWeight()` method?

    a. `weight = weight`

    b. `this.weight = this.weight`

    c. `weight = this.weight`

    d. `this.weight = weight`

13. A static method is also known as a(n) _____ method.
    a. instance   c. private
    b. public   d. class

14. By default, methods contained in a class are _____ methods.
    a. static   c. class
    b. nonstatic   d. public

15. When you instantiate an object, the automatically created method that is called is a _____ .
    a. creator
    b. initiator
    c. constructor
    d. architect

16. Which of the following can be overloaded?
    a. constructors
    b. destructors
    c. both of these
    d. none of these

17. A default constructor is _____ .
    a. another name for a class's automatically created constructor
    b. a constructor that requires no arguments
    c. a constructor that sets a value for every field in a class
    d. the only constructor that is explicitly written in a class

18. When you write a constructor that receives an argument, _____ .
    a. the argument must be numeric
    b. the argument must be used to set a data field
    c. the default constructor no longer exists
    d. the constructor body must be empty

19. A class object can be _____ .
    a. stored in an array
    b. passed to a method
    c. returned from a method
    d. all of the above

20. Most often, a destructor is called when _____ .

a. an object is created

b. an object goes out of scope

c. you make an explicit call to it

d. a value is returned from a class method

EXERCISES

1. Identify three objects that might belong to each of the following classes:

a. `Automobile`

b. `NovelAuthor`

c. `CollegeCourse`

2. Identify three different classes that might contain each of these objects:

a. Wolfgang Amadeus Mozart

b. My pet cat named Socks

c. Apartment 14 at 101 Main Street

3. Design a class named `CustomerRecord` that holds a customer number, name, and address. Include methods to set the values for each data field and print the values for each data field. Create the class diagram and write the pseudocode that defines the class.

4. Design a class named `House` that holds the street address, price, number of bedrooms, and number of baths in a `House`. Include methods to set the values for each data field, and include a method that displays all the values for a `House`. Create the class diagram and write the pseudocode that defines the class.

5. Design a class named `Loan` that holds an account number, name of account holder, amount borrowed, term, and interest rate. Include methods to set values for each data field and a method that prints all the loan information. Create the class diagram and write the pseudocode that defines the class.

6. Complete the following tasks:

a. Design a class named `Book` that holds a stock number, author, title, price, and number of pages for a book. Include methods to set and get the values for each data field. Create the class diagram and write the pseudocode that defines the class.

b. Design an application program that declares two `Book` objects and sets and displays their values.

c. Design an application program that declares an array of 10 `Book`s. Prompt the user for data for each of the `Book`s, then display all the values.

7. Complete the following tasks:

   a. Design a class named `Pizza`. Data fields include a string field for toppings (such as pepperoni) and numeric fields for diameter in inches (such as 12) and price (such as 13.99). Include methods to get and set values for each of these fields. Create the class diagram and write the pseudocode that defines the class.

   b. Design an application program that declares two `Pizza` objects and sets and displays their values.

   c. Design an application program that declares an array of 10 `Pizza`s. Prompt the user for data for each of the `Pizza`s, then display all the values.

8. Complete the following tasks:

   a. Design a class named `HousePlant`. A `HousePlant` has fields for a name (for example, "Philodendron"), a price (for example, 29.99), and a field that indicates whether the plant has been fed in the last month (for example, "Yes"). Create the class diagram and write the pseudocode that defines the class.

   b. Design an application program that declares two `HousePlant` objects and sets and displays their values.

   c. Design an application program that declares an array of 10 `HousePlant`s. Prompt the user for data for each of the `HousePlant`s, then display all the values.

9. Complete the following tasks:

   a. Design a class named `Circle` with fields named `radius`, `area`, and `diameter`. Include a constructor that sets the radius to 1. Include get methods for each field, but include a set method only for the radius. When the radius is set, do not allow it to be zero or a negative number. When the radius is set, calculate the diameter (twice the radius) and the area (the radius squared times pi, which is approximately 3.14). Create the class diagram and write the pseudocode that defines the class.

   b. Design an application program that declares two `Circle`s. Set the radius of one manually, but allow the other to use the default value supplied by the constructor. Then, display each `Circle`'s values.

10. Complete the following tasks:

   a. Design a class named `Square` with fields that hold the length of a side, the length of the perimeter, and the area. Include a constructor that sets the length of a side to 1. Include get methods for each field, but include a set method only for the length of a side, and do not allow a side to be zero or negative. When the side is set, calculate the perimeter length (four times the side length) and the area (a side squared). Create the class diagram and write the pseudocode that defines the class.

   b. Design an application program that declares two `Square`s. Set the side length of one manually, but allow the other to use the default value supplied by the constructor. Then, display each `Square`'s values.

11. Complete the following tasks:

   a. Design a class named `GirlScout` with fields that hold a name, troop number, and dues owed. Include get and set methods for each field. Include a static method that displays the Girl Scout motto ("To obey the Girl Scout law"). Include three overloaded constructors as follows:

   » A default constructor that sets the name to "XXX" and the numeric fields to 0
   » A constructor that allows you to pass values for all three fields
   » A constructor that allows you to pass a name and troop number but sets dues owed to 0

   Create the class diagram and write the pseudocode that defines the class.

   b. Design an application program that declares three `GirlScout` objects using a different constructor version with each object. Display each `GirlScout`'s values. Then display the motto.

12. Complete the following tasks:

   a. Create a class named `Commission` that includes two numeric variables: a sales figure and a commission rate. Also create two overloaded methods named `computeCommission()`. The first method takes two numeric arguments representing sales and rate, multiplies them, and then displays the results. The second method takes a single argument representing sales. When this method is called, the commission rate is assumed to be 7.5 percent and the results are displayed.

   b. Create an application that demonstrates how both method versions can be called.

13. Complete the following tasks:

   a. Create a class named `Pay` that includes five numeric variables: hours worked, rate of pay per hour, withholding rate, gross pay, and net pay. Also create three overloaded `computeNetPay()` methods. When `computeNetPay()` receives values for hours, pay rate, and withholding rate, it computes the gross pay and reduces it by the appropriate withholding amount to produce the net pay. (Gross pay is computed as hours worked, multiplied by pay per hour.) When `computeNetPay()` receives two arguments, they represent the hours and pay rate, and the withholding rate is assumed to be 15 percent. When `computeNetPay()` receives one argument, it represents the number of hours worked, the withholding rate is assumed to be 15 percent, and the hourly rate is assumed to be 6.50.

   b. Create an application that demonstrates all the methods.

CASE PROJECT

You have been developing programs for Cost Is No Object—a car rental service that specializes in lending antique and luxury cars to clients on a short-term basis. Assume you have decided that you will need the following classes: `Name`, `Address`, `Date`, `Employee`, `Customer`, `Automobile`, and `RentalAgreement`.

The `Name` class contains two fields and get and set methods for each field:

» `string firstName`
» `string lastName`

The `Address` class contains the following fields and get and set methods for each field:

» `string streetAddress`
» `string city`
» `string state`
» `string zipCode`

The `Date` class contains the following fields and get and set methods for each field:

» `numeric month`
» `numeric day`
» `numeric year`

The set method for the `month` field prohibits any value of less than 1 or more than 12. The set method for the `day` field prohibits any day that is out of range for the given month.

The `Employee` class contains the following fields and get and set methods for each field:

» `string idNumber`
» `Name name`
» `Address address`
» `Date hireDate`
» `numeric hourlyPayRate`

The `Customer` class contains the following fields and get and set methods for each field:

» `string idNumber`
» `Name name`
» `Address address`

The `Automobile` class contains the following fields and get and set methods for each field:

» `string carId`
» `string make`
» `numeric year`

The `RentalAgreement` class contains the following fields and get and set methods for each field:

» `string rentalAgreementNumber`
» `Customer renter`
» `Employee rentalAgent`
» `Date rentalStartDate`
» `Automobile carRented`
» `numeric dailyFee`
» `numeric numberOfDaysRented`

a. Create a class diagram that could be used to describe data and methods needed for each of these classes.

b. Write pseudocode for each class.

c. Design an application program that declares a `RentalAgreement` object, prompts the user for all necessary values, and displays them.

UP FOR DISCUSSION

1. In this chapter, you learned that instance data and methods belong to objects (which are class members), but that static data and methods belong to a class as a whole. Consider the real-life class named `StateInTheUnitedStates`. Name some real-life attributes of this class that are static attributes and instance attributes. Create another example of a real-life class and discuss what its static and instance members might be.

2. Some programmers use a system called Hungarian notation when naming their variables and class fields. What is Hungarian notation and why do many object-oriented programmers feel it is not a valuable style to use?

3. If you are completing all the programming exercises at the ends of the chapters in this book, you can see how much work goes into planning a full-blown professional program. How would you feel if someone copied your work without compensating you? Investigate the magnitude of software piracy in our society. What are the penalties for illegally copying software? Are there circumstances under which it is acceptable to copy a program? If a friend asked you to make a copy of a program for him, would you? What do you suggest we do about this problem, if anything?

EVENT-DRIVEN PROGRAMMING WITH GRAPHICAL USER INTERFACES

In this chapter, you will:

- Understand the principles of event-driven programming
- Understand the actions that GUI components can initiate
- Be able to design graphical user interfaces
- Be able to modify the attributes of GUI components
- Understand the steps to developing an event-driven application
- Understand multithreading
- Understand how to create animation

UNDERSTANDING EVENT-DRIVEN PROGRAMMING

From the 1950s, when businesses began to use computers to help them perform many jobs, right through the 1960s and 1970s, almost all interactive dialogues between people and computers took place at the command prompt (or on the command line). In Chapter 1 you learned that the command prompt is the location on your computer screen at which you type entries to communicate with the computer's **operating system**—the software that you use to run a computer and manage its resources. In the early days of computing, interacting with a computer operating system was difficult because the user had to know the exact syntax to use when typing commands, and had to spell and type those commands accurately. (Syntax is the correct sequence of words and symbols that form the operating system's command set.) Figure 8-1 shows a command in the Windows operating system.

Figure 8-1 Command prompt screen

> **NOTE** If you use the Windows operating system on a PC, you can locate the command prompt by clicking Start and pointing to the command prompt shortcut on the Start menu. Alternatively, you can point to All Programs in Vista or Windows XP (or Programs in some earlier operating systems), then Accessories, and then click Command Prompt. Still another option is to point to Start, click Run, and type *CMD*.

> **NOTE** Although you frequently use the command line to communicate with the operating system, you also sometimes communicate with software through the command line. For example, when you issue a command to execute some applications, you can include data values that the program uses.

Fortunately for today's computer users, operating system software allows them to use a mouse or other pointing device to select pictures, or **icons**, on the screen. As you learned in Chapter 1, this type of environment is a graphical user interface, or GUI. Computer users can expect to see a standard interface in the GUI programs they use. Rather than memorizing difficult commands that must be typed at a command line, GUI users can select options from menus and click buttons to make their preferences known to a program. Users can select objects that look like their real-world counterparts and get the expected results. For example, users may select an icon that looks like a pencil when they want to write a memo, or they may drag an icon shaped like a folder to another icon that resembles a recycling bin when they want to delete a file. Figure 8-2 shows a Windows program named Paint in which icons representing pencils, paint cans, and so on

Figure 8-2 A GUI application that contains buttons and icons

appear on clickable buttons. Performing an operation on an icon (for example, clicking or dragging it) causes an **event**—an occurrence that generates a message sent to an object.

GUI programs are called **event-driven** or **event-based** because actions occur in response to user-initiated events such as clicking a mouse button. When you program with event-driven languages, the emphasis is on the objects that the user can manipulate, such as buttons and menus, and on the events that the user can initiate with those objects, such as clicking or double-clicking. The programmer writes instructions within modules that correspond to each type of event.

For the programmer, event-driven programs require unique considerations. The program logic you have developed within many of the methods of this book is procedural; each step occurs in the order the programmer determines. In a procedural application, if you issue a prompt and a statement to read the user's response, you have no control over how much time the user takes to enter a response, but you do control the sequence of events—the processing goes no further until the input is completed. In contrast, with event-driven programs, the user might initiate any number of events in any order. For example, if you use an event-driven word-processing program, you have dozens of choices at your disposal at any moment. You can type words, select text with the mouse, click a button to change text to bold or to italics, choose a menu item, and so on. With each word-processing document you create, you choose options in any order that seems appropriate at the time. The word-processing program must be ready to respond to any event you initiate.

» NOTE
You first learned the term *procedural programming* in Chapter 1.

Within an event-driven program, a component from which an event is generated is the **source of the event**. A button that a user can click to cause some action is an example of a source; a text field that one can use to enter typed characters is another source. An object that is "interested in" an event you want it to respond to is a **listener**. It "listens for" events so it knows when to respond. Not all objects can receive all events—you probably have used programs in which clicking many areas of the screen has no effect at all. If you want an object, such as a button, to be a listener for an event such as a mouse click, you must write the appropriate program statements.

» NOTE When an object should listen for events, you must write two types of statements. You write the statement or statements that define the object as a listener, and you write the statements that constitute the event.

Although event-driven programming is relatively new, the instructions that programmers write to correspond to events are still simply sequences, selections, and loops. Event-driven programs still declare variables, use arrays, and contain all the attributes of their procedural-program ancestors. An event-driven program might contain components with labels like "Sort Records," "Merge Files," or "Total Transactions." The programming logic you use when writing code for each of these processes is the same logic you have learned throughout this book. Writing event-driven programs simply involves thinking of possible events as the modules that constitute the program.

» NOTE
In object-oriented languages, the procedural modules that depend on user-initiated events are often called *scripts*.

USER-INITIATED ACTIONS AND GUI COMPONENTS

To understand GUI programming, you need to have a clear picture of the possible events a user can initiate. These include the events listed in Table 8-1.

Event	Description of User's Action
Key press	Pressing a key on the keyboard
Mouse point or mouse over	Placing the mouse pointer over an area on the screen
Mouse click or left mouse click	Pressing the left mouse button
Right mouse click	Pressing the right mouse button
Mouse double-click	Pressing the left mouse button two times in rapid sequence
Mouse drag	Holding the left mouse button down while moving the mouse over the desk surface

Table 8-1 Common user-initiated events

You also need to be able to picture common GUI components. Some are listed in Table 8-2. Figure 8-3 shows a screen that contains several common GUI components.

Component	Description
Label	A rectangular area that displays text
Text field	A rectangular area into which the user can type text
Check box	A label placed beside a small square; you can click the square to display or remove a check mark; this component allows the user to select or deselect an option
Option buttons	A group of options that are similar to check boxes, but that are mutually exclusive. When the options are square, they are often called a check box group. When they are round, they are often called radio buttons.
List box	When the user clicks a list box, a menu of items appears. Depending on the options the programmer sets, you might be able to make only one selection, or you might be able to make multiple selections.
Button	A rectangular object you can click; when you do, it usually appears to be pressed

Table 8-2 Common GUI components

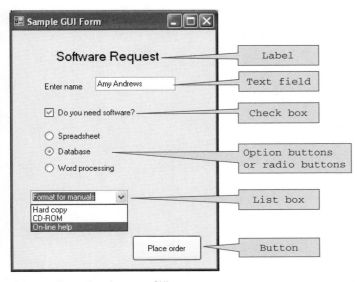

Figure 8-3 Illustration of common GUI components

When you program in a language that supports event-driven logic, you do not create the GUI components you need from scratch. Instead, you call prewritten methods that draw the GUI components on the screen for you. The components themselves are constructed using existing classes complete with names, attributes, and methods. In some programming language environments, you write statements that call the methods that create the GUI objects; in others, you can drag GUI objects onto your screen from a toolbar and arrange them appropriately for your application. Either way, you do not worry about the details of constructing the components. Instead, you concentrate on the actions that you want to take place when a user initiates an event from one of the components. Thus, GUI components are excellent examples of the best principles of object-oriented programming (OOP)—they represent objects with attributes and methods that operate like black boxes, making them easy for you to use.

> **» NOTE** GUI components are often referred to as *widgets*, which some sources claim is a combination of the terms *window* and *gadgets*. Originally, "widget" comes from the 1924 play "Beggar on Horseback," by George Kaufman and Marc Connelly. In the play, a young composer gets engaged to the daughter of a rich businessman, and foresees spending his life doing pointless work in a bureaucratic big business that manufactures widgets, which represent a useless item whose purpose is never explained.

When you use already created GUI components, you are instantiating objects, each of which belongs to a prewritten class. For example, you might use a Button class object when you want the user to be able to click a button to make a selection. Depending on the programming language you use, the Button class might contain attributes or properties such as the text written on the Button and the position of the Button on the screen. The class might also contain methods such as setText() and setPosition(). For example, Figure 8-4 shows how a built-in Button class might have been written.

```
class Button
    private string text
    private numeric x_position
    private numeric y_position

    public void setText(string messageOnButton)
        text = messageOnButton
    return

    public void setPosition(numeric x, numeric y)
        x_position = x
        y_position = y
    return
endClass
```

Figure 8-4 Button class

> **NOTE** The x_position and y_position of the Button object defined in Figure 8-4 refer to horizontal and verti-
> cal coordinates where the Button appears on an object, such as a window that appears on the screen during program
> execution. A **pixel** is one of the tiny dots of light that form a grid on your screen. The term *pixel* derives from combining the
> first syllables of *picture* and *element*. You will use x- and y-positions again when you learn about animation later in this
> chapter.

The Button class shown in Figure 8-4 is an abbreviated version so you can easily see its similarity to classes such as Student and Employee, which you read about in Chapter 7. A working Button class in most programming languages would contain many more fields and methods. For example, you might need to set a Button's font, color, size, and so on.

To create a Button object, you would write a statement similar to the following:

```
Button myProgramButton
```

In this statement, Button represents the type and myProgramButton represents the object you create. To use a Button's methods, you would write statements such as the following:

```
myProgramButton.setText("Click here")
myProgramButton.setPosition(10, 30)
```

Different GUI classes support different attributes and methods. For example, a CheckBox class might contain a method named getChecked() that returns true or false, indicating whether the CheckBox object has been checked. A Button, however, would have no need for such a method.

DESIGNING GRAPHICAL USER INTERFACES

You should consider several general design principles when creating a program that will use a GUI:

>> The interface should be natural and predictable.
>> The interface should be attractive, easy to read, and nondistracting.

» To some extent, it's helpful if the user can customize your applications.

» The program should be forgiving.

» The GUI is only a means to an end.

THE INTERFACE SHOULD BE NATURAL AND PREDICTABLE

The GUI program interface should represent objects like their real-world counterparts. In other words, it makes sense to use an icon that looks like a recycling bin when you want to allow a user to drag files or other components to the bin to delete them. Using a recycling bin icon is "natural" in that people use one in real life when they want to discard real-life items; dragging files to the bin is also "natural" because that's what people do with real-life items they discard. Using a recycling bin for discarded items is also predictable, because users are already familiar with the icon in other programs. Some icons may be natural, but if they are not predictable as well, then they are not as effective. An icon that depicts a recycling truck is just as "natural" as far as corresponding to real-world recycling, but because other programs do not use a truck icon for this purpose, it is not as predictable.

GUIs should also be predictable in their layout. For example, when you use a menu bar, it is at the top of the screen in most GUI programs, and the first menu item is almost always *File*. If you design a program interface in which the menu runs vertically down the right side of the screen, or in which *File* is the last menu option instead of the first, you will confuse users. Either they will make mistakes when using your program, or they may give up using it entirely. It doesn't matter if you can prove that your layout plan is more efficient than the standard one—if you do not use a predictable layout, your program will meet rejection from users in the marketplace.

>>**NOTE** Many studies have proven that the Dvorak keyboard layout is more efficient for typists than the QWERTY keyboard layout that most of us use. The QWERTY keyboard layout gets its name from the first six letter keys in the top row. With the Dvorak layout, which gets its name from its inventor, the most frequently used keys are in the home row, allowing typists to complete many more keystrokes per minute. However, the Dvorak keyboard has not caught on with the computer-buying public because it is not predictable.

>>**NOTE** Stovetops often have an unnatural interface, making unfamiliar stoves more difficult for you to use. Most stovetops have four burners arranged in two rows, but the knobs that control the burners frequently are placed in a single horizontal row. Because there is not a natural correlation between the placement of a burner and its control, you are more likely to select the wrong knob when adjusting the burner's flame or heating element.

THE INTERFACE SHOULD BE ATTRACTIVE, EASY TO READ, AND NONDISTRACTING

>>**NOTE** An excellent way to learn about good GUI design is to pay attention to the design features used in popular applications and in Web sites you visit.

If your interface is attractive, people are more likely to use it. If it is easy to read, they are less likely to make mistakes and more likely to want to use it. And if the interface is easy to read, it will more likely be considered attractive. When it comes to GUI design, fancy fonts and weird color combinations are the signs of amateur designers. In addition, you should make sure that unavailable screen options are either sufficiently dimmed or removed, so the user does not waste time clicking components that aren't functional.

Screen designs should not be distracting. When a screen has too many components, users can't find what they're looking for. When a text field or button is no longer needed, it should be removed from the interface. You also want to avoid distracting users with overly creative design elements. When users click a button to open a file, they might be amused the first time a filename dances across the screen or the speakers play a tune. But after one or two experiences with your creative additions, users find that intruding design elements simply hamper the actual work of the program.

TO SOME EXTENT, IT'S HELPFUL IF THE USER CAN CUSTOMIZE YOUR APPLICATIONS

Every user works in his or her own way. If you are designing an application that will use numerous menus and toolbars, it's helpful if users can position the components in the order that's easiest for them to work with. Users appreciate being able to change features like color schemes. Allowing a user to change the background color in your application may seem frivolous to you, but to users who are color-blind or visually impaired, it might make the difference in whether they use your application at all.

THE PROGRAM SHOULD BE FORGIVING

Perhaps you have had the inconvenience of accessing a voice mail system in which you selected several sequential options, only to find yourself at a dead end with no recourse but to hang up and redial the number. Good program design avoids equivalent problems. You should always provide an escape route to accommodate users who have made bad choices or changed their minds. By providing a Back button or functional Escape key, you provide more functionality to your users.

THE GUI IS ONLY A MEANS TO AN END

The most important principle of GUI design is to always remember that any GUI is only an interface. Using a mouse to click items and drag them around is not the point of any business programs except those that train people how to use a mouse. Instead, the point of a graphical interface is to help people be more productive. To that end, the design should help the user see what options are available, allow the use of components in the ordinary way, and not force the user to concentrate on how to interact with your application. The real work of any GUI program is done after the user clicks a button or makes a list box selection. It is then that actual program tasks take place.

MODIFYING THE ATTRIBUTES OF GUI COMPONENTS

When you design a program with premade or preprogrammed graphical components, you will want to change their appearance to customize them for the current application. Each programming language provides its own means of changing components' appearances, but all involve changing the values stored in the components' attribute fields. Some common changes include setting the following items:

» The size of the component

» The color of the component

» The screen location of the component

» The font for any text contained in or on the component

» The component to be visible or invisible

» The component to be dimmed or undimmed, sometimes called *enabled* or *disabled*

You must learn the exact names of the methods and what type of arguments you are allowed to use in each programming language you learn, but all languages that support creating event-driven applications allow you to set components' attributes and get the values for most of them.

When you use a graphical development environment in which you can drag a component such as a button onto a screen and type its text into a list of properties, program code statements are automatically generated for you. For example, when you drag a `Button` onto a screen, its `setPosition()` method is called automatically and passed the values of the coordinates where you drop it with your mouse. If you move the `Button`, the `setPosition()` method is called again and the new coordinates are passed to it. In graphical languages you always have the option of writing the code statements that set GUI objects' properties yourself instead of allowing them to be automatically generated. In other words, you always have the option of designing the screen "the hard way" by writing code. The drag-and-drop and property list features are available to you as a convenience.

THE STEPS TO DEVELOPING AN EVENT-DRIVEN APPLICATION

In Chapter 1, you first learned the steps to developing a computer program. They are:

1. Identify the objects, design the classes, and establish communication.
2. Plan the logic.
3. Code the program.
4. Translate the program into machine language.
5. Test the program.
6. Put the program into production.

When you develop an event-driven application, you expand on the initial design step, including three new substeps as follows:

1a. Create storyboards.
1b. Define the objects.
1c. Define the connections between the screens the user will see.

For example, suppose you want to create a simple, interactive program that determines premiums for prospective insurance customers. The users should be able to use a graphical interface to select a policy type—health or auto. Next, the users answer pertinent questions, such as how old they are, whether they smoke, and what their driving records are like.

Although most insurance premium amounts would be based on more characteristics than these, assume that policy rates are determined using the factors shown in Table 8-3. The final output of the program is a second screen that shows the semiannual premium amount for the chosen policy.

Health Policy Premiums	Auto Policy Premiums
Base rate: $500	Base rate: $750
Add $100 if over age 50	Add $400 if more than 2 tickets
Add $250 if smoker	Subtract $200 if over age 50

Table 8-3 Insurance premiums based on customer characteristics

CREATING STORYBOARDS

A **storyboard** represents a picture or sketch of a screen the user will see when running a program. Filmmakers have long used storyboards to illustrate key moments in the plots they are developing; similarly, GUI storyboards represent "snapshot" views of the screens the user will encounter during the run of a program. If the user could view up to four screens during the insurance premium program, then you would draw four storyboard cells, or frames.

Figure 8-5 shows two storyboard sketches for the insurance program. They represent the introductory screen at which the user selects a premium type and answers questions, and the final screen that displays the semiannual premium.

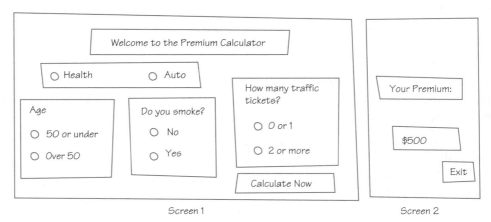

Figure 8-5 Storyboard for insurance program

DEFINING THE OBJECTS IN AN OBJECT DICTIONARY

An event-driven program may contain dozens or even hundreds of objects. To keep track of them, programmers often use an object dictionary. An **object dictionary** is a list of the objects used in a program, including which screens they are used on and whether any code, or script, is associated with them.

Figure 8-6 shows an object dictionary for the insurance premium program. The type and name of each object to be placed on a screen is listed in the left column. The second column shows the screen number on which the object appears. The next column names any variables that are affected by an action on the object. The right column indicates whether any code or script is associated with the object. For example, the label named labelWelcome appears on the first screen. It has no associated actions—it does not call any methods nor change any variables; it is just a label. The calcButton, however, does cause execution of a method named calcRoutine(). This method calculates the semiannual

» NOTE
Some organizations also include the disk location where an object is stored as part of the object dictionary.

Object Name	Screen Number	Variables Affected	Script?
Label labelWelcome	1	none	none
RadioButton radioButtonHealth	1	premiumAmount	none
RadioButton radioButtonAuto	1	premiumAmount	none
Label ageLabel	1	none	none
RadioButton radioButtonLowAge	1	premiumAmount	none
RadioButton radioButtonHighAge	1	premiumAmount	none
Label smokeLabel	1	none	none
RadioButton radioButtonSmokeNo	1	premiumAmount	none
RadioButton radioButtonSmokeYes	1	premiumAmount	none
Label ticketsLabel	1	none	none
RadioButton radioButtonLowTickets	1	premiumAmount	none
RadioButton radioButtonHighTickets	1	premiumAmount	none
Button calcButton	1	premiumAmount	calcRoutine()
Label labelPremium	2	none	none
Label premAmtLabel	2	none	none
Button exitButton	2	none	exitRoutine()

Figure 8-6 Object dictionary for insurance premium program

premium amount and stores it in the `premiumAmount` variable. Depending on the programming language you use, you might need to name `calcRoutine()` something similar to `calcButton.click()` to identify it as the module that executes when the user clicks the `calcButton`.

DEFINING THE CONNECTIONS BETWEEN THE USER SCREENS

The insurance premium program is a small one, so with larger programs you may need to draw the connections between the screens to show how they interact. Figure 8-7 shows an interactivity diagram for the screens used in the insurance premium program. An **interactivity diagram** shows the relationship between screens in an interactive GUI program. Figure 8-7 shows that the first screen calls the second screen, and the program ends.

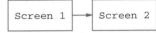

Figure 8-7 Diagram of interaction for insurance premium program

Figure 8-8 shows how a diagram might look for a more complicated program in which the user has several options available at Screens 1, 2, and 3. Notice how each of these three screens may lead to different screens, depending on the options the user selects at any one screen.

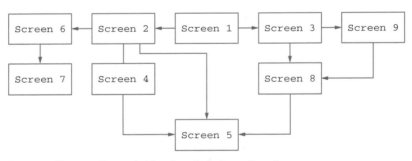

Figure 8-8 Diagram of interaction for a hypothetical complicated program

PLANNING THE LOGIC

In an event-driven program, you design the screens, define the objects, and define how the screens will connect. Then you can start to plan the insurance program class. For example, following the storyboard plan for the insurance program (see Figure 8-5), you need to create the first screen that contains a label, four sets of radio buttons, and a button. Figure 8-9 shows the pseudocode that creates these components.

```
Label labelWelcome
labelWelcome.setText("Welcome to the Premium Calculator")
labelWelcome.setPosition(30, 10)

RadioButton radioButtonHealth
radioButtonHealth.setText("Health")
radioButtonHealth.setPosition(15, 40)

RadioButton radioButtonAuto
radioButtonAuto.setText("Auto")
radioButtonAuto.setPosition(50, 40)

Label ageLabel
ageLabel.setText("Age")
ageLabel.setLocation(5, 60)

RadioButton radioButtonLowAge
radioButtonLowAge.setText("50 or under")
radioButtonLowAge.setPosition(5, 70)

RadioButton radioButtonHighAge
radioButtonHighAge.setText("Over 50")
radioButtonHighAge.setPosition(5, 80)

Label smokeLabel
smokeLabel.setText("Do you smoke?")
smokeLabel.setLocation(40, 60)

RadioButton radioButtonSmokeNo
radioButtonSmokeNo.setText("No")
radioButtonSmokeNo.setPosition(40, 70)

RadioButton radioButtonSmokeYes
radioButtonSmokeYes.setText("Yes")
radioButtonSmokeYes.setPosition(40, 80)

Label ticketsLabel
ticketsLabel.setText("How many traffic tickets?")
ticketsLabel.setLocation(60, 50)

RadioButton radioButtonLowTickets
radioButtonLowTickets.setText("0 or 1")
radioButtonLowTickets.setPosition(60, 70)

RadioButton radioButtonHighTickets
radioButtonHighTickets.setText("2 or more")
radioButtonHighTickets.setPosition(60, 90)

Button calcButton
calcButton.setText("Calculate now")
calcButton.setLocation(60, 100)
calcButton.registerListener(calcRoutine())
```

Figure 8-9 Component definitions for first screen of insurance program

>>**NOTE** Depending on the programming environment in which you are working, you might be able to drag the components in Figure 8-9 onto a screen without explicitly writing all the pseudocode statements. In that case, the coding statements will be generated for you.

>>**NOTE** In Figure 8-9, the statement `calcButton. registerListener (calcRoutine())` specifies that `calcRoutine()` executes when a user clicks the `calcButton`. The syntax of this statement varies among programming languages.

>>**NOTE** In reality, you might generate more code than that shown in Figure 8-9 when you create the insurance program components. For example, each component might require a color and font. You also might want to initialize some components with default values to indicate they are selected. For example, you might want one radio button in a group to be selected already, which allows the user to click a different option only if he does not want the default value.

You also need to create the component onto which all the GUI elements in Figure 8-9 are placed. Depending on the language you are using, you might use a class with a name such as `Screen`, `Form`, or `Window`. Each of these generically is a **container**, or a class of objects whose main purpose is to hold other elements. The container class contains methods that allow you set physical properties such as height and width, as well as methods that allow you to add the appropriate components to a container. Figure 8-10 shows how you would define a `Screen` class, set its size, and add the components it needs.

```
Screen screen1
screen1.setSize(150, 150)
screen1.add(labelWelcome)
screen1.add(radioButtonHealth)
screen1.add(radioButtonAuto)
screen1.add(ageLabel)
screen1.add(radioButtonLowAge)
screen1.add(radioButtonHighAge)
screen1.add(smokeLabel)
screen1.add(radioButtonSmokeNo)
screen1.add(radioButtonSmokeYes)
screen1.add(ticketsLabel)
screen1.add(radioButtonLowTickets)
screen1.add(radioButtonHighTickets)
screen1.add(calcButton)
```

Figure 8-10 Statements that create `screen1`

Similarly, Figure 8-11 shows how you can create the components for the second screen in the insurance program, how to define its components, and how to add the components to the container. Notice the label that holds the user's insurance premium is not filled

```
Screen screen2
screen2.setSize(100, 100)

Label labelPremium
labelPremium.setText("Your Premium")
labelPremium.setPosition(5, 30)

Label premAmtLabel
premAmtLabel.setPosition(20, 50)

Button exitButton
exitButton.setText("Exit")
exitButton.setLocation(60, 80)
exitButton.registerListener(exitRoutine())

screen2.add(labelPremium)
screen2.add(premAmtLabel)
screen2.add(exitButton)
```

Figure 8-11 Statements that define and create `screen2` and its components

with text, because the amount is not known until the user makes all the selections on the first screen.

After the GUI components are designed and arranged, you can plan the logic for each of the modules (or methods or scripts) that the program will use. For example, given the program requirements shown in Table 8-3, you can write the pseudocode for the `calcRoutine()` method of the insurance premium program, as shown in Figure 8-12. The `calcRoutine()` method does not execute until the user clicks the `calcButton`. At that point, the user's choices are sent to the method and used to calculate the premium amount.

```
public static void calcRoutine()
    numeric HEALTH_AMT = 500
    numeric HIGH_AGE = 100
    numeric SMOKER = 250
    numeric AUTO_AMT = 750
    numeric HIGH_TICKETS = 400
    numeric HIGH_AGE_DRIVER_DISCOUNT = 200
    numeric premiumAmount
    if radioButtonHealth.getChecked() then
        premiumAmount = HEALTH_AMT
        if radioButtonHighAge.getChecked() then
            premiumAmount = premiumAmount + HIGH_AGE
        endif
        if radioButtonSmokeYes.getChecked() then
            premiumAmount = premiumAmount + SMOKER
        endif
    else
        premiumAmount = AUTO_AMT
        if radioButtonHighTickets.getChecked() then
            premiumAmount = premiumAmount + HIGH_TICKETS
        endif
        if radioButtonHighAge.getChecked() then
            premiumAmount = premiumAmount - HIGH_AGE_DRIVER_DISCOUNT
        endif
    endif
    premAmtLabel.setText(premiumAmount)
    screen1.remove()
    screen2.display()
return
```

Figure 8-12 Pseudocode for `calcRoutine()` method for insurance premium program

The pseudocode in Figure 8-12 should look very familiar to you—it declares numeric constants and a variable and uses decision-making logic you have used since the early chapters of this book. After the premium is calculated based on the user's choices, it is placed in the label that appears on the second screen. The basic structures of sequence, selection, and looping will continue to serve you well, whether you are programming in a procedural or event-driven environment.

The last two statements in the `calcRoutine()` method indicate that after the insurance premium is calculated and placed in its label, the first screen is removed and the second screen is displayed. Screen removal and display are accomplished differently in different languages; this example assumes that the appropriate methods are named `remove()` and `display()`.

Two more methods are needed to complete the insurance premium program. These methods include the first method that executes when the program starts and the last method that executes when the program ends. For this example, the first method is called `main()`. In many GUI languages, the process is slightly more complicated, but the general logic appears in Figure 8-13. The final method in the program is the one that is associated with the `exitButton` on `screen2`. In Figure 8-13, this method is called `exitRoutine()`. In this program, the initialization method sets up the first screen and the last method removes the last screen.

```
public static void main()
    screen1.display()
return

public static void exitRoutine()
    screen2.remove()
return
```

Figure 8-13 The `main()` and `exitRoutine()` methods for the insurance program

> **NOTE** With most OOP languages, you must **register**, or sign up, components that will react to events initiated by other components. The details vary among languages, but the basic process is to write a statement that links the appropriate method (such as the `calcRoutine()` or `exitRoutine()` method) with an event such as a user's button click. In many development environments, the statement that registers a component to react to a user-initiated event is written for you automatically when you click components while designing your screen.

UNDERSTANDING MULTITHREADING

A **thread** is the flow of execution of one set of program statements. When you execute a program statement by statement, from beginning to end, you are following a thread. Many applications follow a single thread; this means that at any one time the application executes only a single program statement.

Single-thread programs contain statements that execute in very rapid sequence, but only one statement executes at a time. When a computer contains a single central processing unit (CPU, or processor), it can execute only one computer instruction at a time, regardless of its processor speed. When you use a computer with multiple CPUs, the computer can execute multiple instructions simultaneously.

All major OOP languages allow you to launch, or start, multiple threads, no matter which type of processing system you use. Using multiple threads of execution is known as **multithreading**. As already noted, if you use a computer system that contains more than one CPU (such as a very large mainframe or supercomputer), multiple threads can execute simultaneously. Figure 8-14 illustrates how multithreading executes in a multiprocessor system.

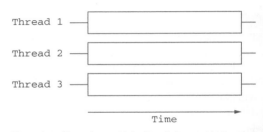

Figure 8-14 Executing multiple threads in a multiprocessor system

If you use a computer with a single processor, the multiple threads share the CPU's time, as shown in Figure 8-15. The CPU devotes a small amount of time to one task, and then devotes a small amount of time to another task. The CPU never actually performs two tasks at the same instant. Instead, it performs a piece of one task and then a piece of another task. The CPU performs so quickly that each task seems to execute without interruption.

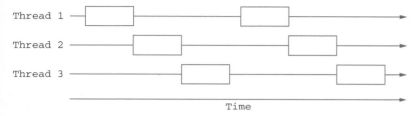

Figure 8-15 Executing multiple threads in a single-processor system

Perhaps you have seen an expert chess player participate in chess games with several opponents at once. The chess player makes a move on the first playing board, and then moves to the second board against a second opponent while the first opponent analyzes his next move. The master can move to the third board, make a move, and return to the first board before the first opponent is even ready to respond. To the first opponent, it might seem as though the expert player is devoting all of her time to him. Because the expert is so fast, she can play other opponents in the first opponent's "downtime." Executing multiple threads on a single CPU is a similar process. The CPU transfers its attention from thread to thread so quickly that the tasks don't even "miss" the CPU's attention.

» NOTE
Programmers sometimes use the terms *thread of execution* or *execution context* to describe a thread. They also describe a thread as a light-weight process because it is not a full-blown program. Rather, a thread must run within the context of a full, heavyweight program.

You use multithreading to improve the performance of your programs. Multithreaded programs often run faster, but more importantly, they are more user-friendly. With a multithreaded program, your user can continue to click buttons while your program is reading a data file. With multithreading, an animated figure can appear on one part of the screen while the user makes menu selections on another part of the screen. When you use the Internet, multithreading increases in importance. For example, you can begin to read a long text file or listen to an audio file while the file is still downloading. Web users are likely to abandon a site if downloading a file takes too long. When you use multithreading to perform concurrent tasks, you are more likely to retain visitors to your Web site—this is particularly important if your site sells a product or service.

Object-oriented languages often contain a built-in `Thread` class that contains methods to help handle multiple threads. For example, one often-needed method is a `sleep()` method that can pause program execution for a specified amount of time. Computer instruction processing speed is so rapid that sometimes you have to slow processing down for human consumption. An application that frequently requires `sleep()` method calls is computer animation.

CREATING ANIMATION

Many object-oriented languages offer built-in classes that contain methods you can use to draw geometric figures on the screen. The methods typically have names like `drawLine()`, `drawCircle()`, `drawRectangle()`, and so on. You place figures on the screen based on a graphing coordinate system. Typically, any component you place on the screen has a horizontal, or **x-axis**, position as well as a vertical, or **y-axis**, position in a screen window. The upper-left corner of any display is position 0, 0. The first, or **x-coordinate**, value increases as you travel from left to right across the window. The second, or **y-coordinate**, value increases as you travel from top to bottom. Figure 8-16 shows four screen coordinate positions. The more to the right a spot is, the higher its x-coordinate value, and the lower a spot is, the higher its y-coordinate value.

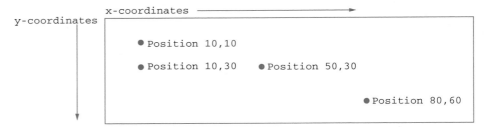

Figure 8-16 Selected screen coordinate positions

Cartoonists create animated films by drawing a sequence of frames or cells. These individual drawings are shown to the audience in rapid succession to give the illusion of natural movement. You create computer animation using the same techniques. If you display computer images as fast as your CPU can process them, you might not be able to see anything. Most computer animation employs a `Thread` class `sleep()` method to pause for short periods of time between animation cells, so the human brain has time to absorb each image's content.

Artists often spend a great deal of time creating the exact images they want to use in an animation sequence. As a simple example, Figure 8-17 shows pseudocode for a `MovingCircle` class. As its name implies, the class moves a circle across the screen. The class contains data fields to hold x- and y-coordinates that identify the location at which a circle appears. The constants `SIZE` and `INCREASE` respectively define the size of the first circle drawn and the relative increase in size and position of each subsequent circle. The `MovingCircle` class

```
public class MovingCircle
    private numeric x = 20
    private numeric y = 20
    private numeric LIMIT = 300
    private numeric SIZE = 40
    private numeric INCREASE = SIZE / 10
    private numeric SLEEP_TIME = 100
    public void main()
        while(true)
            repaintScreen()
        endwhile
    return
    public void repaintScreen()
        drawCircle(x, y, x + SIZE)
        x = x + INCREASE
        y = y + INCREASE
        Thread.sleep(SLEEP_TIME)
    return
endClass
```

Figure 8-17 The `MovingCircle` class

assumes you are working with a language that provides a `drawCircle()` method, which takes care of the details of creating a circle when it is given parameters for horizontal and vertical positions and circle size. Assuming you are working with a language that provides a `sleep()` method that accepts a pause time in milliseconds, the `SLEEP_TIME` constant provides a 100-millisecond gap before the production of each new circle.

The `main()` method in the `MovingCircle` class executes a continuous loop. A similar technique is used in many languages that support GUI interfaces. Program execution will cease only when the user quits the application by clicking a window's close button on the screen, for example. In the `repaintScreen()` method of the `MovingCircle` class, a circle is drawn at the x, y position, then x and y are both increased. The application sleeps for one-tenth of a second (the `SLEEP_TIME` value), and then the `repaintScreen()` method draws a new circle more to the right, further down, and a little larger. The effect is a moving circle that leaves a trail of smaller circles behind as it moves diagonally across the screen. Figure 8-18 shows the output as a Java version of the application executes.

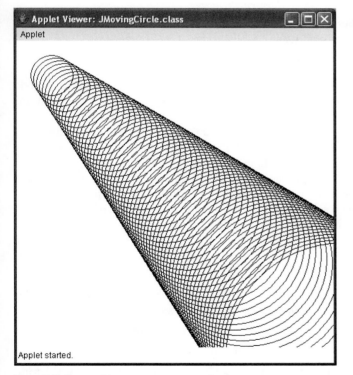

Figure 8-18 Output of the `MovingCircle` application

Although an object-oriented language might make it easy for you to draw geometric shapes, you can also substitute a variety of more sophisticated, predrawn animated images to achieve the graphic effects you want within your programs. An image is loaded in a separate thread of execution; this allows program execution to continue while the image loads. This is a great advantage because loading a large image can be time consuming.

»NOTE
Many animated images are available on the Web for you to use freely. Use your search engine to search for keywords such as *gif files*, *jpeg files*, and *animation* to find sources for shareware and freeware files.

CHAPTER SUMMARY

» Interacting with a computer operating system from the command line is difficult; it is easier to use an event-driven graphical user interface (GUI), in which users manipulate objects such as buttons and menus. Within an event-driven program, a component from which an event is generated is the source of the event. A listener is an object that is "interested in" an event to which you want it to respond.

» The possible events a user can initiate include a key press, mouse point, click, right-click, double-click, and drag. Common GUI components include labels, text fields, buttons, check boxes, check box groups, option buttons, lists, and toolbars. GUI components are excellent examples of the best principles of object-oriented programming (OOP)—they represent objects with attributes and methods that operate like black boxes.

» When you create a program that will use a GUI, the interface should be natural, pre-dictable, attractive, easy to read, and nondistracting. It's helpful if the user can customize your applications. The program should be forgiving, and you should not forget that the GUI is only a means to an end.

» You can modify the attributes of GUI components. For example, you can set the size, color, screen location, font, visibility, and enabled status of the component.

» Developing an event-driven application is more complicated than developing a standard procedural program. You must understand the problem, create storyboards, define the objects, define the connections between the screens the user will see, plan the logic, code the program, translate the program into machine language, test the program, and put the program into production.

» A thread is the flow of execution of one set of program statements. Many applications follow a single thread; using multiple threads of execution is known as multithreading.

» Many object-oriented languages contain built-in classes that contain methods you can use to draw geometric figures on the screen. Typically, any component you place on the screen has a horizontal, or x-axis, position as well as a vertical, or y-axis, position in a screen window. You create computer animation by drawing a sequence of images that are shown in rapid succession.

KEY TERMS

An **operating system** is the software that you use to run a computer and manage its resources.

The **DOS prompt** is the command line in the DOS operating system.

Icons are small pictures on the screen that the user can select with a mouse.

An **event** is an occurrence that generates a message sent to an object.

GUI programs are called **event-driven** or **event-based** because actions occur in response to user-initiated events such as clicking a mouse button.

The **source of an event** is the component from which the event is generated.

A **listener** is an object that is "interested in" an event to which you want it to respond.

A **pixel** is a picture element, or one of the tiny dots of light that form a grid on your screen.

Accessibility issues are the screen design issues that make programs easier to use for people with physical limitations.

A **storyboard** represents a picture or sketch of a screen the user will see when running a program.

An **object dictionary** is a list of the objects used in a program, including which screens they are used on and whether any code, or script, is associated with them.

An **interactivity diagram** shows the relationship between screens in an interactive GUI program.

A **container** is a class of objects whose main purpose is to hold other elements—for example, a window.

In object-oriented programming languages, you **register**, or sign up, components that will react to events initiated by other components.

A **thread** is the flow of execution of one set of program statements.

Multithreading is using multiple threads of execution.

The **x-axis** represents horizontal positions in a screen window.

The **y-axis** represents vertical positions in a screen window.

The **x-coordinate** value increases as you travel from left to right across a window.

The **y-coordinate** value increases as you travel from top to bottom across a window.

REVIEW QUESTIONS

1. As opposed to using a command line, an advantage to using an operating system that employs a GUI is _____ .

   a. you can interact directly with the operating system

   b. you do not have to deal with confusing icons

   c. you do not have to memorize complicated commands

   d. all of the above

2. When users can initiate actions by clicking a mouse on an icon, the program is _____ -driven.

   a. event   c. command

   b. prompt   d. incident

3. A component from which an event is generated is the _____ of the event.

   a. base   c. listener

   b. icon   d. source

4. An object that responds to an event is a _____ .

   a. source   c. transponder

   b. listener   d. snooper

5. All of the following are user-initiated events except a _____ .

    a. key press

    b. key drag

    c. right mouse click

    d. mouse drag

6. All of the following are typical GUI components except a _____ .

    a. label

    b. text field

    c. list box

    d. button box

7. GUI components operate like _____ .

    a. black boxes

    b. procedural functions

    c. looping structures

    d. command lines

8. Which of the following is *not* a principle of good GUI design?

    a. The interface should be predictable.

    b. The fancier the screen design, the better.

    c. The program should be forgiving.

    d. The user should be able to customize your applications.

9. Which of the following aspects of a GUI layout is most predictable and natural for the user?

    a. A menu bar runs down the right side of the screen.

    b. *Help* is the first option on a menu.

    c. A dollar sign icon represents saving a file.

    d. Pressing *Esc* allows the user to cancel a selection.

10. In most GUI programming environments, you can change all of the following attributes of most components except their _____ .

    a. color

    b. screen location

    c. size

    d. You can change all of these attributes.

11. Depending on the programming language you use, you might _____ to change a screen component's attributes.

    a. use an assignment statement

    b. call a module

    c. enter a value into a list of properties

    d. all of the above

12. When you create an event-driven application, which of the following must be done before defining the objects you will use?

    a. Plan the logic.

    b. Create storyboards.

    c. Test the program.

    d. Code the program.

13. A _____ is a sketch of a screen the user will see when running a program.

    a. flowchart

    b. hierarchy chart

    c. storyboard

    d. tale timber

14. A list of objects used in a program is an object _____ .

    a. thesaurus

    b. glossary

    c. index

    d. dictionary

15. A(n) _____ diagram shows the connections between the various screens a user might see during a program's execution.

    a. interactivity

    b. help

    c. cooperation

    d. communication

16. The flow of execution of one set of program statements is a _____ .

    a. thread

    b. string

    c. path

    d. route

17. When a computer contains a single CPU, it can execute _____ computer instruc-
tion(s) at a time.

    a. one

    b. several

    c. an unlimited number of

    d. from several to thousands (depending on the processor speed)

18. Typically, any component you place on the screen has a horizontal, or _____ ,
position as well as a vertical position in a screen window.

    a. x-axis

    b. y-axis

    c. v-axis

    d. h-axis

19. You create computer animation by _____ .

    a. drawing an image and setting its animation property to true

    b. drawing a single image and executing it on a multiprocessor system

    c. drawing a sequence of frames that are shown in rapid succession

    d. Animation is not used in computer applications.

20. You can use sophisticated, predrawn animated images to achieve the graphic effects you
want within your programs _____ .

    a. by loading them in a separate thread of execution

    b. only by subscribing to expensive imaging services

    c. with multiprocessing systems, but not on a computer with a single processor

    d. two of the above

EXERCISES

1. Take a critical look at three GUI applications with which you are familiar—for example, a
spreadsheet, a word-processing program, and a game. Describe how well each conforms
to the GUI design guidelines listed in this chapter.

2. Select one element of poor GUI design in a program with which you are familiar. Describe
how you would improve the design.

3. Select a GUI program that you have never used before. Describe how well it conforms
to the GUI design guidelines listed in this chapter.

4. Design the storyboards, interactivity diagram, object dictionary, and any necessary scripts
for an interactive program for customers of Sunflower Floral Designs.

Allow customers the option of choosing a floral arrangement ($25 base price), cut flowers ($15 base price), or a corsage ($10 base price). Let the customer choose roses, daisies, chrysanthemums, or irises as the dominant flower. If the customer chooses roses, add $5 to the base price. After the customer clicks an Order Now button, display the price of the order.

5. Design the storyboards, interactivity diagram, object dictionary, and any necessary scripts for an interactive program for customers of Toby's Travels.

Allow customers the option of at least five trip destinations and four means of transportation, each with a unique price. After the customer clicks the Plan Trip Now button, display the price of the trip.

6. Design the storyboards, interactivity diagram, object dictionary, and any necessary scripts for an interactive program for customers of The Mane Event Hair Salon.

Allow customers the option of choosing a haircut ($15), coloring ($25), or perm ($45). After the customer clicks a Select button, display the price of the service.

CASE PROJECT

In earlier chapters, you developed classes needed for Cost Is No Object—a car rental service that specializes in lending antique and luxury cars to clients on a short-term basis. You created pseudocode for Employee, Customer, Automobile, and RentalAgreement classes, including attributes and methods to get and set those attributes.

Design an interactive application that displays the following:

» A main screen containing at least the company name, an animated image, and two buttons. One button allows the rental agent to proceed to a data entry screen and enter customer data (name, address, and so on). The other button allows the agent to enter rental agreement data.

» A customer data entry screen.

» A rental agreement data entry screen.

Create storyboards, define the objects you need, and define the connections between the screens the user will see.

UP FOR DISCUSSION

1. Making exciting, entertaining, professional-looking GUI applications becomes easier once you learn to include graphics images. You can copy graphics images from many locations on the Web. Should there be any restrictions on what graphics you use? Does it make a difference if you are writing programs for your own enjoyment as opposed to putting them on the Web where others can see them? Is using photographs different from using drawings? Does it matter if the photographs contain recognizable people? Would you impose any restrictions on images posted to your organization's Web site?

2. Playing computer games has been shown to increase the level of dopamine in the human brain. High levels of this substance are associated with addiction to drugs. Suppose you work for a company that manufactures games and it decides to research how its games can produce more dopamine in the brains of players. Would you support the company's decision?

3. If you are completing all the programming exercises at the ends of the chapters in this book, you are beginning to understand that working programs require a lot of time to plan, write, and test. Professional programs require even more hours of work. In the workplace, programs frequently must be completed by strict deadlines—for example, a tax-calculating program must be completed by year's end or an advertising Web site must be completed by the launch of the product. Programmers often find themselves working into the evenings or weekends to complete rush projects at work. How would you feel about having to do this? What types of compensation would make the extra hours worthwhile for you?

OBJECT CONCEPTS: POLYMORPHISM AND INHERITANCE

In this chapter, you will:

>> Learn about the concept of inheritance
Understand inheritance terminology
Access private members of a parent class
Override base class methods
Understand how constructors are called during inheritance
Learn that a derived class object "is an" instance of the base class
Use inheritance to achieve good software design

UNDERSTANDING INHERITANCE

Understanding classes helps you organize objects in real life. Understanding inheritance helps you organize them more precisely. If you have never heard of a Braford, for example, you would have a hard time forming a picture of one in your mind. When you learn that a Braford is an animal, you gain some understanding of what it must be like. That understanding grows when you learn it is a mammal, and the understanding is almost complete when you learn it is a cow. When you learn that a Braford is a cow, you understand it has many characteristics that are common to all cows. To identify a Braford, you must learn only relatively minor details—its color or markings, for example. Most of a Braford's characteristics, however, derive from its membership in a particular hierarchy of classes: animal, mammal, and cow. All object-oriented programming languages make use of inheritance for the same reasons—to organize the objects programs use, and to make new objects easier to understand based on your knowledge of their inherited traits.

▶▶NOTE
You first learned about the concept of inheritance in Chapter 1.

Inheritance is the principle that you can apply your knowledge of a general category to more specific objects. You are familiar with the concept of inheritance from all sorts of situations. When you use the term *inheritance*, you might think of genetic inheritance. You know from biology that your blood type and eye color are the products of inherited genes. You can say that many other facts about you (your attributes) are inherited. Similarly, you often can attribute your behaviors to inheritance; for example, the way you handle money might be similar to the way your grandmother handles it, and your gait might be the same as your father's—so your methods are inherited, too.

You also might choose to own plants and animals based on their inherited attributes. You plant impatiens next to your house because they thrive in the shade; you adopt a poodle because you know poodles don't shed. Every plant and pet has slightly different characteristics, but within a species, you can count on many consistent inherited attributes and behaviors. In other words, you can reuse the knowledge you gain about general categories and apply it to more specific categories. Similarly, the classes you create in object-oriented programming languages can inherit data and methods from existing classes. When you create a class by making it inherit from another class, you are provided with data fields and methods automatically; you can reuse fields and methods that are already written and tested.

You already know how to create classes and how to instantiate objects that are instances of those classes. For example, consider the Employee class in Figure 9-1. The class

```
class Employee
    private string empNum
    private numeric weeklySalary

    public void setEmpNum(string num)
        empNum = num
    return

    public string getEmpNum()
    return empNum

    public void setWeeklySalary(numeric salary)
        weeklySalary = salary
    return

    public numeric getWeeklySalary()
    return weeklySalary
endClass
```

Figure 9-1 An Employee class

contains two data fields, empNum and weeklySalary, as well as methods that get and set each field.

After you create the Employee class, you can create specific Employee objects, as in the following:

```
Employee receptionist
Employee deliveryPerson
```

These Employee objects can eventually possess different numbers and salaries, but because they are Employee objects, you know that each possesses *some* number and salary.

Suppose you hire a new type of Employee who earns a commission as well as a weekly salary. You can create a class with a name such as CommissionEmployee, and provide this class with three fields (empNum, weeklySalary, and commissionRate) and six methods (to get and set each of the three fields). However, this work would duplicate much of the work that you already have done for the Employee class. The wise and efficient alternative is to create the class CommissionEmployee so it inherits all the attributes and methods of Employee. Then, you can add just the single field and two methods (the get and set methods for the new field) that are additions within the new class. Figure 9-2 depicts these relationships. The complete CommissionEmployee class is shown in Figure 9-3.

NOTE
Recall from Chapter 7 that a plus in a class diagram indicates public access and a minus indicates private access.

NOTE
Figure 9-2 and several other figures in this chapter are examples of UML diagrams. Chapter 11 describes UML diagrams in more detail.

```
Employee

−empNum : string
−weeklySalary : numeric

+setEmpNum(num : string) : void
+getEmpNum() : string
+setWeeklySalary(salary : numeric) : void
+getWeeklySalary() : numeric
```

```
CommissionEmployee

−commissionRate : numeric

+setCommissionRate(rate : numeric) : void
+getCommissionRate() : void
```

Figure 9-2 CommissionEmployee inherits from Employee

```
class CommissionEmployee inheritsFrom Employee
    private numeric commissionRate

    public void setCommissionRate(numeric rate)
        commissionRate = rate
    return

    public numeric getCommissionRate()
    return commissionRate
endClass
```

Figure 9-3 CommissionEmployee class

NOTE The class in Figure 9-3 uses the phrase "inheritsFrom Employee" (see shading) to indicate inheritance. Each programming language uses its own syntax. For example, using Java you would write "extends", in Visual Basic you would write "inherits", and in C++ and C# you would use a colon between the new class name and the one from which it inherits.

When you use inheritance to create the CommissionEmployee class, you acquire the following benefits:

» You save time, because you need not recreate the Employee fields and methods.

» You reduce the chance of errors, because the Employee methods have already been used and tested.

» You make it easier for anyone who has used the `Employee` class to understand the `CommissionEmployee` class because such users can concentrate on the new features only.

» NOTE
In part, the concept of class inheritance is useful because it makes class code reusable. However, you do not use inheritance simply to save work. When properly used, inheritance always involves a general-to-specific relationship.

The ability to use inheritance makes programs easier to write, easier to understand, and less prone to errors. Imagine that besides `CommissionEmployee`, you want to create several other more specific `Employee` classes (perhaps `PartTimeEmployee`, including a field for hours worked, or `DismissedEmployee`, including a reason for dismissal). By using inheritance, you can develop each new class correctly and quickly.

UNDERSTANDING INHERITANCE TERMINOLOGY

A class that is used as a basis for inheritance, like `Employee`, is called a **base class**. When you create a class that inherits from a base class (such as `CommissionEmployee`), it is a **derived** or **extended class**. When presented with two classes that have a base-derived relationship, you can tell which class is the base class and which is the derived class by using the two classes in a sentence with the phrase "is a." A derived class always "is a" case or instance of the more general base class. For example, a `Tree` class may be a base class to an `Evergreen` class. Every `Evergreen` "is a" `Tree`; however, it is not true that every `Tree` is an `Evergreen`. Thus, `Tree` is the base class and `Evergreen` is the derived class. Similarly, a `CommissionEmployee` "is an" `Employee`—not always the other way around—so `Employee` is the base class and `CommissionEmployee` is derived.

You can use the terms **superclass** and **subclass** as synonyms for base class and derived class. Thus, `Evergreen` can be called a subclass of the `Tree` superclass. You also can use the terms **parent class** and **child class**. A `CommissionEmployee` is a child to the `Employee` parent. Use the pair of terms with which you are most comfortable; all of these terms will be used interchangeably in this book.

As an alternative way to discover which of two classes is the base class and which is the derived class, you can try saying the two class names together (although this technique might not work with every base-subclass pair). When people say their names together in the English language, they state the more specific name before the all-encompassing family name, such as "Mary Johnson." Similarly, with classes, the order that "makes more sense" is the child-parent order. Thus, because "Evergreen Tree" makes more sense than "Tree Evergreen," you can deduce that `Evergreen` is the child class.

> **» NOTE** It also is convenient to think of a derived class as building upon its base class by providing the "adjectives" or additional descriptive terms for the "noun." Frequently, the names of derived classes are formed in this way, as in `CommissionEmployee` or `EvergreenTree`.

» NOTE
Do not think of a subclass as a "subset" of another class—in other words, possessing only parts of its base class. In fact, a derived class usually contains more than its parent.

Finally, you usually can distinguish base classes from their derived classes by size. Although it is not required, a derived class is generally larger than its base class, in the sense that it usually has additional fields and methods. A subclass description may look small, but any subclass contains all of its base class's fields and methods as well as its own more specific fields and methods.

A derived class can be further extended. In other words, a subclass can have a child of its own. For example, after you create a `Tree` class and derive `Evergreen`, you might derive a

Spruce class from `Evergreen`. Similarly, a `Poodle` class might derive from `Dog`, `Dog` from `DomesticPet`, and `DomesticPet` from `Animal`. The entire list of parent classes from which a child class is derived constitutes the **ancestors** of the subclass.

> **NOTE** After you create the `Spruce` class, you might be ready to create `Spruce` objects. For example, you might create `theTreeInMyBackYard`, or you might create an array of 1000 `Spruce` objects for a tree farm.

Inheritance is **transitive**, which means a child inherits all the members of all its ancestors. In other words, when you declare a `Spruce` object, it contains all the attributes and methods of both an `Evergreen` and a `Tree`; a `CommissionEmployee` contains all the attributes and methods of an `Employee`. The members of `Employee` and `CommissionEmployee` are as follows:

» `Employee` contains two fields and four methods, as shown in Figure 9-1.

» `CommissionEmployee` contains three fields and six methods, even though you do not see all of them in Figure 9-3.

Although a child class contains all the data fields and methods of its parent, a parent class does not gain any child class members. Therefore, when `Employee` and `CommissionEmployee` classes are defined as in Figures 9-1 and 9-3, the statements in Figure 9-4 are all valid in an application. The `salesperson` object can use all the methods of its parent, plus it can use its own `setCommissionRate()` and `getCommissionRate()` methods. Figure 9-5 shows the output of the program as it would appear in a command-line environment.

```
class EmployeeDemo
   public static void main()
      Employee manager
      CommissionEmployee salesperson
      manager.setEmpNum("111")
      manager.setWeeklySalary(700.00)
      manager.getGreeting()
      salesperson.setEmpNum("222")
      salesperson.setWeeklySalary(300.00)
      salesperson.setCommissionRate(0.12)
      print "Manager ", manager.getEmpNum(), manager.getWeeklySalary()
      print "Salesperson ", salesperson.getEmpNum(),
         salesperson.getWeeklySalary(), salesperson.getCommissionRate()
   return
endClass
```

Figure 9-4 The `EmployeeDemo` application

Figure 9-5 Output of `EmployeeDemo` application

The following statements would not be allowed in the `EmployeeDemo` application in Figure 9-4 because `manager`, as an `Employee`, does not have access to the methods of the `CommissionEmployee` child class:

```
manager.setCommissionRate(0.08)
print manager.getCommissionRate()
```

>> **DON'T DO IT**

These base class objects cannot use methods that belong to their children.

>> **NOTE**
In math, a transitive relationship occurs when something that is true for a and b and for b and c is also true for a and c. For example, equality is transitive. If a = b and b = c, then a = c.

>> **NOTE** When you create your own transitive inheritance chains, you want to place fields and methods at their most general level. In other words, a method named `Grow()` rightfully belongs in a `Tree` class, whereas `LeavesTurnColor()` does not, because the method applies to only some of the `Tree` child classes. Similarly, a `LeavesTurnColor()` method would be better located in a `Deciduous` class than separately within the `Oak` or `Maple` child class.

It makes sense that a parent class object does not have access to its child's data and methods. When you create the parent class, you do not know how many future child classes might be created, or what their data or methods might look like. In addition, derived classes are more specific. A `HeartSurgeon` class and an `Obstetrician` class are children of a `Doctor` class. You do not expect all members of the general parent class `Doctor` to have the `HeartSurgeon`'s `repairHeartValve()` method or the `Obstetrician`'s `performCaesarianSection()` method. However, `HeartSurgeon` and `Obstetrician` objects have access to the more general `Doctor` methods `takeBloodPressure()` and `billPatients()`.

>> **NOTE**
As with subclasses of doctors, it is convenient to think of derived classes as *specialists*. That is, their fields and methods are more specialized than those of the parent class.

>> **NOTE** In some programming languages, such as C#, Visual Basic, and Java, every class you create is a child of one ultimate base class, often called the `Object` class. The `Object` class usually provides you with some basic functionality that all the classes you create inherit—for example, the ability to show its memory location and name.

ACCESSING PRIVATE MEMBERS OF A PARENT CLASS

In Chapter 8 you learned that when you create classes, the most common scenario is for methods to be public but for data to be private. Making data private is an important object-oriented programming concept. By making data fields private and allowing access to them only through a class's methods, you protect the ways in which data can be altered and accessed.

When a data field within a class is private, no outside class can access it directly—including a child class. (Access can be provided through public methods in the parent class, as you will see later in this chapter.) The principle of data hiding would be lost if all you had to do to access a class's private data was to create a child class. However, it can be inconvenient when a child class's methods cannot directly access its own inherited data.

For example, suppose you hire some employees who do not earn a weekly salary as defined in the `Employee` class, but who are paid by the hour. You might create an `HourlyEmployee` class that descends from Employee, as shown in Figure 9-6. The class contains two new fields, hoursWorked and hourlyRate, and a get and set method for each.

```
Employee
─empNum : string
─weeklySalary : numeric

+setEmpNum(num: string) : void
+getEmpNum() : string
+setWeeklySalary(salary : numeric) : void
+getWeeklySalary() : void
```

```
HourlyEmployee
─hoursWorked : numeric
─hourlyRate : numeric

+setHoursWorked(hours : numeric) : void
+getHoursWorked() : numeric
+setHourlyRate(rate : numeric) : void
+getHourlyRate() : numeric
```

Figure 9-6 Class diagram for HourlyEmployee class

Suppose you want to implement the new class as shown in Figure 9-7. Whenever you set either hoursWorked or hourlyRate, you want to modify weeklySalary based on the product of the hours and rate. The logic makes sense, but the code does not compile. The

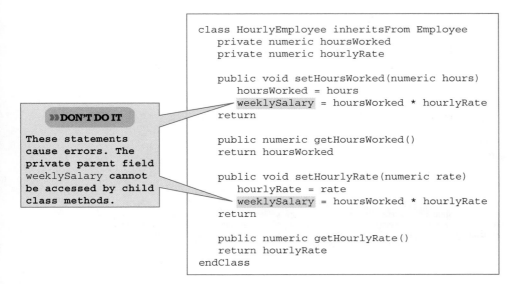

»DON'T DO IT

These statements cause errors. The private parent field weeklySalary **cannot** be accessed by child class methods.

```
class HourlyEmployee inheritsFrom Employee
    private numeric hoursWorked
    private numeric hourlyRate

    public void setHoursWorked(numeric hours)
        hoursWorked = hours
        weeklySalary = hoursWorked * hourlyRate
    return

    public numeric getHoursWorked()
    return hoursWorked

    public void setHourlyRate(numeric rate)
        hourlyRate = rate
        weeklySalary = hoursWorked * hourlyRate
    return

    public numeric getHourlyRate()
    return hourlyRate
endClass
```

Figure 9-7 Implementation of HourlyEmployee class that attempts to access weeklySalary

two shaded statements show that the HourlyEmployee class is attempting to modify the weeklySalary field. Although every HourlyEmployee *has* a weeklySalary field by virtue of being a child of Employee, the HourlyEmployee class methods do not have access to the weeklySalary field, because weeklySalary is private within the Employee class. The weeklySalary field is **inaccessible** to any class other than the one in which it is defined.

One solution to this dilemma would be to make weeklySalary public in the parent Employee class. Then the child class could use it. However, that action would violate the important object-oriented principle of information hiding. When you use information hiding, you are assured that your data will be altered only by the properties and methods you choose and only in ways that you can control. If outside classes could alter an Employee's private fields, then the fields could be assigned values that the Employee class couldn't control. In such a case, the principle of information hiding would be destroyed, causing the behavior of the object to be unpredictable.

Therefore, object-oriented programming languages allow a medium-security access specifier that is more restrictive than public but less restrictive than private. The **protected access** modifier is used when you want no outside classes to be able to use a data field, except classes that are descendents of the original class. Figure 9-8 shows a rewritten

```
class Employee
    private string empNum
    protected numeric weeklySalary

    public void setEmpNum(string num)
        empNum = num
    return

    public string getEmpNum()
    return empNum

    public void setWeeklySalary(numeric salary)
        weeklySalary = salary
    return

    public numeric getWeeklySalary()
    return weeklySalary
endClass
```

Figure 9-8 Employee class with a protected field

>> **NOTE** Although a child class's methods can access data fields originally defined in the parent class, a parent class's methods have no special privileges regarding any of its child's class's data fields. That is, unless the child class's data fields are public, a parent cannot access them, just like any other unrelated class cannot.

`Employee` class that uses the `protected` access modifier on its data fields (see shading). When this modified class is used as a base class for another class such as `HourlyEmployee`, the child class's methods will be able to access any protected items (fields or methods) originally defined in the parent class.

Figure 9-9 contains the class diagram for the version of the `Employee` class shown in Figure 9-8. Notice the `weeklySalary` field is preceded with an octothorpe (#)—the character that is conventionally used in class diagrams to indicate protected class members.

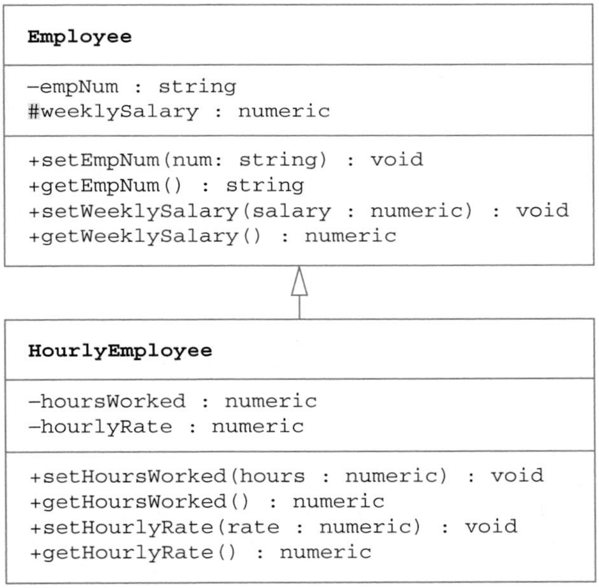

```
Employee
─────────────────────────────────────────────
−empNum : string
#weeklySalary : numeric
─────────────────────────────────────────────
+setEmpNum(num: string) : void
+getEmpNum() : string
+setWeeklySalary(salary : numeric) : void
+getWeeklySalary() : numeric
```

```
HourlyEmployee
─────────────────────────────────────────────
−hoursWorked : numeric
−hourlyRate : numeric
─────────────────────────────────────────────
+setHoursWorked(hours : numeric) : void
+getHoursWorked() : numeric
+setHourlyRate(rate : numeric) : void
+getHourlyRate() : numeric
```

Figure 9-9 `Employee` class with protected member and `HourlyEmployee`, which descends from it

Of course, if `weeklySalary` is defined as protected instead of private in the `Employee` class, then either the creator of the `Employee` class knew that a child class would want to access the field or the `Employee` class was revised after it became known the child class would need access to the field. If the `Employee` class's creator did not foresee that a field would need to be accessible, or if it is not preferable to revise the class, then `weeklySalary` will remain private. It is still possible to set an `HourlyEmployee`'s weekly pay correctly—the `HourlyEmployee` is just required to use the same means as any other class would. That is, the `HourlyEmployee` class can use the public method `setWeeklySalary()` that already exists in the parent class. Any class, including a child, can use a public member of the base

》NOTE
Any class can use a public member of any other class. Public members can include both data fields and methods.

class. So, assuming weeklySalary remains private in Employee, Figure 9-10 shows how HourlyEmployee could be written to set weeklySalary correctly.

```
class HourlyEmployee inheritsFrom Employee
    private numeric hoursWorked
    private numeric hourlyRate

    public void setHoursWorked(numeric hours)
        hoursWorked = hours
        setWeeklySalary(hoursWorked * hourlyRate)
    return

    public numeric getHoursWorked()
    return hoursWorked

    public void setHourlyRate(numeric rate)
        hourlyRate = rate
        setWeeklySalary(hoursWorked * hourlyRate)
    return

    public numeric getHourlyRate()
    return hourlyRate
endClass
```

Figure 9-10 The HourlyEmployee class when weeklySalary remains private

In the version of HourlyEmployee in Figure 9-10, the shaded statements within setHoursWorked() and setHourlyRate() assign a value to the corresponding child class field (hoursWorked or hourlyRate, respectively). Each method then calls the public parent class method setWeeklySalary(). In this example, no protected access modifiers are needed for any fields in the parent class, and the creators of the parent class did not have to foresee that a child class would eventually need to access any of its fields. Instead, any child classes of Employee simply follow the same access rules as any other outside class would. As an added benefit, if the parent class method setWeeklySalary() contained additional code (for example, to require a minimum base weekly pay for all employees) then that code would be enforced even for HourlyEmployees.

So, in summary, when a child class must access a private field of its parent's class, you can take one of several approaches:

» You can modify the parent class to make the field public. Usually, this is not advised, because it violates the principle of information hiding.

» You can modify the parent class to make the field protected so that child classes have access to it, but other outside classes do not. This is necessary if no public methods to modify the field are desired within the parent class.

» The child class can use a public method within the parent class that modifies the field, just as any other outside class would. This is frequently the best option.

Using the protected access modifier for a field can be convenient, and it improves program performance a little by using a field directly instead of "going through" another method. Also, using the protected access modifier is occasionally necessary when no existing public method accesses a field in a way required by the specifications for the child class. However, protected data members should be used sparingly. Whenever possible, the principle of information hiding should be observed, and even child classes should have to go through methods to "get to" their parent's private data.

The likelihood of future errors increases when child classes are allowed direct access to a parent's fields. For example, if the child class is allowed direct access to the `Employee` field `weeklySalary` and a programmer changes the field name to `salaryPerWeek`, then the programmer will have to remember to change the field reference in the child class, too. Worse, the programmer might not be aware of all the child classes that others have derived from the original class, and so might not be aware of all the changes that are required.

>> **NOTE** Classes that depend on field names from parent classes are said to be **fragile** because they are prone to errors—that is, they are easy to "break."

>> **NOTE** Some OOP languages, such as C++, allow a subclass to inherit from more than one parent class. For example, you might create an `InsuredItem` class that contains data fields pertaining to each possession for which you have insurance (for example, value and purchase date) and an `Automobile` class that contains data fields pertaining to an automobile (for example, vehicle identification number, make, model, and year). When you create an `InsuredAutomobile` class for a car rental agency, you might want to include `InsuredItem` information and methods, as well as `Automobile` information and methods, so you might want to inherit from both. The capability to inherit from more than one class is called **multiple inheritance**.

>> **NOTE** Sometimes, a parent class is so general that you never intend to create any specific instances of the class. For example, you might never create an object that is "just" an `Employee`; each `Employee` is more specifically a `SalariedEmployee`, `HourlyEmployee`, or `ContractEmployee`. A class such as `Employee` that you create only to extend from, but not to instantiate objects from, is an abstract class. An **abstract class** is one from which you cannot create any concrete objects, but from which you can inherit.

OVERRIDING BASE CLASS METHODS

>> **NOTE** In Chapter 6 you learned that a method's name and parameter list constitute its signature.

When you create a subclass by extending an existing class, the new subclass contains all the data and methods that were defined in the original superclass and any child class object can use all the nonprivate members of its parent. Sometimes, however, those superclass data fields and methods are not entirely appropriate for the subclass objects; in those cases, you want to override the parent class methods. When you **override a method** in a child class, you create a method with the same identifier and parameter list as the parent's version; the parent's version then becomes hidden from the child class. When you use the method name with a child class object, the child class's version is used, but when you use it with a parent class object, the parent class's version is used.

>> **NOTE** A superclass member that is not hidden by the derived class is **visible** in the derived class.

When you use the English language, you often use the same method name to indicate diverse meanings. For example, if you think of `MusicalInstrument` as a class, you can think of `play()` as a method of that class. If you think of various subclasses such as `Guitar` and `Drum`, you know that you carry out the `play()` method quite differently for each subclass. Using the same method name to indicate different implementations is called polymorphism, a term that means "many forms"; many forms of action take place, even though you use the same word to describe the action. In other words, many forms of the same word exist, depending on the object associated with the word.

>> **NOTE** You first learned the term *polymorphism* in Chapter 6. Polymorphism is one of the basic principles of OOP. If a programming language does not support polymorphism, the language is not considered object-oriented.

For example, suppose you create a `Student` class as shown in Figure 9-11. The class contains three fields: `idNum`, `credits`, and `tuition`. (The fields `credits` and `tuition` are defined as `protected` so that a child class has access to them.) The class also contains a get method for each field. Set methods are in place only for `idNum` and `credits` because clients are not allowed to set `tuition` directly; instead, `tuition` always is calculated based on `credits` at a rate of $100.00 per credit hour. Figure 9-12 shows how the `Student` class is implemented. Whenever a `Student`'s `credits` field is set, `tuition` also is set.

```
class Student
    private string idNum
    protected numeric credits
    protected numeric tuition

    public void setIdNum(string id)
        idNum = id
    return

    public string getIdNum()
    return idNum

    public void setCredits(numeric hours)
        numeric RATE_PER_CREDIT_HOUR = 100.00
        credits = hours
        tuition = credits * RATE_PER_CREDIT_HOUR
    return

    public numeric getCredits()
    return credits

    public numeric getTuition()
    return tuition
endClass
```

Student
−idNum : string #credits : numeric #tuition : numeric
+setIdNum(id : string) : void +getIdNum() : string +setCredits(hours : numeric) : void +getCredits() : numeric +getTuition() : numeric

Figure 9-11 The `Student` class

Figure 9-12 Implementation of `Student` class

Suppose you want to create a class named `ScholarshipStudent` that descends from `Student`. A `ScholarshipStudent` has an ID number and number of credit hours just like a `Student`, but a `ScholarshipStudent`'s `tuition` is calculated differently. If a `ScholarshipStudent` is enrolled in 15 or fewer credit hours, then `tuition` is 0, and if a `ScholarshipStudent` is enrolled in more hours, the tuition rate is $50 per credit hour for the hours over 15. You could handle this problem in one of three ways:

1. You could create a special method in the `ScholarshipStudent` class with a name such as `setScholarshipStudentCredits()` and perform the necessary tuition calculations in this method. This method would not conflict with the parent class method because it has a different identifier, so you could use it with any `ScholarshipStudent` object. However, the parent method would still exist for child class objects, and if a client wrote a program and by mistake used the `setCredits()` method with a `ScholarshipStudent` object (instead of using `setScholarshipStudentCredits()`), then the original method would execute and the `ScholarshipStudent` would be assigned too much tuition.

2. You could create a method in the ScholarshipStudent class with the same name as the parent class method, but a different parameter list. For example, you could create a method with the header setCredits(numeric hours, numeric x). When a client wanted to set a ScholarshipStudent's credits and tuition, the client could use this new method, passing the hours and any other numeric value to it; the second argument would exist simply to distinguish this method from the one in the parent class. In other words, this method would be an overloaded version of the parent class method. However, the client would still have to remember to use this alternate version, could mistakenly use the original version that requires one argument, and could end up assigning incorrect tuition to ScholarshipStudent objects.

»NOTE
In Chapter 6 you learned that over-loaded methods have the same name but different parameter lists.

3. The superior solution is to override the setCredits() method in the child class by creating a new method with the same signature as the parent class method. This action causes the child class version of the method to be the only one used with child class objects. When the parent class method is overridden, a client cannot possibly use the wrong version, and the client has only to remember the simple, logical identifier setCredits() when credit hours and tuition need to be set, whether the client is working with base or derived class objects.

Figure 9-13 shows the class diagram for the ScholarshipStudent class that descends from Student and Figure 9-14 shows the class implementation. ScholarshipStudent contains a

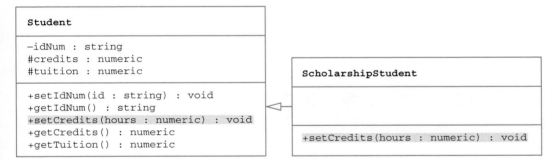

```
Student

−idNum : string
#credits : numeric
#tuition : numeric

+setIdNum(id : string) : void
+getIdNum() : string
+setCredits(hours : numeric) : void
+getCredits() : numeric
+getTuition() : numeric
```

```
ScholarshipStudent


+setCredits(hours : numeric) : void
```

Figure 9-13 Class diagrams for Student and its child, ScholarshipStudent

```
class ScholarshipStudent inheritsFrom Student
    public void setCredits(numeric hours)
        numeric FULLTIME = 15
        numeric REDUCED_RATE = 50
        credits = hours
        if credits <= FULLTIME then
            tuition = 0
        else
            tuition = (credits − FULLTIME) * REDUCED_RATE
    return
endClass
```

»NOTE
If credits and tuition had been declared as private within the Student class, then ScholarshipStu dent would not be able to access them directly.

Figure 9-14 ScholarshipStudent class

single method named setCredits(). Figure 9-15 shows a program that declares a full-time Student and a full-time ScholarshipStudent and displays their tuition values. In the execution in Figure 9-16, you can see that even though both objects use a method named setCredits(), and both use the same value for credits, the tuition values are different and correct for each object type.

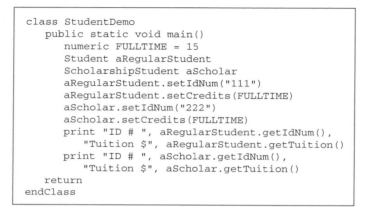

```
class StudentDemo
    public static void main()
        numeric FULLTIME = 15
        Student aRegularStudent
        ScholarshipStudent aScholar
        aRegularStudent.setIdNum("111")
        aRegularStudent.setCredits(FULLTIME)
        aScholar.setIdNum("222")
        aScholar.setCredits(FULLTIME)
        print "ID # ", aRegularStudent.getIdNum(),
            "Tuition $", aRegularStudent.getTuition()
        print "ID # ", aScholar.getIdNum(),
            "Tuition $", aScholar.getTuition()
    return
endClass
```

Figure 9-15 Application that declares a full-time Student and a full-time ScholarshipStudent

Figure 9-16 Execution of application in Figure 9-15

>> **NOTE** It is important to note that each subclass method overrides any method in the parent class that has both the same name and parameter list. If the parent class method has the same name but a different parameter list, the subclass method does not override the parent class version; instead, the subclass method overloads the parent class method and any subclass object has access to both versions. You learned about overloading methods in Chapter 6.

>> **NOTE** In Chapter 6 you learned that the ability of one method name to work correctly with different objects is polymorphism. The type of polymorphism that applies specifically to objects of the same parent class is sometimes called **subtype polymorphism**.

When you write a polymorphic method in an object-oriented programming language, you must write each version of the method, and that can entail a lot of work. The benefits of polymorphism do not seem obvious while you are writing the methods, but the benefits are realized when you can use the methods in all sorts of applications. When you can use a single, simple, easy-to-understand method name such as `setCredits()` with all sorts of objects, such as `Students`, `ScholarshipStudents`, `GraduateStudents`, `WorkStudyStudents`, and so on, then your objects behave more like their real-world counterparts and your programs are easier to understand.

UNDERSTANDING HOW CONSTRUCTORS ARE CALLED DURING INHERITANCE

When you create any object, as in `SomeClass anObject`, you are calling a class constructor method that has the same name as the class itself. When you instantiate an object that is a member of a subclass, you are actually calling at least two constructors: the constructor for the base class and the constructor for the extended, derived class. When you create any subclass object, the superclass constructor must execute first, and then the subclass constructor executes.

When a superclass contains a default constructor, the execution of the superclass constructor when a subclass object is instantiated often is transparent. However, you should realize that when you create an object such as `HourlyEmployee clerk` (where `HourlyEmployee` is a subclass of `Employee`), both the `Employee()` and `HourlyEmployee()` constructors execute.

> **NOTE** In languages in which a class with the name `Object` is the base for all objects (such as Visual Basic, Java, and C#), instantiating a child class object calls three constructors—one for the `Object` class, one for the parent class, and one for the child class.

When you create a class and do not provide a constructor, object-oriented languages automatically supply you with a default constructor—one that never requires arguments. When you write your own constructor, you replace the automatically supplied version. Depending on your needs, a constructor you create for a class might require arguments. When you use a class as a superclass and the class has only constructors that require arguments, you must be certain that any subclasses provide the superclass constructor with the arguments it needs.

When a superclass has a default constructor, you can create a subclass with or without its own constructor. This is true whether the default constructor is the automatically supplied one or one you have written. However, when a superclass contains only constructors that require arguments, you must include at least one constructor for each subclass you create. Your subclass constructors can contain any number of statements, but each constructor must call the superclass constructor. This is accomplished slightly differently in different programming languages, but the principle is the same—a parent constructor must be fully executed before the child class constructor can operate. When a superclass requires parameters upon instantiation, even if you have no other reason to create a subclass constructor, you must write the subclass constructor so it can call its superclass's constructor.

NOTE
You first learned about constructors in Chapter 7.

NOTE
Don't forget that a class can have many constructors. As soon as you create at least one constructor for a class, you can no longer use the automatically supplied version.

NOTE
If a superclass has multiple constructors, but one is a default constructor, you do not have to create a subclass constructor unless you want to. If the subclass contains no constructor, all subclass objects use the superclass default constructor when they are instantiated.

For example, Figure 9-17 shows an Employee class that contains a single constructor that requires two parameters. Because CommissionEmployee descends from Employee, CommissionEmployee must contain a constructor that sends arguments to the parent constructor. In the example in Figure 9-17, the call to the superclass constructor is super("999", 0). The arguments sent to the superclass constructor are constants—the string "999" that becomes every CommissionEmployee object's employee number, and 0, which becomes every CommissionEmployee's default weekly salary.

```
class Employee
    private string empNum
    private numeric weeklySalary

    public Employee(string num, numeric salary)
        empNum = num
        weeklySalary = salary
    return

    public string getEmpNum()
    return empNum

    public numeric getWeeklySalary()
    return weeklySalary
endClass

class CommissionEmployee inheritsFrom Employee
    private numeric commissionRate

    public CommissionEmployee(numeric rate)
        super("999", 0)
        commissionRate = rate
    return

    public numeric getCommissionRate()
    return commissionRate
endClass
```

Figure 9-17 Child class constructor calling base class constructor with constant arguments

> **NOTE** The method used to send parameters to a parent's constructor differs widely among programming languages. For example, in C++ you must call the parent class constructor by name from within the child class constructor header. In C# you also call the parent constructor from the child constructor header, but you use the keyword base. In Visual Basic, a base class constructor is called New, and a child calls myBase.New(). In Java, you use the keyword super. Because Java's format is simple, it is used in the examples in Figures 9-17 and 9-18.

Figure 9-18 shows how the `CommissionEmployee` constructor might be rewritten to receive variable parameters for the employee number and salary, which it then passes along to the base class constructor. Of course, you could also rewrite the `CommissionEmployee` constructor to pass one variable and one constant. The requirement is that the child class constructor "takes care" of the parent class's requirements before performing any other actions.

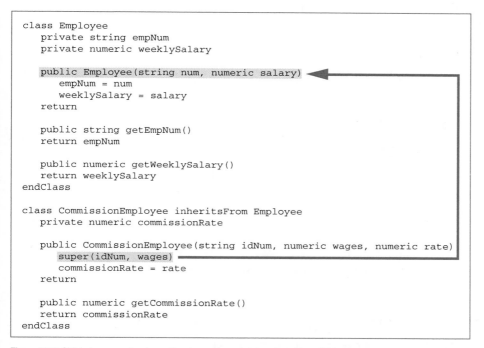

```
class Employee
    private string empNum
    private numeric weeklySalary

    public Employee(string num, numeric salary)
        empNum = num
        weeklySalary = salary
    return

    public string getEmpNum()
    return empNum

    public numeric getWeeklySalary()
    return weeklySalary
endClass

class CommissionEmployee inheritsFrom Employee
    private numeric commissionRate

    public CommissionEmployee(string idNum, numeric wages, numeric rate)
        super(idNum, wages)
        commissionRate = rate
    return

    public numeric getCommissionRate()
    return commissionRate
endClass
```

Figure 9-18 Child class constructor calling base class constructor with variable arguments

The statement that instantiates a `CommissionEmployee` class, as defined in Figure 9-18, requires three arguments. For example, assuming all the variables have been assigned correct values, any of the following statements would work:

```
CommissionEmployee aSalesperson("123", 400.00, 0.12)
CommissionEmployee anAgent(idNumber, salary, rate)
CommissionEmployee aTrader(number, 500.00, percentage)
```

UNDERSTANDING HOW A DERIVED CLASS OBJECT "IS AN" INSTANCE OF THE BASE CLASS

Every derived class object "is a" specific instance of both the derived class and the base class. In other words, `myCar` "is a" `Car` as well as a `Vehicle`, and `myDog` "is a" `Dog` as well as a `Mammal`. You can assign a derived class object to an object of any of its superclass types. When you do, an **implicit conversion** is made from derived class to base class.

For example, when a `ScholarshipStudent` class inherits from `Student`, an object of either type can be passed to a method that accepts a `Student` parameter. In Figure 9-19, the `StudentDemo` application from Figure 9-15 is rewritten to pass both the `Student` and the `ScholarshipStudent` to a method named `display()`. Each is referred to as `stu` within the method, and each is used correctly. The output is the same as shown in Figure 9-16.

```
class StudentDemo2
    public static void main()
        numeric FULLTIME = 15
        Student aRegularStudent
        ScholarshipStudent aScholar
        aRegularStudent.setIdNum("111")
        aRegularStudent.setCredits(FULLTIME)
        aScholar.setIdNum("222")
        aScholar.setCredits(FULLTIME)
        display(aRegularStudent)
        display(aScholar)
    return

    public static void display(Student stu)
        print "ID # ", stu.getIdNum(),
            "Tuition $", stu.getTuition()
    return
endClass
```

Figure 9-19 Application that passes `Student` and `ScholarshipStudent` to the same method

USING INHERITANCE TO ACHIEVE GOOD SOFTWARE DESIGN

When an automobile company designs a new car model, the company does not build every component from scratch. The company might design a new feature completely from scratch; for example, at some point someone designed the first air bag. However, many of a new car's features are simply modifications of existing features. The manufacturer might create a larger gas tank or more comfortable seats, but even these new features still possess many properties of their predecessors in the older models. Most features of new car models are not even modified; instead, existing components such as air filters and windshield wipers are included on the new model without any changes.

Similarly, you can create powerful computer programs more easily if many of their components are used either "as is" or with slight modifications. Inheritance does not give you the ability to write any programs that you could not write without it, because you *could* create every part of a program from scratch. Inheritance simply makes your job easier. Professional programmers constantly create new class libraries for use with OOP languages. Having these classes available to extend makes programming large systems more manageable. When you create a useful, extendable superclass, you and other future programmers gain several advantages:

» Subclass creators save development time because much of the code needed for the class has already been written.

» Subclass creators save testing time because the superclass code has already been tested and probably used in a variety of situations. In other words, the superclass code is **reliable**.

» Programmers who create or use new subclasses already understand how the superclass works, so the time it takes to learn the new class features is reduced.

» When you create a new subclass, neither the superclass source code nor the translated superclass code is changed. The superclass maintains its integrity.

When you consider classes, you must think about the commonalities between them, and then you can create superclasses from which to inherit. You might be rewarded professionally when you see your own superclasses extended by others in the future.

CHAPTER SUMMARY

» Inheritance is the principle that you can apply your knowledge of a general category to more specific objects.

» With inheritance you create new classes that contain all the fields and methods of an existing class, plus any new members you add. The ability to use inheritance makes programs easier to write, easier to understand, and less prone to errors.

» A class that is used as a basis for inheritance is called a base class. When you create a class that inherits from a base class, it is a derived or extended class. You can use the terms *superclass* and *subclass* as synonyms for base class and derived class. You also can use the terms *parent class* and *child class*. A derived class is generally larger than a base class, in the sense that it usually has additional fields and methods. The entire list of parent classes from which a child class is derived constitutes the ancestors of the subclass.

» When a data field within a class is private, no outside class can use it—including a child class. However, it can be inconvenient when a child class's methods cannot directly access its own inherited data. Therefore, object-oriented programming languages allow a medium-security access specifier that is more restrictive than public but less restrictive than private. The `protected` access modifier is used when you want no outside classes to be able to use a data field, except classes that are descendents of the original class. Any class, including a child, can use a public member of the base class; this is frequently the best option. The likelihood of future errors increases when child classes are allowed direct access to a parent's fields.

» When you override a method in a child class, you create a method with the same identifier and parameter list as the parent's version; the parent's version then becomes hidden from the child class. When you use the method name with a child class object, the child class's version is used, but when you use it with a parent class object, the parent class's version is used.

» When you create any object, you are calling a class constructor. When you instantiate an object that is a member of a subclass, you are actually calling at least two constructors: one for the base class and one for the extended, derived class. When you create any subclass object, the superclass constructor must execute first, and then the subclass constructor executes. When a superclass has a default constructor, you can create a subclass with or without its own constructor. However, when a superclass contains only constructors that require arguments, you must include at least one constructor for each subclass you create. Your subclass constructors can contain any number of statements, but it must call the superclass constructor. This is accomplished slightly differently in different programming languages, but the principle is the same—a parent constructor must be fully executed before the child class constructor can operate.

» Every derived class object "is a" specific instance of both the derived class and the base class. You can assign a derived class object to an object of any of its superclass types. When you do, an implicit conversion is made from derived class to base class.

» You can create powerful computer programs more easily if many of their components are used either "as is" or with slight modifications. Inheritance does not give you the ability to write any programs that you could not write without it, because you *could* create every part of a program from scratch. Inheritance simply makes your job easier, saves development time, provides reliable code, and makes it easier for clients to learn to use the new class.

KEY TERMS

Inheritance is the principle that you can apply your knowledge of a general category to more specific objects.

A **base class** is a class that is used as a basis for inheritance.

A **derived** or **extended class** is one that inherits from a base class.

A **superclass** or **parent class** is a base class.

A **subclass** or **child class** is a derived class.

The **ancestors** of a subclass are the entire list of parent classes from which the subclass is derived.

Inheritance is **transitive**, which means a child inherits all the members of all its ancestors.

When a class member is **inaccessible** to a method, it is hidden from the method and cannot be used by it.

The **protected access** modifier is used when you want no outside classes to be able to use a data field, except classes that are descendents of the original class.

Fragile classes are those that depend on field names from parent classes.

The capability to inherit from more than one class is called **multiple inheritance**.

An **abstract class** is one from which you cannot create any concrete objects, but from which you can inherit.

When you **override a method** in a child class, you create a method with the same identifier and parameter list as the parent's version; the parent's version then becomes hidden from the child class.

A superclass member that is not hidden by the derived class is **visible** in the derived class.

The ability of one method name to work appropriately for different subclass objects of the same parent class is sometimes called **subtype polymorphism**.

An **implicit conversion** is a transformation from one type to another that takes place automatically.

When code is **reliable**, it has been tested and is trusted to work correctly.

REVIEW QUESTIONS

1. The principle that you can apply your knowledge of a general category to more specific objects is _____.

   a. polymorphism

   b. inheritance

   c. object orientation

   d. encapsulation

2. Which of the following is *not* an advantage of creating a class that inherits from another?

   a. You save time because subclasses are created automatically from those that come built in as part of a programming language.

   b. You save time because you need not recreate the fields and methods in the original class.

   c. You reduce the chance of errors because the original class's methods have already been used and tested.

   d. You make it easier for anyone who has used the original class to understand the new class.

3. Employing inheritance reduces errors because _____ .

   a. the new classes have access to fewer data fields

   b. the new classes have access to fewer methods

   c. you can copy and paste methods that you already created

   d. many of the methods you need have already been used and tested

4. A class that is used as a basis for inheritance is called a _____ .

   a. derived class

   b. subclass

   c. child class

   d. base class

5. A subclass is also called a _____ .

   a. child class

   b. base class

   c. superclass

   d. parent class

6. Which of the following choices most closely describes a parent class/child class relationship?

   a. Rose/Flower

   b. Present/Gift

   c. Dog/Poodle

   d. Sparrow/Bird

7. A derived class is generally _____ its base class.
   a. larger than
   b. smaller than
   c. the same size as
   d. There are no general rules about the size of derived classes.

8. Which of the following statements is true?
   a. A child class inherits from a parent class.
   b. A parent class inherits from a child class.
   c. Both of the preceding statements are true.
   d. Neither of the preceding statements is true.

9. The entire list of parent classes from which a child class is derived constitutes the _____ of the subclass.
   a. hierarchy
   b. ancestors
   c. family
   d. chain

10. Inheritance is transitive, which means _____ .
    a. the parent class has access to its child's methods
    b. inheritance is temporary
    c. a child inherits all the members of all its ancestors
    d. inheritance changes your view of a class

11. When a data field within a class is private, _____ .
    a. no outside class can use it
    b. no outside class can use it except a child of the class
    c. no outside class can use it except an ancestor of the class
    d. any class can use it

12. Object-oriented programming languages allow a medium-security access level that is more restrictive than public but less restrictive than private. This level is _____ .
    a. intermediate
    b. sheltered
    c. accessible
    d. protected

13. Assume that you are developing a child class that must access a private field of its parent's class. Of the following, the best course of action is to _____ .

    a. modify the parent class to make the field public

    b. modify the parent class to make the field protected

    c. modify the parent class to remove the field

    d. override the parent class field by redefining it in the child class

14. Assume that a child class must access a private field of its parent's class. Of the following, the best course of action is to have the child class _____ .

    a. use the field name directly

    b. use a public parent class method that accesses the field

    c. use a private parent class method that accesses the field

    d. define its own version of the same field

15. Classes that depend on field names from parent classes are _____ .

    a. broken

    b. polymorphic

    c. fragile

    d. sturdy

16. When you override a method in a child class, you create a method with _____ .

    a. the same identifier as the parent's version

    b. the same parameter list as the parent's version

    c. both of these

    d. none of these

17. If a child class method has the same name but a different parameter list than a method in the parent class, the subclass method _____ the parent class version.

    a. oversees

    b. hides

    c. overloads

    d. overrides

18. When you instantiate an object that is a member of a subclass, the _____ constructor executes first.

    a. subclass

    b. child class

    c. extended class

    d. parent class

19. If a superclass constructor requires arguments, its subclass _____ .

    a. must contain a constructor

    b. must not contain a constructor

    c. must contain a constructor that requires arguments

    d. must not contain a constructor that requires arguments

20. Inheritance gives a programmer the ability to _____ .

    a. write programs that otherwise could not be written

    b. develop programs more quickly

    c. both of these

    d. none of these

EXERCISES

1. Complete the following tasks:

    a. In the Exercises in Chapter 7, you designed a class named `Book` that holds a stock number, author, title, price, and number of pages for a book. Design a class named `TextBook` that is a child class of `Book`. Include a new data field for the grade level of the book. Override the `Book` class methods that set and print the data so that you accommodate the new grade-level field.

    b. Design an application that instantiates an object of each type and demonstrates all the methods.

2. Complete the following tasks:

    a. Design a class named `Player` that holds a player number and name for a sports team participant. Include methods to set the values for each data field and print the values for each data field.

    b. Design two classes named `BaseballPlayer` and `BasketballPlayer` that are child classes of `Player`. Include a new data field in each class for the player's position. Include an additional field in the `BaseballPlayer` class for batting average. Include a new field in the `BasketballPlayer` class for free-throw percentage. Override the `Player` class methods that set and print the data so that you accommodate the new fields.

    c. Design an application that instantiates an object of each type and demonstrates all the methods.

3. Complete the following tasks:

    a. Create a class named `Tape` that includes fields for length and width in inches and get and set methods for each field.

    b. Derive two subclasses—`VideoCassetteTape` and `AdhesiveTape`. The `VideoCassetteTape` class includes a numeric field to hold playing time in minutes and get and set methods for the field. The `AdhesiveTape` class includes a numeric field that holds a stickiness factor—a value from 1 to 10—and get and set methods for the field.

c. Design a program that instantiates one object of each of the three classes. Demonstrate how to use all of each class's methods.

4. Complete the following tasks:

a. Create a class named `Rectangle` that contains data fields for `height`, `width`, and `surfaceArea`, and a method named `computeSurfaceArea()`.

b. Create a child class named `Box`. `Box` contains an additional data field named `depth` and a `computeSurfaceArea()` method that overrides the parent method appropriately for a three-dimensional box.

c. Create the logic for an application that instantiates a `Rectangle` object and a `Box` object and displays the surface areas of both objects.

5. Complete the following tasks:

a. Create a class named `Order` that performs order processing of a single item. The class has four fields: customer name, customer number, quantity ordered, and unit price. Include set and get methods for each field. The set methods prompt the user for values for each field. This class also needs a method to compute the total price (quantity multiplied by unit price) and a method to display the field values.

b. Create a subclass named `ShippedOrder` that overrides `computePrice()` by adding a shipping and handling charge of $4.00.

c. Create the logic for an application that instantiates an object of each of these classes. Prompt the user for data for the `Order` object and display the results; then prompt the user for data for the `ShippedOrder` object and display the results.

d. Create the logic for an application that continuously prompts a user for order information until the user enters "ZZZ" for the customer name or 10 orders have been taken, whichever comes first. Ask the user whether each order will be shipped, and create an `Order` or a `ShippedOrder` appropriately. Store each order in an array. When the user is finished entering data, display all the order information taken as well as the total price that was computed for each order.

6. Complete the following tasks:

a. Create a class named `Year` that contains a data field that holds the number of months in a year and the number of days in a year. Include a get method that displays the number of days and a constructor that sets the number of months to 12 and the number of days to 365.

b. Create a subclass named `LeapYear`. `LeapYear`'s constructor overrides `Year`'s constructor and sets the number of days to 366.

c. Design an application that instantiates one object of each class and displays their data.

d. Add a method named `daysElapsed()` to the `Year` class. The `daysElapsed()` method accepts two arguments representing a month and a day; it returns a number indicating the number of days that have elapsed since January 1 of that year. For example, on March 3, 61 days have elapsed (31 in January, 28 in February, and 2 in March). Create a `daysElapsed()` method for the `LeapYear` class that overrides the method in the `Year` class. For example, on March 3 in a `LeapYear`, 62 days have elapsed (31 in January, 29 in February, and 2 in March).

e. Design an application that prompts the user for a month and day, and calculates the days elapsed in a `Year` and in a `LeapYear`.

CASE PROJECT

In earlier chapters you developed classes needed for Cost Is No Object—a car rental service that specializes in lending antique and luxury cars to clients on a short-term basis. You created the logic for the following classes: `Name`, `Address`, `Date`, `Employee`, `Customer`, `Automobile`, and `RentalAgreement`.

Now create the following:

» Create a superclass named `Person` from which both `Employee` and `Customer` can descend. Include attributes and methods that any `Person` should possess—for example, a name and address. Then rewrite the `Employee` and `Customer` classes to descend from `Person`, including only attributes and methods appropriate for each subclass.

» Create at least two subclasses that descend from `Employee` (for example, `PartTimeEmployee`), adding new fields and methods as appropriate. Override at least one parent method.

» Create at least two subclasses that descend from `Customer` (for example, `PreferredCustomer`), adding new fields and methods as appropriate. Override at least one parent method.

» Create at least two subclasses that descend from `Automobile` (for example, `LuxuryCar`), adding new fields and methods as appropriate. Override at least one parent method.

» Create a program that demonstrates each of the classes' methods.

UP FOR DISCUSSION

1. In this chapter, you learned the difference between public, private, and protected class members. Why are some programmers opposed to classifying class members as protected? Do you agree with them?

2. Suppose your organization asks you to develop a code of ethics for the Information Technology Department. What would you include?

3. When you created the `Employee` class in the case problem at the end of Chapter 7, you might have decided to store each employee's Social Security number. Besides using it for tax purposes, many organizations also use this number as an identification number. Is this a good idea? Is a Social Security number unique?

10

EXCEPTION HANDLING

In this chapter, you will:

Understand exceptions
Understand the limitations of traditional error handling
Try code and catch Exceptions
Throw and catch multiple Exceptions
Use the finally block
Understand the advantages of exception handling
Trace Exceptions through the call stack
Create your own Exceptions

LEARNING ABOUT EXCEPTIONS

An **exception** is an unexpected or error condition that occurs while a program is running. The programs you write can generate many types of potential exceptions, such as when you do the following:

» You issue a command to read a file from a disk, but the file does not exist there.

» You attempt to write data to a disk, but the disk is full.

» Your program asks for user input, but the user enters invalid data.

» The program attempts to divide a value by 0, access an array with a subscript that is too large, or calculate a value that is too large for the answer's variable type.

» NOTE
Appendix D provides additional information on handling invalid user-supplied data.

» NOTE
Providing for exceptions involves an oxymoron; you must expect the unexpected.

These errors are called exceptions because, presumably, they are not usual occurrences; they are "exceptional." The object-oriented techniques to manage such errors comprise the group of methods known as **exception handling**. Sometimes, computer programs generate errors from which the programmer cannot possibly recover. For example, a power failure might interrupt production of your paycheck. Exception handling does not deal with these kinds of errors; its concern is predictable errors.

For example, Figure 10-1 contains a `dividingMethod()` method that displays the result of dividing two parameters. When this method executes, it is possible that an attempt will be made to divide by 0. Dividing by 0 is an error in every programming language because it is an operation that is not defined mathematically. Of course, you should never write a method that purposely divides a value by 0. However, this situation certainly could occur by accident—for example, if the variable used as a divisor gets its value as the result of user input.

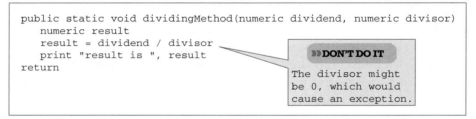

```
public static void dividingMethod(numeric dividend, numeric divisor)
    numeric result
    result = dividend / divisor
    print "result is ", result
return
```

» DON'T DO IT
The divisor might be 0, which would cause an exception.

Figure 10-1 Method that might divide by 0

When you execute the method in Figure 10-1, the method fails if the `divisor` value is 0. When this happens, the application that calls this method typically terminates, control returns to the operating system, and an error message is generated. The method has generated an exception; the error message might even use that term. For example,

Figure 10-2 shows a message generated when the program is implemented in Java. The message explains that an `ArithmeticException` object has been created, and it cites the reason as "/ by zero".

Figure 10-2 Exception message generated in Java when program attempts to divide by 0

> **» NOTE** In Java, an `ArithmeticException` is a type of `Exception`; it is a member of a class (`RuntimeException`) that is a child class of a built-in class named `Exception`. In some languages, for example, C++, when you want to create your own `Exception` classes, you do so from scratch. In others, for example, Java, Visual Basic, and C#, you extend an already created class. You will learn how to create `Exception` classes later in this chapter.

When a method in an object-oriented program causes an exception such as dividing by 0, the method **throws the exception**; you can picture the program tossing out an `Exception` object that "someone else" (another method or the operating system) might handle. Just because a program throws an `Exception`, you don't necessarily have to deal with it. In the `dividingMethod()` method, you can simply let the offending program terminate, as shown in the example in Figure 10-2.

However, program termination is abrupt and unforgiving. When a program divides two numbers (or performs a less trivial task such as balancing a checkbook), the user might be annoyed if the program ends abruptly. However, if the program is used for air-traffic control or to monitor a patient's vital statistics during surgery, an abrupt conclusion could be disastrous. You can handle exceptions either in a traditional manner or in an object-oriented manner. Object-oriented exception-handling techniques provide more elegant (and safer) solutions.

The `Exceptions` automatically created and thrown differ in various programming languages, but some typical examples are:

» `ArithmeticException` or `DivideByZeroException`, thrown when an attempt to divide by 0 occurs

» `ArrayTypeMismatchException`, thrown when you attempt to store an object that is the wrong data type in an array

» `IndexOutOfRangeException`, thrown when you attempt to access an array with an invalid subscript

» `NullReferenceException`, thrown when an object reference does not correctly refer to a created object

» `OverflowException`, thrown when an arithmetic operation produces a result for which the value is greater than the assigned memory location can accommodate

UNDERSTANDING THE LIMITATIONS OF TRADITIONAL ERROR HANDLING

Programmers had to deal with error conditions long before object-oriented methods were conceived. Probably the most often used error-handling solution has been to make a decision before working with a potentially error-causing value. For example, you can change the `dividingMethod()` method to avoid division if the divisor is 0, as shown in Figure 10-3.

```
public static void dividingMethod(numeric dividend, numeric divisor)
   numeric result
   if divisor = 0 then
      print "Cannot divide by 0"
   else
      result = dividend / divisor
      print "result is ", result
   endif
return
```

Figure 10-3 The `dividingMethod()` method using a traditional error-handling technique

In the method in Figure 10-3, an error message is displayed if the divisor is 0 and the division operation only occurs when the `divisor` value is not 0. As another workable alternative, if the divisor is 0, you could force it to 1 or some other acceptable value before dividing, avoiding the error. Another possibility would be to insert a loop into the method and continuously prompt the user to enter a `divisor` value; the loop would execute until the user entered a value other than 0. In short, you could avoid the termination of the `dividingMethod()` method in many ways other than having it abruptly halt and exit the program.

A drawback to using any of these approaches is that any client of the `dividingMethod()` method must accept the method's chosen way of handling the error. If the method prompts the user for a new value, then the method is not useful in an application that gets its values from a file instead of a user. On the other hand, if the method forces the divisor to 1, it is not useful in an application where that answer would be wrong or where the client would prefer that an error message be displayed. In short, using a traditional error-handling method to avoid dividing by 0 prevents the error, but makes the method inflexible. Programmers might have to write multiple versions of the method to fit different clients' needs, wasting time and money.

Exception handling provides a more elegant solution for handling error conditions. In object-oriented terminology, you "try" a procedure that might cause an error. A method that detects an error condition "throws an exception," and, if you choose to create one, the block of code that processes the error "catches the exception."

TRYING CODE AND CATCHING EXCEPTIONS

When you create a segment of code in which something might go wrong, you place the code in a **try block**, which is a block of code you attempt to execute while acknowledging that an exception might occur. A `try` block consists of the keyword `try`, followed by any number of statements, some that might cause exceptions. If a statement in the block causes an exception, the remaining statements in the try block do not execute and the try block is abandoned. For pseudocode purposes, you can end a try block with a sentinel such as endtry.

You almost always code at least one catch block immediately following a try block. A **catch block** is a segment of code that can handle an exception that might be thrown by the try block that precedes it. A **throw statement** is one that sends an Exception object out of a method so it can be handled elsewhere. Each catch block can "catch" one type of exception— that is, one object that is an object of type Exception or one of its child classes. You create a catch block by typing the following elements:

» The keyword catch, followed by parentheses that contain an Exception type and an identifier

» Statements that take the action you want to use to handle the error condition

» For pseudocode purposes, an endcatch statement

Figure 10-4 shows the general format of a method that includes a shaded try...catch pair within the method. In the figure, theExceptionThatWasThrown represents an object of the Exception class or any of its subclasses. If an Exception occurs during the execution of the try block, an Exception object is generated and is sent to the catch block, where it becomes known by the identifier in the catch statement. Then the statements in the catch block execute. If no Exception occurs within the try block (in other words, if the logic reaches endtry), the catch block does not execute. Either way, the statements following the catch block execute normally.

»»NOTE
In some object-oriented program-ming languages, notably C++, you can throw a number or string as well as an Exception.

»»NOTE
A catch block looks a lot like a method named catch() that takes an argument that is some type of Exception. However, it is not a method; it has no return type, and you cannot call it directly.

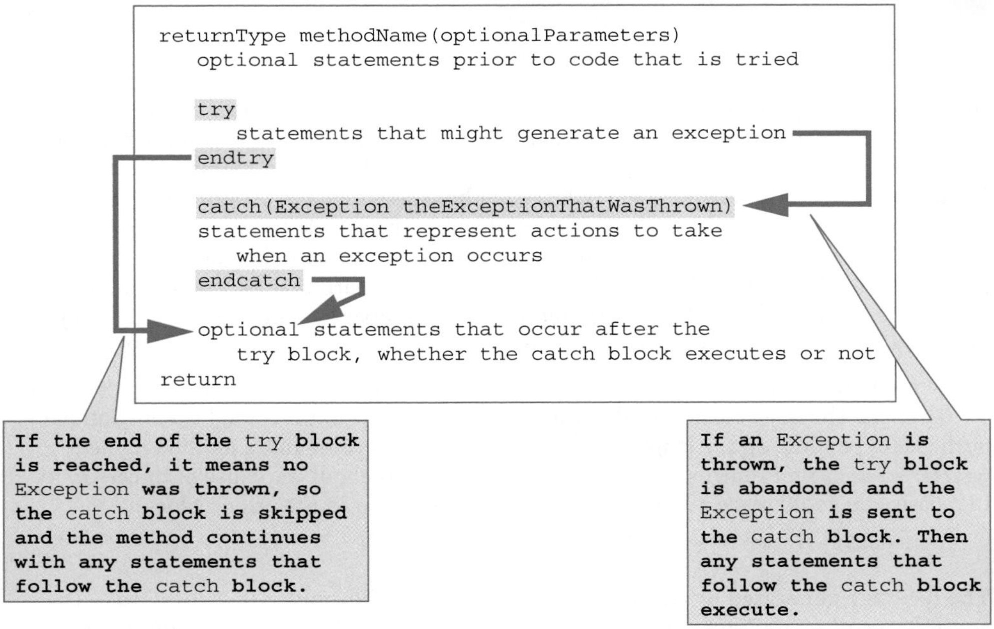

```
returnType methodName(optionalParameters)
    optional statements prior to code that is tried

    try
        statements that might generate an exception
    endtry

    catch(Exception theExceptionThatWasThrown)
    statements that represent actions to take
        when an exception occurs
    endcatch

    optional statements that occur after the
        try block, whether the catch block executes or not
    return
```

If the end of the try block is reached, it means no Exception was thrown, so the catch block is skipped and the method continues with any statements that follow the catch block.

If an Exception is thrown, the try block is abandoned and the Exception is sent to the catch block. Then any statements that follow the catch block execute.

»»NOTE
Some programmers refer to a catch block as a catch clause.

Figure 10-4 General format of a try...catch pair

Figure 10-5 shows a rewritten `dividingMethod()` method with a `try` block that contains code that attempts division. When illegal division by 0 takes place, an `Exception` (an object that contains information about the error) is created automatically by the object-oriented language application. When the `Exception` is created and thrown, the `catch` block (that follows and contains an `Exception` argument) executes.

```
public static void dividingMethod(numeric dividend, numeric divisor)
   numeric result

   try
      result = dividend / divisor
      print "result is ", result
   endtry

   catch(Exception mistake)
      print "Cannot divide by 0"
   endcatch
return
```

Figure 10-5 The `dividingMethod()` method with a `try...catch` pair

> **NOTE** When you learn a programming language, you will learn about subclasses of `Exception` that you might want to use in your code. For example, you saw in Figure 10-2 that in Java an `ArithmeticException` is the type of `Exception` that is automatically created. Therefore, in the code in Figure 10-5, you could catch the more specific `ArithmeticException` instead of the more general `Exception`.

In the application in Figure 10-5, if and when the division-by-0 error occurs, an `Exception` object is created automatically and thrown to the `catch` block. The programmer did not have to write any statement containing the word `throw`; the `throw` operation occurred implicitly. Later in this chapter, you will see methods in which the programmer explicitly throws an exception. Additionally, in this application, the `throw` and `catch` operations reside in the same method. Actually, this is not much different than including an `if...else` pair to handle the mistake. Later in this chapter, you will learn that `throw` statements and their corresponding `catch` blocks frequently reside in separate methods. That technique increases the client's flexibility in error handling.

In the method in Figure 10-5, the variable `mistake` in the `catch` block is an object of type `Exception`. The object is not used within the `catch` block, but it could be. For example, perhaps (depending on the language) the `Exception` class contains a method named `getMessage()` that returns a string that contains details about the cause of the error. In that case, you could place a statement such as the following in the `catch` block:

```
print mistake.getMessage()
```

The message generated by this built-in method would be similar to "/ by zero". As you will recall from Figure 10-2, this message is generated when exception handling occurs automatically.

THROWING AND CATCHING
MULTIPLE EXCEPTIONS

You can place as many statements as you need within a try block, and you can catch as many Exceptions as you want. If you try more than one statement, only the first error-generating statement throws an Exception. As soon as the Exception occurs, the logic transfers to the catch block, which leaves the rest of the statements in the try block unexecuted.

When a program contains multiple catch blocks, they are examined in sequence until a match is found for the type of Exception that occurred. Then, the matching catch block executes and each remaining catch block is bypassed.

For example, consider the application in Figure 10-6. The main() method in the TwoMistakes class throws two types of Exceptions: ArithmeticExceptions and IndexOutOfBoundsExceptions. (An IndexOutOfBoundsException occurs when an array subscript is not within the allowed range.)

```
public class TwoMistakes
    public static void main()
        numeric num[3] = 4, 0, 0

        try
            num[2] = num[0] / num[1]
            num[2] = num[3] / num[0]
        endtry

        catch(ArithmeticException mistake)
            print "Arithmetic mistake"
        endcatch

        catch(IndexOutOfBoundsException mistake2)
            print "Index mistake"
        endcatch

    return
endClass
```

Figure 10-6 The TwoMistakes class

The TwoMistakes class declares a numeric array with three elements. In the main() method, the try block executes, and at the first statement within the try block (shaded), an Exception occurs because the divisor in the division problem, num[1], is 0. The try block is abandoned and the logic transfers to the first catch block (shaded). Division by 0 causes an ArithmeticException, and because the first catch block receives an ArithmeticException, which has the local name mistake, the message "Arithmetic mistake" displays. In this example, the second try statement is never attempted and the second catch block is skipped.

If you make any one of several minor changes to the class in Figure 10-6, you can force the second catch block, the one with the IndexOutOfBoundsException argument, to execute. For example, you can force the division in the try block to succeed by substituting a nonzero value for the divisor in the first shaded arithmetic statement in the try block, as shown in

Figure 10-7. Alternatively, you could reverse the positions of the two arithmetic statements or comment out the first statement. With any of these changes, division by 0 does not take place. In the code in Figure 10-7, the first statement in the `try` block succeeds, and the logic proceeds to the second statement in the `try` block. This shaded statement attempts to access element 3 (the fourth element) of a three-element array (whose subscripts should only be 0, 1, or 2), so it throws an `IndexOutOfBoundsException`. The `try` block is abandoned, and the first `catch` block is examined and found unsuitable because it does not catch an `IndexOutOfBoundsException`. The program logic proceeds to the second `catch` block (shaded), whose `Exception` argument type is a match for the thrown `Exception`, so the message "Index mistake" appears.

```
public class TwoMistakes2
    public static void main()
        numeric num[3] = 4, 0, 0

        try
            num[2] = num[0] / 10
            num[2] = num[3] / num[0]
        endtry

        catch(ArithmeticException mistake)
            print "Arithmetic mistake"
        endcatch

        catch(IndexOutOfBoundsException mistake2)
            print "Index mistake"
        endcatch

    return
endClass
```

Figure 10-7 The `TwoMistakes2` class

Sometimes, you want to execute the same code no matter which `Exception` type occurs. For example, within the `TwoMistakes2` application in Figure 10-7, each of the two `catch` blocks prints a unique message. If both the `ArithmeticException` class and the `IndexOutOfBoundsException` class descend from the same base class, `Exception`, then you can use a single `catch` block to accept both types of objects. For example, Figure 10-8 shows a rewritten `TwoMistakes3` class that uses a single generic `catch` block (shaded) to catch any type of `Exception`.

```
public class TwoMistakes3
    public static void main()
        numeric num[3] = 4, 0, 0

        try
            num[2] = num[0] / 10
            num[2] = num[3] / num[0]
        endtry

        catch(Exception mistake)
            print "Mistake!"
        endcatch

    return
endClass
```

Figure 10-8 The `TwoMistakes3` class

The `catch` block in Figure 10-8 accepts a more generic `Exception` argument type than that thrown by either of the potentially error-causing `try` statements, so the generic `catch` block can act as a "catch-all" block. When either an arithmetic or array error occurs, the thrown exception is "promoted" to an `Exception` error in the `catch` block. Through inheritance, `ArithmeticExceptions` and `IndexOutOfBoundsExceptions` are `Exceptions`.

When you list multiple catch blocks following a try block, you must be careful that some catch blocks don't become unreachable. **Unreachable code** statements are program statements that can never execute under any circumstances. For example, if two successive catch blocks catch an IndexOutOfBoundsException and an ordinary Exception, the IndexOutOfBoundsException errors will cause the first catch to execute and other Exceptions will "fall through" to the more general Exception catch block. However, if you reverse the sequence of the catch blocks so that the code that catches general Exception objects is first, as shown in Figure 10-9, even IndexOutOfBoundsExceptions will be caught by the Exception catch. In this case, the IndexOutOfBoundsException catch block is unreachable because the Exception catch block is in its way and the class will not compile.

>>NOTE
Programmers also call unreachable code **dead code**.

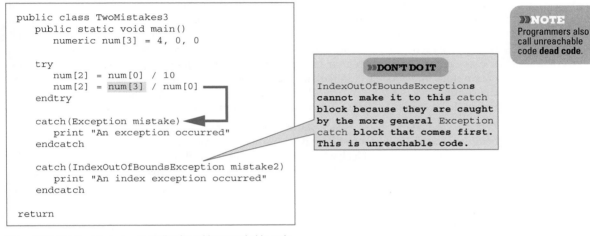

Figure 10-9 The TwoMistakes3 application with unreachable code

USING THE finally BLOCK

When you have actions you must perform at the end of a try...catch sequence, in several languages you can use a **finally block**. The code within a finally block executes whether or not the preceding try block identifies an Exception. Usually, you use a finally block to perform cleanup tasks that must happen whether or not any Exceptions occurred, and whether or not any Exceptions that occurred were caught. Figure 10-10 shows the format of a try...catch sequence that uses a finally block.

```
try
   statements to try
endtry
catch(Exception e)
   actions that occur if exception was thrown
endcatch
finally
   actions that occur whether catch block executed or not
endfinally
```

Figure 10-10 Format of try..catch..finally sequence

Compare Figure 10-10 to Figure 10-4 shown earlier in this chapter. When the `try` code works without error in Figure 10-4, control passes to the statements at the end of the method. Also, when the `try` code fails and throws an `Exception`, and the `Exception` is caught, the `catch` block executes and control again passes to the statements at the end of the method. At first glance, it seems as though the statements at the end of the method always execute. However, the last set of statements in Figure 10-4 might never execute for at least two reasons:

1. An unplanned `Exception` might occur, throwing an `Exception` to the operating system and stopping program execution immediately.

2. The `try` or `catch` block might contain a statement that terminates the program.

Any `try` block might throw an `Exception` for which you did not provide a `catch` block. After all, `Exceptions` occur all the time without your handling them, as one would if you attempted division by 0 without `try` and `catch` blocks. In the case of an unhandled `Exception`, program execution stops immediately, the `Exception` is sent to the operating system for handling, and the current method is abandoned. Likewise, if the `try` block contains an `exit()` statement (or the statement that stops program execution in the programming language you are using), execution stops immediately. Additionally, the `try` block could correctly throw an `Exception` to the `catch` block but the `catch` block could contain an `exit()` statement, or it might throw an unhandled `Exception`; either way, the program would end abruptly.

When you include a `finally` block, you are assured that the `finally` statements will execute before the method is abandoned, even if the method concludes prematurely. For example, programmers often use a `finally` block when the program uses data files that must be closed. Consider the pseudocode in Figure 10-11, which represents part of the logic for a typical file-handling program:

```
try
    Open the file
    Read the file
    Place the file data in an array
    Calculate an average from the data
    Display the average
endtry
catch(IOException e)
    Issue an error message
    System exit
endcatch
finally
    If the file is open, close it
endfinally
```

Figure 10-11 Pseudocode that tries reading a file and handles an `Exception`

The pseudocode in Figure 10-11 represents an application that opens a file; if a file does not exist when you open it, object-oriented languages automatically throw an input/output exception. (This pseudocode assumes the class that contains input/output error information is called `IOException`.) However, because the application uses an array (see the statement "Place the file data in an array"), it is possible that even though the file opened successfully, an uncaught `IndexOutOfBoundsException` might occur. In such an event, you should close the file before proceeding. By using the `finally` block, you ensure that the file is closed because the code in the `finally` block executes before control returns to the operating system. The code in the `finally` block executes no matter which of the following outcomes of the `try` block occurs:

» The `try` ends normally with no exceptions.

» The `try` throws an `IOException` to the `catch` block, which executes and ends the program.

» An `Exception` causes the `try` block to be abandoned prematurely—perhaps the array is not large enough to hold the data, or calculating the average results in division by 0. These `Exceptions` would not allow the `try` block to finish, nor would they cause the `catch` block to execute.

>> **NOTE** You can avoid using a `finally` block, but you would need repetitious code. For example, instead of using the `finally` block in the pseudocode in Figure 10-11, you could insert the statement "If the file is open, close it" as both the last statement in the `try` block and the second-to-last statement in the `catch` block, just before `System exit`. However, writing code just once in a `finally` block is clearer and less prone to error.

>> **NOTE** C++ does not provide a `finally` block, but it does provide a default "catch all" block that can catch any previously uncaught exceptions. C#, Java, and Visual Basic all support a `finally` block.

>> **NOTE** Many well-designed programs that try code do not include any `catch` blocks; instead, they contain only `try-finally` pairs. The `finally` block is used to release resources that other applications might be waiting for, such as database connections.

UNDERSTANDING THE ADVANTAGES OF EXCEPTION HANDLING

Before the inception of OOP languages, potential program errors were handled using somewhat confusing, error-prone methods. For example, a traditional, non-object-oriented, procedural program might perform three methods that depend on each other using code that provides error checking similar to the pseudocode in Figure 10-12.

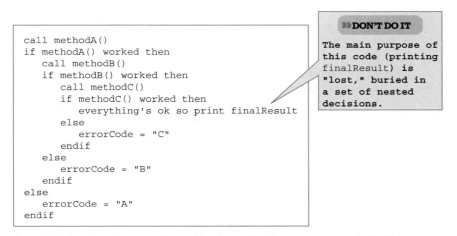

```
call methodA()
if methodA() worked then
    call methodB()
    if methodB() worked then
        call methodC()
        if methodC() worked then
            everything's ok so print finalResult
        else
            errorCode = "C"
        endif
    else
        errorCode = "B"
    endif
else
    errorCode = "A"
endif
```

>> **DON'T DO IT**

The main purpose of this code (printing finalResult) is "lost," buried in a set of nested decisions.

Figure 10-12 Pseudocode representing traditional error checking—not recommended in OO languages

The pseudocode in Figure 10-12 represents an application in which the logic must pass three tests before a final result can be displayed. It performs `methodA()`; it then performs `methodB()` only if `methodA()` is successful. Similarly, `methodC()` executes only when `methodA()` and methodB() are both successful. When any method fails, the program sets an appropriate errorCode to "A", "B", or "C". (Presumably, the errorCode is used later in the application.) The logic in Figure 10-12 is difficult to follow, and the application's purpose and intended outcome—to print the finalResult—is lost in the maze of if statements. Also, you can easily make coding mistakes within such a program because of the complicated nesting and indenting.

Compare the same program logic using the object-oriented, error-handling technique shown in Figure 10-13. Using the try...catch object-oriented technique provides the same results as the traditional method, but the statements of the program that do the "real" work (calling methods A, B, and C, and printing finalResult) are placed together where their logic is easy to follow. The try steps should usually work without generating errors; after all, the errors are "exceptions." It is convenient to see these business-as-usual steps in one location. The unusual, exceptional events are grouped and moved out of the way of the primary action.

» NOTE
In Figure 10-13, each of the methods, methodA(), methodB(), and methodC(), throws a different type of error that is caught by the appropriate catch block.

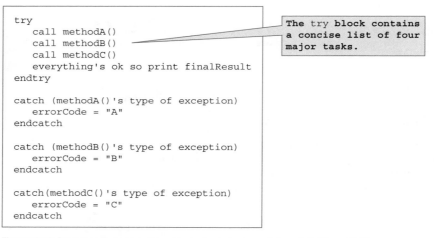

```
try
    call methodA()
    call methodB()
    call methodC()
    everything's ok so print finalResult
endtry

catch (methodA()'s type of exception)
    errorCode = "A"
endcatch

catch (methodB()'s type of exception)
    errorCode = "B"
endcatch

catch(methodC()'s type of exception)
    errorCode = "C"
endcatch
```

> The try block contains a concise list of four major tasks.

Figure 10-13 Pseudocode representing object-oriented approach to code in Figure 10-12

Besides clarity, an advantage to object-oriented exception handling is the flexibility it allows in the handling of error situations. When a method you write throws an Exception, the same method can catch the Exception, although it is not required to do so, and in most object-oriented programs it will not. Often, you will not want a method to handle its own Exception. In many cases, you want the method to check for errors, but you do not want to require a method to handle an error if it finds one; instead, you want a client to be able to handle the exception in the most appropriate way for its application. Just as a police officer can deal with a speeding driver differently depending on circumstances, your client programs can react to Exceptions specifically to suit the current purposes.

Methods are flexible partly because they are reusable—that is, a well-written method might be used by any number of applications. Each calling application might need to handle the same error differently, depending on its purpose. For example, an application that uses a method that divides values might need to terminate if division by 0 occurs. A different program simply might want the user to reenter the data to be used, and a third program might want to force division by 1. The method that contains the division statement can throw the error, but each calling program can assume responsibility for handling the error detected by the method in an appropriate way.

For example, Figure 10-14 shows a `PriceList` class used by a company to hold a list of prices for items it sells. For simplicity, there are only four prices and a single method that displays the price of a single item. The `displayPrice()` method accepts an argument to use as the array subscript, and because the subscript could be out of bounds, the method might throw an exception.

```
public class PriceList
    private numeric price[4] = 15.99, 27.88, 34.56, 45.89
    public static void displayPrice(numeric item)
        print "The price is $", price[item]
    return
endClass
```

Figure 10-14 The `PriceList` class

»NOTE In some languages, for example, Java, if a method throws an `Exception` that it will not catch, but that will be caught by a different method, you must write an **exception specification clause**, which indicates exception types that might be thrown in the method header. In C++ you may write an exception specification, but it is not required. C# and Visual Basic do not allow exception specifications.

Figures 10-15 and 10-16 show two applications in which programmers have chosen to handle the exception differently. In the first class, `PriceListApplication1`, the programmer has

```
public class PriceListApplication1
    public static void main()
        numeric item = 4
        try
            PriceList.displayPrice(item)
        endtry
        catch(IndexOutOfBoundsException e)
            print "Price is $0"
        endcatch
    return
endClass
```

Figure 10-15 The `PriceListApplication1` class

```
public class PriceListApplication2
    public static void main()
        numeric item = 4
        try
            PriceList.displayPrice(item)
        endtry
        catch(IndexOutOfBoundsException e)
            while item < 0 OR item > 3
                print "Please reenter a value 0, 1, 2, or 3"
                read item
            endwhile
            PriceList.displayPrice(item)
        endcatch
    return
endClass
```

Figure 10-16 The `PriceListApplication2` class

»NOTE In C++, you can throw objects that are basic data types, such as numbers and strings, as well as `Exception` class objects.

chosen to handle the exception in the shaded `catch` block by displaying a price of $0. In the second class, `PriceListApplication2`, the programmer has chosen to continue using an input dialog box in the shaded `catch` block to prompt the user for a new item number until it is within the correct range. Other programmers could choose still different actions, but they all can use the flexible `displayPrice()` method because it throws the error but does not limit the calling method's choice of recourse.

TRACING EXCEPTIONS THROUGH THE CALL STACK

When one method calls another, the computer's operating system must keep track of where the method call came from, and program control must return to the calling method when the called method is completed. For example, if `methodA()` calls `methodB()`, the operating system has to "remember" to return to `methodA()` when `methodB()` ends. Likewise, if `methodB()` calls `methodC()`, then after `methodC()` executes, the computer must "remember" to return to `methodB()`, and eventually to `methodA()`. The memory location known as the **call stack** is where the computer stores the list of method locations to which the system must return.

When a method throws an `Exception` and the same method does not `catch` it, the `Exception` is thrown to the next method up the call stack, or in other words, to the method that called the offending method. Figure 10-17 shows how the call stack works.

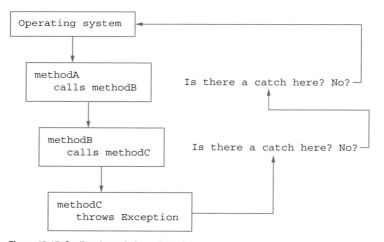

Figure 10-17 Cycling through the call stack

Consider this sequence of events:

1. `methodA()` calls `methodB()`.
2. `methodB()` calls `methodC()`.
3. `methodC()` throws an `Exception`.
4. The program looks first for a `catch` block in `methodC()`.

5. If none exists, then it looks for the same thing in `methodB()`.

6. If `methodB()` does not have a `catch` block for the `Exception`, then the program looks to `methodA()`.

7. If `methodA()` does not catch the `Exception`, then the program terminates and the operating system displays an error message.

This system of passing `Exception`s through the chain of calling methods has great advantages because it allows methods to handle `Exception`s wherever the programmer has decided it is most appropriate—including allowing the operating system to handle the error. However, when a program uses several classes, this system's disadvantage is that the programmer finds it difficult to locate the original source of an `Exception`. Even when you catch an `Exception` instead of allowing it to be thrown to the operating system, object-oriented languages contain an `Exception` class method with a name similar to `printStackTrace()` that allows you to display a list of methods in the call stack so you can determine the location of the `Exception`. Often, you do not want to place a `printStackTrace()` method call in a finished program. The typical application user has no interest in the cryptic messages that display. However, while you are developing an application, printing a list of the method calls in the stack can be a useful tool for diagnosing your application's problems.

A CASE STUDY: TRACING THE SOURCE OF AN EXCEPTION

As an example of when tracing `Exception`s through the stack can be useful, consider the `Tax` class in Figure 10-18. Suppose your company has created or purchased this class to make it easy to calculate tax rates on products sold. For simplicity, assume that only two tax rates are in effect—6 percent for sales of $20 or less and 7 percent for sales over $20. The `Tax` class would be useful for any programmer who wrote a program involving product sales, except for one flaw: in the shaded statement, the subscript is erroneously set to 2 instead of 1 for the higher tax rate. If this subscript is used with the `taxRate` array in the next statement, it will be out of bounds. However, assume that you are provided with this class as a completed package—it has already been written and compiled by someone else and you do not even see the code. In other words, it is a black box to you.

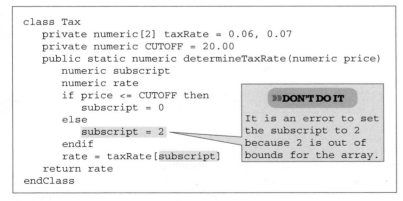

```
class Tax
    private numeric[2] taxRate = 0.06, 0.07
    private numeric CUTOFF = 20.00
    public static numeric determineTaxRate(numeric price)
        numeric subscript
        numeric rate
        if price <= CUTOFF then
            subscript = 0
        else
            subscript = 2
        endif
        rate = taxRate[subscript]
    return rate
endClass
```

>>DON'T DO IT

It is an error to set the subscript to 2 because 2 is out of bounds for the array.

Figure 10-18 The `Tax` class that contains a mistake

Assume your company has also created a `Prices` class, as shown in Figure 10-19. This class contains four prices of items you sell. It contains a single method that accepts an item number (0 through 3, for convenience) and uses it to access one of the prices in the price array. Then, the price is sent to the `determineTaxRate()` method in the `Tax` class so the correct tax can be applied to the price. The correct tax is 6 percent or 7 percent, depending on whether the price is over $20.

```
public class Prices
    private numeric[4] price = {15.99, 27.88, 34.56, 45.89}
    public static void displayPrice(numeric item)
        numeric tax
        numeric total
        numeric pr
        pr = price[item]
        tax = pr * Tax.determineTaxRate(pr)      This statement
        total =  pr + tax                        uses a method in
        print "The total price is ", total       the Tax class.
    return
endClass
```

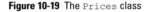

Figure 10-19 The `Prices` class

Suppose you write the application shown in Figure 10-20. This application asks the user to enter a number for an item and passes it to `Prices.displayPrice()`. This program tries the item entry and catches any exception. You created the `try...catch` pair because you knew that if an improper item number (less than 0 or more than 3) was passed to `displayPrice()`, the index would be out of range and an exception would be thrown.

```
class PricesApplication
    public static void main()
        numeric item
        try
            print "Enter an item number from 0 through 3 >> "
            get item
            Prices.DisplayPrice(item)
        endtry
        catch(Exception e)
            print "Error!"                 Your intention
        endcatch                           is to catch bad
    return                                 item numbers.
endClass
```

Figure 10-20 `PricesApplication` class

When you run the program using an out-of-range number such as 5, the "Error!" message is displayed and you consider that test to be correct. When you run the program using what you know to be a valid item number—for example, 1—you might be surprised to see the shaded "Error!" message you have coded in the `catch` block. To attempt to discover what caused the

"Error!" message, you can replace the `catch` block statement with a stack trace call such as the following:

```
e.printStackTrace()
```

In this statement, `e` is the local name for the `Exception` object in the `catch` block and `printStackTrace()` is the name of a method that resides in the `Exception` class. For example, when this program is implemented in C#, the output looks like Figure 10-21. From the list of methods, you can see that the error in your application did not come from the `displayPrice()` method. Rather, it came from the `Tax.DetermineTaxRate()` method, which was called by the `Prices.DisplayPrice()` method, which in turn was called by the `PricesApplication.Main()` method. You might not have even considered that the `Tax` class could have been the source of the problem because it was written by others and provided to you as a working method. If you work in a small organization, you might be allowed to look at the code yourself and fix it. If you work in a larger organization or you purchased the class from an outside vendor, you might be able to contact the programmer or team who created the class for assistance.

```
Command Prompt                              _ □ ×

C:\OOLogic\Chapter.10>PricesApplication

Enter an item number from 0 through 3 >> 1
    at Tax.DetermineTaxRate(Double price)
    at Prices.DisplayPrice(Int32 item)
    at PricesApplication.Main()

C:\OOLogic\Chapter.10>
```

Figure 10-21 Execution of `PricesApplication` program in which the stack trace is displayed in the `catch` block

》NOTE
The stack trace in Figure 10-21 was generated by a C# program. The method names listed begin with uppercase letters because that is the convention in C#.

The classes in this example were small to help you easily follow the discussion. However, a full-blown application might have many more classes that contain many more methods, and so displaying the trace of the stack would become increasingly beneficial.

CREATING YOUR OWN EXCEPTIONS

Many (but not all) OOP languages provide numerous built-in `Exception` types. For example, Java, Visual Basic, and C# each provide dozens of categories of `Exceptions` that you can use in your programs. Those who create the built-in `Exceptions` that are part of a programming language cannot predict every condition that might be an `Exception` in your applications. For example, you might want to declare an `Exception` when your bank balance is negative or when an outside party attempts to access your e-mail account. Most organizations have specific rules for exceptional data; for example, an employee number must not exceed three digits, or an hourly salary must not be less than the legal minimum wage. Of course, you can handle these potential error situations with `if` statements, but you also can create your own `Exceptions`.

To create your own throwable `Exception`, you usually extend a built-in `Exception` class. For example, you might create a class named `NegativeBankBalanceException` or

EmployeeNumberTooLargeException. Each would be a subclass of the more general Exception class. By inheriting from the Exception class, you gain access to methods contained in the parent class, such as those that display a default message describing the Exception and that display the stack trace.

> **» NOTE** When you create an Exception, it is conventional to end its name with Exception, as in NegativeBankBalanceException.

For example, Figure 10-22 shows a HighBalanceException class. This example assumes that the parent class contains a setMessage() method that assigns the passed string to a field in the parent class. Also assume that a parent class getMessage() method can retrieve the message. The HighBalanceException class constructor contains a single statement that sets the error message. This string would be retrieved if you called the getMessage() method using a HighBalanceException object.

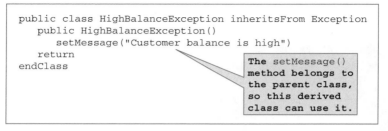

```
public class HighBalanceException inheritsFrom Exception
    public HighBalanceException()
        setMessage("Customer balance is high")
    return
endClass
```

The setMessage() method belongs to the parent class, so this derived class can use it.

Figure 10-22 The HighBalanceException class

Figure 10-23 shows a CustomerAccount class that uses a HighBalanceException. The CustomerAccount class contains an account number, a balance, and a constant that stores a limit for customer credit. If the account balance exceeds the limit, an instance of the HighBalanceException class is created and thrown (see the shaded statements in the figure).

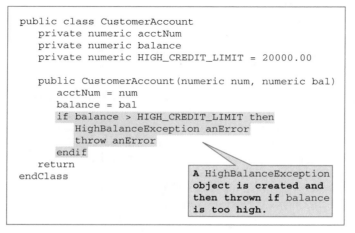

```
public class CustomerAccount
    private numeric acctNum
    private numeric balance
    private numeric HIGH_CREDIT_LIMIT = 20000.00

    public CustomerAccount(numeric num, numeric bal)
        acctNum = num
        balance = bal
        if balance > HIGH_CREDIT_LIMIT then
            HighBalanceException anError
            throw anError
        endif
    return
endClass
```

A HighBalanceException object is created and then thrown if balance is too high.

Figure 10-23 The CustomerAccount class

Figure 10-24 shows an application that instantiates a `CustomerAccount`. In this application, a user is prompted for an account number and balance. After those values are entered, an attempt is made to construct a `CustomerAccount` in a `try` block (as shown in the first shaded section). If the attempt is successful—that is, if the `CustomerAccount` constructor does not throw an `Exception`—the `CustomerAccount` information is displayed. However, if the `CustomerAccount` constructor does throw a `HighBalanceException`, the `catch` block receives it (as shown in the second shaded section) and displays two messages. The `catch` block in this class demonstrates that you can decide to create your own message in the `catch` block, or use the message that is part of every `HighBalanceException`—the one that was set in the constructor in Figure 10-22. A different application could take any number of different actions in its `catch` block; for example, it could display only one of the messages or a different message, construct a new `CustomerAccount` object with a lower balance, or construct a different type of object—perhaps a child of `CustomerAccount` called `PreferredCustomerAccount` that allows a higher balance.

```
public class UseCustomerAccount
    public static void main()
        numeric num
        numeric balance

        print "Enter account number "
        get num
        print "Enter balance "
        get balance

        try
            CustomerAccount newAccount(num, balance)
            print "Customer created"
        endtry

        catch(HighBalanceException hbe)
            print "Customer #", num, "Has a balance that is too high"
            print hbe.getMessage()
        endcatch
    return
endClass
```

> In a full-blown application, you might want to perform other tasks at this point. For example, you might want to save `CustomerAccount` objects to a data file.

Figure 10-24 The `UseCustomerAccount` class

> **NOTE** In Figure 10-24, `balance` is a local variable in the `main()` method. When `balance` is passed to the `CustomerAccount` constructor, its value is assigned to the parameter `bal` as defined in the header of the `CustomerAccount` constructor class. Then, the parameter value is assigned to the `balance` field in the `CustomerAccount` class.

> **NOTE** In the `catch` block in the `main()` method of the `UseCustomerAccount` class in Figure 10-24, the `getMessage()` method is used with the `hbe` object. Because the `hbe` object is a `HighBalanceException`, which is an `Exception`, and because the `HighBalanceException` class defined in Figure 10-22 contains no method named `getMessage()`, you know that `HighBalanceException` must inherit the `getMessage()` method from the more general `Exception` class (or some other class from which `Exception` is derived).

You should not create an excessive number of special Exception types for your classes, especially if the language with which you are working already contains an Exception that will catch the error. Extra Exception types add complexity for other programmers who use your classes. However, when appropriate, specialized Exception classes provide an elegant way for you to handle error situations. They enable you to separate your error code from the usual, nonexceptional sequence of events, they allow errors to be passed up the stack and traced, and they allow clients of your classes to handle exceptional situations in the manner most suitable for their application.

» **NOTE** Exceptions can be particularly useful when you throw them from constructors. Constructors do not have a return type, so they have no other way to send information back to the calling method.

CHAPTER SUMMARY

» An exception is an unexpected or error condition. The object-oriented techniques to manage such errors comprise the group of methods known as exception handling.

» Exception handling provides an elegant solution for handling error conditions. In object-oriented terminology, you "try" a procedure that might cause an error. A method that detects an error condition or exception "throws an exception," and the block of code that processes the error "catches the exception."

» When you create a segment of code in which something might go wrong, you place the code in a try block, which is a block of code you attempt to execute while acknowledging that an exception might occur. You must code at least one catch block immediately following a try block. A catch block is a segment of code that can handle an exception that might be thrown by the try block that precedes it.

» You can place as many statements as you need within a try block, and you can catch as many Exceptions as you want. If you try more than one statement, only the first error-generating statement throws an Exception. As soon as the Exception occurs, the logic transfers to the catch block, which leaves the rest of the statements in the try block unexecuted. When a program contains multiple catch blocks, they are examined in sequence until a match is found for the type of Exception that occurred. Then, the matching catch block executes and each remaining catch block is bypassed.

» When you have actions you must perform at the end of a try...catch sequence, in some languages you can use a finally block. The code within a finally block executes whether or not the preceding try block identifies an Exception. Usually, you use a finally block to perform cleanup tasks that must happen whether or not any Exceptions occurred, and whether or not any Exceptions that occurred were caught.

» Besides clarity, an advantage to object-oriented exception handling is the flexibility it allows in the handling of error situations. Each calling application might need to handle the same error differently, depending on its purpose.

» When one method calls another, the computer's operating system must keep track of where the method call came from, and program control must return to the calling method when the called method is completed. The memory location known as the call stack is where the computer stores the list of method locations to which the system must return.

» Those who create the built-in Exceptions that are part of a programming language cannot predict every condition that might be an Exception in your applications, so you can create your own Exceptions. Usually you accomplish this by creating a subclass based on a built-in Exception class.

KEY TERMS

An **exception** is an unexpected or error condition that occurs while a program is running.

Exception handling is an object-oriented technique for managing errors.

Throwing an exception is the process of tossing out an Exception object that another method or the operating system might handle.

A **try block** is a block of code you attempt to execute while acknowledging that an exception might occur.

A **catch block** is a segment of code that can handle an exception that might be thrown by the try block that precedes it.

A **throw statement** is one that sends an Exception out of a method so it can be handled elsewhere.

Unreachable code statements are program statements that can never execute under any circumstances.

Programmers also call unreachable code **dead code**.

A **finally block** holds statements that execute at the end of a try...catch sequence.

An **exception specification clause** is a declaration of a method's possible throw types.

The **call stack** is the memory location where the computer stores the list of method locations to which the system must return.

REVIEW QUESTIONS

1. In object-oriented programming terminology, an unexpected or error condition is a(n) _____ .

   a. anomaly

   b. aberration

   c. deviation

   d. exception

2. A programmer can recover from _____ errors.

   a. all

   b. some

   c. only unpredictable

   d. no

3. When a program might generate an exception, you _____ .

   a. must write statements to handle it

   b. must write a class to handle it

   c. can choose to handle it or not

   d. cannot handle it; the operating system must do so

4. Which of the following is *not* a typical example of a situation in which an `Exception` would be automatically created and thrown?

   a. You attempt to access an array element using an illegal subscript.

   b. You attempt to store an object in an array that is an incorrect data type.

   c. An arithmetic operation produces a result for which the value is greater than the assigned memory location can accommodate.

   d. You store an employee's Social Security number that contains only eight digits instead of nine.

5. In object-oriented terminology, you _____ a series of steps or a procedure when you think it might throw an exception.

   a. `try`

   b. `catch`

   c. `handle`

   d. `encapsulate`

6. A `catch` clause _____ an `Exception`.

   a. tries

   b. returns

   c. handles

   d. encapsulates

7. A `try` block can include all of the following elements except _____.

   a. the keyword `try`

   b. the keyword `catch`

   c. statements that might cause `Exceptions`

   d. statements that cannot cause `Exceptions`

8. The segment of code that handles or takes appropriate action after an exception is thrown is a _____ block.

   a. `try`

   b. `catch`

   c. `throws`

   d. `class`

9. You _____ within a `try` block.

   a. must place only a single statement

   b. can place any number of statements

   c. must place at least two statements

   d. must place a `catch` block

10. If you try three statements and include three `catch` blocks, and the second statement that is tried throws an `Exception`, _____ .

    a. the first `catch` block executes

    b. the first two `catch` blocks execute

    c. only the second `catch` block executes

    d. the first matching `catch` block executes

11. When a `try` block does not generate an `Exception` and you have included multiple `catch` blocks, _____ .

    a. they all execute

    b. only the first one executes

    c. only the first matching one executes

    d. no `catch` blocks execute

12. In most languages, a `catch` block that begins `catch (Exception e)` probably can catch `Exceptions` of type _____ .

    a. `IndexOutOfBoundsException`

    b. `ArithmeticException`

    c. both of the above

    d. none of the above

13. The code within a `finally` block executes when the `try` block _____ .

    a. identifies one or more `Exceptions`

    b. does not identify any `Exceptions`

    c. either a or b

    d. neither a nor b

14. An advantage to using a `try...catch` block is that exceptional events are _____ .

    a. eliminated

    b. reduced

    c. integrated with regular events

    d. isolated from regular events

15. Which methods can throw an `Exception`?

    a. only methods with a `throws` clause

    b. only methods with a `catch` block

    c. only methods with both a `throws` clause and a `catch` block

    d. any method

16. In object-oriented programming, you usually want a method that might generate an exception to _____ .

    a. throw the exception to the calling method

    b. handle the exception

    c. either of the above

    d. neither of the above

17. If `method1()` calls `method2()` and `method2()` throws an exception, then _____ .

    a. `method1()` must catch the exception

    b. `method2()` must catch the exception

    c. `method2()` must catch the exception and then throw it to `method1()`

    d. None of these is true.

18. The memory location where the computer stores the list of method locations to which the system must return is known as the _____ .

    a. registry   c. chronicle

    b. call stack   d. archive

19. You can get a list of the methods through which an `Exception` has traveled by displaying the method's _____ .

    a. constructor

    b. `getMessage()` value

    c. stack trace

    d. `path`

20. To create your own `Exception` class from which you create objects that you can throw, in most object-oriented languages you must create _____ .

    a. a subclass of an existing `Exception` class

    b. an overloaded constructor for the existing `Exception` class

    c. a new class that does not descend from any class

    d. additional methods for the class that will throw the new `Exception` type

EXERCISES

1. Design an application in which you declare an array of five numbers and store five values in the array. Write a `try` block in which you loop to display each successive element of the array, increasing a subscript by one on each pass through the loop. Assume you are working with a language that automatically creates an `ArrayIndexOutOfBoundsException` when a subscript is not correct for an array. Create a `catch` block that catches the exception if it is generated and displays the message, "Now you've gone too far."

2. Design a class that contains public methods named add(), subtract(), multiply(), and divide(). Each of the methods accepts two numeric arguments and returns a number that represents the result of the appropriate arithmetic operation. Design a main() method that prompts the user for two numbers and tries each of the methods. Assume you are working in a language in which a NumberFormatException is automatically created and thrown when a method's argument is not numeric, and in which an ArithmeticException is created and thrown when division by 0 is attempted. Display an appropriate message when an Exception is caught.

3. Design an application that prompts the user to enter a number to use as an array size, and then attempt to declare an array using the entered size. If the array is created successfully, display an appropriate message. Assume you are working with a language that generates a NegativeArraySizeException if you attempt to create an array with a negative size, and a NumberFormatException if you attempt to create an array using a nonnumeric value for the size. Use a catch block that executes if the array size is nonnumeric or negative, displaying a message that indicates the array was not created.

4. Design an application that throws and catches an automatically generated ArithmeticException when you attempt to take the square root of a negative value. Prompt the user for an input value and try a squareRoot() method that accepts a numeric argument and returns its square root. (You do not need to design the implementation of the squareRoot() method.) The application either displays the square root or catches the thrown Exception and displays an appropriate message.

5. Complete the following tasks:

   a. Design an EmployeeException class whose constructor receives a string that consists of an employee's ID and pay rate. Include a getMessage() method that returns a string that contains the employee's data.

   b. Create an Employee class with two numeric fields, idNum and hourlyWage. The Employee constructor requires values for both fields. Upon construction, throw an EmployeeException if the hourlyWage is less than $6.00 or more than $50.00.

   c. Write an application that establishes an array of 20 Employees. Prompt the user for ID numbers and hourly wages for each Employee. Display an appropriate message when an Employee is successfully created as well as when one is not.

6. Complete the following tasks:

   a. Create an IceCreamConeException class whose constructor receives a string that consists of an ice cream cone's flavor and an integer representing the number of scoops in the IceCreamCone. Create a getMessage() method that returns a string that contains the IceCreamCone information.

   b. Create an IceCreamCone class with two fields—flavor and scoops. The IceCreamCone constructor calls two data-entry methods—setFlavor() and setScoops(). The setScoops() method throws an IceCreamConeException when the scoop quantity exceeds three.

   c. Write an application that establishes an array of 10 IceCreamCone objects and handles the Exceptions that occur as a user enters data.

d. Create an `IceCreamCone2` class in which you modify the `IceCreamCone` `setFlavor()` method to ensure that the user enters a valid flavor. Allow at least four flavors of your choice. If the user's entry does not match a valid flavor, throw an `IceCreamConeException`.

e. Write an application that establishes an array of 10 `IceCreamCone` objects and demonstrates the handling of the new `Exception`.

7. Write an application that displays a series of five student ID numbers that you store in an array: 1023, 1045, 2134, 2768, and 3478. Ask the user to enter a numeric test score for each student. Create a `ScoreException` class and throw a `ScoreException` if the user does not enter a valid score (greater than or equal to 0 and less than or equal to 100). Catch the `ScoreException` and then display an appropriate message. In addition, if an exception is thrown, store a 0 for the student's score. At the end of the application, display all the student IDs and scores.

8. Write an application that displays a series of 10 student ID numbers that you have stored in an array: 1023, 1045, 2134, 2768, 3478, 3712, 4198, 4367, 5510, and 5672. Ask the user to enter a test letter grade for each student. Create an `Exception` class named `GradeException` that contains an array of valid grade letters ('A', 'B', 'C', 'D', 'F', and 'I') you can use to determine whether a grade input from the application is valid. In your application, throw a `GradeException` if the user does not enter a valid letter grade. Catch the `GradeException` and then display an appropriate message. In addition, store an 'I' (for Incomplete) for any student for whom an exception is caught. At the end of the application, display all the student IDs and grades.

CASE PROJECT

In earlier chapters, you developed classes needed for Cost Is No Object—a car rental service that specializes in lending antique and luxury cars to clients on a short-term basis. You created the logic for `Name`, `Address`, `Date`, `Person`, `Employee`, `Customer`, `Automobile`, `RentalAgreement`, and several other subclasses.

In Chapter 7, you created the `RentalAgreement` class to contain all the attributes and methods associated with one rental contract. Specifically, a `RentalAgreement` contains the following:

» `string rentalAgreementNumber`
» `Customer renter`
» `Employee rentalAgent`
» `Date rentalStartDate`
» `Automobile carRented`
» `numeric dailyFee`
» `numeric numberOfDaysRented`

Now do the following:

» Design a `RentalAgreementException` class. The class contains a string field that holds an error message. The constructor accepts a string message that it can return with a `getMessage()` method.

» Modify the `RentalAgreement` class so that each set method throws a `RentalAgreementException` that contains an appropriate message if any of the method's arguments are out of range, as follows:

   » The rental agreement number must be a string between "10000" and "99999" inclusive.

   » The customer ID number must be a string between "100" and "999" inclusive.

   » The car ID number must be a string between "100" and "999" inclusive.

   » The starting date for the rental agreement is not prior to today's date, the month is between 1 and 12 inclusive, and the date is appropriate for the month (for example, the date for June is between 1 and 30 inclusive).

   » The number of days rented is between 1 and 30 days inclusive; the set method also calculates the ending month, day, and year based on the starting date and length of the agreement.

» Design an application that creates an array of 10 `RentalAgreement` objects. In a loop, prompt the user to enter the needed data for each object. If a `RentalAgreementException` is thrown, display the `RentalAgreementException`'s message and end the application.

» Design a second application that creates an array of 10 `RentalAgreement` objects. In a loop, prompt the user to enter the needed data for each object. If a `RentalAgreementException` is thrown after the user enters data for any field, display the `RentalAgreementException`'s message, and continue to prompt the user for data until a valid value for the erroneous field is entered. After all the objects are entered, display all 10 `RentalAgreement` objects.

» Design a third application that creates an array of 10 `RentalAgreement` objects. In a loop, prompt the user to enter the needed data for each object. If a `RentalAgreementException` is thrown after the user enters data for any field, force the user to reenter all the data for that object, continuing until there are 10 completely valid objects. After all the objects are entered, display all 10 `RentalAgreement` objects.

UP FOR DISCUSSION

1. Have you ever been victimized by a computer error? For example, were you ever incorrectly denied credit, billed for something you did not purchase, or assigned an incorrect grade in a course? How did you resolve the problem? On the Web, find the most outrageous story you can involving a computer error.

2. Search the Web for information about educational video games in which historical simulations are presented in an effort to teach students about history. For example, Civilization IV is a game in which players control a society as it progresses through time. Do you believe such games are useful to history students? Does the knowledge gained warrant the hours it takes to master the games? Do the makers of the games have any obligations to present history factually? Do they have a right to penalize players who choose options of which the game writers disapprove (such as using nuclear weapons or allowing slavery)? Do game creators have the right to create characters who possess negative stereotypical traits—for example, a person of a specific nationality portrayed as being stupid, weak, or evil? Would you like to take a history course that uses similar games?

SYSTEM MODELING WITH THE UML

In this chapter, you will:

Understand the need for system modeling
Learn about the UML
Work with use case diagrams
Use class and object diagrams
Use sequence and communication diagrams
Use state machine diagrams
Use activity diagrams
Use component and deployment diagrams
Diagram exception handling
Decide when to use UML and which UML
    diagrams to use

UNDERSTANDING THE NEED FOR SYSTEM MODELING

Computer programs often stand alone to solve a user's specific problem. For example, a program might exist only to print paychecks for the current week. Most computer programs, however, are part of a larger system. Your company's payroll system might consist of dozens of programs, including programs that produce employee paychecks, apply raises to employee records, alter employee deduction options, and print federal and state tax forms at the end of the year. Each program you write as part of a system might be related to several others. Some programs depend on input from other programs in the system or produce output to be fed into other programs. Similarly, an organization's accounting, inventory, and customer ordering systems all consist of many interrelated programs. Producing a set of programs that operate together correctly requires careful planning. **System design** is the detailed specification of how all the parts of a system will be implemented and coordinated.

Many textbooks cover the theories and techniques of system design. If you continue to study in a Computer Information Systems program at a college or university, you will probably be required to take a semester-long course in system design. Explaining all the techniques of system design is beyond the scope of this book. However, some of the basic principles parallel those you have used throughout this book in designing individual programs:

» Large systems are easier to understand when you break them down into subsystems.

» Good modeling techniques are increasingly important as the size and complexity of systems increase.

» Good models promote communication among technical and nontechnical workers while ensuring good business solutions.

In other words, developing a model for a single program or an entire business system requires organization and planning. In this chapter, you learn the basics of one popular design tool, the UML, which is based on these principles. The UML, or Unified Modeling Language, allows you to envision systems with an object-oriented perspective, breaking a system into subsystems, focusing on the big picture, and hiding the implementation details. In addition, the UML provides a means for programmers and businesspeople to communicate about system design. It also provides a way to plan to divide responsibilities for large systems. Understanding the UML's principles helps you design a variety of system types and talk about systems with the people who will use them.

WHAT IS THE UML?

The **UML** is a standard way to specify, construct, and document systems that use object-oriented methods. (The UML is a modeling language, not a programming language. The systems you develop using the UML will probably be implemented later in object-oriented programming languages such as Java, C++, C#, or Visual Basic.) As with flowcharts, pseudocode, hierarchy charts, and class diagrams, the UML has its own notation that consists of a set of specialized shapes and conventions. You can use the UML's shapes to construct different kinds of software diagrams and model different kinds of systems. Just as you can use a flowchart or hierarchy chart to diagram real-life activities, organizational relationships, or computer programs, you also can use the UML for many purposes, including modeling business activities, organizational processes, or software systems.

> **» NOTE** The UML was created at Rational Software by Grady Booch, Ivar Jacobson, and Jim Rumbaugh. The Object Management Group (OMG) adopted the UML as a standard for software modeling in 1997. The OMG includes more than 800 software vendors, developers, and users who seek a common architectural framework for object-oriented programming. The UML is in its second major version; the current version is UML 2.1.1. You can view or download the entire UML specification and usage guidelines from the OMG at *www.uml.org*.

> **» NOTE** You can purchase compilers for most programming languages from a variety of manufacturers. Similarly, you can purchase a variety of tools to help you create UML diagrams, but the UML itself is vendor-independent.

When you draw a flowchart or write pseudocode, your purpose is to illustrate the individual steps in a process. When you draw a hierarchy chart, you use more of a "big picture" approach. As with a hierarchy chart, you use the UML to create top-view diagrams of business processes that let you hide details and focus on functionality. This approach lets you start with a generic view of an application and introduce details and complexity later. UML diagrams are useful as you begin designing business systems, when customers who are not technically oriented must accurately communicate with the technical staff members who will create the actual systems. The UML was intentionally designed to be nontechnical so that developers, customers, and implementers (programmers) could all "speak the same language." If business and technical people can agree on what a system should do, chances improve that the final product will be useful.

The UML is very large; its documentation is more than 800 pages. The UML provides 13 diagram types that you can use to model systems. Each of the diagram types lets you see a business process from a different angle, and appeals to a different type of user. Just as an architect, interior designer, electrician, and plumber use different diagram types to describe the same building, different computer users appreciate different perspectives. For example, a business user most values a system's use case diagrams because they illustrate who is doing what. On the other hand, programmers find class and object diagrams more useful because they help explain details of how to build classes and objects into applications.

The UML superstructure defines six structure diagrams, three behavior diagrams, and four interaction diagrams. The 13 UML diagram types are:

» **Structure diagrams** that emphasize the "things" in a system. These include:
  » Class diagrams
  » Object diagrams
  » Component diagrams
  » Composite structure diagrams
  » Package diagrams
  » Deployment diagrams
» **Behavior diagrams** that emphasize what happens in a system. These include:
  » Use case diagrams
  » Activity diagrams
  » State machine diagrams

» **Interaction diagrams** that emphasize the flow of control and data among the things in the system being modeled:

> » Sequence diagrams
> » Communication diagrams
> » Timing diagrams
> » Interaction overview diagrams

» NOTE You can categorize UML diagrams as those that illustrate the dynamic, or changing, aspects of a system and those that illustrate the static, or steady, aspects of a system. Dynamic diagrams include use case, sequence, communication, state machine, and activity diagrams. Static diagrams include class, object, component, and deployment diagrams.

» NOTE Diagram names have evolved. For example, in UML 1.5, communication diagrams were called collaboration diagrams, and state machine diagrams were called statechart diagrams.

Each of the UML diagram types supports multiple variations, and explaining them all would require an entire textbook. This chapter presents an overview and simple examples of several diagram types, which provides a good foundation for further study of the UML.

USING USE CASE DIAGRAMS

The **use case diagram** shows how a business works from the perspective of those who approach it from the outside, or those who actually use the business. This category includes many types of users—for example, employees, customers, and suppliers. Although users can also be governments, private organizations, machines, or other systems, it is easiest to think of them as people, so users are called actors and are represented by stick figures in use case diagrams. The actual use cases are represented by ovals.

Use cases do not necessarily represent all the functions of a system; they are the system functions or services that are visible to the system's actors. In other words, they represent the cases by which an actor uses and presumably benefits from the system. Determining all the cases for which users interact with systems helps you divide a system logically into functional parts.

Establishing use cases usually follows from analyzing the main events in a system. For example, from a librarian's point of view, two main events are `acquireNewBook()` and `checkOutBook()`. Figure 11-1 shows a use case diagram for these two events.

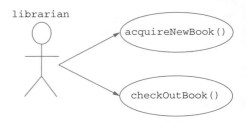

Figure 11-1 Use case diagram for librarian

» NOTE Many system developers would use the standard English form to describe activities in their UML diagrams—for example, `check out book` instead of `checkOutBook()`, which looks like a programming method call. Because you are used to seeing method names in camel casing and with trailing parentheses throughout this book, this discussion of the UML continues with that same format.

In many systems, there are variations in use cases. The three possible types of variations are:

» Extend

» Include

» Generalization

An **extend variation** is a use case variation that shows functions beyond those found in a base case. In other words, an extend variation is usually an optional activity. For example, checking out a book for a new library patron who doesn't have a library card is slightly more complicated than checking out a book for an existing patron. Each variation in the sequence of actions required in a use case is a **scenario**. Each use case has at least one main scenario, but might have several more that are extensions or variations of the main one. Figure 11-2 shows how you would diagram the relationship between the use case checkOutBook() and the more specific scenario checkOutBookForNewPatron(). Extended use cases are shown in an oval with a dashed arrow pointing to the more general base case.

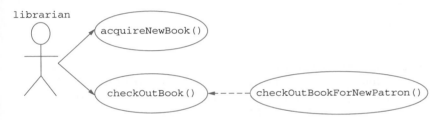

Figure 11-2 Use case diagram for librarian, with scenario extension

For clarity, you can add "<<extend>>" near the line that shows a relationship extension. Such a feature, which adds to the UML vocabulary of shapes to make them more meaningful for the reader, is called a **stereotype**. Figure 11-3 includes a stereotype.

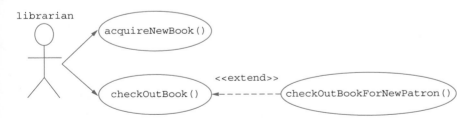

Figure 11-3 Use case diagram for librarian, using stereotype

In addition to extend relationships, use case diagrams also can show include relationships. You use an **include variation** when a case can be part of multiple use cases. This concept is very much like that of a subroutine or submodule. You show an include use case in an oval with a dashed arrow pointing to the subroutine use case. For example, `issueLibraryCard()` might be a function of `checkOutBook()`, which is used when the patron checking out a book is new, but it might also be a function of `registerNewPatron()`, which occurs when a patron registers at the library but does not want to check out books yet. See Figure 11-4.

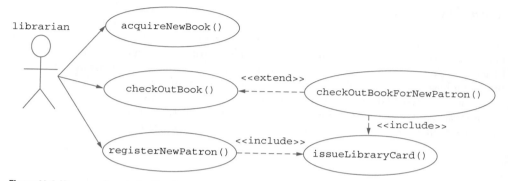

Figure 11-4 Use case diagram for librarian, using include relationship

You use a **generalization variation** when a use case is less specific than others are, and you want to be able to substitute the more specific case for a general one. For example, a library has certain procedures for acquiring new materials, whether they are videos, tapes, CDs, hardcover books, or paperbacks. However, the procedures might become more specific during a particular acquisition—perhaps the librarian must procure plastic cases for circulating videos or assign locked storage locations for CDs. Figure 11-5 shows the generalization

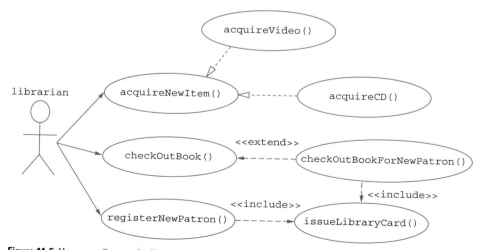

Figure 11-5 Use case diagram for librarian, with generalizations

`acquireNewItem()` with two more specific situations: acquiring videos and acquiring CDs. The more specific scenarios are attached to the general scenario with open-headed dashed arrows.

Many use case diagrams show multiple actors. For example, Figure 11-6 shows that a library clerk cannot perform as many functions as a librarian; the clerk can check out books and register new patrons but cannot acquire new materials.

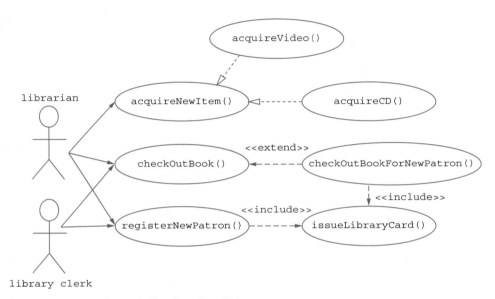

Figure 11-6 Use case diagram for librarian, with multiple actors

While designing an actual library system, you could add many more use cases and actors to the use case diagram. The purpose of such a diagram is to encourage discussion between the system developer and the library staff. Library staff members do not need to know any of the technical details of the system that the analysts will eventually create, and they certainly do not need to understand computers or programming. However, by viewing the use cases, the library staff can visualize activities they perform while doing their jobs and correct the system developer if inaccuracies exist. The final software products developed for such a system are far more likely to satisfy users than those developed without this design step.

A use case diagram is only a tool to aid communication. No single "correct" use case diagram exists; you might correctly represent a system in several ways. For example, you might choose to emphasize the actors in the library system, as shown in Figure 11-7, or to emphasize system requirements, as shown in Figure 11-8. Diagrams that are too crowded are neither visually pleasing nor very useful. Therefore, the use case diagram in Figure 11-7

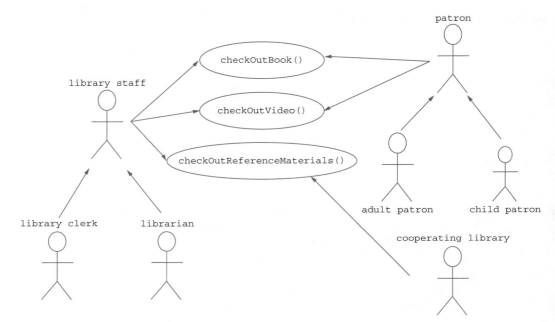

Figure 11-7 Use case diagram emphasizing actors

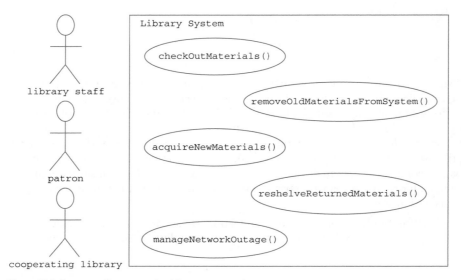

Figure 11-8 Use case diagram emphasizing system requirements

shows all the specific actors and their relationships, but purposely omits more specific system functions, whereas Figure 11-8 shows many actions that are often hidden from users but purposely omits more specific actors. For example, the activities carried out to `manageNetworkOutage()`, if done properly, should be invisible to library patrons checking out books.

In Figure 11-8, the relationship lines between the actors and use cases have been removed because the emphasis is on the system requirements, and too many lines would make the diagram confusing. When system developers omit parts of diagrams for clarity, they refer to the missing parts as **elided**. For the sake of clarity, eliding extraneous information is perfectly acceptable. The main purpose of UML diagrams is to facilitate clear communication.

USING CLASS AND OBJECT DIAGRAMS

You use a class diagram to illustrate the names, attributes, and methods of a class or set of classes. Class diagrams are more useful to a system's programmers than to its users because they closely resemble code the programmers will write. A class diagram illustrating a single class contains a rectangle divided into three sections: the top section contains the name of the class, the middle section contains the names of the attributes, and the bottom section contains the names of the methods. Figure 11-9 shows the class diagram for a `Book` class. Each `Book` object contains an `idNum`, `title`, and `author`. Each `Book` object also contains methods to create a `Book` when it is acquired and to retrieve or get `title` and `author` information when the `Book` object's `idNum` is supplied.

Book
idNum
title
author
create()
getInfo(idNum)

Figure 11-9 `Book` class diagram

> **NOTE**
> You first used class diagrams in Chapter 7.

In the preceding section, you learned how to use generalizations with use case diagrams to show general and more specific use cases. With use case diagrams, you drew an open-headed arrow from the more specific case to the more general one. Similarly, you can use generalizations with class diagrams to show inheritance; that is, you can show more general (or parent) classes along with more specific (or child) classes that inherit attributes from parents. For example, Figure 11-10 shows `Book` and `Video` classes that are more specific than the general `LibraryItem` class. All `LibraryItem` objects contain an `idNum` and `title`, but each `Book` item also contains an `author`, and each `Video` item also contains a `runningTime`. In addition, `Video` items contain a `rewind()` method not found in the more general `LibraryItem` class. Child classes contain all the attributes of their parents and usually contain additional attributes not found in the parent.

> **NOTE**
> You learned about inheritance and parent and child classes in Chapter 9. There, you learned that the `create()` and `getInfo()` methods in the `Book` and `Video` classes override the version in the `LibraryItem` class.

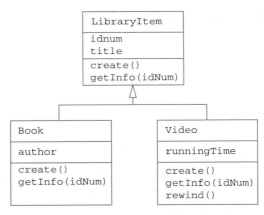

Figure 11-10 `LibraryItem` class diagram showing generalization

Class diagrams can include symbols that show the relationships between objects. You can show two types of relationships:

» An association relationship
» A whole-part relationship

An **association relationship** describes the connection or link between objects. You represent an association relationship between classes with a straight line. Frequently, you include information about the arithmetical relationship or ratio (called **cardinality** or **multiplicity**) of the objects. For example, Figure 11-11 shows the association relationship between a Library and the LibraryItems it lends. Exactly one Library object exists, and it can be associated with any number of LibraryItems from 0 to infinity, which is represented by an asterisk. Figure 11-12 adds the Patron class to the diagram and shows how you indicate that any number of Patrons can be associated with the Library, but that each Patron can borrow only up to five LibraryItems at a time, or currently might not be borrowing any. In addition, each LibraryItem can be associated with one Patron at most, but at any given time might not be on loan.

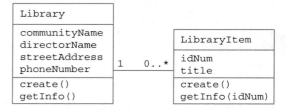

Figure 11-11 Class diagram with association relationship

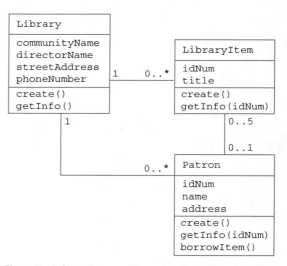

Figure 11-12 Class diagram with several association relationships

A **whole-part relationship** describes an association in which one or more classes make up the parts of a larger whole class. For example, 50 states "make up" the United States, and 10 departments might "make up" a company. This type of relationship is also called an **aggregation** and is represented by an open diamond at the "whole part" end of the line that indicates the relationship. You also can call a whole-part relationship a **has-a relationship** because the phrase describes the association between the whole and one of its parts; for example,

"The library has a Circulation Department." Figure 11-13 shows a whole-part relationship for a Library.

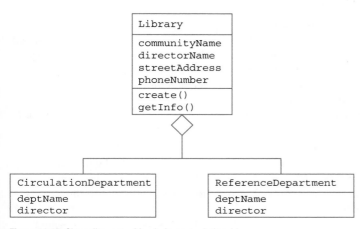

Figure 11-13 Class diagram with whole-part relationship

Object diagrams are similar to class diagrams, but they model specific instances of classes. You use an object diagram to show a snapshot of an object at one point in time, so you can more easily understand its relationship to other objects. Imagine looking at the travelers in a major airport. If you try to watch them all at once, you see a flurry of activity, but it is hard to understand all the tasks (buying a ticket, checking luggage, and so on) a traveler must accomplish to take a trip. However, if you concentrate on one traveler and follow his or her actions through the airport from arrival to takeoff, you get a clearer picture of the required activities. An object diagram serves the same purpose; you concentrate on a specific instance of a class to better understand how the class works.

Figure 11-14 contains an object diagram showing the relationship between one Library, LibraryItem, and Patron. Notice the similarities between Figures 11-12 and 11-14. If you need to describe the relationship among three classes, you can use either model—a class diagram or an object diagram—interchangeably. You simply use the model that seems clearer to you and your intended audience.

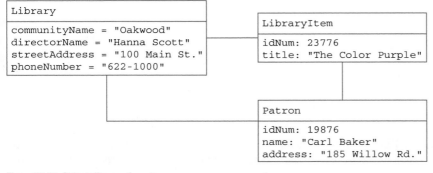

Figure 11-14 Object diagram for Library

USING SEQUENCE AND COMMUNICATION DIAGRAMS

You use a **sequence diagram** to show the timing of events in a single use case. A sequence diagram makes it easier to see the order in which activities occur. The horizontal axis (x-axis) of a sequence diagram represents objects, and the vertical axis (y-axis) represents time. You create a sequence diagram by placing objects that are part of an activity across the top of the diagram along the x-axis, starting at the left with the object or actor that begins the action. Beneath each object on the x-axis, you place a vertical dashed line that represents the period of time the object exists. Then, you use horizontal arrows to show how the objects communicate with each other over time.

For example, Figure 11-15 shows a sequence diagram for a scenario that a librarian can use to create a book check-out record. The librarian begins a `create()` method with `Patron idNum` and `Book idNum` information. The `BookCheckOutRecord` object requests additional `Patron` information (such as `name` and `address`) from the `Patron` object with the correct `Patron idNum`, and additional `Book` information (such as `title` and `author`) from the `Book` object with the correct `Book idNum`. When `BookCheckOutRecord` contains all the data it needs, a completed record is returned to the librarian.

»NOTE
In Figures 11-15 and 11-16, `patronInfo` and `bookInfo` represent group items that contain all of a `Patron`'s and `Book`'s data. For example, `patronInfo` might contain `idNum`, `name`, and `address`, all of which have been defined as attributes of that class.

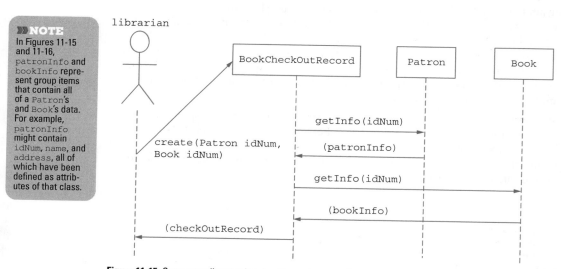

Figure 11-15 Sequence diagram for checking out a `Book` for a `Patron`

A **communication diagram** emphasizes the organization of objects that participate in a system. It is similar to a sequence diagram, except that it contains sequence numbers to represent the precise order in which activities occur. Communication diagrams focus on object roles instead of the times that messages are sent. Figure 11-16 shows the same sequence of events as Figure 11-15, but the steps to creating a `BookCheckOutRecord` are clearly numbered (see the shaded sections of the figure). Decimal numbered steps (1.1, 1.2, and so on) represent substeps of the main steps. Checking out a library book is a fairly straightforward event, so a sequence diagram sufficiently illustrates the process. Communication diagrams become more useful with more complicated systems.

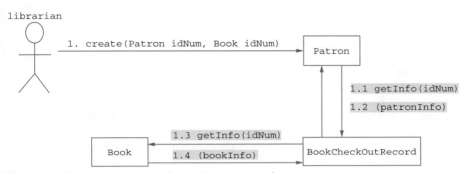

Figure 11-16 Communication diagram for checking out a `Book` for a `Patron`

USING STATE MACHINE DIAGRAMS

A **state machine diagram** shows the different statuses of a class or object at different points in time. You use a state machine diagram to illustrate aspects of a system that show interesting changes in behavior as time passes. Conventionally, you use rounded rectangles to represent each state and labeled arrows to show the sequence in which events affect the states. A solid dot indicates the start and stop states for the class or object. Figure 11-17 contains a state machine diagram you can use to describe the states of a `Book`.

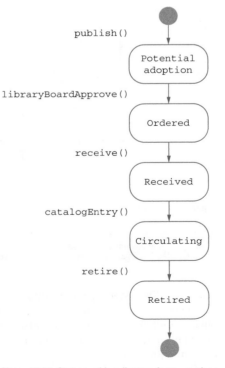

Figure 11-17 State machine diagram for `Book` class

> **NOTE** So that your diagrams are clear, you should use the correct symbol in each UML diagram you create, just as you should use the correct symbol in each program flowchart. However, if you create a flowchart and use a rectangle for an input or output statement where a parallelogram is conventional, others will still understand your meaning. Similarly, with UML diagrams, the exact shape you use is not nearly as important as the sequence of events and relationships between objects.

USING ACTIVITY DIAGRAMS

The UML diagram that most closely resembles a conventional flowchart is an activity diagram. In an **activity diagram**, you show the flow of actions of a system, including branches that occur when decisions affect the outcome. Conventionally, activity diagrams use flowchart start and stop symbols (called lozenges) to describe actions and solid dots to represent start and stop states. Like flowcharts, activity diagrams use diamonds to describe decisions. Unlike the diamonds in flowcharts, the diamonds in UML activity diagrams are usually empty; the possible outcomes are documented along the branches emerging from the decision symbol. As an example, Figure 11-18 shows a simple activity diagram with a single branch.

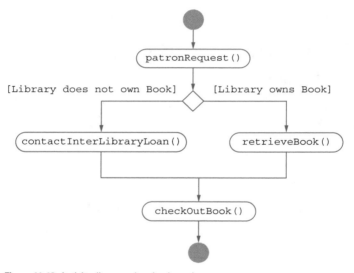

Figure 11-18 Activity diagram showing branch

> **NOTE** In the first major version of the UML (UML 1.0), each lozenge was an activity. Starting with the second major version (UML 2.0), each lozenge is an action and a group of actions is an activity.

Many real-life systems contain actions that are meant to occur simultaneously. For example, when you apply for a home mortgage with a bank, a bank officer might perform a credit or background check while an appraiser determines the value of the house you are buying. When both actions are complete, the loan process continues. UML activity diagrams use forks and joins to show simultaneous activities. A fork is similar to a decision, but whereas the flow of control follows only one path after a decision, a fork defines a branch in which all paths are followed simultaneously. A join, as its name implies, reunites the flow of control after a fork. You indicate forks and joins with thick straight lines. Figure 11-19 shows how you might model the way an interlibrary loan system processes book requests. When a request is received, simultaneous searches begin at three local libraries that are part of the library system.

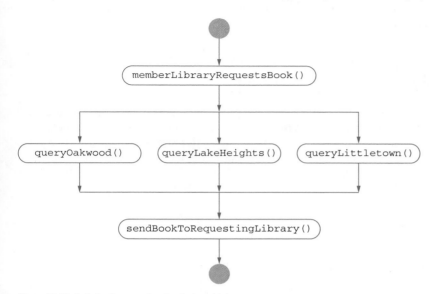

Figure 11-19 Activity diagram showing fork and join

An activity diagram can contain a time signal. A **time signal** indicates that a specific amount of time should pass before an action starts. The time signal looks like two stacked triangles (resembling the shape of an hourglass). Figure 11-20 shows a time signal indicating that if a

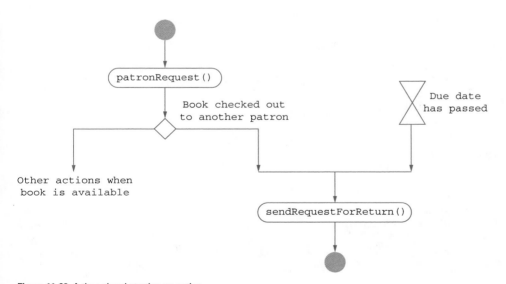

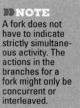

Figure 11-20 A time signal starting an action

patron requests a book, and the book is checked out to another patron, then only if the book's due date has passed should a request to return the book be issued. In activity diagrams for other systems, you might see explanations at time signals, such as "10 hours have passed" or "at least January 1st." If an action is time-dependent, whether by a fraction of a second or by years, using a time signal is appropriate.

USING COMPONENT AND DEPLOYMENT DIAGRAMS

Component and deployment diagrams model the physical aspects of systems. You use a **component diagram** when you want to emphasize the files, database tables, documents, and other components that a system's software uses. You use a **deployment diagram** when you want to focus on a system's hardware. You can use a variety of icons in each type of diagram, but each icon must convey meaning to the reader. Figures 11-21 and 11-22 show component and deployment diagrams that illustrate aspects of a library system. Figure 11-21 contains

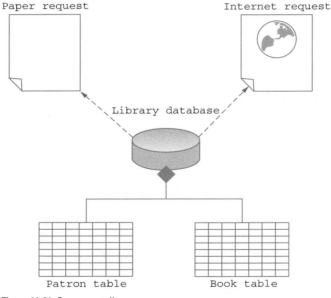

Figure 11-21 Component diagram

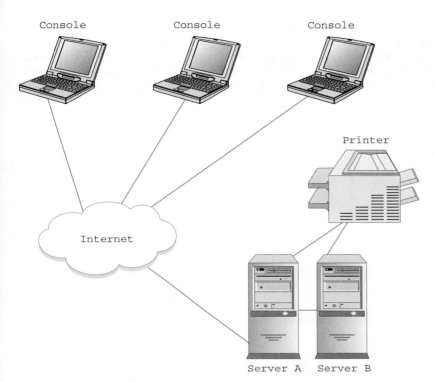

Figure 11-22 Deployment diagram

icons that symbolize paper and Internet requests for library items, the library database, and two tables that constitute the database. Figure 11-22 shows some commonly used icons that represent hardware components.

DIAGRAMMING EXCEPTION HANDLING

Exception handling is a set of the object-oriented techniques used to handle program errors. In Chapter 10, you learned that when a segment of code might cause an error, you can place that code in a `try` block. If the error occurs, an object called an exception is thrown, or sent, to a `catch` block where appropriate action can be taken. For example, depending on the application, a `catch` block might display a message, assign a default value to a field, or prompt the user for direction.

In the UML, a `try` block is called a **protected node** and a `catch` block is a **handler body node**. In a UML diagram, a protected node is enclosed in a rounded rectangle and any exceptions that might be thrown are listed next to lightning bolt-shaped arrows that extend to the appropriate handler body node.

Figure 11-23 shows an example of an activity that uses exception handling. When a library patron tries to check out a book, the patron's card is scanned and the book is scanned. These actions might cause three errors—the patron owes fines, and so cannot check out new books; the patron's card has expired, requiring a new card application; or the book might be on hold for another patron. If no exceptions occur, the activity proceeds to the `checkOutBook()` process.

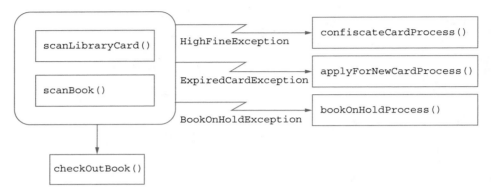

Figure 11-23 Exceptions in the `Book` check-out activity

DECIDING WHEN TO USE UML AND WHICH UML DIAGRAMS TO USE

The UML is widely recognized as a modeling standard, but it is also frequently criticized. The criticisms include:

- » *Size*—The UML is often criticized as being too large and complex. Many of the diagrams are infrequently used, and some critics claim several are redundant.
- » *Imprecision*—The UML is a combination of rules and casual English; it is not as precise as a programming language. In particular, problems occur when the diagrams are applied to tasks other than those implemented in object-oriented programming languages.
- » *Complexity*—Because of its size and imprecision, the UML is relatively difficult to learn.

Still, under the right circumstances, the UML can increase communication between developers and users of a system. Each of the UML diagram types provides a different view of a system. Just as a portrait artist, psychologist, and neurosurgeon each prefer a different conceptual view of your head, the users, managers, designers, and technicians of computer and business systems each prefer specific system views. Very few systems require diagrams of all 13 types; you can illustrate the objects and activities of many systems by using a single diagram, or perhaps one that is a hybrid of two or more basic types. No view is superior to the others; you can achieve the most complete picture of any system by using several views. The most important reason you use any UML diagram is to communicate clearly and efficiently with the people for whom you are designing a system.

CHAPTER SUMMARY

» System design is the detailed specification of how all the parts of a system will be implemented and coordinated. Good designs make systems easier to understand. The UML (Unified Modeling Language) provides a means for programmers and businesspeople to communicate about system design.

» The UML is a standard way to specify, construct, and document systems that use object-oriented methods. The UML has its own notation, with which you can construct software diagrams that model different kinds of systems. The UML provides 13 diagram types that you use at the beginning of the design process.

» A use case diagram shows how a business works from the perspective of those who approach it from the outside, or those who actually use the business. The diagram often includes actors, represented by stick figures, and use cases, represented by ovals. Use cases can include variations such as extend relationships, include relationships, and generalizations.

» You use a class diagram to illustrate the names, attributes, and methods of a class or set of classes. A class diagram of a single class contains a rectangle divided into three sections: the name of the class, the names of the attributes, and the names of the methods. Class diagrams can show generalizations and the relationships between objects. Object diagrams are similar to class diagrams, but they model specific instances of classes at one point in time.

» You use a sequence diagram to show the timing of events in a single use case. The horizontal axis (x-axis) of a sequence diagram represents objects, and the vertical axis (y-axis) represents time. A communication diagram emphasizes the organization of objects that participate in a system. It is similar to a sequence diagram, except that it contains sequence numbers to represent the precise order in which activities occur.

» A state machine diagram shows the different statuses of a class or object at different points in time.

» In an activity diagram, you show the flow of actions of a system, including branches that occur when decisions affect the outcome. UML activity diagrams use forks and joins to show simultaneous activities.

» You use a component diagram when you want to emphasize the files, database tables, documents, and other components that a system's software uses. You use a deployment diagram when you want to focus on a system's hardware.

» Each of the UML diagram types provides a different view of a system. Very few systems require diagrams of all 13 types; the most important reason to use any UML diagram is to communicate clearly and efficiently with the people for whom you are designing a system.

KEY TERMS

System design is the detailed specification of how all the parts of a system will be implemented and coordinated.

Reverse engineering is the process of creating a model of an existing system.

The **UML** is a standard way to specify, construct, and document systems that use object-oriented methods. UML is an acronym for Unified Modeling Language.

Structure diagrams emphasize the "things" in a system.

Behavior diagrams emphasize what happens in a system.

Interaction diagrams emphasize the flow of control and data among the things in the system being modeled.

The **use case diagram** is a UML diagram that shows how a business works from the perspective of those who approach it from the outside, or those who actually use the business.

An **extend variation** is a use case variation that shows functions beyond those found in a base case.

Each variation in the sequence of actions required in a use case is a **scenario**.

A feature that adds to the UML vocabulary of shapes to make them more meaningful for the reader is called a **stereotype**.

An **include variation** is a use case variation that you use when a case can be part of multiple use cases in a UML diagram.

You use a **generalization variation** in a UML diagram when a use case is less specific than others, and you want to be able to substitute the more specific case for a general one.

When system developers omit parts of UML diagrams for clarity, they refer to the missing parts as **elided**.

An **association relationship** describes the connection or link between objects in a UML diagram.

Cardinality and **multiplicity** refer to the arithmetic relationships between objects.

A **whole-part relationship** describes an association in which one or more classes make up the parts of a larger whole class. This type of relationship is also called an **aggregation**. You can also call a whole-part relationship a **has-a relationship** because the phrase describes the association between the whole and one of its parts.

Object diagrams are UML diagrams that are similar to class diagrams, but they model specific instances of classes.

A **sequence diagram** is a UML diagram that shows the timing of events in a single use case.

A **communication diagram** is a UML diagram that emphasizes the organization of objects that participate in a system.

A **state machine diagram** is a UML diagram that shows the different statuses of a class or object at different points in time.

An **activity diagram** is a UML diagram that shows the flow of actions of a system, including branches that occur when decisions affect the outcome.

A **time signal** is a UML diagram symbol that indicates that a specific amount of time has passed before an action is started.

A **connector** is a UML diagram symbol used to connect diagrams that continue on a new page; it is represented by a small circle.

A **component diagram** is a UML diagram that emphasizes the files, database tables, documents, and other components that a system's software uses.

A **deployment diagram** is a UML diagram that focuses on a system's hardware.

A **protected node** is the UML diagram name for an exception-throwing `try` block.

A **handler body node** is the UML diagram name for an exception-handling `catch` block.

REVIEW QUESTIONS

1. The detailed specification of how all the parts of a system will be implemented and coordinated is called _____ .

   a. programming   c. system design

   b. paraphrasing   d. structuring

2. The primary purpose of good modeling techniques is to _____ .

   a. promote communication

   b. increase functional cohesion

   c. reduce the need for structure

   d. reduce dependency between modules

3. The Unified Modeling Language provides standard ways to do all of the following to business systems except to _____ them.

   a. construct   c. describe

   b. document   d. destroy

4. The UML is commonly used to model all of the following except _____ .

   a. computer programs   c. organizational processes

   b. business activities   d. software systems

5. The UML was intentionally designed to be _____ .

   a. low-level and detail-oriented

   b. used with Visual Basic

   c. nontechnical

   d. inexpensive

6. The UML diagrams that show how a business works from the perspective of those who actually use the business, such as employees or customers, are _____ diagrams.

   a. communication   c. state machine

   b. use case   d. class

7. Which of the following examples would be portrayed as an extend relationship in a use case diagram for a hospital?

   a. the relationship between the head nurse and the floor nurses

   b. admitting a patient who has never been admitted before

   c. serving a meal

   d. scheduling the monitoring of patients' vital signs

8. The people shown in use case diagrams are called _____ .

    a. workers   c. actors

    b. clowns   d. relatives

9. One aspect of use case diagrams that makes them difficult to learn about is that _____ .

    a. they require programming experience to understand

    b. they use a technical vocabulary

    c. there is no single right answer for any case

    d. all of the above

10. At most colleges, the arithmetic association relationship between a student and courses would be expressed as _____ .

    a. 1 0   c. 1 0..*

    b. 1 1   d. 0..* 0..*

11. In the UML, object diagrams are most similar to _____ diagrams.

    a. use case   c. class

    b. activity   d. sequence

12. In any given situation, you should choose the type of UML diagram that is _____ .

    a. shorter than others

    b. clearer to users than others

    c. more detailed than others

    d. closest to the programming language you will use to implement the system

13. A whole-part relationship can be described as a(n) _____ relationship.

    a. parent-child   c. has-a

    b. is-a   d. creates-a

14. The timing of events is best portrayed in a(n) _____ diagram.

    a. sequence   c. communication

    b. use case   d. association

15. A communication diagram is closest to a(n) _____ diagram.

    a. activity   c. deployment

    b. use case   d. sequence

16. A(n) _____ diagram shows the different statuses of a class or object at different points in time.

    a. activity   c. sequence

    b. state machine   d. deployment

17. The UML diagram that most closely resembles a conventional flowchart is a(n) _____ diagram.

    a. activity   c. sequence

    b. state machine   d. deployment

18. You use a _____ diagram when you want to emphasize the files, database tables, documents, and other components that a system's software uses.

    a. state machine   c. deployment

    b. component   d. use case

19. The UML diagram that focuses on a system's hardware is a(n) _____ diagram.

    a. deployment   c. activity

    b. sequence   d. use case

20. When using the UML to describe a single system, most designers would use _____ .

    a. a single type of diagram

    b. at least three types of diagrams

    c. most of the available types of diagrams

    d. all 13 types of diagrams

EXERCISES

1. Complete the following tasks:

    a. Develop a use case diagram for a convenience food store. Include an actor representing the store manager and use cases for `orderItem()`, `stockItem()`, and `sellItem()`.

    b. Add more use cases to the diagram you created in Exercise 1a. Include two generalizations for `stockItem(): stockPerishable()` and `stockNonPerishable()`. Also include an extension to `sellItem()` called `checkCredit()` for when a customer purchases items using a credit card.

    c. Add a customer actor to the use case diagram you created in Exercise 1b. Show that the customer participates in `sellItem()`, but not in `orderItem()` or `stockItem()`.

2. Develop a use case diagram for a department store credit card system. Include at least two actors and four use cases.

3. Develop a use case diagram for a college registration system. Include at least three actors and five use cases.

4. Develop a class diagram for a `Video` class that describes objects a video store customer can rent. Include at least four attributes and three methods.

5. Develop a class diagram for a `Shape` class. Include generalizations for child classes `Rectangle`, `Circle`, and `Triangle`.

6. Develop a class diagram for a `BankLoan` class. Include generalizations for child classes `Mortgage`, `CarLoan`, and `EducationLoan`.

7. Develop a class diagram for a college registration system. Include at least three classes that cooperate to achieve student registration.

8. Develop a sequence diagram that shows how a clerk at a mail-order company places a customer `Order`. The `Order` accesses `Inventory` to check availability. Then, the `Order` accesses `Invoice` to produce a customer invoice that returns to the clerk.

9. Develop a state machine diagram that shows the states of a `CollegeStudent` from `PotentialApplicant` to `Graduate`.

10. Develop a state machine diagram that shows the states of a `Book` from `Concept` to `Publication`.

11. Develop an activity diagram that illustrates how to build a house.

12. Develop an activity diagram that illustrates how to prepare dinner.

13. Develop the UML diagram of your choice that illustrates some aspect of your life.

14. Complete the following tasks:

    a. Develop the UML diagram of your choice that best illustrates some aspect of a place you have worked.

    b. Develop a different UML diagram type that illustrates the same functions as the diagram you created in Exercise 14a.

CASE PROJECT

In earlier chapters, you developed classes needed for Cost Is No Object—a car rental service that specializes in lending antique and luxury cars to clients on a short-term basis. Now, complete the following tasks:

a. Develop a use case diagram for renting a car. Include actors representing the fleet mechanic, rental agent, and a customer, and use cases for `reportMechanicalProblems()`, `orderRepairs()`, `makeRepairs()`, `makeReservation()`, `rentCar()`, and `returnCar()`.

b. Develop an activity diagram that illustrates how to rent a car.

UP FOR DISCUSSION

1. What are the education requirements for a career in system design? What are the job prospects and average salaries?

2. Find any discussion you can on the advantages and disadvantages of the UML as a system design tool. Summarize your findings.

3. Which do you think you would enjoy doing more on the job—designing large systems that contain many programs, or writing the programs themselves? Why?

4. In Chapter 3, you considered ethical dilemmas in writing a program that selects candidates for organ transplants. Are the ethical responsibilities of a system designer different from those of a programmer? If so, how?

12

ADVANCED ARRAY CONCEPTS

In this chapter, you will:

Understand the need for sorting data
Swap two values in computer memory
Understand the bubble sort
Understand the insertion sort
Understand the selection sort
Declare an array of objects
Sort arrays of objects
Use two-dimensional and multidimensional arrays
Use a built-in `Array` class

UNDERSTANDING THE NEED FOR SORTING RECORDS

When you store data records, they exist in some sort of order; that is, one record is first, another second, and so on. When records are in **sequential order**, they are arranged one after another on the basis of the value in some field. Examples of records in sequential order include employee records stored in numeric order by Social Security number or department number, or in alphabetical order by last name or department name. Even if the records are stored in a random order—for example, the order in which a data-entry clerk felt like entering them—they still are in *some* order, although probably not the order desired for processing or viewing. When this is the case, the data records need to be **sorted**, or placed in order, based on the contents of one or more fields. When you sort data, you can sort either in **ascending order**, arranging records from lowest to highest value, or **descending order**, arranging records from highest to lowest value. Here are some examples of occasions when you would need to sort records:

» A college stores students' records in ascending order by student ID number, but the registrar wants to view the data in descending order by credit hours earned so he can contact students who are close to graduation.

» A department store maintains customer records in ascending order by customer number, but at the end of a billing period, the credit manager wants to contact customers whose balances are 90 or more days overdue. The manager wants to list these overdue customers in descending order by the amount owed so the customers with the biggest debt can be contacted first.

» A sales manager keeps records for her salespeople in alphabetical order by last name, but needs to list the annual sales figure for each salesperson so she can determine the median annual sale amount. The **median** value in a list is the value of the middle item when the values are listed in order; it is not the same as the arithmetic average, or **mean**.

» **NOTE** To help you understand the difference between median and mean, consider the following five values: 0, 7, 10, 11, 12. The median value is the middle position's value when the values are listed in numerical order; in this example, the median is 10. The mean, however, is the sum (40) divided by the number of values (5), which evaluates to 8. The median is used as a statistic in many cases because it represents a more typical case than the mean—half the values are below it and half are above it. Unlike the median, the mean is skewed by a few very high or low values.

» **NOTE** Sorting is usually reserved for a relatively small number of data items. If thousands of customer records are stored and they frequently need to be accessed in order based on different fields (alphabetical order by customer name one day, zip code order the next), the records would probably not be sorted at all, but would be connected by another process. For example, some systems use an **index**, or list of key fields, which are manipulated instead of altering the positions of much larger records. Other systems use **linked lists** in which each record contains a field that holds the address of the next logical record.

When computers sort data, they always use numeric values when making comparisons between values. This is clear when you sort records by fields such as a numeric customer ID or balance due. However, even alphabetic sorts are numeric, because everything that is stored in a computer is stored as a number using a series of 0s and 1s. In every popular computer coding scheme, "B" is numerically one greater than "A", and "y" is numerically one less than "z". Unfortunately, it depends on your system whether the number that represents "A" is greater or smaller than the number that represents "a". Therefore, to obtain the most useful and accurate list of alphabetically sorted records, either the data-entry personnel should be consistent in the use of capitalization or the programmer should convert all the data to consistent capitalization.

UNDERSTANDING HOW TO SWAP TWO VALUES

Many sorting techniques have been developed. **Swapping** two values is a concept that is central to most sorting techniques. When you swap the values stored in two variables, you reverse their positions—you set the first variable equal to the value of the second, and the second variable equal to the value of the first. However, there is a trick to reversing any two values. Assume you have declared two variables as follows:

```
numeric score1 = 90
numeric score2 = 85
```

You want to swap the values so that score1 is 85 and score2 is 90. If you first assign score1 to score2 using a statement such as score2 = score1, both score1 and score2 hold 90 and the value 85 is lost. Similarly, if you first assign score2 to score1 using a statement such as score1 = score2, both variables hold 85 and the value 90 is lost.

The solution to swapping the values lies in creating a temporary variable to hold one of the scores; then, you can accomplish the swap as shown in the program segment in Figure 12-1.

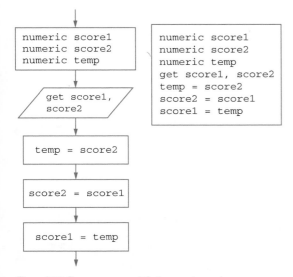

```
numeric score1
numeric score2
numeric temp
get score1, score2
temp = score2
score2 = score1
score1 = temp
```

Figure 12-1 Program segment that swaps two values

First, the value in `score2`, 85, is assigned to a temporary holding variable named `temp`. Then, the `score1` value, 90, is assigned to `score2`. At this point, both `score1` and `score2` hold 90. Then, the 85 in `temp` is assigned to `score1`. Therefore, after the swap process, `score1` holds 85 and `score2` holds 90.

USING A BUBBLE SORT

One of the simplest sorting techniques to understand is a bubble sort. You can use a bubble sort to arrange records in either ascending or descending order. In a **bubble sort**, items in a list are compared with each other in pairs, and when an item is out of order, it swaps values with the item below it. With an ascending bubble sort, after each adjacent pair of items in a list has been compared once, the largest item in the list will have "sunk" to the bottom. After many passes through the list, the smallest items rise to the top like bubbles in a carbonated drink.

Assume that you want to sort five student test scores in ascending order. Figure 12-2 shows a program in which an array is declared to hold five scores. Three main procedures are called—one to get the five scores, one to sort them, and the final one to display the sorted result.

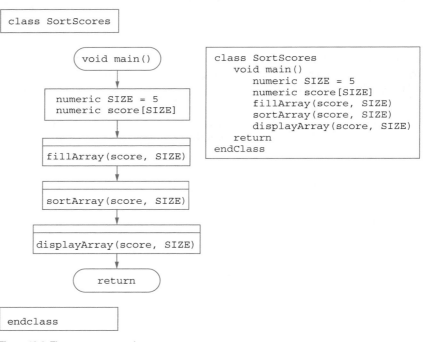

Figure 12-2 The `SortScores` class

> **»NOTE** In the application in Figure 12-2, each method receives the array and its size. Recall from Chapter 5 that many programming languages provide a built-in constant that represents the size of each declared array. If the program in Figure 12-2 was implemented in one of those languages, there would be no need to pass the array size to the methods because it would automatically "come with" the array.

Figure 12-3 shows the fillArray() method. The method receives the array and its size. A subscript is initialized to 0 and each array element is filled in turn. After five scores have been entered, control returns to the main program. Recall from Chapter 6 that when an array is passed to a method, its address is passed, so there is no need to return anything from the method in order for the main method to have access to the newly entered array values.

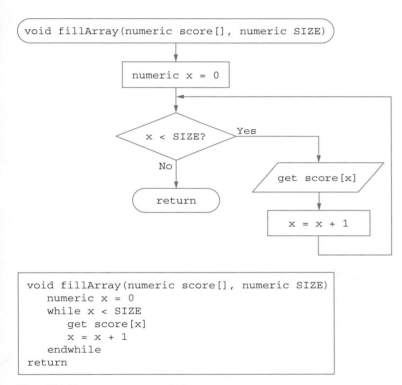

```
void fillArray(numeric score[], numeric SIZE)
    numeric x = 0
    while x < SIZE
        get score[x]
        x = x + 1
    endwhile
return
```

Figure 12-3 The fillArray() method

The `sortArray()` method in Figure 12-4 sorts the array elements by making a series of comparisons of adjacent element values and swapping them if they are out of order. For example, assume the five entered scores are:

```
score[0]  =  90
score[1]  =  85
score[2]  =  65
score[3]  =  95
score[4]  =  75
```

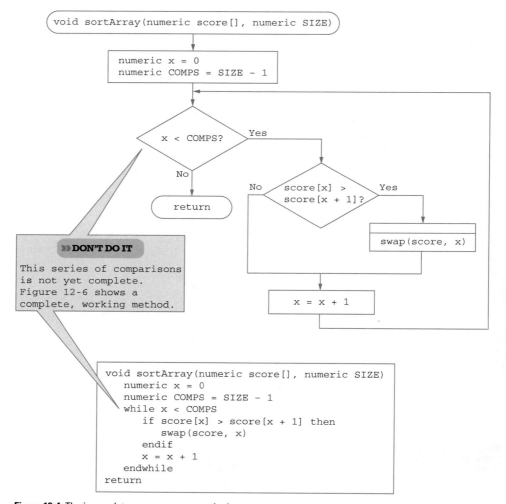

Figure 12-4 The incomplete `sortArray()` method

>> NOTE   For a descending sort in which you want to end up with the highest value first, write the decision so that you perform the switch when `score[x]` is less than `score[x + 1]`. In other words, all that needs to be changed is the relational comparison.

To begin sorting this list of scores, you compare the first two scores, score[0] and score[1]. If they are out of order—that is, if score[0] is larger than score[1]—you want to reverse their positions, or swap their values. For example, if score[0] is 90 and score[1] is 85, then you want score[0] to assume the value 85 and score[1] to take on the value 90. Therefore, you call the swap() method that reverses the values of the two elements. After this swap, the scores are in slightly better order than they were originally.

In Figure 12-4, a constant named COMPS is declared and assigned the value of SIZE − 1. That is, for an array of size 5, the COMPS constant will be 4. The while loop in the method continues as long as x is less than COMPS. The comparisons that are made, therefore, are as follows:

```
score[0] > score[1] ?
score[1] > score[2] ?
score[2] > score[3] ?
score[3] > score[4] ?
```

Each element in the array is compared to the one that follows it. When x becomes COMPS, the while loop ends. If it continued when x became equal to COMPS, then the next comparison would be score[4] > score[5] ?. This would cause an error because the highest allowed subscript in a five-element array is 4. You must execute the decision score[x] > score[x + 1] ? four times—when x is 0, 1, 2, and 3.

For an ascending sort, you need to perform the swap() method whenever any given element x of the score array has a value greater than the next element, x + 1, of the score array. For any x, if the xth element is not greater than the element at position x + 1, the swap should not take place. For example, when score[x] is 90 and score[x + 1] is 85, a swap should occur. On the other hand, when score[x] is 65 and score[x + 1] is 95, then no swap should occur.

>> NOTE In the sortArray() method, you could use either the greater-than (>) or greater-than-or-equal-to (>=) sign to compare adjacent values and you would achieve the same results. Using the greater-than comparison to determine when to switch values in the sort is more efficient than using greater-than-or-equal-to, because if two compared values are equal, there is no need to swap them.

Figure 12-5 shows the swap() method. This module switches any two adjacent elements in the score array when the variable x represents the position of the first of the two elements, and the value x + 1 represents the subsequent position.

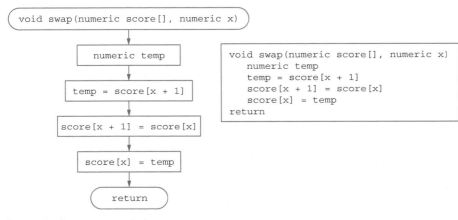

```
void swap(numeric score[], numeric x)
   numeric temp
   temp = score[x + 1]
   score[x + 1] = score[x]
   score[x] = temp
return
```

Figure 12-5 The swap() method

>> NOTE
Notice the similarities between Figure 12-1 and the swap() method in Figure 12-5.

As an example of how the `SortScores` application works, suppose you have these original scores:

```
score[0]  =  90
score[1]  =  85
score[2]  =  65
score[3]  =  95
score[4]  =  75
```

The logic of the `sortArray()` method proceeds like this:

1. Set x to 0.
2. The value of x is less than 4 (COMPS), so enter the loop.
3. Compare `score[x]`, 90, to `score[x + 1]`, 85. The two scores are out of order, so they are switched.

   The list is now:
   ```
   score[0]  =  85
   score[1]  =  90
   score[2]  =  65
   score[3]  =  95
   score[4]  =  75
   ```

4. After the swap, add 1 to x so that x is 1.
5. Return to the top of the loop. The value of x is less than 4, so enter the loop a second time.
6. Compare `score[x]`, 90, to `score[x + 1]`, 65. These two values are out of order, so swap them.

   Now the result is:
   ```
   score[0]  =  85
   score[1]  =  65
   score[2]  =  90
   score[3]  =  95
   score[4]  =  75
   ```

7. Add 1 to x, so that x is now 2.
8. Return to the top of the loop. The value of x is less than 4, so enter the loop.
9. Compare `score[x]`, 90, to `score[x + 1]`, 95. These values are in order, so no switch is made.
10. Add 1 to x, making it 3.
11. Return to the top of the loop. The value of x is less than 4, so enter the loop.
12. Compare `score[x]`, 95, to `score[x + 1]`, 75. These two values are out of order, so switch them.

Now the list is as follows:

```
score[0]  =  85
score[1]  =  65
score[2]  =  90
score[3]  =  75
score[4]  =  95
```

13. Add 1 to x, making it 4.
14. Return to the top of the loop. The value of x is 4, which equals COMPS, so do not enter the loop again.

When x reaches 4, every element in the list has been compared with the one adjacent to it. The highest score, 95, has "sunk" to the bottom of the list. However, the scores still are not in order. They are in slightly better ascending order than they were when the process began, because the largest value is at the bottom of the list, but they are still out of order. You need to repeat the entire procedure so that 85 and 65 (the current score[0] and score[1] values) can switch places, and 90 and 75 (the current score[2] and score[3] values) can switch places. Then, the scores will be 65, 85, 75, 90, and 95. You will have to go through the list yet again to swap 85 and 75.

As a matter of fact, if the scores had started out in the worst possible order (95, 90, 85, 75, 65), the comparison process would have to take place four times. In other words, you would have to pass through the list of values four times, making appropriate swaps, before the numbers would appear in perfect ascending order. You need to place the loop in Figure 12-4 within another loop that executes four times.

Figure 12-6 shows the complete logic for the sortArray() method. The method uses a loop control variable named y to cycle through the list of scores four times. (The initialization, comparison, and alteration of this loop control variable are shaded in the figure.) With an array of five elements, it takes four comparisons to work through the array once, comparing each pair, and it takes four sets of those comparisons to ensure that every element in the entire array is in sorted order.

When you sort the elements in an array this way, you use nested loops—an inner loop within an outer loop. The general rule is that, whatever the number of elements in the array, the greatest number of pair comparisons you need to make during each loop is *one less* than the number of elements in the array. You use an inner loop to make the pair comparisons. In addition, the number of times you need to process the list of values is *one less* than the number of elements in the array. You use an outer loop to control the number of times you walk through the list. As an example, if you want to sort a 10-element array, you make nine pair comparisons on each of nine rotations through the loop, executing a total of 81 score comparison statements.

> **»NOTE** In many cases, you do not want to sort a single data item such as a score. Instead, you might want to sort data records that contain fields such as ID number, name, and score, placing the records in score order. The sorting procedure remains basically the same, but you need to store entire records in an array. Then, you make your comparisons based on a single field, but you make your swaps using entire objects. You will learn how to sort objects later in this chapter.

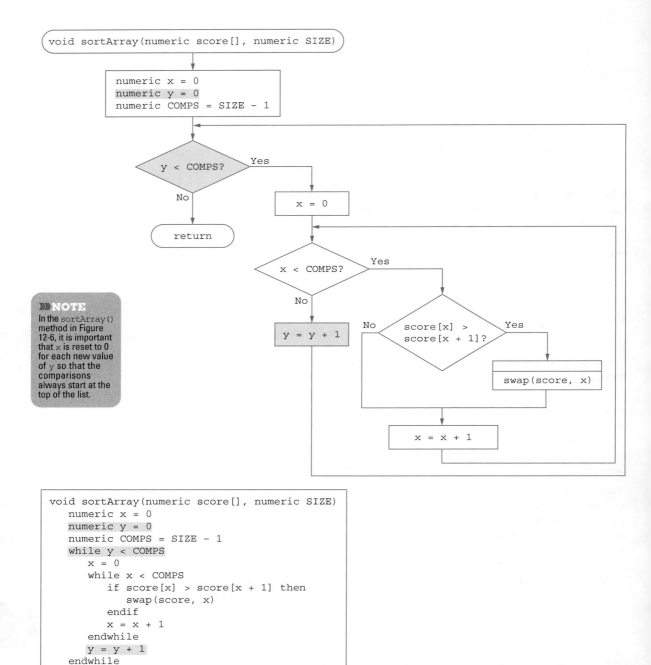

> **》NOTE**
> In the sortArray()
> method in Figure
> 12-6, it is important
> that x is reset to 0
> for each new value
> of y so that the
> comparisons
> always start at the
> top of the list.

```
void sortArray(numeric score[], numeric SIZE)
   numeric x = 0
   numeric y = 0
   numeric COMPS = SIZE - 1
   while y < COMPS
      x = 0
      while x < COMPS
         if score[x] > score[x + 1] then
            swap(score, x)
         endif
         x = x + 1
      endwhile
      y = y + 1
   endwhile
return
```

Figure 12-6 The completed sortArray() method

The last method called by the SortScores application in Figure 12-2 is the one that displays the sorted array contents. Figure 12-7 shows this method.

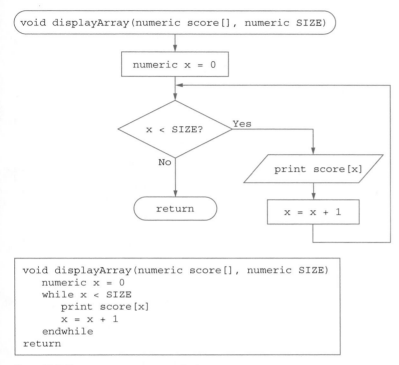

```
void displayArray(numeric score[], numeric SIZE)
    numeric x = 0
    while x < SIZE
        print score[x]
        x = x + 1
    endwhile
return
```

Figure 12-7 The displayArray() method

SORTING A LIST OF VARIABLE SIZE

In the score-sorting application in the previous section, a SIZE constant was initialized to the number of elements to be sorted at the start of the program. Sometimes, you do not want to create a value to represent the number of elements to be sorted at the start of the program because you might not know how many array elements will hold valid values. For example, sometimes when you run the program, you might want to sort only three or four scores, and sometimes you might want to sort 20. In other words, the size of the list to be sorted might vary. Rather than initializing a constant to a fixed value, you can count the input scores, and then give a variable the value of the number of array elements to use after you know how many scores exist.

To keep track of the number of elements stored in an array, you can create the application shown in Figure 12-8. In this example, the score array is created to hold 100 elements, a number larger than you anticipate you will need. As in the original version of the program, you pass the array and its size to the fillArray() method. Within the method, when you get each score, you increase x by 1 in order to place each new score into a successive element of the score array. The variable x is initialized to 0. After you read one score value and

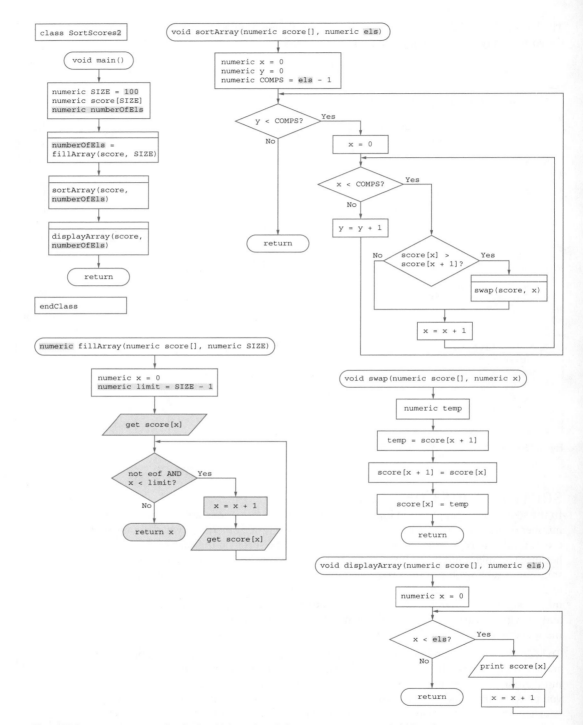

Figure 12-8 SortScores2 application in which number of elements to sort can vary (*continued*)

```
class SortScores2
   void main()
      numeric SIZE = 100
      numeric score[SIZE]
      numeric numberOfEls
      numberOfEls = fillArray(score, SIZE)
      sortArray(score, numberOfEls)
      displayArray(score, numberOfEls)
   return

   numeric fillArray(numeric score[], numeric SIZE)
      numeric x = 0
      numeric limit = SIZE - 1
      get score[x]
      while not eof AND x < limit
         x = x + 1
         get score[x]
      endwhile
   return x

   void sortArray(numeric score[], numeric els)
      numeric x = 0
      numeric y = 0
      numeric COMPS = els - 1
      while y < COMPS
         x = 0
         while x < COMPS
            if score[x] > score[x + 1] then
               swap(score, x)
            endif
            x = x + 1
         endwhile
         y = y + 1
      endwhile
   return

   void swap(numeric score[], numeric x)
      numeric temp
      temp = score[x + 1]
      score[x + 1] = score[x]
      score[x] = temp
   return

   void displayArray(numeric score[], numeric els)
      numeric x = 0
      while x < els
         print score[x]
         x = x + 1
      endwhile
   return
endClass
```

Figure 12-8 SortScores2 application in which number of elements to sort can vary

>> **NOTE**
In the fillArray() method in Figure 12-8, notice that a loop ending limit is calculated as SIZE − 1. That is because 1 is added to x when the loop is entered, possibly increasing the value of x to equal limit, and that is the last legal array element in which you can store a value.

>> **NOTE**
In the fillArray() method in Figure 12-8, notice that a priming read has been added to the method. If eof is encountered when an attempt is made to read the first record, then the number of elements to be sorted will be 0. Within the loop, 1 is added to x before the next score is read. When eof finally is encountered, x represents the number of scores in the array.

>> **NOTE** When you count the input records and use the numberOfEls variable, it does not matter if an insufficient number of scores exist to fill the array. However, it does matter if there are more scores than the array can hold. Every array must have a finite size, and it is an error to try to store data past the end of the array. When you do not know how many elements will be stored in an array, you must overestimate the number of elements you declare. If the number of scores in the score array can be 100 or fewer, then you can declare the score array to have a size of 100, and you can use 100 elements or fewer.

place it in the first element of the array, x is increased to 1. After a second score is read and placed in `score[1]`, x is increased to 2, and so on. After you reach the end of input (`eof`), x holds the number of scores that have been placed in the array, so you can return x to the main method where it is stored in `numberOfEls`. With this approach, it does not matter if there are not enough `score` values to fill the array. You simply pass `numberOfEls` to both `sortArray()` and `displayArray()` instead of passing `SIZE`. In the sorting process, you make one fewer pair comparison than the number of the value held in `numberOfEls`. Using this technique, you avoid always making a larger fixed number of pair comparisons. For example, if 35 scores are input, `numberOfEls` will be set to 35 in the `fillArray()` method, and when the program sorts, it will use 34 (`els - 1`) as a cutoff point for the number of pair comparisons to make. In other words, the highest pair comparison will be between the 34th and 35th array elements (elements with subscripts 33 and 34). The sorting program will never make pair comparisons on array elements 36 through 100—those elements will just "sit there," never being involved in a comparison or swap.

REFINING THE BUBBLE SORT BY REDUCING UNNECESSARY COMPARISONS

You can make additional improvements to the bubble sort created in the previous sections. As illustrated in Figure 12-8, when you perform the sorting module for a bubble sort, you pass through a list, making comparisons and swapping values if two adjacent values are out of order. If you are performing an ascending sort, then after you have made one pass through the list, the largest value is guaranteed to be in its correct final position at the bottom of the list. Similarly, after the second pass through the list, the second-largest element is guaranteed to be in its correct second-to-last position, and so on. If you continue to compare every element pair in the list on every pass through the list, you are comparing elements that are already guaranteed to be in their final correct position. In other words, after the first pass through the list, there is no longer a need to check the bottom element; after the second pass, there is no need to check the two bottom elements.

On each pass through the array, you can afford to stop your pair comparisons one element sooner. You can avoid comparing the already-in-place values by creating a new variable, `pairsToCompare`, and setting it equal to the value of `els - 1`. On the first pass through the list, every pair of elements is compared, so `pairsToCompare` *should* equal `els - 1`. In other words, with five array elements to sort, there are four pairs to compare, and with 50 elements to sort, there are 49 pairs to compare. On each subsequent pass through the list, `pairsToCompare` should be reduced by 1, because after the first pass there is no need to check the bottom element anymore. See Figure 12-9 to examine the use of the `pairsToCompare` variable.

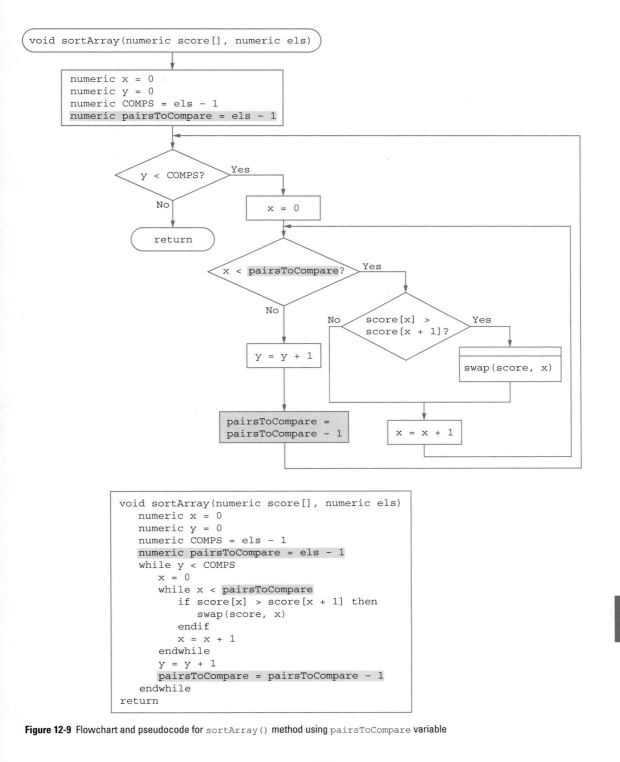

Figure 12-9 Flowchart and pseudocode for `sortArray()` method using `pairsToCompare` variable

REFINING THE BUBBLE SORT BY ELIMINATING UNNECESSARY PASSES

Another improvement you could make to the bubble sort module in Figure 12-9 is one that reduces the number of passes through the array. If array elements are so badly out of order that they are in reverse order, then it takes many passes through the list to place it in order. It takes one fewer pass than the value in els to complete all the comparisons and swaps needed to get the list sorted. However, when the array elements are in order or nearly in order to start, all the elements might be correctly arranged after only a few passes through the list; all subsequent passes result in no swaps. For example, assume there are five scores as follows:

```
score[0]  =  65
score[1]  =  75
score[2]  =  85
score[3]  =  90
score[4]  =  95
```

The bubble sort module in Figure 12-9 would pass through the array list four times, making four sets of pair comparisons. It would always find that each score[x] is *not* greater than the corresponding score[x + 1], so no switches would ever be made. The scores would end up in the proper order, but they *were* in the proper order in the first place; therefore, a lot of time would be wasted.

A possible remedy is to add a flag variable that you set to a "continue" value on any pass through the list in which any pair of elements is swapped (even if just one pair), and that holds a different "finished" value when no swaps are made—that is, all elements in the list are already in the correct order. For example, you can create a variable named switchOccurred and set it to "No" at the start of each pass through the list. You can change its value to "Yes" each time the swap() method is performed (that is, each time a swap is necessary).

If you ever make it through the entire list of pairs without making a switch, the switchOccurred flag will *not* have been set to "Yes", meaning that no switch has occurred and that the array elements must already be in the correct order. This *might* be on the first or second pass through the array list, or it might not be until a much later pass. If the array elements are already in the correct order at any point, there is no need to make more passes through the list. You can stop making passes through the list when switchOccurred is "No" after a complete trip through the array.

Figure 12-10 illustrates a method that sorts scores and uses a switchOccurred flag. At the beginning of the sortArray() method, you initialize switchOccurred to "Yes" before entering the comparison loop the first time. Then, you immediately set switchOccurred to "No". When a switch occurs—that is, when the swap() module executes—set switchOccurred to "Yes".

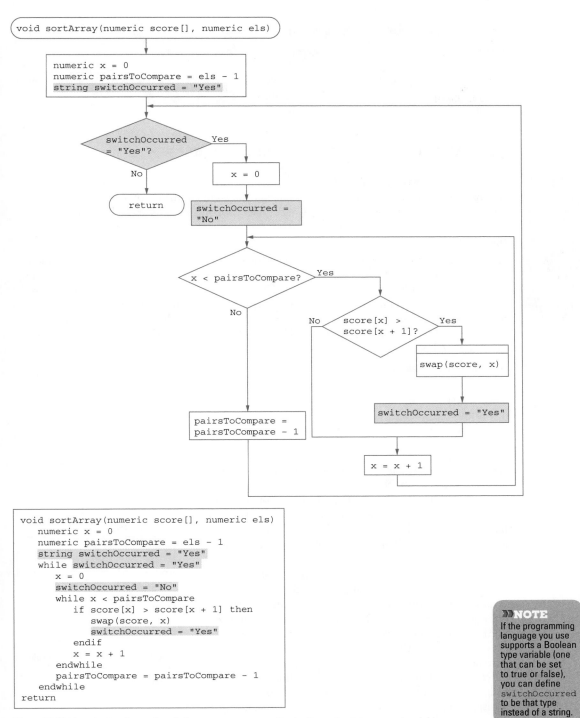

```
void sortArray(numeric score[], numeric els)
    numeric x = 0
    numeric pairsToCompare = els - 1
    string switchOccurred = "Yes"
    while switchOccurred = "Yes"
        x = 0
        switchOccurred = "No"
        while x < pairsToCompare
            if score[x] > score[x + 1] then
                swap(score, x)
                switchOccurred = "Yes"
            endif
            x = x + 1
        endwhile
        pairsToCompare = pairsToCompare - 1
    endwhile
return
```

>> NOTE
If the programming language you use supports a Boolean type variable (one that can be set to true or false), you can define switchOccurred to be that type instead of a string.

Figure 12-10 Flowchart and pseudocode for sortArray() method using switchOccurred variable

>> **NOTE** With the addition of the flag variable in Figure 12-10, you no longer need the variable y, which was keeping track of the number of passes through the list. You also no longer need the constant COMPS, which kept track of the number of comparisons to be made. Instead, you just keep going through the list until you can make a complete pass without any switches. For a list that starts in perfect order, you go through the loop only once. For a list that starts in the worst possible order, you will make a switch with every pair each time through the loop until pairsToCompare has been reduced to 0. In this case, on the last pass through the loop, x is set to 0, switchOccurred is set to "No", x is no longer less than or equal to pairsToCompare, and the inner loop is exited. In the outer loop, switchOccurred is not "Yes", so the method ends.

USING AN INSERTION SORT

>> **NOTE**
Although a sort such as the bubble sort might be inefficient, it is easy to understand. When programming, you frequently weigh the advantages of using simple solutions against writing more complicated ones that perform more efficiently.

The bubble sort works well and is relatively easy for novice array users to understand and manipulate, but even with all the improvements you added to the original bubble sort in previous sections, it is actually one of the least efficient sorting methods available. An insertion sort provides an alternate method for sorting data, and it usually requires fewer comparison operations.

As with the bubble sort, when using an **insertion sort**, you also look at each pair of elements in an array. When you find an element that is smaller than the one before it (for an ascending sort), this element is "out of order." As soon as you locate such an element, search the array backward from that point to see where an element smaller than the out-of-order element is located. At that point, you open a new position for the out-of-order element by moving each subsequent element down one position. Then, you insert the out-of-order element into the newly opened position.

For example, consider these scores:

```
score[0]  = 65
score[1]  = 80
score[2]  = 95
score[3]  = 75
score[4]  = 90
```

If you want to rearrange the scores in ascending order using an insertion sort, you begin by comparing score[0] and score[1], which are 65 and 80, respectively. You determine that they are in order, and leave them alone. Then, you compare score[1] and score[2], which are 80 and 95, and leave them alone. When you compare score[2], 95, and score[3], 75, you determine that the 75 is "out of order." Next, you look backward from the score[3] of 75. The value of score[2] is not smaller than score[3], nor is score[1]; however, because score[0] is smaller than score[3], score[3] should follow score[0]. So you store score[3] in a temporary variable, then move score[1] and score[2] "down" the list to higher subscripted positions. You move score[2], 95, to the score[3] position. Then, you move score[1], 80, to the score[2] position. Finally, you assign the value of the temporary variable, 75, to the score[1] position. Figure 12-11 is a diagram of the movements as 75 moves up to the second position and 80 and 95 move down.

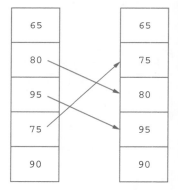

Figure 12-11 Movement of the value 75 to a "better" array position in an insertion sort

After the sort finds the first element that was out of order and inserts it in a "better" location, the results are:

```
score[0]  =  65
score[1]  =  75
score[2]  =  80
score[3]  =  95
score[4]  =  90
```

You then continue down the list, comparing each pair of variables. A complete insertion sort method is shown in Figure 12-12.

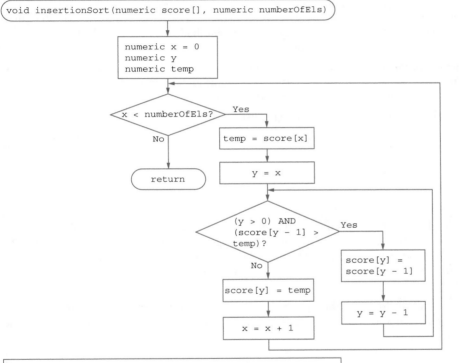

»NOTE
In Figure 12-12, parentheses enclose each half of the Boolean expression (y > 0) AND (score[y - 1] > temp) so you can more clearly discern the two parts of the question.

```
void insertionSort(numeric score[], numeric numberOfEls)
    numeric x = 0
    numeric y
    numeric temp
    while x < numberOfEls
        temp = score[x]
        y = x
        while (y > 0) AND (score[y - 1] > temp)
            score[y] = score[y - 1]
            y = y - 1
        endwhile
        score[y] = temp
        x = x + 1
    endwhile
return
```

Figure 12-12 Insertion sort

The logic for the insertion sort is slightly more complicated than that for the bubble sort, but the insertion sort is more efficient because, for the average out-of-order list, it takes fewer "switches" to put the list in order.

USING A SELECTION SORT

A selection sort provides another sorting option. In an ascending **selection sort**, the first element in the array is assumed to be the smallest. Its value is stored in a variable—for example, smallest—and its position in the array, 0, is stored in another variable—for example, position. Then, every subsequent element in the array is tested. If an element with a smaller value than smallest is found, smallest is set to the new value, and position is set to that element's position. After the entire array has been searched, smallest holds the smallest value and position holds its position.

The element originally in position[0] is then switched with the smallest value, so at the end of the first pass through the array, the lowest value ends up in the first position, and the value that was in the first position is where the smallest value used to be.

For example, assume you have the following list of scores:

```
score[0]  = 95
score[1]  = 80
score[2]  = 75
score[3]  = 65
score[4]  = 90
```

First, you place 95 in smallest. Then check score[1]; it is less than 95, so place 1 in position and 80 in smallest. Then test score[2]; it is smaller than smallest, so place 2 in position and 75 in smallest. Then test score[3]; because it is smaller than smallest, place 3 in position and 65 in smallest. Finally, check score[4]; it *is not* smaller than smallest.

So at the end of the first pass through the list, position is 3 and smallest is 65. You move the value 95 to score[position] , or score[3], and the value of smallest, 65, to score[0]. The list becomes:

```
score[0]  = 65
score[1]  = 80
score[2]  = 75
score[3]  = 95
score[4]  = 90
```

>> **NOTE** Besides the bubble, insertion, and selection sorts, there are many other sorting algorithms with colorful names such as the cocktail sort, gnome sort, and quick sort.

Now that the smallest value is in the first position, you repeat the whole procedure starting with the second array element, `score[1]`. After you have passed through the list `numberOfEls` - 1 times, all elements will be in the correct order. Walk through the logic shown in Figure 12-13.

Like the insertion sort, the selection sort almost always requires fewer switches than the bubble sort, but the variables might be a little harder to keep track of because the logic is a little more complex. Thoroughly understanding at least one of these sorting techniques provides you with a valuable tool for arranging data and increases your understanding of the capabilities of arrays.

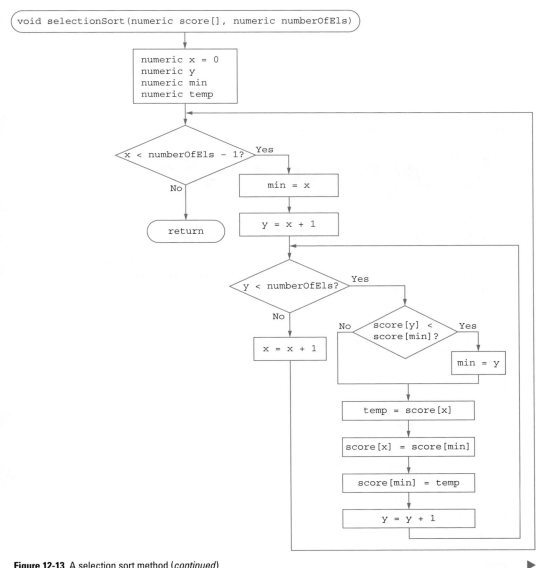

Figure 12-13 A selection sort method (*continued*)

```
void selectionSort(numeric score[], numeric numberOfEls)
   numeric x = 0
   numeric y
   numeric min
   numeric temp
   while x < numberOfEls - 1
      min = x
      y = x + 1
      while y < numberOfEls
         if score[y] < score[min] then
            min = y
         endif
         temp = score[x]
         score[x] = score[min]
         score[min] = temp
         y = y + 1
      endwhile
      x = x + 1
   endwhile
return
```

Figure 12-13 A selection sort method

>>NOTE Remember that you might never have to write your own sorting method. Many languages come with already-created sorting methods that you use as black boxes. However, taking the time to understand some sorting procedures increases your ability to work with arrays.

DECLARING AN ARRAY OF OBJECTS

You can declare arrays that hold elements of any type, including objects. For example, consider the Employee class in Figure 12-14. This class has two data fields (empNum and sal) and methods to get and set each field.

```
class Employee
   private string empNum
   private numeric sal

   public void setEmpNum(string num)
      empNum = num
   return

   public string getEmpNum()
   return empNum

   public void setSal(numeric salary)
      sal = salary
   return

   public numeric getSal()
   return sal
endClass
```

Figure 12-14 An Employee class

412

You can create separate `Employee` objects with unique names, such as `Employee painter`, `electrician`, or `plumber`, but for many applications it is far more convenient to create an array of `Employee` objects. The syntax to declare an array named `emp` that holds five `Employee` objects varies slightly between languages, but the statement is similar to the following, including the data type (the class), the array name, and the size:

```
Employee emp[5]
```

Alternatively, if you have declared a symbolic constant such as numeric `NUM_EMPLOYEES = 5`, you can write:

```
Employee emp[NUM_EMPLOYEES]
```

These declaration statements reserve enough computer memory for five `Employee` objects named `emp[0]` through `emp[4]`.

When a class contains only a nondefault constructor—that is, when the only constructors available for a class require one or more arguments—then you must provide those values when you create an array, just as you must when you declare an individual object. For example, if the only constructor available for the `Employee` class requires both an employee number and salary as arguments, then the declaration of the array might be similar to the following pseudocode:

```
Employee emp[NUM_EMPLOYEES] = {101, 12.45}, {103, 7.50},
    {119, 13.25}, {213, 15.00}, {218, 8.40}
```

The declaration includes five pairs of constructor values. The syntax differs among languages, but the pairs usually can be grouped using punctuation such as curly braces.

To use a method that belongs to an object that is part of an array, you insert the appropriate subscript notation after the array name and before the dot that precedes the method name. For example, to print data for five `Employees` stored in the `emp` array, you can write the following:

```
numeric MAX = NUM_EMPLOYEES - 1
for x = 0 to MAX
    print emp[x].getEmpNum(), " ", emp[x].getSal()
endfor
```

> **>> NOTE**
> Although the syntax differs in various programming languages, declaring an array always includes the size. For example, in Java, you write `Employee[] emp = new Employee[5] ;`, but in C++ you write `Employee emp[5] ;`.

> **>> NOTE**
> You learned to use a `for` loop in Chapter 6.

> **>> NOTE** Pay attention to the syntax of the `Employee` objects' method calls, such as `emp[x].getEmpNum()`. Although you might be tempted to place the subscript at the end of the expression after the method name, as in `emp.getEmpNum[x]`, you cannot—the values in `x` (0 through 4) refer to a particular `emp`, each of which has access to a single `getEmpNum()` method. Placement of the bracketed subscript so it follows `emp` means the method "belongs" to a particular `emp`.

SORTING ARRAYS OF OBJECTS

You can sort arrays of objects in much the same way that you sort arrays of primitive types. The major difference occurs when you make the comparison that determines whether you want to swap two array elements. When you construct an array of a primitive element type, you compare the two array elements to determine whether they are out of order. When array elements are objects, you usually want to sort based on a particular object field.

You can write a program that contains an array of five Employee objects using the statement Employee someEmps[5]. Assume that after you assign employee numbers and salaries to the Employee objects, you want to sort them in order by salary. You can pass the array and its length to a sortArray() method that is prepared to receive Employee objects. Figure 12-15 shows the method.

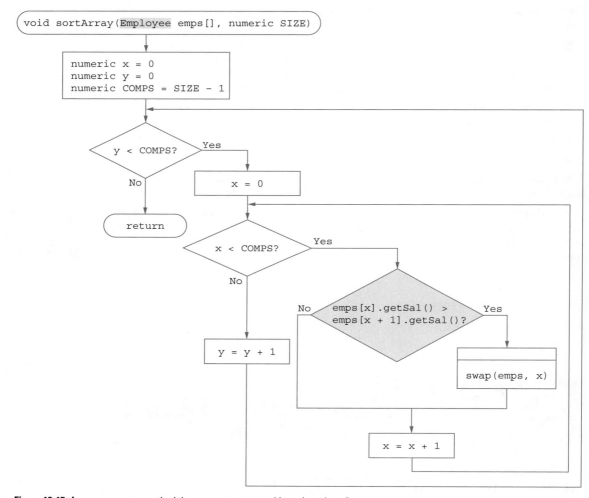

Figure 12-15 A sortArray() method that sorts Employee objects (*continued*)

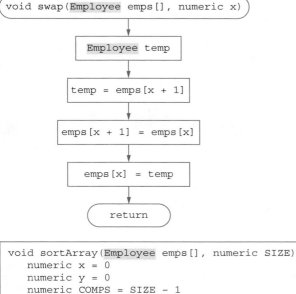

```
void sortArray(Employee emps[], numeric SIZE)
    numeric x = 0
    numeric y = 0
    numeric COMPS = SIZE - 1
    while y < COMPS
        x = 0
        while x < COMPS
            if emps[x].getSal() > emps[x + 1].getSal() then
                swap(emps, x)
            endif
            x = x + 1
        endwhile
        y = y + 1
    endwhile
return

void swap(Employee emps [], numeric x)
    Employee temp
    temp = emps[x + 1]
    emps[x + 1] = emps[x]
    emps[x] = temp
return
```

Figure 12-15 A `sortArray()` method that sorts `Employee` objects

Examine Figure 12-15 carefully and notice that the `sortArray()` method is similar to the method you use to sort an array of any primitive type (for example, like the numeric sort shown in Figure 12-6), but there are three major differences:

» The method headers for `sortArray()` and `swap()` show that they each receive an array of type `Employee`.

» The comparison for determining whether a swap should occur uses method calls to the `getSal()` method to compare the returned salary for each `Employee` object in the array with the salary of the adjacent `Employee` object.

» In the `swap()` method, the `temp` variable created for swapping is type `Employee`. The `temp` variable will hold an `Employee` object, not just one number or one field.

> **»»NOTE** Note that even though only employee salaries are compared, you do not swap employee salaries. You do not want to substitute one employee's salary for another's. Instead, you swap the entire `Employee` object so that each `Employee` object's `empNum` and `sal` are swapped as a unit.

> **»»NOTE** Some programming languages allow you to define relational comparison operators such as > and < so they work with objects. When you create the methods that do this, you define the specific field or fields that are the basis of the comparison.

USING TWO-DIMENSIONAL AND MULTIDIMENSIONAL ARRAYS

> **»»NOTE**
> You can think of the single dimension of a single-dimensional array as the height of the array.

When you declare an array such as `numeric someNumbers[3]`, you can envision the three declared numbers as a column of numbers in memory, as shown in Figure 12-16. In other words, you can picture the three declared numbers stacked one on top of the next. An array that you can picture as a column of values, and whose elements you can access using a single subscript, is a **one-dimensional** or **single-dimensional array**.

someNumbers[0]
someNumbers[1]
someNumbers[2]

Figure 12-16 View of a single-dimensional array in memory

Most object-oriented programming (OOP) languages also support two-dimensional arrays. **Two-dimensional arrays** have both rows and columns of values, as shown in Figure 12-17. You must use two subscripts when you access an element in a two-dimensional array. When mathematicians use a two-dimensional array, they often call it a **matrix** or a **table**; you might have used a two-dimensional array called a spreadsheet.

someNumbers[0] [0]	someNumbers[0] [1]	someNumbers[0] [2]	someNumbers[0] [3]
someNumbers[1] [0]	someNumbers[1] [1]	someNumbers[1] [2]	someNumbers[1] [3]
someNumbers[2] [0]	someNumbers[2] [1]	someNumbers[2] [2]	someNumbers[2] [3]

Figure 12-17 View of a two-dimensional array in memory

> **»»NOTE**
> You can think of the two dimensions of a two-dimensional array as height and width. You also can think of a two-dimensional array as an array of arrays because each row holds an array of values, and the rows themselves are an array.

When you declare a one-dimensional array, you type a set of square brackets after the array type. To declare a two-dimensional array, many languages require you to type two sets of brackets after the array type. For example, the array in Figure 12-17 can be declared as `numeric someNumbers[3] [4]`, creating an array named `someNumbers` that holds three rows and four columns.

In many OOP languages, if you do not provide initial values for a numeric array, then each element is 0 by default. However, just as you can assign values to a one-dimensional array when you create it or elements later, you can assign other values to a two-dimensional array when you create it or elements later. For example, `someNumbers[0] [0]   = 14` assigns the value 14 to the element of the someNumbers array that is in the first column of the first row. Alternatively, you can initialize a two-dimensional array with values when it is created, as in the following pseudocode:

```
numeric someNumbers[3][4] = {8,  9,  10,  11},
                            {1,  3,  12,  15},
                            {5, 33,  44,  99}
```

In this example, the values that are assigned to each row are enclosed in braces to help you picture the placement of each number in the array. The first row of the array holds the four integers 8, 9, 10, and 11. Similarly, 1, 3, 12, and 15 make up the second row, and 5, 33, 44, and 99 are the values in the third row. The value of someNumbers[0][0] is 8. The value of someNumbers[0][1] is 9. The value of someNumbers[2][3] is 99. The value within the first pair of brackets following the array name always refers to the row; the value within the second pair of brackets refers to the column.

As an example of how useful two-dimensional arrays can be, assume you own an apartment building with four floors—a basement, which you refer to as floor zero, and three other floors numbered one, two, and three. In addition, each of the floors has studios (with no bedroom) and one- and two-bedroom apartments. The monthly rent for each type of apartment is different—the higher the floor, the higher the rent (the view is better), and the rent is higher for apartments with more bedrooms. Table 12-1 shows the rental amounts.

Floor	Zero Bedrooms ($)	One Bedroom ($)	Two Bedrooms ($)
0	400	450	510
1	500	560	630
2	625	676	740
3	1,000	1,250	1,600

Table 12-1 Rents charged

NOTE
Because the rent values will not change during the program's execution, the RENTS array is created as a constant array and uses the all-uppercase naming convention. Just like any other variables, arrays can be variable or constant.

To determine a tenant's rent, you need to know two pieces of information: the floor on which the tenant rents an apartment and the number of bedrooms in the apartment. Within a rent-determining application, you can declare an array of rents using the following code:

```
numeric RENTS[4][3] = {400,  450,  510},
                      {500,  560,  630},
                      {625,  676,  740},
                      {1000, 1250, 1600}
```

NOTE
Just as within a one-dimensional array, each element in a multidimensional array must be the same data type.

Assuming you declare two variables to hold the floor number and bedroom count as numeric floor and numeric bedrooms, any tenant's rent is RENTS[floor] [bedrooms].

NOTE Some languages access two-dimensional array elements with commas separating the subscript values; for example, the first-floor, two-bedroom rate might be written RENT[1, 2]. In every language, you provide a subscript for the row first and for the column second.

As another example, suppose a library is trying to decide whether to charge a fee for videos checked out on weekends because demand seems higher than during the week.

Figure 12-18 shows an example in which a user can enter a number that represents a day of the week (0 through 6 for Sunday through Saturday) and can enter the number of videos checked out by the patron (0 through 4, because some patrons do not take out videos and 4 is the maximum number allowed).

```
class LibraryStatistics
    void main()
        numeric day
        numeric videos
        numeric LOWDAY = 0
        numeric HIGHDAY = 7
        numeric LOWVIDEOS = 0
        numeric HIGHVIDEOS = 5
        numeric count[HIGHDAY][HIGHVIDEOS] = {0, 0, 0, 0, 0},
                                             {0, 0, 0, 0, 0},
                                             {0, 0, 0, 0, 0},
                                             {0, 0, 0, 0, 0},
                                             {0, 0, 0, 0, 0},
                                             {0, 0, 0, 0, 0},
                                             {0, 0, 0, 0, 0}
        numeric QUIT = 999
        string DAYNAME[HIGHDAY] = "Sunday", "Monday", "Tuesday",
            "Wednesday", "Thursday", "Friday", "Saturday"

        print "Please enter the day number, or ", QUIT, " to quit"
        get day
        while day not = QUIT
            while day < LOWDAY OR day >= HIGHDAY
                print "Please reenter day "
                get day
            endwhile
            print "Please enter number of videos "
            get videos
            while videos < LOWVIDEOS OR videos >= HIGHVIDEOS
                print "Please reenter videos "
                get videos
            endwhile
            count[day][videos] = count[day][videos] + 1
            print "Please enter next day, or ", QUIT, " to quit "
        endwhile

        print "Weekly Statistics"
        day = 0
        videos = 0
        while day < HIGHDAY
            print DAYNAME[day]
            videos = 0
            while videos < HIGHVIDEOS
                print "Number of videos ", videos,
                    " Count: ", count[day][videos]
                videos = videos + 1
            endwhile
            day = day + 1
        endwhile
    return
endClass
```

Figure 12-18 The LibraryStatistics class

In the program in Figure 12-18, variables are created to hold a day number and a number of videos checked out, and constants are declared for the minimum and maximum values for each. Then, in the first shaded statement, an array is declared that contains seven rows (one for each day of the week) and five columns (one for each number of possible videos checked out, 0 through 4). All of the array elements are initialized to 0 so that they can be incremented as each patron checks out.

When the actual work of the `LibraryStatistics` program begins, the user is prompted for a day number. While the day number is out of range, the user continues to be reprompted. This assures that the final value for `day` will be a usable subscript. Next, the user enters a number of videos, and a loop again assures that the value is valid.

In the second shaded statement in Figure 12-18, a 1 is added to one of the 35 `count` array elements, depending on the day number (which determines the row) and the number of videos (which determines the column). Because the program uses a two-dimensional array, the tedious process of making 35 separate decisions is avoided, and the appropriate `count` element can be accessed directly using `day` and `videos` as subscripts. After 1 is added to the correct `count`, the user can enter the next set of values, and the process repeats.

In the last section of the application in Figure 12-18, a heading is printed, and then a nested loop prints each of the 35 `count` values. For example, when `day` is 0, DAYNAME[0] ("Sunday") is printed, and each of the five `count` values for that day is displayed. Then `day` is increased and DAYNAME[1] ("Monday") is displayed, followed by its five `count` values. Because the program uses a two-dimensional array, two loops produce all the output. Figure 12-19 shows the beginning of a sample report the program might produce.

```
Weekly Statistics

Sunday
    Number of videos: 0    Count: 315
    Number of videos: 1    Count: 102
    Number of videos: 2    Count: 145
    Number of videos: 3    Count:  25
    Number of videos: 4    Count:  16
Monday
    Number of videos: 0    Count: 120
    Number of videos: 1    Count:  78
    Number of videos: 2    Count:  43
    Number of videos: 3    Count:  12
    Number of videos: 4    Count:   7
Tuesday
    Number of videos: 0    Count: 135
    Number of videos: 1    Count:  54
```

Figure 12-19 Sample report produced by the `LibraryStatistics` class

Besides one- and two-dimensional arrays, many programming languages also support **multidimensional arrays**, which might contain any number of dimensions. For example, if you own an apartment building with a number of floors and different numbers of bedrooms available in apartments on each floor, you can use a two-dimensional array to store the rental fees. If you own several apartment buildings, you might want to employ a third dimension to store the building number. An expression such as RENTS[building] [floor] [bedrooms] refers to a specific rent figure for a building whose building number is stored in the `building` variable, and whose floor and bedroom numbers are stored in the `floor` and `bedrooms` variables.

» NOTE
Technically, a two-dimensional array is a multidimensional array, but programmers are likely to reserve the prefix "multi" for references to three dimensions or more.

Specifically, RENTS[5] [1] [2] refers to a two-bedroom apartment on the first floor of building 5 (which is the sixth building in an array in which the first building is referenced with a 0 subscript).

USING A BUILT-IN Array CLASS

When you fully understand the power of arrays, you will want to use them to store all kinds of objects. Frequently, you will want to perform similar tasks with different arrays—for example, filling them with values and sorting their elements. Many OOP languages provide an **Array class**, which contains many useful methods for manipulating arrays. One of the advantages of using modern object-oriented languages is the vast libraries of classes that contain useful built-in methods that are available to you. The Array class is just one of many examples.

> **» NOTE** If a language provides a class to help you work with arrays, it might have a name other than Array. For example, in C# and Visual Basic, the class is Array, but in Java, the corresponding class is Arrays.

Table 12-2 shows some of the typically included, useful methods of the Array class. The most useful Array class would contain an overloaded version of each method for each appropriate data type. For example, you would want versions of the sort() method to sort numeric, string, and object elements.

Method	Purpose
numeric binarySearch (type a[], type key)	Searches the specified array (name a of type type) for the specified key value using the binary search algorithm
boolean equals(type a[], type a2[])	Returns true if the two specified arrays of the same type are equal to one another and false if they are not; this means that the programmer will have to define what "equal" means for two objects
void fill(type a[], type val)	Assigns the specified value val to each element of the specified array
void sort(type a[])	Sorts the specified array into ascending numerical order

Table 12-2 Typical useful methods of the Array class

If you are using an object-oriented language that does not provide a built-in Array class to perform common array-based tasks, you could write one yourself. Doing so would require a lot of code-writing up front, but the future availability of useful methods to handle common array tasks would be well worth the effort.

CHAPTER SUMMARY

» Frequently, data records need to be sorted, or placed in order, based on the contents of one or more fields. When you sort data, you can sort either in ascending order, arranging records from lowest to highest value, or descending order, arranging records from highest to lowest value.

» Swapping two values is a concept that is central to most sorting techniques. When you swap the values stored in two variables, you reverse their positions using a temporary variable to hold one of the values during the swap process.

» In a bubble sort, items in a list are compared with each other in pairs, and when an item is out of order, it swaps values with the item below it. With an ascending bubble sort, after each adjacent pair of items in a list has been compared once, the largest item in the list will have "sunk" to the bottom. After many passes through the list, the smallest items rise to the top like bubbles in a carbonated drink.

» Sometimes, the size of the list to be sorted might vary. Rather than initializing a constant to a fixed value, you can count the values to be sorted, and then give a variable the value of the number of array elements to use after you know how many scores exist.

» You can improve a bubble sort by stopping pair comparisons one element sooner on each pass through the array being sorted.

» You can improve a bubble sort by adding a flag variable that you set to a "continue" value on any pass in which any pair of elements is swapped (even if just one pair), and that holds a different "finished" value when no swaps are made—that is, all elements in the list are already in the correct order.

» An insertion sort provides an alternate method for sorting data, and it usually requires fewer comparison operations. As with the bubble sort, when using an insertion sort, you also look at each pair of elements in an array. When you find an element that is smaller than the one before it (for an ascending sort), this element is "out of order." As soon as you locate such an element, search the array backward from that point to see where an element smaller than the out-of-order element is located. At that point, you open a new position for the out-of-order element by moving each subsequent element down one position. Then, you insert the out-of-order element into the newly opened position.

» In an ascending selection sort, the first element in the array is assumed to be the smallest. Its value is stored in a variable—for example, smallest—and its position in the array, 0, is stored in another variable—for example, position. Then, every subsequent element in the array is tested. If an element with a smaller value than smallest is found, smallest is set to the new value, and position is set to that element's position. After the entire array has been searched, smallest holds the smallest value and position holds its position. The element originally in position[0] is then switched with the smallest value, so at the end of the first pass through the array, the lowest value ends up in the first position, and the value that was in the first position is where the smallest value used to be.

» You can declare arrays that hold elements of any type, including objects. When a class contains only a nondefault constructor—that is, when the only constructors available for a class require one or more arguments—then you must provide those values when you create an array just as you must when you declare an individual object. To use a method that belongs to an object that is part of an array, you insert the appropriate subscript notation after the array name and before the dot that precedes the method name.

» You can sort arrays of objects in much the same way that you sort arrays of primitive types. The major difference occurs when you make the comparison that determines whether you want to swap two array elements. When array elements are objects, you usually want to sort based on a particular object field.

» An array that you can picture as a column of values, and whose elements you can access using a single subscript, is a one-dimensional or single-dimensional array. Most object-oriented programming (OOP) languages also support two-dimensional arrays. Two-dimensional arrays have both rows and columns of values. You must use two subscripts when you access an element in a two-dimensional array.

» Many OOP languages provide an `Array` class, which contains many useful methods for manipulating arrays.

KEY TERMS

When records are in **sequential order**, they are arranged one after another on the basis of the value in some field.

When data records are **sorted**, they are placed in order based on the contents of one or more fields.

Ascending order is an arrangement from lowest to highest value.

Descending order is an arrangement from highest to lowest value.

The **median** value in a list is the value of the middle item when the values are listed in order.

The **mean** of a list of values is the arithmetic average.

An **index** is a construct used as an alternative to sorting large numbers of records; it is a list of key fields that are manipulated instead of altering the positions of much larger records.

Linked lists are used as an alternative to physically sorting large records; in a linked list, each record contains a field that holds the address of the next logical record.

Swapping two values is the act of reversing their positions.

In a **bubble sort**, items in a list are compared with each other in pairs, and when an item is out of order, it swaps values with the item below it.

A bubble sort is sometimes called a **sinking sort**.

An **algorithm** is a list of instructions that accomplish some task.

In an **insertion sort**, each pair of elements in an array is compared. When an out-of-order element is found, a backward search is made for an element smaller than the out-of-order element. When the smaller element is located, a new position is opened for the out-of-order element and each subsequent element is moved down one position.

In an ascending **selection sort**, the first element in the array is assumed to be the smallest. Its value is stored in a variable and its position in the array is stored in another variable. Then, every subsequent element in the array is tested. If an element with a smaller value is found, the variable storing the smallest value is set to the new value and its position is stored. The procedure is repeated for each subsequent value.

A **one-dimensional** or **single-dimensional array** is a list accessed using a single subscript.

Two-dimensional arrays have both rows and columns of values; you must use two subscripts when you access an element in a two-dimensional array.

When mathematicians use a two-dimensional array, they often call it a **matrix** or a **table**.

Multidimensional arrays can have any number of dimensions.

An **Array class** is a class provided with many OOP languages that contains useful methods for manipulating arrays.

REVIEW QUESTIONS

1. Records that are in sequential order are in _____ .

   a. alphabetical order

   b. ascending numerical order

   c. descending numerical order

   d. Any of these can be true.

2. When computers sort data, they always use _____ values when making comparisons between values.

   a. alphabetic   c. string

   b. numeric   d. null

3. When you _____ two values, you reverse their positions.

   a. sort   c. replace

   b. compare   d. swap

4. Arranging items from the one with the highest value to the one with the lowest value places them in _____ order.

   a. ascending   c. cascading

   b. descending   d. reference

5. How does a bubble sort begin its operation on an array list?

   a. Each element in a list is compared with an average value and placed above or below that point.

   b. Each element in a list is compared with the value in the middle position and placed above or below that point.

   c. Each element in a list is compared with the one following it, and their values are exchanged if they are out of order.

   d. The first and last elements in a list are compared and then exchanged if they are out of order. Then the second and second-to-last items are compared, and so on.

6. With an ascending bubble sort, after each pair of items in a list has been compared once, the largest item in the list will _____ .

   a. have been removed from the list

   b. have risen to the top

   c. have "sunk" to the bottom

   d. have been placed in the middle

7. With a bubble sort, after one pass through the list, the items _____ .

   a. are in order from lowest to highest

   b. are in order from highest to lowest

   c. are in slightly better order than they were at the start

   d. are in slightly worse order than they were at the start

8. In a descending bubble sort of an array named `array` with size `SIZE`, you switch the positions of `array[a]` and _____ .

   a. `array[a + 1]` whenever the value of `array[a]` is higher

   b. `array[a + 1]` whenever the value of `array[a]` is lower

   c. `array[SIZE - 1]` whenever `array[a]` is higher

   d. none of the above

9. With a(n) _____ you compare pairs of elements in an array, looking for those that are out of order.

   a. bubble sort   c. both of these

   b. insertion sort   d. none of these

10. The sort that begins with the assumption that the first element is the smallest is the _____ .

    a. ascending bubble sort

    b. ascending insertion sort

    c. ascending selection sort

    d. all of the above

11. The least efficient of the following sort algorithms is the _____ .

    a. bubble   c. insertion

    b. selection   d. All of these are equally efficient.

12. You can declare arrays of _____ .

    a. numbers   c. objects

    b. strings   d. all of the above

13. What does the following statement declare?

    ```
    Product inventory[1000]
    ```

    a. 1,000 numbers in an array named `Product`

    b. 1,000 `Product` objects in an array named `inventory`

    c. A class named `inventory` that contains 1,000 fields

    d. A class named `Product` that contains strings representing 1,000 inventory items

14. Assume `Student` is a class that contains fields for an ID number, last name, and grade level. It also contains get and set methods for each field and a single constructor that requires a numeric ID number argument. Which of the following declares an array of three `Student` objects?

    a. `numeric Student[3] = 1234, 2345, 3456`

    b. `Student students[3]`

    c. `Student students[3] = 1234, 2345, 3456`

    d. two of the above

15. Assume `Student` is a class that contains fields for an ID number, last name, and grade level. It also contains a nonstatic public `getGPA()` method that returns a `Student`'s grade point average. Which of the following prints the grade point average of the second `Student` in an array declared as `Student stu[3]` ?

    a. `print Student[1]`

    b. `print stu[1]`

    c. `print stu.getGpa()[1]`

    d. `print stu[1].getGpa()`

16. Assume a class named `Business` contains a name, address, number of employees, and annual revenue figure for a business. The class contains a nonstatic, public `getName()` method that returns the name of the business. You have declared an array as `Business bus[50]`. Which of the following prints the name of the last `Business` in the array?

    a. `print Business[50].getName()`

    b. `print bus[50].getName()`

    c. both of these

    d. none of these

17. Assume you declare an array as `numeric values[5][12]`. Which of the following is true?

    a. The array contains five columns.

    b. The array contains 44 elements (4 times 11).

    c. The array contains 12 rows.

    d. The array cannot contain strings.

18. Assume you declare an array as follows:

```
string names[2][4]  = {"Amy", "Brian", "Carol", "Dan"},
    {"Emily", "Frank", "Georgette", "Hank"}
```

Which of the following is true?

a. "Carol" is in location [1][3].

b. "Emily" is in location [2][1].

c. "Georgette" is in location [1][2].

d. Two of these are true.

19. Many OOP languages provide an `Array` class, which _____ .

a. contains useful methods for manipulating arrays

b. is used as the data type when you declare any array

c. is used as the data type when you declare any array with more than one dimension

d. is the child class of all declared arrays

20. If you use a programming language that does not provide a built-in `Array` class, you _____ .

a. cannot declare arrays

b. can declare arrays of simple data types, but not of objects

c. can declare arrays of objects, but not of simple data types

d. could write one yourself

EXERCISES

1. Design an application that allows you to enter 10 numbers from the keyboard and display them in descending order.

2. Design an application that allows you to enter eight friends' first names and display them in alphabetical order.

3. Professor Zak allows students to drop the two lowest scores on the ten 100-point quizzes she gives during the semester. Based on this information, complete the following tasks.

a. Design a usable `Student` class that contains ID number, last name, first name, and 10 quiz scores. Include methods to get and set these fields.

b. Design an application that allows the professor to enter records for 20 students. The output lists each student ID, name, and total points for each student's eight highest-scoring quizzes.

c. Modify the application in Exercise 3b so that the students are displayed in alphabetical order by last name.

d. Modify the application in Exercise 3b so that the students are displayed in alphabetical order by total for the eight high-scoring quizzes.

e. Modify the application in Exercise 3b so that the end of the list of students displays the mean and median total points for the class.

4. The Hinner College Foundation holds an annual fundraiser for which the foundation director maintains records. Based on this information, complete the following tasks.

   a. Design a usable class that contains a donor name and contribution amount. Include get and set methods for these fields.

   b. Develop the logic for a program that sorts the donations by amounts in descending order. Assume a maximum of 300 donors. Output lists the five highest donation amounts (or fewer if at least five are not entered).

5. The Spotless Reputation Dry Cleaning Store maintains customer records with data fields for first name, last name, address, and annual cleaning bill in dollars. At the end of the year, the store manager sends a $25 coupon to each of the 100 customers with the highest annual purchases. Based on this information, complete the following tasks.

   a. Design a usable class that contains customer data. Include get and set methods for these fields.

   b. Develop the logic for a program that reads in and sorts up to 1,000 customer records by annual cleaning bill and prints the names and addresses for the top 100 customers (or fewer if at least 100 are not entered).

6. The village of Ringwood has taken a special census. Every census record contains a household ID number, number of occupants, and income. Ringwood has exactly 75 households. Village statisticians are interested in the median household size and the median household income. Develop the logic for a program that allows census data to be entered and that determines these statistics.

7. The village of Marengo has taken a special census and collected records that contain a household ID number, number of occupants, and income for each village household. The exact number of household records has not yet been determined, but you know that Marengo has fewer than 1,000 households. Develop the logic for a program that determines the median household size and the median household income.

8. The MidAmerica Bus Company charges fares to passengers based on the number of travel zones they cross. Additionally, discounts are provided for multiple passengers traveling together. Ticket fares are shown in Table 12-3.

Passengers	Zones Crossed			
	1	2	3	4
1	7.50	10.00	12.00	12.75
2	14.00	18.50	22.00	23.00
3	20.00	21.00	32.00	33.00
4	25.00	27.50	36.00	37.00

Table 12-3 Fares charged by MidAmerica Bus Company

Based on this information, complete the following tasks.

   a. Develop a class that holds a travel party's last name, number in the party, and zones crossed. Include get and set methods for each field.

b. Design the logic for an application that reads in travel party records and displays the travel party data, the ticket charge per person, and ticket charge per party.

9. In golf, par represents a standard number of strokes a player needs to complete a hole. Instead of using an absolute score, players can compare their scores on a hole to the par figure and determine whether they are above or below par. Families can play nine holes of miniature golf at the Family Fun Miniature Golf Park. So that family members can compete fairly, the course provides a different par for each hole based on the player's age. The par figures are shown in Table 12-4.

| Age | Holes | | | | | | | | |
	1	2	3	4	5	6	7	8	9
4 and under	8	8	9	7	5	7	8	5	8
5–7	7	7	8	6	5	6	7	5	6
8–11	6	5	6	5	4	5	5	4	5
12–15	5	4	4	4	3	4	3	3	4
16 and over	4	3	3	3	2	3	2	3	3

Table 12-4 Par for holes at Family Fun Miniature Golf Park

Based on this information, complete the following tasks.

a. Design a class that holds a player's name, age, nine individual hole scores, and a total score. Include set methods for all the fields except total score, which is calculated any time an individual hole field is set. Include get methods for all the fields.

b. Develop the logic for an application that prints a score summary for each player. The summary contains the player's name and score on each of the nine holes, with one of the phrases "Over par", "Par", or "Under par" next to each score.

c. Modify the program in Exercise 9b so that at the end of each golfer's report, the golfer's total score displays. Include a number indicating how many strokes over or under par the player is for the entire course.

10. The It's Greek to Me Translation Service pays its translators a per-page rate based on two criteria—number of pages to be translated and years of service the translator has provided. The salary schedule is shown in Table 12-5.

| Years of Service | Pages in Document | | | |
	1–10	11–20	21–40	41 or more
1	1.50	1.75	2.00	2.20
2	2.00	2.25	2.95	3.30
3	2.50	3.00	3.50	4.00
4	3.50	4.25	5.00	5.65
5 or more	5.50	6.75	8.25	11.00

Table 12-5 Pay rates for It's Greek to Me Translation Service

Based on this information, complete the following tasks.

a. Create a class to hold translator employee records including ID numbers, last and first names, year hired, and years of service. Include set methods for the first three fields but calculate the years-of-service field by subtracting the year hired from the current year. Include get methods for all the fields.

b. Create a `Job` class that holds an `Employee`, a number of pages to be translated, and the per-page rate for the `Job`. Include appropriate get and set methods.

c. Develop the logic for an application program that reads a file of `Jobs` and displays each `Job`'s employee ID number, name, and pay rate. Assume there are no more than 50 `Jobs`. At the end of the report, display a count of the `Jobs` entered as well as the average pay rate.

11. The Roadmaster Driving School allows students to sign up for any number of driving lessons. The school allows up to four attempts to pass the driver's license test; otherwise, the student's tuition is returned. The school maintains an archive that contains student records for those who have successfully passed the licensing test over the last 10 years. Each record contains a student ID number, name, number of driving lessons completed, and the number of attempts the student needed to pass the licensing test. The records are stored in alphabetical order by student name. The school administration is interested in examining the correlation between the number of lessons taken and the number of attempts required to pass the test. Develop the logic for a program that would produce a table for the school that would help administrators analyze test performance. Each row represents the number of lessons taken: 0–9, 10–19, 20–29, and 30 or more. Each column represents the number of test attempts in order to pass—1 through 4.

12. The Stevens College Testing Center creates a record each time a student takes a placement test. Students can take a test in any of 12 subject areas: English, Math, Biology, Chemistry, History, Sociology, Psychology, Art, Music, Spanish, German, or Computer Science. Each record contains the date the test was taken, the student's ID number, the test subject area, and a percent score on the test. Records are maintained in the order they are entered as the tests are taken. The college would like a report that lists each of the 12 tests along with a count of the number of students who have received scores in each of the following categories: at least 90 percent, 80 through 89 percent, 70 through 79 percent, and below 70 percent. Develop the logic that produces the report.

CASE PROJECT

In earlier chapters you developed classes needed for Cost Is No Object—a car rental service that specializes in lending antique and luxury cars to clients on a short-term basis. You created the logic for `Name`, `Address`, `Date`, `Person`, `Employee`, `Customer`, `Automobile`, `RentalAgreement`, and several other subclasses.

In Chapter 4, you learned that valid `Employee` insurance plan codes are 1 or 2. In Chapter 5, you added job descriptions to the `Employee` class. These descriptions appear in Table 12-6. The pay rates based on the job descriptions appear in Table 12-7.

Job Code	Title
10	Desk clerk
11	Credit checker
12	Billing
13	Car cleaner
14	Chauffeur
15	Marketer
16	Accountant
17	Mechanic
18	CEO
19	Contract

Table 12-6 Job titles for Cost Is No Object

Job Code	Hourly Pay Rate ($)
10–13	9.00
14–15	14.50
16–17	20.00
18	65.00
19	0.00

Table 12-7 Hourly pay rates for Cost Is No Object

Complete the following tasks:

» Design an `Employee` class that contains at least an ID number, first name, last name, insurance plan code, job code, and pay rate. You might use a class you developed in a previous chapter as a basis for this class.

» Create an application in which you create an array of 25 `Employee` objects.

» Prompt a user for data for any number of employees up to 25. In turn, pass each `Employee` object to a method that accepts an `Employee`, prompts the user for necessary data, and returns a "filled" `Employee` object to the array.

» Pass the `Employee` array to a method that counts the number of employees in each of the 10 job description categories and displays a count of each.

» Pass the `Employee` array to a method that counts the number of employees in each of the two insurance plans and displays a count of each.

» Pass the `Employee` array to a method that sorts the `Employees` in ascending ID number order and display a list of the employees' first and last names in ID number order.

» Pass the `Employee` array to a method that displays the last names and pay rates of the employees with the five highest pay rates. If there are fewer than five employees, then display all of them. If displaying only the five highest-paid employees would exclude some employees whose pay rate "tied" for any of the five highest, then display as many as needed.

UP FOR DISCUSSION

1. In Chapter 3, you considered the criteria you would use to select organ transplant recipients. This chapter discusses sorting data. Suppose a large hospital hires you to write a program that displays lists of potential organ recipients, and that the hospital administrators instruct you to sort potential recipients by last name and to display them sequentially in alphabetical order. If more than 10 patients are waiting for a particular organ, the first 10 patients are displayed; a doctor can either select one of these or move on to view the next set of 10 patients. You worry that this system gives an unfair advantage to patients with last names that start with A, B, C, and D. Should you write and install the program? If you do not, many transplant opportunities will be missed while the hospital searches for another programmer to write the program. Are there different criteria you would want to use to sort the patients?

2. This chapter discusses sorting data. Suppose your supervisor asks you to create a report that lists all employees sorted by salary. Suppose you also know that your employer will use this report to lay off the highest-paid employee in each department. Would you agree to write the program? Instead, what if the report's purpose was to list the worst performer in each department in terms of sales? What if the report grouped employees by gender? What if the report grouped employees by race? Suppose your supervisor asks you to sort employees by the dollar value of medical insurance claims they have in a year, and you fear the employer will use the report to eliminate workers who are driving up the organization's medical insurance costs. Do you agree to write the program even if you know that the purpose of the report is to eliminate workers?

APPENDIX A

SOLVING DIFFICULT STRUCTURING PROBLEMS

In Chapter 2, you learned that you can solve any logical problem using only the three standard structures—sequence, selection, and loop. Often it is a simple matter to modify an unstructured program method to make it adhere to structured rules. Sometimes, however, it is a challenge to structure a more complicated method. Still, no matter how complicated, large, or poorly structured a problem is, the same tasks can *always* be accomplished in a structured manner.

Consider the flowchart segment in Figure A-1. Is it structured?

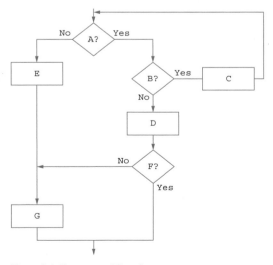

Figure A-1 Unstructured flowchart segment

No, it is not. To straighten out the flowchart segment, making it structured, you can use the "spaghetti" method. Using this method, you untangle each path of the flowchart as if you were attempting to untangle strands of spaghetti in a bowl. The objective is to create a new flowchart segment that performs exactly the same tasks as the first, but using only the three structures—sequence, selection, and loop.

To begin to untangle the unstructured flowchart segment, you start at the beginning with the decision labeled A, shown in Figure A-2. This step must represent the beginning of either a selection or a loop, because a sequence would not contain a decision.

Figure A-2 Structuring, Step 1

If you follow the logic on the "No," or left, side of the question in the original flowchart, you can pull up on the left branch of the decision. You encounter process E, followed by G, followed by the end, as shown in Figure A-3. Compare the "No" actions after Decision A in the first flowchart (Figure A-1), and the actions after Decision A in Figure A-3; they are identical.

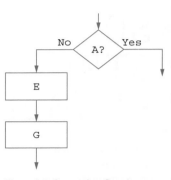

Figure A-3 Structuring, Step 2

Now continue on the right, or "Yes," side of Decision A in Figure A-1. When you follow the flowline, you encounter a decision symbol, labeled B. Pull on B's left side, and a process, D, comes up next. See Figure A-4.

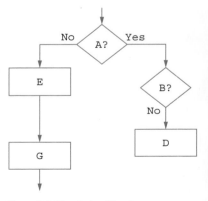

Figure A-4 Structuring, Step 3

After Step D in the original diagram, a decision labeled F comes up. Pull on its left, or "No," side and get a process, G, and then the end. When you pull on F's right, or "Yes," side in the original flow-chart, you simply reach the end, as shown in Figure A-5. Notice in Figure A-5 that the G process now appears in two locations. When you improve unstructured flowcharts so that they become structured, you must often repeat steps. This eliminates crossed lines and difficult-to-follow spaghetti logic.

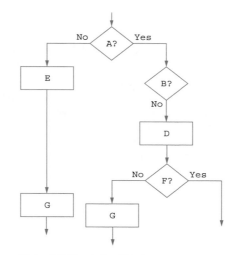

Figure A-5 Structuring, Step 4

The biggest problem in structuring the original flowchart segment from Figure A-1 follows the right, or "Yes," side of the B decision. When the answer to B is Yes, you encounter process C, as shown in both Figures A-1 and A-6. The structure that begins with Decision C looks like a loop because it doubles back, up to Decision A. However, the rules of a structured loop say that it must have the appearance shown in Figure A-7: a question, followed by a structure,

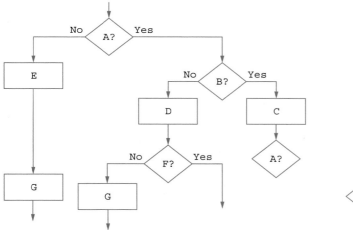

Figure A-6 Structuring, Step 5

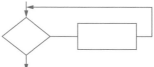

Figure A-7 A structured loop

returning right back to the question. In Figure A-1, if the path coming out of C returned right to B, there would be no problem; it would be a simple, structured loop. However, as it is, Question A must be repeated. The spaghetti technique says if things are tangled up, start repeating them. So repeat an A decision after C, as Figure A-6 shows.

In the original flowchart segment in Figure A-1, when A is Yes, Question B always follows. So, in Figure A-8, after A is Yes, B is Yes, Step C executes, and A is asked again; when A is Yes, B repeats. In the original, when B is Yes, C executes, so in Figure A-8, on the right side of B, C repeats. After C, A occurs. On the right side of A, B occurs. On the right side of B, C occurs. After C, A should occur again, and so on. Soon you should realize that, in order to follow the steps in the same order as in the original flowchart segment, you will repeat these same steps forever. See Figure A-8.

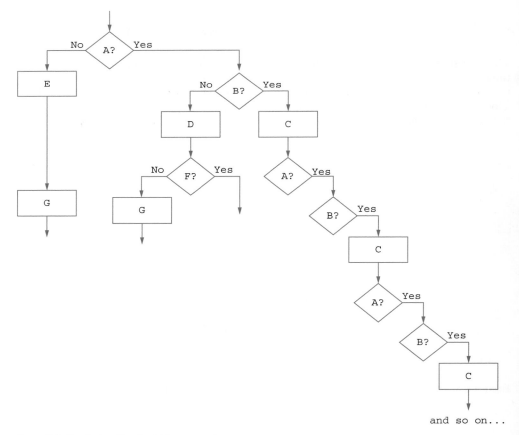

and so on...

Figure A-8 Structuring, Step 6, which never ends

If you continue with Figure A-8, you will never be able to end; every C is always followed by another A, B, and C. Sometimes, in order to make a program segment structured, you have to add an extra flag variable to get out of an infinite mess. A flag is a variable that you set to indicate a true or false state. Typically, a variable is called a flag when its only purpose is to tell you whether some event has occurred. You can create a flag variable named shouldRepeat and set its value to "Yes" or "No", depending on whether it is appropriate to repeat Decision A. When A is No, the shouldRepeat flag should be set to "No" because, in this situation, you never want to repeat Question A again. See Figure A-9.

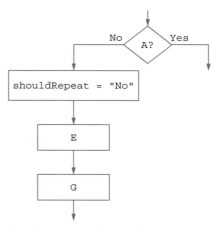

Figure A-9 Adding a flag to the flowchart

Similarly, after A is Yes, but when B is No, you never want to repeat Question A again. Figure A-10 shows that you set shouldRepeat to "No" when the answer to B is No. Then you continue with D and the F decision that executes G when F is No.

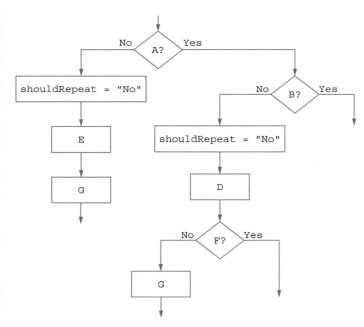

Figure A-10 Adding a flag to a second path in the flowchart

However, in the original flowchart segment in Figure A-1, when the B decision result is Yes, you *do* want to repeat A. So when B is Yes, perform the process for C and set the `shouldRepeat` flag equal to "Yes", as shown in Figure A-11.

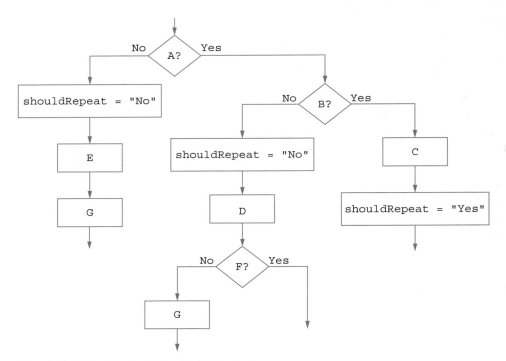

Figure A-11 Adding a flag to a third path in the flowchart

Now all paths of the flowchart can join together at the bottom with one final question: Is `shouldRepeat` equal to "Yes"? If it is not, exit; but if it is, extend the flowline to go back to repeat Question A. See Figure A-12. Take a moment to verify that the steps that would execute following Figure A-12 are the same steps that would execute following Figure A-1.

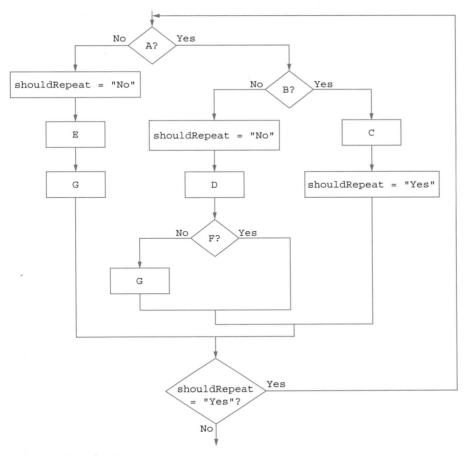

Figure A-12 Tying up the loose ends

> **NOTE** Figure A-12 contains three nested selection structures. In this figure, notice how the F decision begins a complete selection structure whose Yes and No paths join together when the structure ends. This F selection structure is within one path of the B decision structure; the B decision begins a complete selection structure, the Yes and No paths of which join together at the bottom. Likewise, the B selection structure resides entirely within one path of the A selection structure.

» When A is No, E and G always execute.
» When A is Yes and B is No, D and Decision F always execute.
» When A is Yes and B is Yes, C always executes and A repeats.

The flowchart segment in Figure A-12 performs identically to the original spaghetti version in Figure A-1. However, is this new flowchart segment structured? There are so many steps in the diagram, it is hard to tell. You may be able to see the structure more clearly if you create a method named aThroughG(). If you create the method shown in Figure A-13, then the original flowchart segment can be drawn as in Figure A-14.

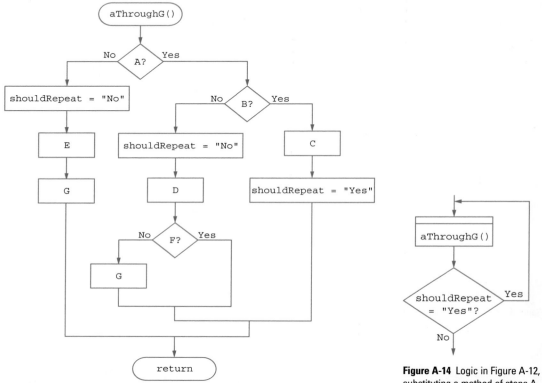

Figure A-13 The aThroughG() method

Figure A-14 Logic in Figure A-12, substituting a method of steps A through G

Now you can see that the completed flow-chart segment in Figure A-14 is a do-until loop. If you prefer to use a while loop, you can redraw Figure A-14 to perform a sequence followed by a while loop, as shown in Figure A-15.

It has taken some effort, but any logical problem can be made to conform to structured rules. It may take extra steps, including repeating specific steps and using some flag variables, but every logical problem can be solved using the three structures: sequence, selection, and loop.

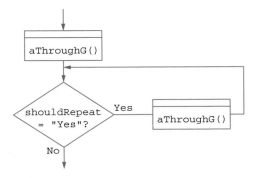

Figure A-15 Logic in Figure A-14, substituting a sequence and a while loop for the do-until loop

APPENDIX B

UNDERSTANDING NUMBERING SYSTEMS AND COMPUTER CODES

The numbering system with which you are most familiar is the decimal system—the system based on ten digits, 0 through 9. When you use the decimal system, there are no other symbols available; if you want to express a value larger than 9, you must resort to using multiple digits from the same pool of ten, placing them in columns.

When you use the decimal system, you analyze a multicolumn number by mentally assigning place values to each column. The value of the rightmost column is 1, the value of the next column to the left is 10, the next column is 100, and so on, multiplying the column value by 10 as you move to the left. There is no limit to the number of columns you can use; you simply keep adding columns to the left as you need to express higher values. For example, Figure B-1 shows how the value 305 is represented in the decimal system. You simply sum the value of the digit in each column after it has been multiplied by the value of its column.

Column value:	100	10	1
Number:	3	0	5
Evaluation:	3*100	+0*10	+5*1

Figure B-1 Representing 305 in the decimal system

The **binary numbering system** works in the same way as the decimal numbering system, except that it uses only two digits, 0 and 1. When you use the binary system and you want to express a value greater than 1, you must resort to using multiple columns, because no single symbol is available that represents any value other than 0 or 1. However, instead of each new column to the left being 10 times greater than the previous column, each new column in the binary system is only two times the value of the previous column. For example,

443

Figure B-2 shows how the number 9 is represented in the binary system, and Figure B-3 shows how the value 305 is represented. Notice that in both figures that show binary numbers, as well as in the decimal system, it is perfectly acceptable—and often necessary—to write a number containing 0 as some of the digits. As with the decimal system, there is no limit to the number of columns you can use in the binary system—you use as many as it takes to express a value.

Column value:	8	4	2	1
Number:	1	0	0	1

```
Conversion to decimal:     1*8  = 8
                          +0*4  = 0
                          +0*2  = 0
                          +1*1  = 1
                      Total:      9
```

Figure B-2 Representing 9 in the binary system

>> **NOTE**
Mathematicians call decimal numbers **base 10 numbers** and binary numbers **base 2 numbers**.

Column value:	256	128	64	32	16	8	4	2	1
Number:	1	0	0	1	1	0	0	0	1

```
Conversion to decimal:     1*256  = 256
                          +0*128  =   0
                          +0* 64  =   0
                          +1* 32  =  32
                          +1* 16  =  16
                          +0*  8  =   0
                          +0*  4  =   0
                          +0*  2  =   0
                          +1*  1  =   1

              Total:                305
```

Figure B-3 Representing 305 in the binary system

Every computer stores every piece of data it ever uses as a set of 0s and 1s. Each 0 or 1 is known as a **bit**, which is short for **bi**nary dig**it**. Every computer uses 0s and 1s because all values in a computer are stored as electronic signals that are either on or off. This two-state system is most easily represented using just two digits.

Every computer uses a set of binary digits to represent every character it can store. If computers used only one binary digit to represent characters, then only two different characters could be represented, because the single bit could be only 0 or 1. If computers used only two digits, then only four characters could be represented—one that used each of the four codes 00, 01, 10, and 11, which in decimal values are 0, 1, 2, and 3, respectively. Many computers use sets of eight binary digits to represent each character they store, because using eight binary digits provides 256 different combinations. One combination can represent an "A", another a "B", and still others "a" and "b", and so on. Two hundred fifty-six combinations are enough so that each capital letter, small letter, digit, and punctuation mark used in English has its own code; even a space has a code. For example, in some computers 01000001 represents the character "A". The

>> **NOTE**
A set of eight bits is called a **byte**. Half a byte, or four bits, is a **nibble**.

binary number 01000001 has a decimal value of 65, but this numeric value is not important to ordinary computer users; it is simply a code that stands for "A". The code that uses 01000001 to mean "A" is the **American Standard Code for Information Interchange**, or **ASCII**.

The ASCII code is not the only computer code; it is just a typical one, and it is the one used in most personal computers. The Extended Binary Coded Decimal Interchange Code, or **EBCDIC**, is an eight-bit code that is used in IBM mainframe computers. In these computers, the principle is the same—every character is stored as a series of binary digits. The only difference is that the actual values used are different. For example, in EBCDIC, an "A" is 11000001, or 193.

Another code used by languages such as Java and C# is **Unicode**; with this code, 16 bits are used to represent each character. The character "A" in Unicode has the same decimal value as the ASCII "A" (65), but it is stored as 0000000001000001. Using 16 bits provides many more possible combinations than using only eight—65,536 to be exact. With Unicode, not only are there enough available codes for all English letters and digits, there are plenty for characters from many international alphabets.

Ordinary computer users seldom think about the numeric codes behind the letters, numbers, and punctuation marks they enter from their keyboards or see displayed on a monitor. However, they see the consequence of the values behind letters when they see data sorted in alphabetical order. When you sort a list of names, "Andrea" comes before "Brian" and "Caroline" comes after "Brian", because the numeric code for "A" is lower than that for "B" and the numeric code for "C" is higher than that for "B", no matter whether you use ASCII, EBCDIC, or Unicode.

Table B-1 shows the decimal and binary values behind the most commonly used characters in the ASCII character set—the letters, numbers, and punctuation marks you can enter from your keyboard using a single key press.

> **NOTE**
> Each binary number in Table B-1 is shown containing two sets of four digits; this convention makes the long eight-digit numbers easier to read.

> **NOTE** Most of the values not included in Table B-1 have a purpose, even though they do not represent common printed characters. For example, the decimal value 7 represents a bell—a dinging sound your computer can make, often used to notify you of an error or some other unusual condition.

Decimal Number	Binary Number	ASCII Character
32	0010 0000	Space
33	0010 0001	! Exclamation point
34	0010 0010	" Quotation mark, or double quote
35	0010 0011	# Number sign, also called an octothorpe or a pound sign
36	0010 0100	$ Dollar sign
37	0010 0101	% Percent
38	0010 0110	& Ampersand
39	0010 0111	' Apostrophe, single quote
40	0010 1000	(Left parenthesis
41	0010 1001	) Right parenthesis
42	0010 1010	* Asterisk

Table B-1 Decimal and binary values for common ASCII characters (*continued*) ▶

Decimal Number	Binary Number	ASCII Character
43	0010 1011	+ Plus sign
44	0010 1100	, Comma
45	0010 1101	- Hyphen or minus sign
46	0010 1110	. Period or decimal point
47	0010 1111	/ Slash or front slash
48	0011 0000	0
49	0011 0001	1
50	0011 0010	2
51	0011 0011	3
52	0011 0100	4
53	0011 0101	5
54	0011 0110	6
55	0011 0111	7
56	0011 1000	8
57	0011 1001	9
58	0011 1010	: Colon
59	0011 1011	; Semicolon
60	0011 1100	< Less-than sign
61	0011 1101	= Equal sign
62	0011 1110	> Greater-than sign
63	0011 1111	? Question mark
64	0100 0000	@ At sign
65	0100 0001	A
66	0100 0010	B
67	0100 0011	C
68	0100 0100	D
69	0100 0101	E
70	0100 0110	F
71	0100 0111	G
72	0100 1000	H
73	0100 1001	I
74	0100 1010	J
75	0100 1011	K
76	0100 1100	L

Table B-1 Decimal and binary values for common ASCII characters (*continued*) ▶

Decimal Number	Binary Number	ASCII Character
77	0100 1101	M
78	0100 1110	N
79	0100 1111	O
80	0101 0000	P
81	0101 0001	Q
82	0101 0010	R
83	0101 0011	S
84	0101 0100	T
85	0101 0101	U
86	0101 0110	V
87	0101 0111	W
88	0101 1000	X
89	0101 1001	Y
90	0101 1010	Z
91	0101 1011	[Opening or left bracket
92	0101 1100	\ Backslash
93	0101 1101	] Closing or right bracket
94	0101 1110	^ Caret
95	0101 1111	_ Underline or underscore
96	0110 0000	` Grave accent
97	0110 0001	a
98	0110 0010	b
99	0110 0011	c
100	0110 0100	d
101	0110 0101	e
102	0110 0110	f
103	0110 0111	g
104	0110 1000	h
105	0110 1001	i
106	0110 1010	j
107	0110 1011	k
108	0110 1100	l
109	0110 1101	m
110	0110 1110	n

Table B-1 Decimal and binary values for common ASCII characters (*continued*) ▶

Decimal Number	Binary Number	ASCII Character
111	0110 1111	o
112	0111 0000	p
113	0111 0001	q
114	0111 0010	r
115	0111 0011	s
116	0111 0100	t
117	0111 0101	u
118	0111 0110	v
119	0111 0111	w
120	0111 1000	x
121	0111 1001	y
122	0111 1010	z
123	0111 1011	{ Opening or left brace
124	0111 1100	| Vertical line or pipe
125	0111 1101	} Closing or right brace
126	0111 1110	~ Tilde

Table B-1 Decimal and binary values for common ASCII characters

KEY TERMS

The **binary numbering system** uses only two digits, 0 and 1. Each new column is two times the value of the previous column.

Base 10 numbers are decimal numbers.

Base 2 numbers are binary numbers.

A **bit** is a **bi**nary digi**t**.

The **American Standard Code for Information Interchange**, or **ASCII**, is an eight-bit binary code used to represent characters in many computer systems.

A **byte** is a set of eight bits.

A **nibble** is half a byte, or four bits.

EBCDIC is an eight-bit computer code used to represent characters in some computer systems.

Unicode is a 16-bit code used to represent characters in some computer systems.

APPENDIX C

USING A LARGE DECISION TABLE

In Chapter 3, you learned to use a simple decision table, but real-life problems often require many decisions. A complicated decision process is represented by the instructions in the memo in Figure C-1, which outlines a year-end bonus plan. Appendix C will walk you through the process of solving this problem by using a large decision table.

```
To: Programming staff
From: The boss
I need a report listing every employee and the
bonus I plan to give him or her. Everybody gets
at least $100. All the employees in Department 2
get $200, unless they have more than 5 dependents.
Anybody with more than 5 dependents gets $1000
unless they're in Department 2. Nobody with an ID
number greater than 800 gets more than $100 even
if they're in Department 2 or have more than 5
dependents.
P.S. I need this by 5 o'clock.
```

Figure C-1 Memo of the outlined bonus plan

Drawing the flowchart or writing the pseudocode for this task may seem daunting. You can use a decision table to help you manage all the decisions, and you can begin to create one by listing all the possible decisions you need to make to determine an employee's bonus. They are:

» `empDept = 2?`

» `empDepend > 5?`

» `empIdNum > 800?`

Next, determine how many possible Boolean value combinations exist for the conditions. In this case, there are eight possible combinations, shown in Figure C-2. An employee can be in Department 2, have over five dependents, and have an ID number greater than 800. Another employee can be in Department 2, have over five dependents, but have an ID number that is 800 or less. Because each condition has two outcomes and there are three conditions, there are 2 * 2 * 2, or eight possibilities. Four conditions would produce 16 possible outcome combinations, five would produce 32, and so on.

Condition	Outcome							
empDept = 2	T	T	T	T	F	F	F	F
empDepend > 5	T	T	F	F	T	T	F	F
empIdNum > 800	T	F	T	F	T	F	T	F

Figure C-2 Possible outcomes of bonus conditions

> **» NOTE** In Figure C-2, notice how the pattern of Ts and Fs varies in each row. The bottom row contains one T and F, repeating four times, the second row contains two of each, repeating twice, and the top row contains four of each without repeating. If a fourth decision was required, you would place an identical grid of Ts and Fs to the right of this one, then add a new top row containing eight Ts (covering all eight columns you see currently) followed by eight Fs (covering the new copy of the grid to the right).

Next, list the possible outcome values for the bonus amounts. If you declare a numeric variable named `bonus` by placing the statement `num bonus` in your list of variables at the beginning of the program, then the possible outcomes can be expressed as:

» `bonus = 100`

» `bonus = 200`

» `bonus = 1000`

Finally, choose one required outcome for each possible combination of conditions. For example, the first possible outcome is a $100 bonus. As Figure C-3 shows, you place Xs in the bonus = 100 row each time empIdNum > 800 is true, no matter what other conditions exist, because the memo from the boss said, "Nobody with an ID number greater than 800 gets more than $100, even if they're in Department 2 or have more than 5 dependents."

Condition	Outcome							
empDept = 2	T	T	T	T	F	F	F	F
empDepend > 5	T	T	F	F	T	T	F	F
empIdNum > 800	T	F	T	F	T	F	T	F
bonus = 100	X		X		X		X	
bonus = 200								
bonus = 1000								

Figure C-3 Decision table for bonuses, part 1

Next, place an X in the bonus = 1000 row under all remaining columns (that is, those without a selected outcome) in which empDepend > 5 is true unless the empDept = 2 condition is true, because the memo stated, "Anybody with more than 5 dependents gets $1000 unless they're in Department 2." The first four columns of the decision table do not qualify, because the empDept value is 2; only the sixth column in Figure C-4 meets the criteria for the $1000 bonus.

Condition	Outcome							
empDept = 2	T	T	T	T	F	F	F	F
empDepend > 5	T	T	F	F	T	T	F	F
empIdNum > 800	T	F	T	F	T	F	T	F
bonus = 100	X		X		X		X	
bonus = 200								
bonus = 1000						X		

Figure C-4 Decision table for bonuses, part 2

Place Xs in the bonus = 200 row for any remaining columns in which empDept = 2 is true and empDepend > 5 is false, because "All the employees in Department 2 get $200, unless they have more than 5 dependents." Column 4 in Figure C-5 satisfies these criteria.

Condition	Outcome							
empDept = 2	T	T	T	T	F	F	F	F
empDepend > 5	T	T	F	F	T	T	F	F
empIdNum > 800	T	F	T	F	T	F	T	F
bonus = 100	X		X		X		X	
bonus = 200				X				
bonus = 1000						X		

Figure C-5 Decision table for bonuses, part 3

Finally, fill any unmarked columns with an X in the bonus = 100 row because, according to the memo, "Everybody gets at least $100." The only columns remaining are the second column and the last column on the right. See Figure C-6.

Condition	Outcome							
empDept = 2	T	T	T	T	F	F	F	F
empDepend > 5	T	T	F	F	T	T	F	F
empIdNum > 800	T	F	T	F	T	F	T	F
bonus = 100	X	X	X		X		X	X
bonus = 200				X				
bonus = 1000						X		

Figure C-6 Decision table for bonuses, part 4

The decision table is complete. When you count the Xs, you will find there are eight possible outcomes. Take a moment and confirm that each bonus is the appropriate value based on the specifications in the original memo from the boss. Now you can start to plan the logic. If you choose to use a flowchart, you start by drawing the path to the first outcome, which occurs when empDept = 2, empDepend > 5, and empIdNum > 800 are all true, and which corresponds to the first column in the decision table. See Figure C-7.

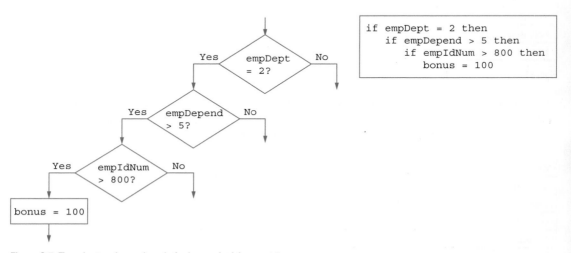

Figure C-7 Flowchart and pseudocode for bonus decision, part 1

To continue creating the diagram started in Figure C-7, add the "false" outcome to the `empIdNum > 800` decision; this corresponds to the second column in the decision table. When an employee's department is 2 and the employee has more than five dependents and an ID number not greater than 800, the employee's bonus should be $100. See Figure C-8.

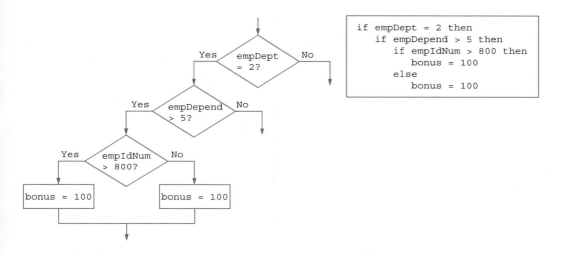

```
if empDept = 2 then
    if empDepend > 5 then
        if empIdNum > 800 then
            bonus = 100
        else
            bonus = 100
```

Figure C-8 Flowchart and pseudocode for bonus decision, part 2

Continue the diagram in Figure C-8 by adding the "false" outcome when the `empDepend > 5` decision is No and the `empIdNum > 800` decision is Yes, which is represented by the third column in the decision table. In this case, the bonus is again $100. See Figure C-9.

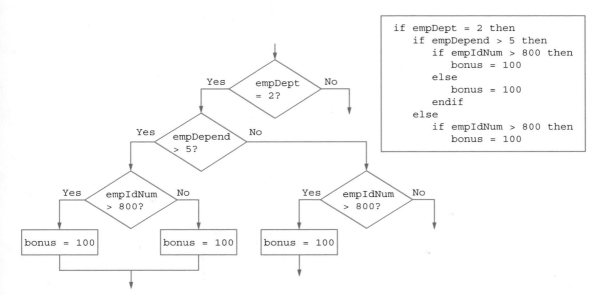

```
if empDept = 2 then
    if empDepend > 5 then
        if empIdNum > 800 then
            bonus = 100
        else
            bonus = 100
        endif
    else
        if empIdNum > 800 then
            bonus = 100
```

Figure C-9 Flowchart and pseudocode for bonus decision, part 3

Continue adding decisions until you have drawn all eight possible outcomes, as shown in Figure C-10.

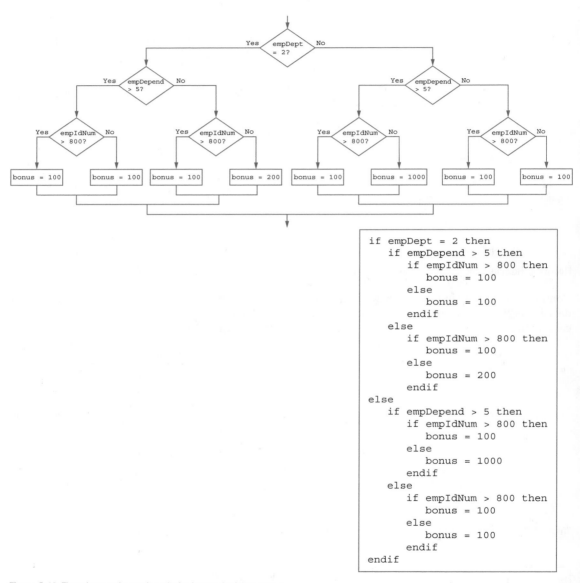

```
if empDept = 2 then
    if empDepend > 5 then
        if empIdNum > 800 then
            bonus = 100
        else
            bonus = 100
        endif
    else
        if empIdNum > 800 then
            bonus = 100
        else
            bonus = 200
        endif
else
    if empDepend > 5 then
        if empIdNum > 800 then
            bonus = 100
        else
            bonus = 1000
        endif
    else
        if empIdNum > 800 then
            bonus = 100
        else
            bonus = 100
        endif
    endif
endif
```

Figure C-10 Flowchart and pseudocode for bonus decision, part 4

The logic shown in Figure C-10 correctly assigns a bonus to any employee, no matter what combination of characteristics the employee's record holds. However, you can eliminate many of the decisions shown in Figure C-10; you can eliminate any decision that does not make any difference. For example, if you look at the far left side of Figure C-10, you see that when empDept is 2 and empDepend is greater than 5, the outcome of empIdNum > 800 does not matter; the bonus value is 100 either way. You might as well eliminate the selection. Similarly, on the far right, the question empIdNum > 800 makes no difference. Finally, many programmers prefer the True, or Yes, side of a flowchart decision always to appear on the right side. The result is Figure C-11.

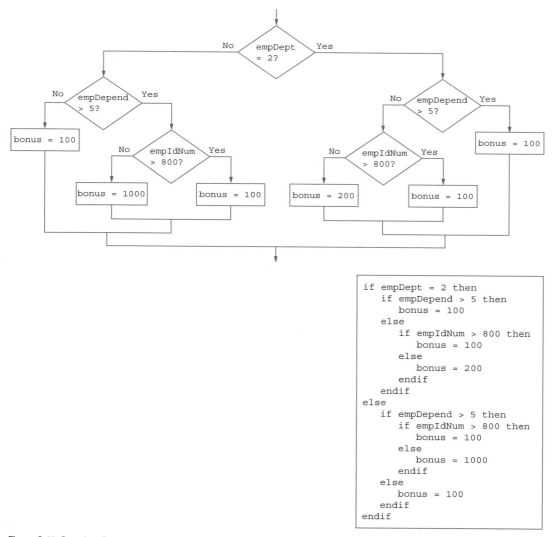

```
if empDept = 2 then
    if empDepend > 5 then
        bonus = 100
    else
        if empIdNum > 800 then
            bonus = 100
        else
            bonus = 200
        endif
    endif
else
    if empDepend > 5 then
        if empIdNum > 800 then
            bonus = 100
        else
            bonus = 1000
        endif
    else
        bonus = 100
    endif
endif
```

Figure C-11 Complete flowchart and pseudocode for bonus decision

APPENDIX D

SOFTWARE TESTING AND DATA VALIDATION

Computer programming is an error-prone task. When you start to write computer programs, it is likely that even your first, small programs that require no more than 10 or 20 statements will contain some small error. Fortunately, if your mistakes are simply typographical errors, such as a misspelled programming language keyword, the language translator will identify the errors and list them for you. For example, Figure D-1 shows a program written in C# that contains two mistakes, and Figure D-2 shows an attempt to compile the program.

» DON'T DO IT
In C#, the `WriteLine` method begins with an uppercase *W*.

```
public class Hello
{
    public static void Main()
    {
        System.Console.Out.writeLine("Hello!")
    }
}
```

» DON'T DO IT
In C#, every statement must end with a semicolon.

Figure D-1 A C# program that contains two mistakes

Figure D-2 Attempt to compile the program in Figure D-1

After some copyright information, Figure D-2 shows an error message explaining that the program named Hello.cs contains a mistake in line 5 (of the seven lines in the file), position 45 (counting from left to right). The error number is CS1002, which you could look up in the language documentation if necessary. The brief explanation of the error is "; expected". A C# programmer would immediately realize that the semicolon was missing at the end of line 5 of the program. The programmer would insert the semicolon, save the program, and attempt to compile it again. Figure D-3 shows the results.

```
Command Prompt                                               _ □ ×

C:\Logic5e\Appendices>csc Hello.cs
Microsoft (R) Visual C# 2005 Compiler version 8.00.50727.42
for Microsoft (R) Windows (R) 2005 Framework version 2.0.50727
Copyright (C) Microsoft Corporation 2001-2005. All rights reserved.

Hello.cs(5,26): error CS0117: 'System.IO.TextWriter' does not contain a
        definition for 'writeLine'

C:\Logic5e\Appendices>
```

Figure D-3 Attempt to recompile the program in Figure D-1 after adding a semicolon to the end of the fifth line

The error message in Figure D-3 states that the compiler does not recognize `'writeLine'`. If you were a C# programmer, you would immediately recognize that the correct method name begins with an uppercase letter, and you would fix the problem. At your next attempt to compile the program, there would be no error messages.

Although *WriteLine* was typed incorrectly when the program was first compiled in Figure D-2, that error was masked by the more serious error of omitting the end-of-statement semicolon. When you write computer programs, you will often think you have fixed all the mistakes, only to see new errors uncovered that were not apparent at first.

After all the syntax errors in a program are fixed, you do not necessarily have a working program. As a very simple example, if the C# program in Figure D-1 was supposed to print "Goodbye" instead of "Hello", then users will be dissatisfied or perhaps confused. In this case, although you have included no syntax errors in your program, you have committed a logical error. To fix all the logical errors in a program, you have two additional responsibilities:

» Debugging
» Software testing

Debugging and software testing are closely related terms, and many years ago they actually meant the same thing. However, in modern programming terminology, debugging is performed by the programmer(s) who wrote the application and **software testing** is performed by users (or test users) who do not know or care what the program code includes—they care only that the program performs as expected.

> **» NOTE** The testing that programmers perform is called **white box testing**, because programmers can "see inside the box" to understand how the code works. The testing that users perform is **black box testing**, because they do not know how the program works; they simply test whether the program *does* work.

Both debugging and testing are important phases of software development. Although you might be annoyed if a program prints "Hellloo" when you wanted it to print "Hello", computers and software are used in much more critical applications such as navigating airplanes and monitoring patients' vital signs during surgery. In these applications, the result of an error in the software could literally be a matter of life or death.

As a simple example, suppose you write a program in which the user should enter a value no greater than 5. You might write pseudocode for this part of the program, as shown in Figure D-4. This program contains a loop that continuously accepts a user's number until it does not exceed 5.

```
numeric inputValue
numeric MAX = 5
print "Enter a number no bigger than ", MAX
get inputValue
while inputValue > MAX
    print "Number too large - please reenter "
    get inputValue
endwhile
```

Figure D-4 Pseudocode that forces a user to reenter a number if it is more than MAX

A programmer who understands the code might test the program by executing it several times. A good testing process would be to run the program at least three times, entering a number under 5 (such as 4), a number over 5 (such as 7), and 5. Testing at the exact limit of the MAX value is important because the programmer might have inadvertently used >= in the comparison that controls the loop instead of =. The programmer might conclude that the code works correctly and add it to a complete application.

What the programmer might not foresee is that a user might enter a negative value, which might not be acceptable according to the program specifications. Even worse, the user might enter a non-numeric value, which definitely is not allowed as the program is written. A good software tester, however, would enter all kinds of values, including letters, punctuation marks, function key presses, and so on, because a user might inadvertently take any of those actions.

> **NOTE** Software testing can be **alpha testing**, which is testing by potential users at the developers' site. Beta testing occurs after alpha testing. With **beta testing**, software is tested by a limited group of trial customers, or sometimes by the public in general.

Because user data entry is such an error-prone activity, programmers can eliminate a lot of potential trouble by including several standard tests in their code. Many of these techniques are discussed in the next section. However, software testing involves many additional issues such as:

» Is the software easy to understand and use?
» Is there a way to back up or escape? Are there other ways to recover from user errors?
» Are the results consistent with what was expected?

Software testing is not a mature science. It is an art, because each newly written application might present new problems never before encountered. Software testing can be expensive, but not testing is even more expensive, especially in applications that involve high-priced equipment or human lives. Most programmers agree we can never be sure that a piece of software is completely correct; we simply must try to come as close as possible.

VALIDATING INPUT

Menu programs rely on a user's input to select one of several paths of action. Other types of programs also require a user to enter data. Unfortunately, you cannot count on users to enter valid data, whether they are using a menu or supplying information to a program. Users will make incorrect choices because they do not understand the valid choices, or simply because they make typographical errors. Therefore, the programs you write will be improved if you employ **defensive programming**, which means trying to prepare for all possible errors before they occur. Incorrect user entries are by far the most common source of computer errors.

>> NOTE
Validating input is also called *editing* data.

You can circumvent potential problems caused by invalid data entries by validating the user's input. **Validating input** involves checking the user's responses to ensure they fall within acceptable bounds. Validating input does not eliminate all program errors. For example, if a user can choose option *1* or option *2* from a menu, validating the input means you check to make sure the user response is *1* or *2*. If the user enters a *3*, you can issue an error message. However, if the user enters a *2* when she really wants a *1*, there is no way you can validate the response. Similarly, if a user must enter his birth date, you can validate that the month falls between 1 and 12; you usually cannot verify that the user has typed his true birth date.

>> NOTE
Programmers employ the acronym GIGO for "garbage in, garbage out." It means that if your input is incorrect, your output is worthless.

The correct action to take when you find invalid data depends on the application. Within an interactive program, you might require the user to reenter the data. If your program uses a data file, you might print a message so someone can correct the invalid data. Alternatively, you can force the invalid data to a default value. **Forcing** a field to a value means you override incorrect data by setting the field to a specific value. For example, you might decide that if a month value does not fall between 1 and 12, you will force the field to 0 or 99. This indicates to users of the data that no valid value exists.

The data you use within computer programs is varied. It stands to reason that validating data requires a variety of methods. Some of the techniques you want to master include validating:

- Data type
- Data range
- Reasonableness and consistency of data
- Presence of data

VALIDATING A DATA TYPE

Some programming languages allow you to check data items to make sure they are the correct data type. Although this technique varies from language to language, you can often make a statement like the one shown in Figure D-5. In this program segment, `isNumeric()` represents a method call; it is used to check whether the entered employee `salary` falls within the

>> NOTE
Some languages require you to check data against the actual machine codes used to store the data, to determine if the data is the appropriate type.

```
numeric salary
print "Enter salary "
get salary
while not isNumeric(salary)
   print "Invalid entry - try again "
   get salary
endwhile
```

Figure D-5 Method for checking data for correct type

category of numeric data. A method such as `isNumeric()` is most often provided with the language translator you use to write your programs. Such a method operates as a black box; you can use its results without understanding its internal statements.

Besides allowing you to check whether a value is numeric, some languages contain methods with names like the following:

» `isChar()`—Is the value a character data type?

» `isWhitespace()`—Is the value a nonprinting character such as a space, a tab, or the Enter key?

» `isUpper()`—Is the value a capital letter?

» `isLower()`—Is the value a lowercase letter?

In many languages, you accept all user data as a string of characters, and then use built-in methods to attempt to convert the characters to the correct data type for your application. When the conversion methods succeed, you have useful data; when the conversion methods fail because the user has entered the wrong data type, you can take appropriate action, such as issuing an error message, reprompting the user, or forcing the data to a default value.

VALIDATING A DATA RANGE

Sometimes, a user response or other data must fall within a range of values. For example, when a user enters a month, you typically require it to fall between 1 and 12, inclusive.

» **NOTE**
Chapter 4 describes range-checking in detail.

VALIDATING REASONABLENESS AND CONSISTENCY OF DATA

Data items can be the correct type and within range, but still be incorrect. You have experienced this phenomenon yourself if anyone has ever misspelled your name or overbilled you. The data might have been the correct type—that is, alphabetic letters were used in your name—but the name itself was incorrect. Many data items cannot be checked for reasonableness; it is just as reasonable that your name is Catherine as it is that your name is Katherine or Kathryn.

However, there are many data items that you can check for reasonableness. If you make a purchase on May 3, 2010, then the payment cannot possibly be due prior to that date. Perhaps within your organization, if you work in Department 12, you cannot possibly make more than $20.00 per hour. If your zip code is 90201, your state of residence cannot be New York. If your pet's breed is stored as "Great Dane," then its species cannot be "bird." Each of these examples involves comparing two data fields for reasonableness and consistency. You should consider making as many such comparisons as possible when writing your own programs.

Frequently, testing for reasonableness and consistency involves using additional data files. For example, to check that a user has entered a valid county of residence for a state, you might use a file that contains every county name in every state in the United States, and check the user's county against those listed in the file.

VALIDATING PRESENCE OF DATA

Sometimes, data is missing from a file, either for a reason or by accident. A job applicant might fail to submit an entry for the `salaryAtPreviousJob` field, or a client might have no entry for the `emailAddress` field. A data-entry clerk might accidentally skip a field when typing records. Many programming languages allow you to check for missing data and take appropriate action with a statement similar to `if emailAddress is blank perform noEmailModule()`. You can place any instructions you like within `noEmailModule()`, including forcing the field to a default value or issuing an error message.

Good defensive programs try to foresee all possible inconsistencies and errors. The more accurate your data is, the more useful it will be when produced as output from your programs.

KEY TERMS

Software testing is testing performed by users (or test users) who do not know or care what the program code includes, but care only that the program performs as expected.

White box testing is the type of testing programmers perform; they can "see inside the box" to understand how the code works.

Black box testing is the type of testing users perform. They do not know how the program works; they simply test whether the program does work.

Alpha testing is software testing by potential users at the developers' site.

Beta testing is software testing by a limited group of trial customers, or sometimes by the public in general.

Defensive programming is a technique in which the programmer tries to prepare for all possible errors before they occur.

Validating input involves checking the user's responses to ensure they fall within acceptable bounds.

Forcing a field to a value means you override incorrect data by setting the field to a specific value.

GLOSSARY

A

abstract class—a class from which you cannot create any concrete objects, but from which you can inherit objects.

abstract data type (ADT)—a programmer-defined type. Also see *user-defined type*.

abstraction—the programming feature that allows you to use a method name to encapsulate a series of statements.

access modifier—the adjective that defines the type of access outside classes will have to an attribute or method. Also see *access specifier*.

access specifier—the adjective that defines the type of access outside classes will have to an attribute or method. Also see *access modifier*.

accessibility—describes issues that make programs easier to use for people with physical limitations.

accessor methods—methods that get values from class fields. Contrast with *mutator methods*.

accumulator—a variable that you use to gather or accumulate values.

activity diagram—a UML diagram that shows the flow of actions of a system, including branches that occur when decisions affect the outcome.

actual parameters—the arguments in a method call.

aggregation—describes an association in which one or more classes make up the parts of a larger whole class.

algorithm—a list of instructions or sequence of steps necessary to accomplish a task or solve a problem.

alpha testing—software testing by potential users at the developers' site.

ambiguous—describes methods for which the compiler cannot determine which version to use.

American Standard Code for Information Interchange (ASCII)—an 8-bit binary code used to represent characters in many computer systems.

ancestors—the entire list of parent classes from which a subclass is derived.

AND decision—a decision in which two conditions must both be true for an action to take place.

AND operator—a symbol you use to combine decisions so that two or more conditions must be true for an action to occur. Also see *conditional AND operator*.

application—a program that accomplishes some task.

application software—the set of all programs you apply to a task. Contrast with *system software*.

arguments—the data items sent to methods. Contrast with *parameters*.

array—a series or list of variables in computer memory, all of which have the same name and data type but are differentiated with special numbers called subscripts.

Array class—a class provided with many OOP languages that contains useful methods for manipulating arrays.

ascending order—an arrangement from lowest to highest value. Contrast with *descending order*.

assignment operator—the equal sign; it always requires the name of a memory location on its left side.

assignment statement—a program statement that stores the result of any value or calculation performed on its right side to the named location on its left side.

association relationship—describes the connection or link between objects in a UML diagram.

attributes of an object—the features an object "has"; an object's data.

B

base 2 numbers—binary numbers, or numbers formed from the digits 0 and 1 in which each new column is two times the value of the previous column. Also see *binary numbering system*.

base 10 numbers—decimal numbers, or numbers formed from the digits 0 through 9 in which each new column is 10 times the value of the previous column.

base class—a class that is used as a basis for inheritance. Also see *parent class* and *superclass*.

behaviors of an object—the things an object "does"; an object's methods.

beta testing—software testing by a limited group of trial customers, or sometimes by the public in general.

binary decision—a decision with two possible outcomes.

binary numbering system—a number system that uses only two digits, 0 and 1, and in which each new column is two times the value of the previous column. Also see *base 2 numbers*.

bit—a unit of computer storage represented by a binary digit.

black box—a metaphor for hidden implementation details.

black box testing—the type of testing users perform; they do not know how the program works, they simply test whether the program does work.

block—a group of statements that execute as a single unit.

Boolean expression—an expression that represents only one of two states, usually expressed as true or false.

bubble sort—a sorting algorithm in which items in a list are compared with each other in pairs; when an item is out of order, it swaps values with the item below it. Also see *sinking sort*.

byte—a unit of computer storage that is a set of eight bits.

C

call—to execute a method from another method. Also see *invoke*.

call stack—a memory location where the computer stores the list of method locations to which the system must return.

called method—a method that is invoked by another method.

calling method—a method that invokes another method.

camel casing—the format for naming variables and other program components in which multiple-word variable names are run together, the initial letter is lowercase, and each new word within the variable name begins with an uppercase letter.

cardinality—refers to the arithmetic relationship between objects, or the number of objects in a set.

cascading `if` statement—a series of nested `if` statements.

case structure—a structure used when several possible values exist for a single variable you are testing, and each requires a different course of action.

`catch` block—in exception handling, a segment of code that can handle an exception that might be thrown by the `try` block that precedes it.

central processing unit (CPU)—the hardware component that processes data.

character constant—a single character enclosed in single quotation marks.

character variables—named memory locations that hold single character values.

child class—a derived class. Also see *extended class* and *subclass*.

class—a general category of objects.

class client—a program or class that instantiates objects of another prewritten class. Also see *class user*.

class definition—a set of program statements that tell you the characteristics of the class's objects and the methods that can be applied to its objects.

class diagram—a design tool that consists of a rectangle divided into three sections that show a class's name, data, and methods.

class header—the first line in a class definition; it contains the keyword `class` and an identifier for the class.

class level—describes variables and constants known to an entire class.

class method—a static method. Class methods are not instance methods and they do not receive a `this` reference. Contrast with *instance method*.

class user—a program or class that instantiates objects of another prewritten class. Also see *class client*.

coding—the process of writing statements in a programming language.

command prompt—the text-based interface that you can use to communicate with a computer's operating system.

communication diagram—a UML diagram that emphasizes the organization of objects that participate in a system.

comparison operators—the symbols that express Boolean comparisons, such as =, >, <, >=, <=, and <>. Also see *relational operators* and *relational comparison operators*.

compiler—translates a high-level language into machine language and tells you if you have used a programming language incorrectly. A compiler translates an entire program before executing it. Contrast with *interpreter*.

component diagram—a UML diagram that emphasizes the files, database tables, documents, and other components that a system's software uses.

composition—the act of using a class object as a field within another class. Also see *has-a relationship*.

compound condition—a requirement that multiple questions must be asked before determining an outcome.

conditional AND operator—a symbol you use to combine decisions so that two or more

conditions must be true for an action to occur. Also see *AND operator*.

conditional OR operator—a symbol you use to combine decisions when any one condition can be true for an action to occur. Also see *OR operator*.

connector—a UML diagram symbol used to connect diagrams that continue on a new page; it is represented by a small circle.

constant array—an array whose values are assigned permanently when you write the program code. Contrast with *variable array*.

constructor—an automatically called method that establishes an object.

container—a class of objects whose main purpose is to hold other elements—for example, a window.

conversion—the entire set of actions an organization must take to switch over to using a new program or set of programs.

counted loop—a loop for which the number of repetitions is a fixed value. Also see *definite loop*.

counter—any numeric variable you use to count the number of times an event has occurred.

D

data—facts that are input to a program.

data hiding—the concept that other classes should not alter an object's attributes—only the methods of an object's own class should have that privilege. Also see *information hiding*.

data modeling—the act of identifying all the objects you want to manipulate and how they relate to each other.

database—a group of related files stored using software that provides easy organization and retrieval.

dead code—program statements that can never execute under any circumstances. Also see *unreachable code*.

dead path—a logical path that can never be traveled.

decision structure—a structure in which you ask a question, and, depending on the answer, you take one of two courses of action. Then, no matter which path you follow, you continue with the next event. Also see *selection structure*.

decision symbol—a flowchart symbol that is shaped like a diamond and contains a question.

decision table—a problem-analysis tool that lists conditions, Boolean outcomes when those conditions are tested, and possible actions based on the outcomes.

decrementing—the act of decreasing a variable by a constant value, frequently 1. Contrast with *incrementing*.

default constructor—a constructor that requires no arguments.

default value—an automatically supplied value.

defensive programming—a technique in which the programmer tries to prepare for all possible errors before they occur.

definite loop—a loop for which the number of repetitions is a fixed value. Also see *counted loop*. Contrast with *indefinite loop*.

deployment diagram—a UML diagram that focuses on a system's hardware.

derived class—one that inherits from a base class. Also see *subclass*, *child class*, and *extended class*.

descending order—an arrangement from highest to lowest value. Contrast with *ascending order*.

destructor—an automatically called method that contains the actions that occur when an instance of a class is destroyed.

DOS prompt—the command line in the DOS operating system.

do-until loop—a posttest loop in which you ensure that a procedure executes at least once; then, as long as the answer to the controlling question is false, the loop continues to execute additional times.

do-while loop—a posttest loop in which you ensure that a procedure executes at least once; then, as long as the answer to the controlling question is true, the loop continues to execute additional times.

dual-alternative ifs—statements that define one action to be taken when the tested condition is true, and another action to be taken when it is false. Contrast with *single-alternative if*.

dummy value—a value that does not represent real data; often it is just a signal to stop processing. Also see *sentinel*.

dynamic arrays—arrays whose size (number of elements) can be altered. Also see *dynamically allocated*.

dynamically allocated—describes arrays whose size (number of elements) can be altered. Also see *dynamic arrays*.

E

early exit—the act of leaving a loop as soon as some criterion is met rather than letting the loop come to its original end after the maximum number of iterations.

EBCDIC—the Extended Binary Coded Decimal Interchange Code; an eight-bit computer code used to represent characters in some computer systems.

element—an individual component of an array that is differentiated from others by a subscript.

elided—describes the missing parts when system developers omit parts of UML diagrams for clarity.

else clause—part of a decision that holds the action or actions that execute only when the Boolean expression in the decision is false.

encapsulated—contained.

encapsulation—the feature of methods that provides for their instructions and data to be contained in the method.

eof—short for "end of file"; a marker that automatically acts as a sentinel.

event—an occurrence that generates a message sent to an object.

event-driven or **event-based**—describes GUI programs in which actions occur in response to user-initiated events such as clicking a mouse button.

exception—in object-oriented terminology, an unexpected or error condition that occurs while a program is running.

exception handling—an object-oriented technique for managing errors.

exception specification clause—a declaration of a method's possible `throw` types.

executed—describes a written and translated program that has been run.

extend variation—in a UML diagram, a use case variation that shows functions beyond those found in a base case.

extended class—one that inherits from a base class. Also see *derived class*, *subclass*, and *child class*.

external storage—permanent storage outside the main memory of the machine, on a device such as a floppy disk, hard disk, or magnetic tape. Contrast with *internal storage*.

F

facilitators—methods that perform tasks within a class; usually as opposed to get or set methods. Also see *help methods* and *work methods*.

field—a term used to describe data items or object attributes within a class.

finally block—a group of statements that execute at the end of a `try...catch` sequence.

flag—a variable that you set to indicate whether some event has occurred.

flat file—describes data files that are not part of a database.

floating-point—describes a numeric value that contains a decimal point.

flowchart—a pictorial representation of the logical steps it takes to solve a problem.

flowlines—the arrows in a flowchart that show the sequence of steps carried out.

for loop—a loop that contains a loop control variable that is automatically initialized, evaluated, and incremented.

for statement—a statement used to control definite loops. It contains a loop control variable that is automatically initialized, evaluated, and incremented.

forcing—the act of assigning a value to a field by overriding incorrect data and setting the field to a specific value.

formal parameters—the variables in a method declaration that accept values from the actual parameters.

fragile classes—classes that depend on field names from parent classes.

G

garbage value—an unknown value in an uninitialized variable.

generalization variation—in a UML diagram, a variation that you use when a use case is less specific than others, and you want to be able to substitute the more specific case for a general one.

get method—in a class, a method that returns a value from a data field. Contrast with *set method*.

global—describes a variable or constant that is known to an entire class. Contrast with *local*.

go-to-less—a style of programming written without "go to" statements; structured programs are written with such statements.

graphical user interface (**GUI**)—a system that allows users to interact with a program in a graphical environment.

H

handler body node—the UML diagram name for an exception-handling `catch` block.

hard copy—printed computer output. Contrast with *soft copy*.

hard-coded—describes values that are explicitly assigned.

hardware—the equipment of a computer system.

has-a relationship—describes the association between the whole and one of its parts; also the type of relationship that exists when using composition.

help methods—methods that perform tasks within a class; usually as opposed to get or set methods. Also see *work methods* and *facilitators*.

high-level programming languages—describes languages that are English-like. Contrast with *low-level machine language*.

I

icons—small pictures on the screen that the user can select with a mouse.

IDE—Integrated Development Environment; the visual development environment in some programming languages.

identifier—the name of a programming object—a class, method, or variable.

if clause—part of a decision that holds the action that results when a Boolean expression in the decision is true.

if-then—a single-alternative selection.

if-then-else—a selection structure.

implementation hiding—a principle of OO programming that describes the encapsulation of method details within a class.

implementing a method—the act of writing the statements that constitute a method.

implicit conversion—a transformation from one type to another that takes place automatically.

implicitly sized—describes an array that is automatically given a size based on a list of provided values.

in scope—describes the area in which a data item or method is usable. Compare with *visible*.

inaccessible—quality of a method that is hidden from and cannot be used by a method.

include variation—in a UML use case diagram, a variation that you use when a case can be part of multiple use cases.

incrementing—the act of adding a constant value to a variable, frequently 1. Contrast with *decrementing*.

indefinite loop—a loop for which you cannot predetermine the number of executions. Contrast with *definite loop*.

index—1. a number that indicates the position of an element item within an array. Also see *subscript*. 2. A construct used as an alternative to sorting large numbers of records; it is a list of key fields that are manipulated instead of altering the positions of much larger records.

infinite loop—a repeating flow of logic with no end.

information—data that has been processed and is ready for output.

information hiding—the concept that other classes should not alter an object's attributes—only the methods of an object's own class should have that privilege. Also see *data hiding*.

inheritance—the principle that you can apply your knowledge of a general category to more specific objects; the process of acquiring the traits of one's predecessors.

initialization loop—a loop structure that provides initial values for every element in any array.

initializing—the act of declaring a variable and providing an initial value.

inner loop—a loop contained within another loop. Contrast with *outer loop*. Also see *nested loops*.

input devices—hardware devices through which data enters a computer system. Common examples are keyboards and mice.

input symbol—a shape in a flowchart that contains an input statement and is represented by a parallelogram.

insertion sort—a sorting algorithm in which each pair of elements in an array is compared; when an out-of-order element is found, a backward search is made for an element smaller than the out-of-order element. When that element is found, a new position is opened for the out-of-order element and each subsequent element is moved down one position.

instance—one tangible example of a class; an object.

instance method—a method that operates correctly yet differently for each class object. An instance method is nonstatic and receives a `this` reference. Contrast with *class method*.

instance variables—within a class, the data components that belong to every instantiated object.

instantiation—one instance or object of a class.

integer—a whole number.

interactivity diagram—a design tool that shows the relationship between screens in an interactive GUI program.

interface to a method—the part of a method that a client sees and uses, including a method's return type, name, and arguments.

internal storage—temporary, volatile storage within a computer system. Also see *memory*, *main memory*, and *primary memory*. Contrast with *external storage*.

interpreter—translates a high-level language into machine language and tells you if you have used a programming language incorrectly. An interpreter translates and executes each line of a program one at a time. Contrast with *compiler*.

invoke—to execute a method from another method. Also see *call*.

is-a relationship—the relationship that exists between an object and its class.

iteration—a loop structure.

libraries—stored collections of classes that serve related purposes.

linked lists—constructs used as an alternative to physically sorting large records; in a linked list, each record contains a field that holds the address of the next logical record.

L

listener—an object that is "interested in" an event that occurs on an object and to which you want the object to respond.

local—describes a variable or constant that is known only within the boundaries of a method. Contrast with *global*.

logic—the processes you develop to give instructions to a computer in a specific sequence, without leaving any instructions out or adding extraneous instructions.

logical error—an error that occurs when incorrect instructions are performed, or when instructions are performed in the wrong order.

logical NOT operator—a symbol that reverses the meaning of a Boolean expression.

loop control variable—a variable that determines whether a loop will continue.

loop structure—a programming structure in which you ask a question; if the answer requires an action, you perform the action and ask the original question again.

loop's body—the statements within a loop.

low-level machine language—the set of statements made up of 1s and 0s that the computer understands. Contrast with *high-level programming languages*.

lozenge—a flowchart symbol that marks the beginning or end of a flowchart segment, method, or program.

M

machine language—a computer's on-off circuitry language, most often expressed in 1s and 0s.

magic numbers—unnamed numeric constants.

main memory—temporary, volatile storage within a computer system. Also see *memory*, *internal storage*, and *primary memory*.

matrix—a two-dimensional array.

mean—arithmetic average.

median—the middle item in a list when the values are listed in order.

memory—temporary, volatile storage within a computer system. Also see *internal storage*, *main memory*, and *primary memory*.

method—a self-contained program module that contains a series of statements that carry out a task or group of tasks.

method body—holds the method's statements.

method declaration—describes a method. In some languages, it is the first line of the method; in others, it is a separate statement.

method header—the first line in a method. Typically, a method header contains a method's return type, identifier, and parameter list.

method's client—a program or other method that uses the method.

method's implementation—the set of statements within a method.

method's type—the feature of a method that is the data type for any value it returns. Also see *return type*.

mnemonic—a memory device; variable identifiers act as mnemonics for hard-to-remember memory addresses.

multidimensional arrays—arrays with two or more dimensions.

multiple inheritance—a programming feature that describes the capability of inheriting from more than one base class.

multiplicity—refers to the arithmetic relationships between objects, or the number of objects in a set.

multithreading—using multiple threads of execution.

mutator methods—methods that set values in a class. Contrast with *accessor methods*.

N

named constant—a named memory location, similar to a variable, except that its value never changes during the execution of a program.

nested decision—a decision "inside of" another decision. Also see *nested if*.

nested if—a decision "inside of" another decision. Also see *nested decision*.

nested loops—structures in which a loop exists within another loop. Also see *inner loop* and *outer loop*.

nesting structures—structures that are placed within other structures.

nibble—half a byte, or four bits.

nonstatic methods—methods that exist to be used with an object created from a class; they are instance methods and they receive a `this` reference. Contrast with *static methods*.

null case—the branch of a decision in which no action is taken.

numeric constant—a specific numeric value.

numeric variables—named memory locations that hold numeric values.

O

object diagrams—UML diagrams that are similar to class diagrams, but they model specific instances of classes.

object dictionary—a list of the objects used in a program, including which screens they are used on and whether any code, or script, is associated with them.

object-oriented analysis (OOA)—the process of analyzing a system using an object-oriented approach.

object-oriented approach—a methodology that includes defining the objects needed to accomplish a task and developing the objects so that each maintains its own data and carries out tasks when another object requests them.

object-oriented design (OOD)—the process of designing a system using an object-oriented approach.

object-oriented programming (OOP)—a style of programming that focuses on objects, or "things." OOP describes the objects' features, or attributes, and their behaviors. Contrast with *procedural programming*.

one-dimensional array—a list accessed using a single subscript.

operating system—the software that you use to run a computer and manage its resources.

OR decision—a decision that contains two or more decisions; if at least one condition is met, the resulting action takes place.

OR operator—a symbol that you use to combine decisions when any one condition can be true for an action to occur. Also see *conditional OR operator*.

out of bounds—describes an array subscript when it is not within the range of acceptable subscripts.

outer loop—a loop that contains another loop. Contrast with *inner loop*. Also see *nested loops*.

output device—hardware that provides information so that people can view, interpret, and work with processed results. Common examples are printers and monitors.

output symbol—a shape in a flowchart that contains an output statement and is represented by a parallelogram.

overload a method—to write multiple methods with a shared name but different parameter lists.

overloading—the act of supplying diverse meanings for a single item.

override a method—to create a method with the same identifier and parameter list as a parent class version; the parent's version then becomes hidden from the child class.

P

packages—another name for libraries in some languages.

parallel arrays—two or more arrays in which each element in one array is associated with the element in the same relative position in the other array or arrays.

parameter list—all the parameters passed into a method.

parameters—the data items received by methods. Contrast with *arguments*.

parent class—a base class. Also see *superclass*.

Pascal casing—the format for naming variables and other program components in which multiple-word variable names are run together, the initial letter is uppercase, and each new word within the variable name begins with an uppercase letter.

pass the data—the act of sending values from one method to another; the act of sending arguments to method parameters.

passed by reference—describes values passed to a method when the method receives the actual memory address item. Contrast with *passed by value*.

passed by value—describes how a variable is sent to a method when a copy of its value is stored in a new memory location accessible to the method. Contrast with *passed by reference*.

pixel—a picture element, or one of the tiny dots of light that form a grid on your screen.

polymorphism—the ability of a method to act appropriately depending on the context.

populating an array—the act of assigning values to array elements.

portable—describes program features that can more easily be reused in multiple programs.

posttest loop—a loop in which a condition is tested after the loop body has executed once. Both `do-while` and `do-until` loops are posttest loops.

pretest loop—a loop in which a condition is tested before entering the loop body even once. A `while` loop is a pretest loop.

primary key—a unique identifier for each object in a file or database.

primary memory—temporary, volatile storage within a computer system. Also see *memory*, *main memory*, and *internal storage*.

priming read (or **priming input**)—the first read or data input statement that occurs before and outside of the loop that performs the rest of the input statements.

primitive data types—simple numbers and characters that are not class types.

private access—as applied to a class's data or methods, specifies that the data or method cannot be used by any method that is not part of the same class.

procedural programming—a style of writing programs that focuses on the procedures that programmers create to manipulate data. Contrast with *object-oriented programming*.

processing—the act of handling and manipulating data items, such as organizing them, checking them for accuracy, or performing mathematical operations on them.

processing symbol—a shape in a flowchart that contains a processing statement and is represented by a rectangle.

programmer-defined type—a class. Also see *user-defined type* and *abstract data type*.

programming languages—languages (sets of syntax and rules) used to write source code for programs. Examples include Visual Basic, C#, C++, Java, Pascal, COBOL, RPG, and Fortran.

prompt—a message displayed on a monitor, asking the user for a response.

property—a programming language feature that provides methods that allow you to get and set a class field value using a simple syntax.

protected access—describes a modifier that is used when you want no outside classes to be able to use a data field, except classes that are descendents of the original class.

protected node—the UML diagram name for an exception-throwing `try` block.

pseudocode—an English-like representation of the logical steps it takes to solve a problem.

public access—as applied to a class's data or methods, specifies that other programs and methods may use the specified data or methods.

R

range check—a comparison of a variable to a series of values that mark the limiting ends of ranges.

range of values—every value between a high and low limit.

register—to sign up components as listeners that will react to events initiated by other components.

relational comparison operators—the symbols that express Boolean comparisons, such as =, >, <, >=, <=, and <>. Also see *relational operators* and *comparison operators*.

relational operators—the symbols that express Boolean comparisons, such as =, >, <, >=, <=, and <>. Also see *comparison operators* and *relational comparison operators*.

reliable—describes code that has been tested and is trusted to work correctly.

repetition—a loop structure.

return statement—a statement that marks the end of the method; sometimes it includes a value to be returned.

return type—the feature of a method that is the data type for any value it returns. Also see *method's type*.

returning a value—the act of sending a data value from a called method back to the calling method.

reverse engineering—the process of creating a model of an existing system.

rules of precedence—a set of laws that dictate the order in which operations in the same statement are carried out.

run—the act of executing a computer program that has been written and translated.

S

save—to store a program by placing a copy on some nonvolatile medium.

scenario—in a UML use case diagram, each variation in the sequence of actions required.

selection sort—a sorting algorithm in which the first element in the array is assumed to be the smallest. Its value is stored in a variable and its position in the array is stored in another variable. Then, every subsequent element in the array is tested. If an element with a smaller value is found, the variable storing the smallest value is set to the new value, and its position is stored. The procedure is repeated for each subsequent value.

selection structure—a structure in which you ask a question, and, depending on the answer, you take one of two courses of action. Then, no matter which path you follow, you continue with the next event. Also see *decision structure*.

semantic errors—logical errors.

sentinel—a value that is an entry or exit point in a program. Also see *dummy value*.

sequence diagram—a UML diagram that shows the timing of events in a single use case.

sequence structure—a programming structure that can contain any number of events, but there is no chance to branch off and skip any of the events.

sequential order—data records arranged one after another on the basis of the value in some field.

set method—in a class, a method that sets the values of a data field. Contrast with *get method*.

short-circuit evaluation—a logical feature in which each part of a larger expression is evaluated only as far as necessary to determine the final outcome.

signature—a method's name and argument list. Contrast with *interface to a method*.

single-alternative `ifs`—statements that take action on just one branch of a decision. Contrast with *dual-alternative `ifs`*.

single-dimensional array—a list accessed using a single subscript.

sinking sort—alternate name for a bubble sort.

size of the array—the number of elements the array can hold.

soft copy—screen output. Contrast with *hard copy*.

software—the set of instructions written by programmers that tell the computer what to do; software is computer programs.

software testing—testing performed by users (or test users) who do not know or care what the program code includes, but care only that the program performs as expected.

sorted—the condition of records that have been placed in order based on the contents of one or more fields.

source of an event—the component from which an event is generated.

spaghetti code—snarled, unstructured program statements.

stacking structures—structures that are attached end-to-end.

state—the current values or conditions of an object's attributes.

state machine diagram—a UML diagram that shows the different statuses of a class or object at different points in time.

static methods—methods for which no object needs to exist. Static methods are not instance methods and they do not receive a `this` reference. Contrast with *nonstatic methods*.

step value—a number used to increase a loop control variable on each pass through a loop.

stereotype—a feature that adds to the UML vocabulary of shapes to make them more meaningful for the reader.

storage devices—hardware on which you can store output information for later use. Examples include magnetic disks, compact discs, and USB drives.

storyboard—a design tool that represents a picture or sketch of a screen the user will see when running a program.

string constant—a literal set of characters enclosed within quotation marks.

string variables—named memory locations that hold a series of characters.

structure—a basic unit of programming logic; each structure is a sequence, selection, or loop. Each structure has a single entry and exit point.

subclass—a derived class. Also see *extended class* and *subclass*.

subscript—a number that indicates the position of an element within an array. Also see *index*.

subtype polymorphism—the ability of one method name to work appropriately for different subclass objects of the same parent class.

summary report—a report that lists only totals, without individual detail records.

superclass—a base class. Also see *parent class*.

swapping—the act of reversing the positions of two values.

syntax—the rules of a language.

syntax error—an error in language or grammar.

system design—the detailed specification of how all the parts of a system will be implemented and coordinated.

system software—the set of all programs you use to manage your computer, including operating systems such as Windows or UNIX and other utility programs not directly used by end users. Contrast with *application software*.

T

table—a two-dimensional array.

testing a value—the process of comparing a value to another value to make a decision.

`this` reference—an automatically created variable that holds the address of an object that is passed to every instance method used with the object.

thread—the flow of execution of one set of program statements.

`throw` statement—a statement that sends an `Exception` out of a method so it can be handled elsewhere.

throwing an exception—the process of tossing out an exception object that another method or the operating system might handle.

time signal—a UML diagram symbol that indicates a specific amount of time has passed before an action is started.

transitive—a quality of inheritance that means a child inherits all the members of all its ancestors.

trivial—describes a Boolean expression that always evaluates to the same result.

truth tables—diagrams used in mathematics and logic to help describe the truth of an entire expression based on the truth of its parts.

try block—in exception handling, a block of code you attempt to execute while acknowledging that an exception might occur.

two-dimensional arrays—arrays that have both rows and columns of values; you must use two subscripts when you access an element in a two-dimensional array. Also see *matrix* and *table*.

U

UML—Unified Modeling Language; a standard way to specify, construct, and document systems that use object-oriented methods.

undeclared variables—variables that have not been provided with a data type or identifier; attempting to use one is an error.

undefined variables—variables that have not been provided with a value before you attempt to use them.

Unicode—a 16-bit code used to represent characters in some computer systems.

unreachable code—program statements that can never execute under any circumstances. Also see *dead code* and *unreachable path*.

unreachable path—a logical path that can never be traveled. Also see *dead code* and *unreachable code*.

use case diagram—a UML diagram that shows how a business works from the perspective of those who approach it from the outside, or those who actually use the business.

user interface—the user's means of interacting with the computer. Also see *graphical user interface* and *command prompt*.

user-defined type—a class. Also see *programmer-defined type* and *abstract data type*.

V

validate data—to make sure data meets specific criteria or falls within an acceptable range.

validating input—the act of checking the user's responses to ensure they fall within acceptable bounds.

variable array—an array whose values change during program execution. Contrast with *constant array*.

variable declaration—a statement that names a variable and assigns a data type.

variables—named memory locations whose contents can vary over time.

visible—describes the area in which a data item or method is usable. Compare with *in scope*.

visual development environment—an environment in which you can create programs by dragging components such as buttons and labels onto a screen and arranging them visually.

void method—a method that returns no value.

volatile—the condition that describes the loss of memory contents when a computer loses power.

W

while loop (or **while-do loop)**—a structure in which a process continues while some condition continues to be true.

white box testing—the type of testing programmers perform; they can "see inside the box" to understand how the code works.

whole-part relationship—describes an association in which one or more classes make up the parts of a larger whole class.

work methods—methods that perform tasks within a class; usually as opposed to get or set methods. Also see *help methods* and *facilitators*.

X

x-axis—a representation of horizontal positions in a screen window.

x-coordinate—describes values that increase as you travel from left to right across a window.

Y

y-axis—a representation of vertical positions in a screen window.

y-coordinate—describes values that increase as you travel from top to bottom across a window.

INDEX

Note: Page numbers in **bold** reflect key words in text.